Universal-International Westerns,
1947–1963

For Catherine

Universal-International Westerns, 1947–1963

THE COMPLETE FILMOGRAPHY

by

GENE BLOTTNER

McFarland & Company, Inc., Publishers

Jefferson, North Carolina, and London

Library of Congress cataloguing data are available

Blottner, Gene, 1938–
    Universal-International westerns, 1947–1963 : the complete
filmography / by Gene Blottner.
        p.   cm.
    Includes bibliographical references and index.
    ISBN 0-7864-0791-3 (library binding : 50# alkaline paper) ∞
    1. Western films — Catalogs.   2. Universal-International
(Firm).   I. Title.
PN1995.9.W4B59   2000
016.79143'6278 — dc21   00-30538

British Library cataloguing data are available

Manufactured in the United States of America

*McFarland & Company, Inc., Publishers
    Box 611, Jefferson, North Carolina 28640
    www.mcfarlandpub.com*

Contents

Acknowledgments

Many people assisted in obtaining information for this book. I would like to thank the stars who had the patience to allow me to interview them either by phone, in person or by correspondence through the mail: Keith Andes, Earl Bellamy, James Best, Budd Boetticher, Peter Breck, Polly Burson, Johnny Carpenter, Harry Carey Jr., Fred Carson, Kathleen Crowley, Rosemary De Camp, Myrna Dell, Penny Edwards, John Ericson, Gene Evans, Nina Foch, Dianne Foster, Beverly Garland, Coleen Gray, Gary Gray, John Hart, Myron Healey, Robert Hoy, Kathleen Hughes, Whitey Hughes, Russell Johnson, Andrea King, Marc Lawrence, Donna Martell, Jan Merlin, Colleen Miller, Lori Nelson, Gregg Palmer, Michael Pate, House Peters Jr., Paul Picerni, Mala Powers, William Pullen, Walter Reed, Dale Robertson, John Saxon, William Schallert, Lee Sholem, Marjorie Stapp, Warren Stevens, Gale Storm, and Marie Windsor.

A special thanks to those people who willingly shared their knowledge, memorabilia and information or assisted me in obtaining information: Catherine Blottner, Woody Blottner, Jim Cook, Roger Crowley, Myrna Dell, Michael Fitzgerald, Larry Floyd, Jim Goldrup, Tom Goldrup, Sue Gossett, Boyd Magers, Donna Magers, Don Meade, Ray Nielsen, Cindy Peery, Bill Sasser, Dorothy Sink, Kenneth Stier, Neil Summers, and Tinsley Yarbrough; the staffs of the Kirn Memorial Library and the Old Dominion Library in Norfolk, Virginia; the Library of Congress; and the TAA (Tidewater Automobile Association) in Norfolk.

American Movie Classics provided most of the films for my viewing and the subsequent impetus for writing about those films. Finally, I would like to thank those individuals who were kind enough to share photographs or other illustrative materials with me: Roger Crowley, Penny Edwards, Sue Gossett, Robert Hoy, Donna Martell, and Jan Merlin.

Preface

What is a western? No one person seems to have a clear definition of a western. Some films are obvious: They take place in what is known as the Old West, with cowboys, outlaws, cavalry, and Indians. But other writers add Northwest logging, oil well drilling, pioneer and Civil War stories to the genre. Some historians include stories that start in the West but take place mainly in the East, such as a cowboy coming to grips with gangsters in the big city.

For the most part, the selection of films to be covered in this book was obvious. Only two films that were ultimately included did not meet my first pass criteria. Those films were *Feudin', Fussin' and a-Fightin'* and *One Desire*. Universal-International's ad copy for *Feudin'* proclaimed "The West at its Wild and Wackiest Best." That settled that controversy. Michael Fitzgerald, author of *Universal Pictures* (Arlington House, 1977), remarked that *One Desire* should be included and Phil Hardy's *The Western* (William Morrow and Company, 1983) seconded this. Therefore, both films were included.

Other sources mentioned two other titles as western films. Michael Fitzgerald considered *Meet Me at the Fair* (Universal-International, 1953) a musical western-comedy drama. I could find no other source that agreed with this. On viewing this film, *Meet Me at the Fair* turned out to be a delicious slice of turn-of-the-century Americana. Michael Pitts listed *Arctic Manhunt* (Universal-International, 1949) in his book *Western Movies* (McFarland, 1986), but no other source listed it as a western. In reading two synopses of this film, I found that the feel of the story is definitely of a crime melodrama. Therefore, these films were not included.

One hundred and fourteen feature films became the basis for this book. For the most part, these films cannot be called great. The exceptions are some of the films of James Stewart and Kirk Douglas. The majority of these films promised and delivered solid entertainment, probably due to the directing talents of such men as Budd Boetticher, Jack Arnold and Raoul Walsh. As in any grouping of this kind, there are always some films best left unmade.

For those of you who are unfamiliar with these films, American Movie Classics (AMC) and the Western Channel show most of them. Other titles are available at your local video store or through the mail from various video distributors.

To give the reader an insight to the entry style and primary sources used for the films covered in this book, the following information may be helpful.

Above the title of each film covered, there is an example of a "blurb" used in the advertising copy for the film. All release dates were taken from Charles Aaronson's *The International Motion Picture Almanac* with the exception of *Ride Clear of Diablo*. The release date for that title came from Adams and Rainey's *The Shoot-Em-Ups*. If a film is in color or any wide-screen process, this is noted. Of the 114 westerns covered in this book, 101 were filmed in Technicolor, Eastman Color or Cinecolor. As acknowledged, photographs, title cards, and scene cards used as illustrations are courtesy of Roger Crowley, Penny Edwards, Sue Gossett, Robert Hoy, Donna Martell, Jan Merlin, and the author.

Alternate Title: If a film used a title other than that given on initial release, this title is listed. Working titles will be found in the "Notes and Commentary" section of the entry.

Cast: All cast members listed before the designation "//" were identified in either the beginning or end credits or both. All cast members listed after that designation were identified either by the author or by people considered knowledgeable about the western and Universal Studios personnel.

Credits: Each person listed received on-screen billing.

Song(s): All identifiable songs have been named with composers and artists, if known.

Location Filming: Tinsley Yarbrough's *Those Great B-Western Locations*; Sue Gossett's *The Films and Career of Audie Murphy*; *Hollywood Reporter*; Kenneth Stier; and interviews with the stars and directors helped to provide much of this information. Although most films are covered, there are a few in which this information was unavailable.

Running Time: All running times appeared in Jack Alicoate's *Film Daily Yearbook of Motion Pictures*. It was important, for consistency, to use only one source for this information.

Source: If a film was derived from a published work, either a novel or story, this is stated along with the name(s) of the author.

Story: This is an encapsulation of the happenings on the silver screen and not an attempt to describe every scene in detail. The author has watched each film with the exception of *The Raiders*, which is unavailable for viewing.

Notes and Commentary: For the most part, this is information obtained from those stars and directors who graciously consented to allow me to interview them, and facts published in *Hollywood Reporter*.

Reviews: To give the reader a flavor of how critics received the film at the time of release, selected reviews are printed. Also, retrospective views from various authors on the western or on film in general are included.

Summation: My overall appraisal of the film, with which I can only hope that the reader might agree.

Historical Overview

Pre–Universal-International Years (1912–1946)

From 1912 through 1946, Universal Studios was known for providing entertaining films. These films included comedies, melodramas and especially the westerns.

On June 8, 1912, Carl Laemmle founded the Universal Film Manufacturing Company. The merger of Laemmle's Independent Motion Picture Company (IMP), Picture Plays, Bison Life Motion Pictures and Rex Company accomplished this.

Laemmle had been a theater owner and had run a film rental service. In 1909, he established his own motion picture company to ensure a supply of motion pictures for his theaters.

Laemmle initially built two studios in California because its climate would be conducive to year-round motion picture production.

Being a visionary, in 1914 Laemmle purchased the Taylor Ranch in Lankershim Township for $165,000. The ranch was located at the east end of the San Fernando Valley and covered 230 acres. It was the site of the treaty signed by Mexican General Andres Pico and U.S. Army Colonel John C. Frémont that ceded California to the United States. The largest movie studio of its day would be erected; everything that would be needed to produce motion pictures could be gathered there.

The new facility officially opened on March 15, 1915, and was proclaimed to be Universal City. It was even legally designated as a town.

Laemmle had a fascination with the American West and the first Universal western was forthcoming. The film was titled *Just Jim* (1915) and starred Harry Carey. Even though Hobart Bosworth and Monroe Salisbury would also star in some of these early Universal westerns, Harry Carey became their first western star. Carey would usually play a character named

Cheyenne Harry in his pictures and most of these films would be directed by Jack (later John) Ford. In one film, *The Ace of the Saddle* (1919), Cheyenne Harry acquired the last name of Henderson. Probably the most memorable of Carey's westerns would be *Straight Shooting* (1917), *The Three Godfathers* (1916) and *The Outcasts of Poker Flat* (1919).

In 1921, a new western star emerged at Universal. He had doubled Carey, played supporting roles in the Carey westerns and finally received starring roles in *Action* (1921) and *Sure Fire* (1921). His name was Ed "Hoot" Gibson. Because of Hoot's popularity, Carey's contract was not renewed. Hoot was Universal's reigning cowboy star of the 1920s. Gibson had a knack for comedy as well as being able to handle the action scenes.

In 1922, the studio underwent a name change, becoming known as Universal Pictures.

With the surge of popularity in the early and mid-twenties for westerns, Universal had to employ other saddle aces to fill the void. William Desmond, Jack Hoxie, Art Acord, Pete Morrison, Fred Humes, Ted Wells and Jack Perrin were some of the cowboys riding the Universal western trails.

In the late twenties, there was a decline in popularity for the western. In addition, the movies had found a voice. Fox's *The Cisco Kid,* the first all-talking western to be released, won an Academy Award for Warner Baxter as Best Actor in 1929. Laemmle decided he not only wanted sound in his westerns, he wanted them all talking. Universal's series western stars now were Hoot Gibson and Ken Maynard. Both series' entries currently had budgets of $75,000 each. Sound added additional expense to the already established budgets. With independent companies able to produce sound westerns at a fraction of the Universal budgets, profits were falling. Westerns were discontinued at Universal for the 1930-31 season.

In 1930, *All Quiet on the Western Front* won an Academy Award as Best Picture. Carl Laemmle had turned over the daily responsibility for running the studio to his son, Carl Jr.

Due to the success of *All Quiet on the Western Front*, the junior Laemmle had a vision that Universal could compete with MGM, Paramount and possibly Warner Bros. No longer would the studio emphasize "entertainments," but the expensive prestige pictures instead. But the "entertainments" were what the theater owners wanted.

In 1932, one of the top western stars, and possibly the greatest of them all, Tom Mix, was signed for a series of westerns. Mix's westerns were extremely popular. Western historian Jon Tuska, in his fine book *The Filming of the West* (Doubleday, 1976), stated that no western series of the thirties or forties surpassed the Mix series. Tuska also thought that Mix's *Riders of Death Valley* (1932) was perhaps the best "B" western of the sound era. Mix was able to complete only nine films, however, before the second of two disastrous falls made him unable to fulfill his contract. He asked out, and recommended Hoot Gibson as a replacement, but Ken Maynard was chosen instead.

Ken Maynard's pictures were popular despite outrageous plots that stretched the viewer's credibility. Perhaps the best of Ken's series was *Trail Drive* (1933). *The Strawberry Roan* (1933) should be mentioned as the culmination of Maynard's vision of the musical western, which would gain enormous popularity with the films of Gene Autry, Tex Ritter and Roy Rogers a few years later. Maynard's pictures were produced on budgets of over $90,000 as compared to the budgets of $25,000–$30,000 for the most popular western star of the time, Buck Jones. The films of both Maynard and Jones attained similar grosses. Maynard's disposition made him a difficult star to handle. Eventually Carl Jr. and his father made the decision not to continue the Maynard series and wooed Buck Jones from Columbia.

Jones' series ran from 1934 to 1937 and was extremely popular at the box office. In the first *Motion Picture Herald* poll of top moneymaking western stars for 1936, Buck placed first. By the next year, Jones had slipped to third place behind Gene Autry and William Boyd. Jones' stories began to stress plot over action and met with less critical favor. *The Ivory Handled Gun* (1935) and *Stone of Silver Creek* (1935) were two stories that showed Jones in top form.

A western paved the way for Carl Laemmle's retirement. *Sutter's Gold* (1936) was to be *the* epic for Universal. No expense was spared to show these gold rush days. The film would turn out to be a box office disaster due primarily to a non–western type leading man in Edward Arnold and a rambling plot line. When a subsequent film, *Show Boat* (1936), began to run into financial difficulties while in production, the studio was forced to reorganize. Standard Capital purchased Universal; Robert H. Cochrane became the studio head and Charles Rogers the production head. An austerity program was put into effect; Universal was now known as the New Universal.

Into this climate, Jones began negotiations on a new three-year contract. Jones knew William Boyd was making $25,000 per picture and wanted a similar contract. Universal would not give in to Jones' demands.

Jones then entered into a contract with an independent company who would have his films distributed by Columbia. In retrospect, this was an unwise decision for Jones, as he never again matched his box office status of the early and mid-thirties.

Universal decided to join the parade of the companies producing musical westerns. Bob Baker was hired over Roy Rogers. Baker's films were pleasant but did not have the continuous rugged action expected in the programmers. After twelve films, Johnny Mack Brown was brought in to headline the western series with Baker in support. After six films, Baker was dropped from the series.

New management took over in 1938, as the austerity policy proved to be ineffective. The new studio head was Nate J. Blumberg and the production head was Cliff Work.

The epic western became the vogue in 1939 and Universal released *Destry Rides Again*. The film starred Marlene Dietrich and James Stewart and became a classic western. Dietrich's career, which had been floundering, was given new life.

In 1940, Universal began producing medium budgeted westerns with running times between 70 and 89 minutes. Some of the more memorable titles were: *When the Daltons Rode* (1940), *Trail of the Vigilantes* (1940), *Badlands of Dakota* (1941), *The Lady from Cheyenne* (1941), *Men of Texas* (1942), *The Spoilers* (1942), *Frontier Badman* (1943) and *Frontier Gal* (1945).

The "B" western was a staple for Universal into 1946 with Johnny Mack Brown first riding solo and then teaming up with Tex Ritter to be heralded as "The West's Greatest Star Team." Brown left Universal for his own starring series at Monogram with Ritter slated to have his own series with Universal. An injury to Ritter gave Russell Hayden the opportunity to be star of *Frontier Law* (1943). Ritter did star in three Universal westerns, one with Hayden as co-star, before moving over to PRC. Universal concluded their "B" western series with entries starring Rod Cameron, Eddie Dew and Kirby Grant from 1944 to 1946.

Technicolor finally came to the Universal western in 1944. The first color western was *Can't Help Singing* with the popular singing star, Deanna Durbin. Other Technicolor westerns were *Salome, Where She Danced* (1945), the previously mentioned *Frontier Gal* (1945) and *Canyon Passage* (1946).

In 1945, Universal began negotiations to merge with the independent studio, International Pictures. The merger and the subsequent reorganization was completed on November 12, 1946, with Universal-International Pictures as the studio's new name. A new policy would go into effect: All releases would have a minimum running time of 70 minutes; there would be no "B" pictures, which doomed the serials and programmer westerns; more films were to be lensed in Technicolor. In addition, the studio entered into an agreement with J. Arthur Rank to acquire and distribute prestigious British films such as *Black Narcissus* (1947), *Nicholas Nickleby* (1947), *Great Expectations* (1946) and *Hamlet* (1948), which garnered an Oscar for Best Picture.

Therefore in 1947, all films had Universal-International logos, with two prominent exceptions. The westerns *Michigan Kid* and *The Vigilantes Return* had the Universal logo, even though *The Vigilantes Return* had been scheduled to be released under the Universal-International banner. Both starred Jon Hall, both were in Cinecolor and both ran slightly under 70 minutes.

With the October 1947 release of *The Wistful Widow of Wagon Gap*, a western satire with Abbott and Costello, the era of the Universal-International westerns was underway.

Universal-International Years (1947–1963)

Within this new regime, Leo Spitz and William Goetz became the production heads. J. Cheever Cowdin and Nate J. Blumberg were the heads of the parent company, Universal Picture Company. In addition to the agreement made with J. Arthur Rank, Universal-International arranged to have several independent production units supply films to the moviegoing public. The studio signed agreements with The Fairbanks Company, Karem Productions, Walter Wanger and Mark Hellinger.

Westerns and other escapist fare during these early years were not emphasized, but a few westerns of note did emerge, including *Black Bart* (1948), *Red Canyon* (1949) and *Calamity Jane and Sam Bass* (1949). Yvonne De Carlo was probably Universal-International's biggest western star. She starred in four of the seven westerns released in 1948-49. De Carlo had taken over Maria Montez' crown as the Queen of Technicolor.

Several prestige films such as *Another Part of the Forest* (1949) and *All My Sons* (1948) failed to live up to expectations at the box office. Even *Tap Roots* (1948), a Civil War western that was touted as the successor to *Gone with the Wind* (Metro-Goldwyn-Mayer, 1939), became a major disappointment. The studio was set to offer this film only as a roadshow attraction in its initial run but made the decision to release it at the regular admission price.

By 1949, Universal-International fortunes were looking bleak as losses mounted to $4.3 million. Fortunately, a longtime employee, Edward Muhl, was present to reverse the studio's fortunes. Muhl, the studio manager, led the company back to presenting entertainments, the type of films that had made the studio famous. Led by the Francis the Talking Mule and the Ma and Pa Kettle series, action films were also produced which included a steady supply of westerns.

Equally important to Universal-International was the Supreme Court's decision that the motion picture studios (e.g., Metro-Goldwyn-Mayer and Warner Bros.) could no longer be associated with the theater chains. Now the Universal-International product could be shown in movie houses that had previously been closed to them.

From 1950 to 1954, veteran western star Joel McCrea could be seen in six outdoor films. James Stewart climbed in to the saddle for the classic western drama *Winchester '73* (1950). Stewart would be headlined in three more superior westerns during these Universal-International (U-I) years. But the king of the U-I range had emerged: Audie Murphy—a soft-spoken, baby-faced Texan who captivated the action audience. This new cowpoke was the most decorated soldier of World War II. Murphy would star in westerns and a few non-westerns at the studio until 1966.

Decca Records gained control of 28 percent of Universal's stock in 1951. A year later, Decca purchased enough stock to gain control of the studio. Cowdin had resigned two years previously and now Milton Rachmil succeeded Blumberg as president. Edward Muhl became the new production head with the resignations of Spitz and Goetz.

Muhl's "magic touch" continued with blockbuster pictures such as *The Glenn Miller Story* (1954), *To Hell and Back* (1955), and two westerns from the early fifties, *Bend of the River* (1952) and *Mississippi Gambler* (1953). Under Muhl's guidance, the quota of western features was increased. From 1952 through 1957, there was an average of almost a dozen westerns released each year.

The leads in some of these westerns were up-and-coming stars like Jeff Chandler and Rock Hudson. Chandler could be seen to good advantage in *The Battle at Apache Pass* (1952), *Pillars of the Sky* (1956) and *Man in the Shadow* (1958). This latter film co-starred Orson Welles in his only western role. Hudson starred in *Seminole* (1953) and *Taza, Son of Cochise* (1954) but it was *The Lawless Breed* (1953) that really boosted

Hudson's stock by landing him plum roles in *Magnificent Obsession* (1954) and *Giant* (Warner Bros., 1956).

Joel McCrea's last film for Universal-International, *Border River*, was released in early 1954. By the latter part of the year, Rory Calhoun was signed for six westerns. Coinciding with the release of Calhoun's fifth oater, *Red Sundown* in 1956, television's Range Rider, Jock Mahoney, became the studio's newest cowboy star. Universal-International had the highest hopes for Mahoney but he never lived up to the studio's expectations. With the release of *The Saga of Hemp Brown* (1958) and *Money, Women and Guns* (1959), both Calhoun and Mahoney moved on to other pastures.

Audie Murphy still remained the studio's most popular and durable cowboy star. Murphy was seen to good advantage in *No Name on the Bullet* (1959), *Walk the Proud Land* (1956) and *Destry* (1955). By the early sixties, Murphy's films were now destined to play in double-feature houses and drive-in theaters. The proliferation of western programming on television began to satisfy most of the public who were looking for Wild West thrills.

In 1956, RKO studios ceased operation and had a number of films ready for moviegoers. Universal-International distributed eleven of these in 1957-58 two of which had western or pioneer stories. One was *Run of the Arrow* (1957), which starred Rod Steiger and had a cameo by western great Tim McCoy. The other was *All Mine to Give* (1958) with Glynis Johns and Cameron Mitchell top-billed.

In the late fifties, as westerns became more and more of a staple on television, the popularity of the western film, primarily those not featuring sex and violence, began to diminish. From 1959 through 1963, Universal-International released only 14 westerns as the studio drastically cut the total number of films to be released annually.

With sound stages remaining empty, U-I was able to sell studio space to the Music Corporation of America (MCA). The agreement allowed U-I to lease space, as it might be required. In 1961, MCA bought Decca Records and gained control of Universal.

Even with reduced film production, the years from 1959 through 1962 were some of the most profitable in the long history of Universal Pictures. Unfortunately, the western film played only a small part in this success. *Operation Petticoat* (1959), *Midnight Lace* (1960), *Spartacus* (1960), *Imitation of Life* (1959) and *Pillow Talk* (1959) were some of the studio's major moneymakers.

Showdown (1963), with Audie Murphy in the lead, was the last Universal-International western. All the advertising indicated that this was a

Universal Picture, but when the picture unfolded on movie screens around the country, the Universal-International logo was in evidence. Not expecting any blockbuster returns from this release, producer Gordon Kay shot the film in black and white to the displeasure of Murphy.

Thus ended the Universal-International years. The next western from the studio, *He Rides Tall* (1964), would have the new Universal logo but would be lensed in black and white.

Post–Universal-International Years (1963–1998)

The tastes of moviegoers continued to change, not necessarily for the better. Relaxation of censorship allowed nudity, sex and violence to run rampant on the silver screen. Audiences flocked to sexploitation, blaxploitation and gratuitously violent films. Italian producers changed the complexion of the western, churning out "spaghetti" westerns in which violence, blood and gore were the watchword.

Up against this permissiveness, Universal still stayed with the entertainment programmers that had always been offered. The theater owners were not enthusiastic about these westerns. Some of the films never played the large theatergoing markets and had to settle for the smaller or largely rural trade. The films that did make some of the larger markets were usually placed on the bottom half of a double bill and were fortunate to last out a week.

Shenandoah (1965), *War Wagon* (1967), *Texas Across the River* (1966) and *Coogan's Bluff* (1968) were the Universal westerns that made an impact on the moviegoing public in the mid to late sixties. John Wayne was and still is a household name and Clint Eastwood was gaining popularity. James Stewart showed that even some Universal big-budgeted westerns were beginning to slip when *The Rare Breed* (1966) was paired with a second feature. Just a year earlier, that film would have probably played as a single feature. Dean Martin scored well with the light comedy-western *Texas Across the River* but couldn't duplicate the success with the violent *Rough Night in Jerico* (1967).

Still convinced the public would buy these western entertainments that had been popular so long, Universal decided to take television episodes, string a few of them together and present them as a feature film. Thus *Three Guns for Texas* (1968, three *Laredo* episodes), *Backtrack* (1969, a *Virginian* episode that introduced the *Laredo* characters) and *This Savage Land* (1969, the first two-part episode of *The Road West*) saw the light of day.

The seventies weren't much kinder to the Universal western. Clint Eastwood had great success with *High Plains Drifter* (1973), *Joe Kidd* (1972) and *Two Mules for Sister Sara* (1970) but *The Beguiled* (1971) was too arty to draw the necessary action trade. John Wayne put on the eye patch from *True Grit* (Paramount, 1969) and reprised his Rooster Cogburn character in a film aptly titled *Rooster Cogburn* (1975). The chemistry between Wayne and fellow screen great Katharine Hepburn made this a most entertaining film that performed well at the box office.

Joel McCrea, at age 70, climbed into the saddle for *Mustang Country* (1976). This was a good family film that failed to find an audience because not many theater owners were interested in showing it. This was Universal's last western feature for a few years.

The late seventies and early eighties saw Universal's last western hurrah. *The Electric Horseman* (1979) made some noise at the box office. The studio distributed two ITC productions, *The Legend of the Lone Ranger* (1981) and *Barbarosa* (1982). The new Lone Ranger film without Clayton Moore but with newcomer Klinton Spillsbury received some immediate playdates upon release. In some situations the film quickly disappeared but still was able to draw enough fans to the theaters to make the studio happy. *Barbarosa* with Willie Nelson and Gary Busey played situations in which only the star names and the title were mentioned. The public had to guess what type of film this might be; consequently, it vanished quickly. Despite some good reviews, *Cattle Annie and Little Britches* (1981) with Burt Lancaster also had a hard time finding receptive theaters in many areas of the country.

There has been no true out-and-out western released by Universal since that time. There have been four films that would qualify in our list of western films. *Back to the Future III* (1990) was a science fiction comedy that sent Michael J. Fox back to the wild and woolly West. An animated feature, *An American Tail: Fievel Goes West* (1991), featured the cartoon mouse on a westward trek. Tom Cruise and Nicole Kidman starred in an epic, *Far and Away* (1992), that sent two Irish immigrants to the American shore and finally to the Oklahoma land rush. The last film, *The Cowboy Way* (1994), had cowboys Woody Harrelson and Kiefer Sutherland using western ways to bring sinister, violent criminals to justice. This film was as western as the studio's earlier *Coogan's Bluff* (1968).

On June 5, 1995, The Seagram Company Ltd. acquired an 80 percent interest in Universal Studios Holding I Corporation (formerly MCA Holding I Corporation) from Matsushita Electric Industrial Co. Ltd. Matsushita had purchased MCA in 1990. Universal Studios Holding I Corporation is the indirect parent of Universal Studios. Even with this new ownership, westerns have not been forthcoming from Universal.

Indeed over the past fifteen or twenty years, only a handful of westerns have met with the moviegoers' approval. This fact would have certainly distressed the studio's founder, Carl Laemmle.

Universal can feel proud that they released countless films with some of the greatest western stars who ever appeared on the silver screen. Harry Carey, Hoot Gibson, Ken Maynard, Tom Mix, Buck Jones, Johnny Mack Brown, Randolph Scott, John Wayne, Rod Cameron, Joel McCrea, Audie Murphy and Clint Eastwood thrilled and entertained millions of fans as they made the West a safer place in which to live.

The Western Films

Six kids on a true and Wonderful Adventure...
In a Truly Remarkable Film...

All Mine to Give

ALTERNATE TITLE: *The Day They Gave Babies Away;* RKO Radio Pictures/Universal-International (January 1958); COLOR by Technicolor; RUNNING TIME: 102 min.

CAST: Mamie, **Glynis Johns**; Robert, **Cameron Mitchell**; Robbie, **Rex Thompson**; Annabella, **Patty McCormack**; Dr. Delbert, **Ernest Truex**; Mrs. Pugmire, **Hope Emerson**; Tom Cullen, **Alan Hale**; Lelia Delbert, **Sylvia Field**; Howard Tyler, **Royal Dano**; Mrs. Runyon, **Reta Shaw**; Jimmie, **Stephen Wootten**; Kirk, **Butch Bernard**; Elizabeth, **Yolanda White**; Katie Tyler, **Rita Johnson**; Mrs. Raiden, **Ellen Corby**; Mrs. Stephens, **Rosalyn Boulter**; Mr. Stephens, **Francis de Sales**; Bobbie, **Jon Provost**; Jane, **Terry Ann Ross**

CREDITS: Director, **Allen Reisner**; Assistant Director, **Russell Llewellyn**; Producer, **Sam Wiesenthal**; Screenwriters, **Katherine** and **Dale Eunson**; Editorial Supervisor, **Allan Crosland, Jr.**; Editor, **Bettie Mosher**; Set Decorator, **Glen Daniels**; Art Decorators, **Albert S. D'Agostino** and **Frank T. Smith**; Cinematographer, **William Skall**; Costumes, **Bernice Fentrelli**; Hair Stylist, **Larry Germain**; Makeup, **Harry Maret Jr.**; Sound, **James S. Thompson** and **Terry Nellum**; Music, **Max Steiner**; Orchestrations, **Murray Cutter**

SOURCE: Novel and *Cosmopolitan* magazine story, *The Day They Gave Babies Away* by **Dale Eunson**

STORY: Scottish immigrants Mamie (Glynis Johns) and Robert (Cameron Mitchell) venture to Wisconsin to start a new life with Mamie's uncle. Upon their arrival, Johns finds that not only is her uncle dead but his cabin has burned to the ground. Realizing Johns is ready to deliver their first child in a few weeks, Mitchell hurriedly starts to build a new cabin. With the neighbors' help the cabin is completed and Mitchell finds a job at

15

SIX KIDS ON A TRUE, WONDERFUL ADVENTURE!

The heartwarming story of six brothers
and sisters without parents or home
...but with the courage of the very young
they walk a street where strangers live
to find a bright new future of their own!

"All
Mine
To
Give"

TECHNICOLOR®

STARRING
GLYNIS JOHNS · CAMERON MITCHELL
REX THOMPSON · PATTY McCORMACK
with
ERNEST TRUEX · HOPE EMERSON · ALAN HALE
SYLVIA FIELD · RETA SHAW

All Mine to Give (1958). Title card: left side (*top to bottom*)—Rex Thompson, Stephen Wooten, Butch Bernard, Cameron Mitchell, and Glynis Johns; right side (*top to bottom*)—Patty McCormack, Yolanda White, and Terry Ann Ross.

a nearby lumber camp. Through the next few years, Johns has a total of six children, three boys and three girls. The youngest child, Kirk (Butch Bernard), contracts diphtheria. Even though Bernard pulls through, Mitchell comes down with the disease and dies. Johns takes on dressmaking and the oldest child, Robbie (Rex Thompson), obtains a job at the lumber camp to make ends meet. Johns becomes very ill and is diagnosed with typhoid fever. Knowing she is about to die, Johns gives Thompson the responsibility of find-

ing good homes for his brothers and sisters. On Christmas Day, Thompson finds homes for his siblings and plans to live and work at the lumber camp.

NOTES AND COMMENTARY: When this film was completed, all production at RKO Radio Pictures had been terminated. Universal-International became the distribution arm for the more important RKO features. Even though *All Mine to Give* was not released in the United States until January 1958, the film had its world premiere in England in April 1957.

Glynis Johns' statue as an international film star and a favorite of the British public probably accounted for the British premiere. Available cast listings have Glynis Johns' cast name as Mamie while Cameron Mitchell distinctly calls her Jo. Also, Hope Emerson is called Mrs. Pugmeister while the same cast listings indicate Mrs. Pugmire.

REVIEWS: "Heart warming and very well done family movie; recommended." *Western Movies*, Pitts; "Genuine pathos and touching sentiment." *New York Times*, 8/4/58.

SUMMATION: *All Mine to Give* is a very good, heartwarming pioneer story. Cameron Mitchell and Glynis Johns are excellent as the immigrant couple. Mitchell can be both gentle and rough as the father. Johns gives a fine realistic performance as the mother. Rex Thompson is quite good as the oldest son especially in the scenes in which he has to find homes for his siblings. Mention has to be made of the fine job that Stephen Wooten as the second child delivers. With the benefit of a well-crafted script by Katherine and Dale Eunson and a fine cast throughout, director Allen Reisner has fashioned a tearjerker of the first order.

All the Fury of the Apache Wars!
All the Glory of Those Who Fought at Spanish Boot!
Down from the forbidden mesas they rode...
the most savage Indians of all...

Apache Drums

Universal-International (June 1951); COLOR by Technicolor; RUNNING TIME: 75 min.

CAST: Sam Leeds, **Stephen McNally**; Sally, **Coleen Gray**; Joe Madden, **Willard Parker**; Reverend Griffin, **Arthur Shields**; Lt. Glidden, **James Griffith**; Pedro-Peter, **Armando Silvestre**; Mrs. Keon, **Georgia Backus**; Jeru, **Clarence Muse**; Betty Careless, **Ruthelma Stevens**; Bert Keon, **James Best**; Chaco, **Chinto Guzman**; Mr. Keon, **Ray Bennett**, Little Girl, **Sherry Jackson**

CREDITS: Director, **Hugo Fregonese**; Producer, **Val Lewton**; Screenwriter, **David Chandler**; Editor, **Milton Carruth**; Art Directors, **Bernard Herzbrun** and **Robert Clatworthy**; Set Decorators, **Russell A. Gausman** and **A. Roland Fields**; Cinematographer, **Charles P. Boyle**; Costumes, **Bill Thomas**; Hair Stylist, **Joan St. Oegger**; Makeup, **Bud Westmore**; Sound, **Leslie I. Carey** and **Glenn E. Anderson**; Music, **Hans I. Salter**; Technicolor Color Consultant, **William Fritzsche**

SONG: "The Bells of St. Clements" (traditional Welsh song)—sung by **Coleen Gray**

Apache Drums (1951). Scene card: Willard Parker (*right*) gives gambler Stephen McNally a rifle to lead townspeople into Apache country to obtain water; left border shows Stephen McNally and Coleen Gray.

LOCATION FILMING: Red Rock Canyon, California

SOURCE: Novel, *Stand at Spanish Boot* by **Harry Brown**

STORY: Mayor Madden (Willard Parker) and Reverend Griffin (Arthur Shields) decide to clean up the town of Spanish Boot by banishing gambler Sam Leeds (Stephen McNally) and saloon owner Betty Careless (Ruthelma Stevens) and her dance hall girls. Just outside town Mescalero Apaches massacre the girls. McNally rides back to Spanish Boot to warn the townspeople that the Apaches are on the warpath. The townspeople refuse to believe McNally until a stagecoach comes in with all the passengers murdered. In a skirmish with the Apaches, McNally wounds their chief. In retaliation, the Indians attack the town. The townsmen take refuge in an adobe church. The Indians need a doctor to tend to their chief's wounds. In an attempt to buy time, Parker poses as a doctor but is unable to keep the chief alive. Parker is killed and the Indians attack the church in force. As the situation looks hopeless, the cavalry arrives. McNally and Coleen Gray plan to spend the rest of their lives together.

NOTES AND COMMENTARY: Coleen Gray felt the script told an interesting aspect of the drug culture of the Mescalero Apache. Drugs were used to highlight their resentment of the white man, and gave a dimension of desperation and religious fervor usually not seen in the western film.

The scene in which Coleen Gray sang "The Bells of St. Clements" with the children was edited prior to the film's release. In the picture, the last line that you hear Gray sing is, "Here comes a candle to light you your bed." The scene then moves to another part of the church. The last line Gray actually sang was, "and here comes a chopper to chop off your..." Gray stops singing because the horror of those words, remembering the mutilated body of the young man found in the well, and also because the mother is sitting near her in the church. In fact, the mutilation of James Best is never mentioned in the film. Best's dead body is just found in the well. Therefore the line Coleen Gray sang that stopped her in horror was also removed from the picture. James Best was disappointed in his role in the film because it was so small. Best, when asked about the film, said, "I think they killed me and threw me in the well. I never saw the movie."

Coleen Gray became friends with Willard Parker and his wife, Virginia Field. Parker reminded Gray of buckskin. I asked her why and she replied, "Willard Parker wore buckskin, I think. My mental picture of him is the blondish hair, deeply tanned skin, the color of buckskin, and wearing buckskin ... and blue eyes."

Footage of Indians beating the drums was used in *The Stand at Apache River* (Universal-International, 1953), *Drums Across the River* (Universal-International, 1954) and *Kiss of Fire* (Universal-International, 1955).

REVIEWS: "Frontier days western with good climax." *Variety*, 4/25/51; "A literate screenplay which does not overlook opportunities for vivid and exciting action." *Hollywood Reporter*, 4/20/51.

SUMMATION: This is a sturdy, suspenseful western in the Val Lewton tradition. Lewton was known for his intelligent well-crafted horror films for RKO in the early to mid–40s. He believed that the unseen is more gripping to an audience than what is actually presented on the screen. By having the climactic Indian attack in a building where the inhabitants are unable to see outside accomplishes Lewton's objective. Good performances are given by Stephen McNally, Coleen Gray, Willard Parker, Arthur Shields and James Griffith. The film is well directed by Hugo Fregonese.

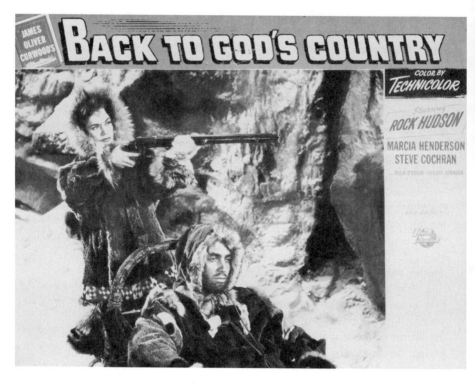

Back to God's Country (1953). Scene card: Marcia Henderson protects an ill Rock Hudson from dangers on the trail.

JAMES OLIVER CURWOOD'S GREAT CLASSIC OF THE NORTH!
...the saga of Peter Keith, the mighty conquest he dared
and the reckless woman he won!

Back to God's Country

Universal-International (November 1953); COLOR by Technicolor; RUNNING TIME: 78 min.

CAST: Peter Keith, **Rock Hudson**; Dolores Keith, **Marcia Henderson**; Paul Blake, **Steve Cochran**; Frank Hudson, **Hugh O'Brian**; Shorter, **Chubby Johnson**; Fitzsimmons, **Tudor Owen**; Carstairs, **Arthur Space**; Lagi, **Bill Radovich**; Joe, **John Cliff**; Uppy, **Pat Hogan**; Reinhardt, **Ivan Triesault**; Nelson, **Charles Horvath**; Wapi, **Wapi**

CREDITS: Director, **Joseph Pevney**; Assistant Director, **Ronnie Rondell**; Producer, **Howard Christie**; Screenwriter, **Tom Reed**; Editor, **Milton Carruth**; Art Directors, **Bernard Herzbrun** and **Hilyard Brown**; Set Decorators, **Russell A. Gausman** and **Oliver Emert**; Cinematographer, **Maury Gertsman**; Costumes, **Bill Thomas**; Hair Stylist, **Joan St. Oegger**; Makeup, **Bud Westmore**; Sound, **Leslie I. Carey** and **Joe Lapis**; Music, **Frank Skinner**; Technicolor Color Consultant, **William Fritzsche**

SONG: "Beyond the Horizon" (Herbert and Hughes)—sung by **Hugh O'Brian**

LOCATION FILMING: Colorado and Sun Valley, Idaho

SOURCE: Story, *Back to God's Country* by **James Oliver Curwood**

STORY: An Eskimo is attacked and killed by two assailants to obtain the map to a valuable gold mine. The Eskimo's Great Dane, Wapi, tries to defend his master but before he is rendered unconscious is able to bite one of the murderers. In Franklin Bay, sea captain Keith (Rock Hudson) decides he has enough furs on board and plans to sail to the United States at midnight. Trader Blake (Steve Cochran) tries to convince Hudson and his wife, Marcia Henderson, to stay. Cochran has lecherous designs on Henderson. Hudson receives a letter from the Canadian government telling him not to sail until his cargo can be inspected. Hudson plans to ignore the letter and later finds that it was a forged letter sent by Cochran. Before Hudson can sail, two crewmen are lured into the interior with the promise of obtaining gold. Hudson and his cook, Shorter (Chubby Johnson), find them and the men start back to the ship. Since their dogsled has been stolen, the men have to make the trip back on foot. A hired assassin paid to shoot Hudson mistakenly shoots Johnson instead. Thinking Hudson dead, Cochran makes an unsuccessful attempt to make love to Henderson. On his return, Hudson confronts Cochran and a rugged fistfight ensues. Hudson is getting the upper hand in the fight until he is struck on his head by Cochran's bookkeeper, Hudson (Hugh O'Brian). Cochran then throws Hudson from an upper landing to the ground floor with the fall breaking Hudson's leg. Hudson is in need of medical attention and he and his wife leave Franklin Bay by dogsled. By trickery, Hudson travels in a circle giving Cochran a chance to catch up to them. Cochran plans to kill Hudson and force Henderson to live with him. As Cochran catches up, Wapi lies in wait. At the exact spot his original master was killed, Wapi confronts Cochran, one of the men responsible for his master's death. Wapi exacts his revenge and Hudson is able to complete his journey.

NOTES AND COMMENTARY: Universal-International borrowed Steve Cochran from Warner Bros. to play villain Paul Blake in this motion picture. James Oliver Curwood's story had been filmed twice previously, both as silents. The first version was a Canadian Photoplays/First National production in 1919 starring Wheeler Oakman, Nell Shipman and Charles Arling. Universal filmed the second in 1927 with Robert Frazer, Renée Adorée and Walter Long. The 1953 version, at least, had the correct character names for all three leads.

REVIEWS: "Color and the villainy

of Steve Cochran greatly help the adaptation of the James Oliver Curwood story" *Western Movies*, Pitts; "Some good outdoor photography is about all to recommend this, other than Cochran's leering, sneering performance," *The Motion Picture Guide*, Nash and Ross.

SUMMATION: *Back to God's Country* is a slightly above average Northwest saga highlighted by a tough fistic encounter between hero Rock Hudson and villain Steve Cochran. Although Hudson and Marcia Henderson turn in good performances, Steve Cochran stands out in his villainous role as Paul Blake. For all the scenic location shots, which add to enjoyment of this picture, the number of outdoor scenes filmed on a soundstage somewhat blunt the overall impact of the film.

The Story of JIM SLATER
...who followed The Trail of Empty Graves
...past Apache ambush
...through Treachery's silken net, to the shadows of a frightened town,
where the Sixth Man waited
...the man he must destroy even if he destroyed himself!
SUSPENSE THAT CUTS LIKE A WHIP!

Backlash

Universal-International (April 1956); COLOR by Technicolor; RUNNING TIME: 84 min.

CAST: Jim Slater, **Richard Widmark**; Karyl Orton, **Donna Reed**; Johnny Cool, **William Campbell**; Jim Bonniwell, **John McIntire**; Sergeant Lake, **Barton MacLane**; Tony Welker, **Harry Morgan**; Jeff Welker, **Robert J. Wilke**; Benton, **Jack Lambert**; Major Carson, **Roy Roberts**; Sheriff Marson, **Edward C. Platt**; Sheriff Olson, **Robert Foulk**; Dobbs, **Phil Chambers**; Sleepy, **Gregg Barton**; Ned McCloud, **Fred Graham**; Cassidy, **Frank Chase**; Tom Welker, **Reg Parton**; Stage Driver, **Glenn Strange**; Gang Members, **I. Stanford Jolley, Lee Roberts** and **Kermit Maynard**

CREDITS: Director, **John Sturges**; Assistant Director, **John Sherwood**; Producer, **Aaron Rosenberg**; Screenwriter, **Borden Chase**; Editor, **Sherman Todd**; Art Directors, **Alexander Golitzen** and **Eric Orbom**; Set Decorators, **Russell A. Gausman** and **Ray Jeffers**; Cinematographer, **Irving Glassberg**; Costumes, **Rosemary Odell**; Hair Stylist, **Joan St. Oegger**; Makeup, **Bud Westmore**; Sound, **Leslie I. Carey** and **Corson Jowett**; Music Supervisor, **Joseph Gershenson**; Technicolor Color Consultant, **William Fritzsche**

LOCATION FILMING: Arizona

SOURCE: Novel, *Fort Starvation* by **Frank Gruber**

STORY: Karyl (Donna Reed)

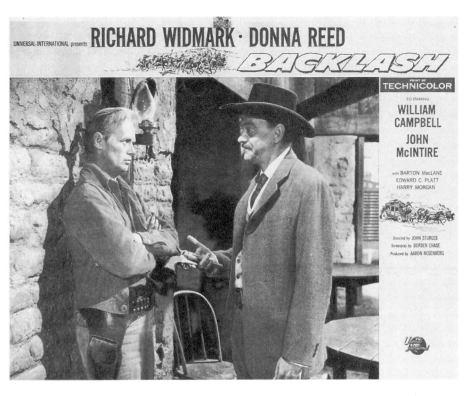

UNIVERSAL-INTERNATIONAL presents **RICHARD WIDMARK · DONNA REED**

BACKLASH

PRINT BY TECHNICOLOR

CO STARRING

WILLIAM CAMPBELL
JOHN McINTIRE

with BARTON MacLANE
EDWARD C. PLATT
HARRY MORGAN

Directed by JOHN STURGES
Screenplay by BORDEN CHASE
Produced by AARON ROSENBERG

Backlash (1956). Scene card: John McIntire (*right*) returns Richard Widmark's pistol.

discovers Jim (Richard Widmark) digging in Gila Valley, Arizona. Reed thinks Widmark is seeking gold but Widmark just wants to find how many bodies were buried there. Five men were buried at the site, but six men found $60,000 in gold. Cavalry sergeant Lake (Barton MacLane) gives Widmark a clue to the sixth man. Reed wants the gold since her husband was one of the men involved and uses her womanly charms to convince Widmark to allow her to accompany him in his quest. Widmark believes this sixth man was responsible for the death of his father.

The trail leads to Major Carson's (Roy Roberts) ranch. Roberts tells Widmark that Jim Bonniwell (John McIntire) came to Texas with $60,000, bought land and suddenly had cattle appear on his range. Now McIntire is trying to start a range war. Widmark finally confronts McIntire and discovers McIntire is his father. McIntire allowed Indians to murder his partners so all the gold, which actually was spoils from a bank robbery, could be taken by him. McIntire plans to ambush Roberts and his men to ensure his victory in the range war. Widmark tries to stop his father, and when McIntire steps out to meet Widmark in a gun duel, McIntire is shot down by a Roberts' ranch hand. Widmark and Reed decide to make a life together.

NOTES AND COMMENTARY: The working title for *Backlash* was *Fort Starvation*.

REVIEWS: "John Sturges should have looked more closely at the script. Aaron Rosenberg missed when he put this one together for Universal" *The Motion Picture Guide*, Nash and Ross; "Unevenly directed but picturesque western, regulation western drama." *Variety*, 3/7/56.

SUMMATION: *Backlash* is not a completely satisfying western. Bor-

den Chase's script is not up to his standards in his collaborations with Anthony Mann. Even Richard Widmark is not able to bring the depth to his performance that is needed to elevate a film trying to be more than an action western. Director John Sturges allows most of his actors to act tough, and the end result is a lot of actors trying to act tough, nothing more. Only Roy Roberts, Robert Foulk and Harry Morgan shine in an otherwise unspectacular cast. Donna Reed is beautiful, probably too much so in the arid and dusty locations. The film is a disappointment considering the talent used in the making of this picture.

The courage of COCHISE!
The vengeance of GERONIMO!
The glory of the U.S. CAVALRY!

The Battle at Apache Pass

ALTERNATE TITLE: *The Battle of Apache Pass*; Universal-International (April 1952); COLOR by Technicolor; RUNNING TIME: 85 min.

CAST: Major Jim Colton, **John Lund**; Cochise, **Jeff Chandler**; Nona, **Susan Cabot**; Neil Baylor, **Bruce Cowling**; Mary Kearny, **Beverly Tyler**; Sgt. Bernard, **Richard Egan**; Geronimo, **Jay Silverheels**; Lt. George Bascomb, **John Hudson**; Mescal Jack, **Jack Elam**; Dr. Carter, **Regis Toomey**; Little Elk, **Tommy Cook**; Lt. Hartley, **Hugh O'Brian**; Cpl. Hassett, **James Best**; Culver, **Richard Garland**; Joe Bent, **Palmer Lee**; Lem Bent, **William Reynolds**; Ross, **Paul Smith**; Johnny Ward, **Jack Ingram**; Pvt. Bolin, **John Baer**; Negai, **Fred Carson**

CREDITS: Director, **George Sherman**; Producer, **Leonard Goldstein**; Associate Producer, **Ross Hunter**; Story/Screenwriter, **Gerald Drayson Adams**; Editor, **Ted J. Kent**; Art Directors, **Bernard Herzbrun** and **Richard H. Riedel**; Set Decorators, **Russell A. Gausman** and **Oliver Emert**; Cinematographer, **Charles Boyle**; Costumes, **Rosemary Odell**; Hair Stylist, **Joan St. Oegger**; Makeup, **Bud Westmore**;

The Battle at Apache Pass (1952). Scene card: Regis Toomey (*center*) bandages Jeff Chandler's wound as John Lund looks on.

Sound, **Leslie I. Carey** and **Corson Jowett**; Music, **Hans J. Salter**; Technicolor Color Consultant, **William Fritzsche**

LOCATION FILMING: Arches National Park, Utah

STORY: Peace between the Apache Indians and the white settlers is the result primarily of a deep friendship between Indian Chief Cochise (Jeff Chandler) and Army Major Jim Colton (John Lund). When soldiers are deployed to the east to fight in the Civil War, Geronimo (Jay Silverheels) believes this would be a good time to rid the territory of all whites. Indian agent Baylor (Bruce Cowling) arrives at the fort. Cowling wants to make the Indians wards of the government and manipulate his way to become governor of the territory. Cowling arranges for Silverheels to attack some white settlers and throw the blame on Chandler. When Lund leaves the fort to find the responsible parties, Cowling talks Lt. Bascomb (John Hudson) into arresting Chandler, Nona (Susan Cabot) and Little Elk (Tommy Cook). Chandler escapes but the others are taken captive. Chandler retaliates and war begins between the Indians and the whites. Lund returns and places Cowling under arrest. Lund decides to move all personnel to another fort. The route the soldiers take is through Apache Pass. A battle ensues in which Cabot is injured. Under a flag of truce, Chandler brings Cabot to Lund for medical assistance. Silverheels declares he is the Apache leader. Chandler defeats Silverheels in a hand-to-hand fight and allows Lund and his soldiers to continue their journey without further incident. Chandler declares there will be peace talks at a later date after there has been time for hatreds to subside.

NOTES AND COMMENTARY: In the climactic fight between Cochise and Geronimo at the end of the picture, Al Wyatt doubled Jeff Chandler and Fred Carson doubled Jay Silverheels. Wyatt was sitting on his horse. Carson had to run up a rock, jump from that rock and take Wyatt off his horse. There was a potential problem. Carson couldn't see anything until he reached the edge and had to hope Wyatt would be where he should. The scene went just like it had been planned. After the scene was over, someone decided to measure the distance Carson actually leapt. The distance was measured as 27 feet.

In an earlier fight scene, Carson played the Indian who issued a challenge to Jeff Chandler. Chandler had come for Beverly Tyler as Mary, who had been captured by renegade Indians. Carson threw the spear into the ground and Chandler broke the spear over his knee. The fight started with Al Wyatt doubling Chandler, except for the close-ups.

The Battle at Apache Pass was Palmer Lee's first movie under contract to Universal. The company was on location and Lee as Bent was to lead a wagon train out. Beverly Tyler was sitting on the buckboard seat next to Lee. Tyler was sitting there and looking around at the desert. The wind machines and the mock prop road of canvas were ready. Director George Sherman was ready to start the cameras rolling. The wind machines were turned on and the winds began to blow. Immediately Tyler's hair became disheveled and the scene was stopped. The makeup people came over and began repairing the damage. Lee had to make way to give the makeup people room and found himself sitting on the wrought iron handle on the side, which he found very uncomfortable. After a few minutes of being bounced up and down on the handle, Lee decided to get down and go into the tent that was set up for relaxation between takes. Jeff Chandler came in and began to talk with Lee, commenting on how a lot of time is wasted during filming. Lee agreed and mentioned he had been sitting in the tent for twenty minutes. Chandler looked at Lee and said, "They're waiting on you." Lee had the dubious distinction of being the latest example of time wasted between scenes. As he reached the set, Sherman said, "Are you ready, Mr. Lee?" All Lee could say was that he was sorry and filming was then resumed. Palmer Lee would later in his career be billed as Gregg Palmer.

Jeff Chandler and Jay Silverheels had played the parts of Cochise and Geronimo, respectively in *Broken Arrow* (20th Century–Fox, 1950). Jeff Chandler would have a death scene as Cochise in *Taza, Son of Cochise* (Universal-International, 1954). Jay Silverheels would be seen as Geronimo once more in *Walk the Proud Land* (Universal-International, 1956). In a number of cast listings in various publications, Susan Cabot's part is listed as Nono. The "a" can be distinctly heard each time her name is spoken. The burning fort scene at the beginning of the picture was previously seen in *Tomahawk* (Universal-International, 1951).

REVIEWS: "Interesting outdoor drama." *Variety*, 4/2/52; "A colorful, rousing saga of the war against the Apache." *Hollywood Reporter*, 4/2/52.

SUMMATION: This is a solid cavalry and Indians saga with many exciting action sequences. Jeff Chandler reprises his Cochise role admirably while John Lund delivers a nice performance as the cavalry officer who is a friend to Chandler. Jay Silverheels makes a fine bloodthirsty Geronimo. Richard Egan, Beverly Tyler, Susan Cabot and John Hudson, in particular, give fine support. George Sherman's direction is on the mark for this type of action picture. The screenplay, while full of action, stresses the interaction of Chandler and Lund over the nefarious doings of Bruce Cowling. It must be mentioned that the battle scenes are first-rate.

The greatness ... the glory ... the fury ...
of the last Untamed Frontier!

Bend of the River

ALTERNATE TITLE: *Where the River Bends*; Universal-International (February 1952); COLOR by Technicolor; RUNNING TIME: 91 min.

CAST: Glyn McLyntock, **James Stewart**; Emerson Cole, **Arthur Kennedy**; Laura Baile, **Julia Adams**; Trey Wilson, **Rock Hudson**; Marjie Baile, **Lori Nelson**; Jeremy Baile, **Jay C. Flippen**; Cap'n Mello, **Chubby Johnson**; Shorty, **Harry Morgan**; Long Tom, **Royal Dano**; Mrs. Prentiss, **Frances Bavier**; Tom Hendricks, **Howard Petrie**; Adam, **Stepin Fetchit**; Don Grundy, **Frank Ferguson**; Aunt Tildy, **Lillian Randolph**; Red, **Jack Lambert**; Miner, **Gregg Barton**; Prospectors, **Philo McCullough** and **George Taylor**; Roustabout, **Britt Wood**; Wasco, **Frank Chase**; Barker, **Donald Kerr**; Willie, **Cliff Lyons**

CREDITS: Director, **Anthony Mann**; Producer, **Aaron Rosenberg**; Associate Producer, **Frank Cleaver**; Screenwriter, **Borden Chase**; Editor, **Russell Schoengarth**; Art Directors, **Bernard Herzbrun** and **Nathan Juran**; Set Decorators, **Russell A. Gausman** and **Oliver Emert**; Cinematographer, **Irving Glassberg**; Costumes, **Rosemary Odell**; Hair Stylist, **Joan St. Oegger**; Makeup, **Bud Westmore**; Sound, **Leslie I. Carey** and **Joe Lapis**; Music, **Hans J. Salter**; Technicolor Color Consultant, **William Fritzsche**

LOCATION FILMING: Mt. Hood, the Sandy River, and Timberline, Oregon

SOURCE: Novel, *Bend of the Snake* by **Bill Gulick**

STORY: While leading settlers to farmland in Oregon, McLyntock (James Stewart) saves Cole (Arthur Kennedy) from being hanged as a horse thief. The settlers stop in Portland to order supplies to see them through the winter. When the supplies haven't arrived as promised, Stewart and settler leader Baile (Jay C. Flippen) decide to return to Portland. They find gold fever has hit the city and their supplies are now worth a small fortune in the gold fields. Stewart, with help from Kennedy and gambler Wilson (Rock Hudson), takes the supplies by force and starts back to the farmers' camp. Kennedy decides to take over the supply wagons and sell the supplies in the gold fields. Kennedy leaves Stewart on foot with enough provisions for a return trip to Portland. Stewart vows

Lori Nelson, James Stewart, Jay C. Flippen, and Julia Adams (*left to right*) in a portrait photograph from *Bend of the River* (1952).

that Kennedy has not seen the last of him. Stewart is able to catch up to the wagons and he defeats Kennedy in a hand-to-hand struggle. Stewart and Flippen bring the supplies to the farmers. In the process, Stewart wins pretty Julia Adams as Laura.

NOTES AND COMMENTARY: This film had a lot of exciting memories for Lori Nelson, as it was her first movie. While on location, Nelson celebrated her eighteenth birthday. Nelson's mother and father paid a surprise visit and the cast and crew gave Nelson a surprise birthday party. Rock Hudson became one of Lori Nelson's best friends. Nelson said, "I suppose I had a crush on him in those days." Lori Nelson had this comment about *Bend of the River*, "That was one of the better westerns made in those days. I don't think it got the critical acclaim that it deserved."

Bend of the Snake, the title of the novel from which the movie was adapted, was the working title for the film. The film performed well at the box office and finished in a tie for 13th place in the list of top box office attractions for 1952. *Bend of the River* took in three million dollars. Ted Mapes was Stewart's double for his dangerous scenes in the movie.

The scene in which James Stewart and his group ambush Howard Petrie and his men would be utilized again in Audie Murphy's *Gunsmoke* (Universal-International, 1953).

REVIEWS: "Top-notch pioneer adventure." *Variety*, 1/23/52; "A stunning outdoor drama, filled with rousing action material." *Hollywood Reporter*, 1/22/52.

SUMMATION: This is an excellent western that is full of action, well-written, acted and directed. James Stewart gives a great performance as a man trying to live down a violent past. Arthur Kennedy almost matches Stewart in his role as a man who still prefers to live a life of violence. Julia Adams, Rock Hudson and Jay C. Flippen add good support. Anthony Mann's hard-edged direction to Borden Chase's superior script is outstanding. This was the second western in the Stewart-Mann collaboration.

The lady known as LOLA—*exotic dancing queen of a frontier where love was made at gun-point...*

Black Bart

ALTERNATE TITLE: *Black Bart Highwayman*; Universal-International (April 1948); COLOR by Technicolor; RUNNING TIME: 80½ min.

CAST: Lola Montez, **Yvonne De Carlo**; Charles E. Boles/Black Bart, **Dan Duryea**; Lance Hardeen, **Jeffrey Lynn**; Jersey Brady, **Percy Kilbride**; Sheriff Gordon, **Lloyd Gough**; Lorimer, **Frank Lovejoy**; Clark, **John McIntire**; J.T. Hall, **Don Beddoe**; MacFarland, **Ray**

Walker; Teresa, **Soledad Jiminez**; Mason, **Eddy C. Waller**; Mrs. Harmon, **Anne O'Neal**; Indian, **Chief Many Treaties**; Elkins, **Eddie Acuff**; Sheriff Mix, **Douglas Fowley**; Mamacita, **Nina Campana**; Agent Clayton, **Russ Conway**; Bartender, **Reed Howes**; Pete, **Ray Teal**; Henry, **Ray Bennett**

CREDITS: Director, **George Sherman**; Assistant Director, **William Holland**; Producer, **Leonard Goldstein**; Story, **Luci Ward** and **Jack Natteford**; Screenwriters, **Luci Ward, Jack Natteford** and **William Bowers**; Editor, **Russell Schoengarth**; Art Directors, **Bernard Herzbrun** and **Emrich Nicholson**; Set Decorators, **Russell A. Gausman** and **William Stevens**; Cinematographer, **Irving Glassberg**; Costumes, **Yvonne Wood**; Hair Stylist, **Carmen Dirigo**; Sound, **Leslie I. Carey** and **Corson Jowett**; Music for Miss De Carlo's dances, **Frank Skinner**; Choreography, **Val Raset**; Technicolor Color Director, **Natalie Kalmus**; Associate Color Director, **Clemens Finley**

LOCATION FILMING: Kanab, Utah, and Iverson's Ranch, California

STORY: Jersey Brady (Percy Kilbride) saves fellow outlaws, Boles (Dan Duryea) and Hardeen (Jeffrey Lynn) from being hanged for bank robbery and other assorted crimes. The trio decides to split up, with Lynn and Kilbride leaving Duryea afoot. Duryea already has the money in his possession that Lynn and Kilbride are riding to get. Duryea goes to California and enters into a scheme with Clark (John McIntire) to break the Wells Fargo branch in Sacramento. McIntire supplies the information and Duryea then holds up the stagecoaches as the nefarious outlaw, Black Bart. Dancer Lola Montez (Yvonne De Carlo), Lynn and Kilbride come to California. Duryea and Lynn become rivals for the affections of De Carlo but De Carlo prefers Duryea. Knowing Duryea is Black Bart, Lynn also wants to rob stagecoaches. De Carlo discovers that Duryea is Black Bart but decides not to tell the authorities. Duryea wants to commit one more robbery that will ruin Wells Fargo. Duryea gets the strongbox but the box is empty. Lynn doesn't believe the box was empty and wants a share of the money. Duryea thinks the money is being held at a stage station and suggests that Lynn steal the money. De Carlo has convinced Duryea to quit his life of crime but Lynn forces Duryea to accompany him to the station. J.T. Hall (Don Beddoe), a Wells Fargo detective, has set a trap to thwart any robbery attempt. In a blazing gunfight, Duryea and Lynn are killed as they try to escape capture.

NOTES AND COMMENTARY: This film had working titles of *Adventures of Black Bart*, *Black Bart Highwayman* and *Legend of Black Bart* before *Black Bart* became the final title. Some of the music score contains elements previously heard in earlier Universal westerns and serials and also in some Columbia western features.

Look at the newspaper columns in the film; one article mentions

Black Bart (1948) scene card: Dan Duryea as Black Bart (*right*) holds up stage-coach driver Eddy C. Waller (*left*) and an unidentified actor; left, border shows Dan Duryea.

automobiles. The time line of the film is around 1849! Dan Duryea was nervous about his role in this film. The role of Black Bart was a departure from his previous roles as a straight villain with Duryea having his first leading man–type love scenes. One web site states that Black Bart was an African-American. The real Black Bart/Charles E. Boles was, in fact, a dapper white gentleman in his mid-fifties when he was finally brought to justice in November 1883. Again Universal used dramatic license in having a romantic encounter between Boles

and dancer Lola. In all their travels, Boles and Montez never met. Montez' earlier life was as notorious as alluded to in the script. Montez died in Australia in 1861 at age 43.

Black Bart was remade in 1967 as *Ride to Hangman's Tree* (Universal, 1967) with Jack Lord, James Farentino and Don Galloway as the outlaw trio. Jeffrey Lynn had a brief nude swimming scene in the original while Melodie Johnson returns the favor in the remake.

Black Bart marked Frank Lovejoy's movie debut. Lovejoy primarily appeared in non-western films, al-though he would be seen in *The Charge at Feather River* (Warner Bros., 1953) and *The Americano* (RKO, 1955) and would star in *Cole Younger, Gunfighter* (Allied Artists, 1958).

A montage scene contains footage previously shown in *Can't Help Singing* (Universal, 1944) and *Frontier Gal* (Universal, 1945).

REVIEWS: "First-rate entertain-ment, lushly mounted actionful out-door melodrama." *Variety*, 2/4/48; "This is an action picture and of that there is plenty topped off by a blaz-ing climax." *New York Times*, 3/4/48.

SUMMATION: A good action-western with fine performances from principals Dan Duryea, Yvonne De Carlo, Jeffrey Lynn and Percy Kil-bride. George Sherman's direction is first-rate and moves the film along nicely. Irving Glassberg's outstand-ing photography captures the spec-tacular scenic backgrounds.

HE CHALLENGED AN OUTLAW STALLION'S WILDERNESS KINGDOM!
To Conquer the knife-hooved killer no corral could hold!
To Defy the men whose treachery ruled a lawless wasteland!
To Win the fiery beauty no other man could tame!

Black Horse Canyon

Universal-International (June 1954); COLOR by Technicolor; RUN-NING TIME: 81½ min.

CAST: Del Rockwell, **Joel Mc-Crea**; Aldis Spain, **Mari Blan-chard**; Ti, **Race Gentry**; Jennings, **Murvyn Vye**; Doc, **Irving Bacon**; Duke, **John Pickard**; Sheriff, **Ewing Mitchell**; Juanita, **Pilar del Rey**

CREDITS: Director, **Jesse Hibbs**; Assistant Director, **John Sherwood**; Producer, **John W. Rogers**; Screen-writer, **Geoffrey Homes**; Adapta-tion, **David Lang**; Editor, **Frank Gross**; Art Decorators, **Bernard Herzbrun** and **Robert Clatworthy**; Set Decorators, **Russell A. Gaus-man** and **Ruby R. Levitt**; Cine-matographer, **George Robinson**; Costumes, **Bill Thomas**; Hair Stylist, **Joan St. Oegger**; Makeup, **Bud Westmore**; Sound, **Leslie I. Carey** and **Corson Jowett**; Music Director, **Joseph Gershenson**; Technicolor Color Consultant, **Monroe W. Bur-bank**

LOCATION FILMING: Arizona; SOURCE: Novel, *The Wild Horse* by **Lee Savage, Jr.**

STORY: Outlaw, a wild stallion and leader of a large herd of horses, is actually owned by rancher Aldis Spain (Mari Blanchard). Outlaw has the ability to open corral gates and consequently adds to his herd by stealing ranchers' horses. Rival rancher Jennings (Murvyn Vye) and struggling ranchers Rockwell (Joel McCrea) and Ti (Race Gentry) covet Outlaw. To capture Outlaw, McCrea and Gentry drive his herd into their corral. Before they have a chance to

Black Horse Canyon (1954) scene card: Race Gentry and Mari Blanchard discuss Outlaw, a wild stallion, and Joel McCrea.

cut out the branded stock, Vye accuses them of rustling. Vye and his men take McCrea and Gentry to Blanchard's ranch since some of her stock was found with the herd. Blanchard tells Vye that Outlaw was responsible for taking the horses. Vye makes an attempt to capture Outlaw which results in one of his men being killed by Outlaw before the stallion escapes. Vye wants Outlaw hunted down and killed as a killer horse. McCrea intervenes and gets Blanchard one week to capture and break Outlaw to show that the charge of killer is unfounded. Gentry, who has fallen in love with Blan-

chard, wants to stay and help her. McCrea finally agrees and the three capture Outlaw. Through this, Blanchard and McCrea are gradually falling in love. The stallion is brought back to Blanchard's ranch and the process of breaking him is begun. Gentry attempts to ride Outlaw in order to impress Blanchard and is thrown. Then Gentry finds McCrea and Blanchard in an embrace, which causes a rift between the two men. When Blanchard calls Gentry a child, Gentry reacts by leaving the two of them. McCrea decides to attempt to ride Outlaw. Vye and his ranch hand, Duke (Pickard), open the corral gate and start firing their guns in the air in an attempt to have McCrea thrown and the horse escape into the hills. Gentry, who has not traveled far, comes to McCrea's rescue by fighting Pickard and Vye. McCrea dismounts and joins the fray in which McCrea and Gentry emerge victorious. When Blanchard joins them, Gentry announces that McCrea is going to marry Blanchard, which is fine with them.

NOTES AND COMMENTARY: The working title for *Black Horse Canyon* was *Echo Canyo*. Footage from *Red Canyon* (Universal-International, 1949) is used in this film with some of the scenes later seeing use in Joel McCrea's final starring western, *Mustang Country* (Universal, 1976).

Geoffrey Homes was the pseudonym for Daniel Mainwaring. Billed as Homes, Mainwaring wrote the scripts for *The Big Steal* (RKO, 1949), *The Tall Target* (Metro-Goldwyn-Mayer, 1951), *A Bullet for Joey* (United Artists, 1955) and *Out of the Past* (RKO, 1947), a film noir classic adapted from the novel *Build My Gallows High*, also written by Mainwaring. Under his own name, Mainwaring received screen credit for delivering scripts for *Invasion of the Body Snatchers* (Allied Artists, 1956) and *Baby Face Nelson* (United Artists, 1957).

A nice dialogue exchange happened between Joel McCrea and Mari Blanchard after McCrea had been abrupt with Race Gentry. *Blanchard:* "Do you find it easy to be disagreeable or do you have to work for it?" *McCrea:* "You know, I got a kind of talent for it."

REVIEWS: "Entertaining hoss opera, a sterling outdoor story." *Variety*, 5/19/54; "A pleasant horse-opera of a Western." *The Western*, Hardy.

SUMMATION: *Black Horse Canyon* is a pleasant, entertaining outdoor saga of two men and a woman chasing a wild stallion. Agreeable performances are given by Joel McCrea, Mari Blanchard and Race Gentry as the leads. Irving Bacon chips in with some light comedy and Murvyn Vye capably handles the mild villainy. Director Jesse Hibbs keeps the story moving along nicely, easily holding the audience's interest.

THEY HAD A DATE WITH DESTINY IN THE POWDER KEG OF THE WEST ... ZONA LIBRE!

Border River

Universal-International (January 1954); COLOR by Technicolor; RUNNING TIME: 80½ min.

CAST: Clete Mattson, **Joel McCrea**; Carmelita Carias, **Yvonne De Carlo**; General Calleja, **Pedro Armendariz**; Captain Vargas, **Alfonso Bedoya**; Newland, **Howard Petrie**;

Annina Strasser, **Erika Nordin**; Sanchez, **George J. Lewis**; Lopez, **Nacho Galindo**; Baron Von Hollden, **Ivan Triesault**; Fletcher, **George Wallace**; Anderson, **Lane Chandler**; Guzman, **Martin Garralaga**; Stanton, **Joe Bassett**; General Robles, **Salvador Baguez**; Pablo, **Felipe Turich**; Cavalry Sergeant, **Robert Hoy**; Crowe, **Charles Horvath**; Union Sympathizer, **Britt Wood**

CREDITS: Director, **George Sherman**; Assistant Director, **Frank Shaw**; Producer, **Albert J. Cohen**; Story, **Louis Stevens**; Screenwriters, **William Sackheim** and **Louis Stevens**; Editor, **Frank Gross**; Art Directors, **Bernard Herzbrun** and **Richard H. Reidel**; Set Decorators, **Russell A. Gausman** and **John Austin**; Cinematographer, **Irving Glassberg**; Costumes, **Rosemary Odell**; Hair Stylist, **Joan St. Oegger**; Makeup, **Bud Westmore**; Sound, **Leslie I. Carey** and **Corson Jowett**; Music Director, **Joseph Gershenson**; Technicolor Color Consultant, **William Fritzsche**

Border River (1954) scene card: Joel McCrea retrieves Yvonne De Carlo from the floor after an altercation in the saloon.

LOCATION FILMING: Moab area (Professor Valley, Colorado River, White's Ranch, Courthouse Wash), Utah

STORY: A wounded Clete Mattson barely makes it across a river to safety in Zona Libre. Zona Libre, though in Mexico, is under rule by General Calleja (Pedro Armendariz) and offers sanctuary to people seeking refuge from the law. McCrea, a Confederate officer, wants to purchase rifles, ammunition, food and clothing for the Confederacy with the two million in gold that has been stolen from the Union. Complicating matters for McCrea is Carmelita (Yvonne De Carlo), who runs a saloon in partnership with Armendariz. Both men are in love with De Carlo, who does not want to be involved in any cause. As McCrea gets closer to obtaining the supplies that he needs, other Confederate soldiers bring the gold to Zona Libre. Armandariz' second-in-command, Vargas (Alfonso Bedoya), catches McCrea in the act of hiding the gold but is killed. Armendariz discovers that De Carlo is now aiding McCrea and uses De Carlo to find the gold. McCrea and his men attack Armendariz and his small band of soldiers as they are trying to move the gold. The soldiers are shot but Armendariz drowns in a quicksand bog during a fight with McCrea. The new regime in Zona Libre makes a fair bargain with McCrea. McCrea and De Carlo leave Zona Libre to take the supplies to the Confederate soldiers.

NOTES AND COMMENTARY: Robert Hoy was quite busy during the filming of *Border River*. In addition to playing the role of a Cavalry Sergeant, Hoy doubled both Pedro Armendariz and Alfonso Bedoya. Pedro Armendariz was needed to finish the fight sequence with Joel McCrea. The fight had been completed but close-ups of the principals were needed. Hoy, who had doubled Armendariz for the fight, was told that he would fill in for Armendariz. Cinematographer Irving Glassberg told Hoy, "Whatever we do, Bobby, we can't see your head not even your profile." The punch that Hoy was to throw was choreographed but Joel McCrea stepped the opposite way and Hoy's punch hit McCrea in the mouth. Assistant Director Frank Shaw was horrified and jumped all over Hoy, "Bobby, how dare you. How could you!" McCrea stepped in and said, "Frank, shut up. It wasn't Bobby's fault, it was mine. Not only that, Frank, you've got people moving behind the camera." The camera had been set over Hoy's shoulder to catch McCrea and McCrea was distracted. The incident cost the studio $10,000 because McCrea had a swollen lip and couldn't do a love scene with Yvonne De Carlo. Al Wyatt doubled Joel McCrea in the fight in the mud hole with Pedro Armendariz.

Robert Hoy made this comment about director George Sherman, "Georgie was a man. When I say he was a man, he was about five-feet six-inches tall. He had control and respect. Good guy."

REVIEWS: "Well made actioner." *Variety*, 1/6/54; "Colorful outing that provides good entertainment." *Western Movies*, Pitts.

SUMMATION: *Border River* is a good action-western set at the end of the Civil War. The principals, Joel McCrea, Yvonne De Carlo and Pedro Armendariz, acquit themselves well but Alfonso Bedoya steals the show as Armendariz' second-in-command. Bedoya is able to show craftiness and intelligence in a loutish, stupid-looking individual. As usual, George Sherman directs economically with not a wasted scene and with a firm hand on some rousing action scenes.

The Thrill Story of THE MEN WHO RIDE DANGER...
AND THE WOMEN WHO DARE TO LOVE THEM!
The Roaring Spectacle of the Most Dangerous Sport in the World!

Bronco Buster

Universal-International (May 1952); COLOR by Technicolor; RUNNING TIME: 81 min.

CAST: Tom Moody, **John Lund**; Bart Eaton, **Scott Brady**; Judy Bream, **Joyce Holden**; Dan Bream, **Chill Wills**; Dobie Carson, **Don Haggerty**; Casey Tibbs, **Casey Tibbs**; Pete Crump, **Pete Crump**; Dan Poore, **Dan Poore**; Bill Williams, **Bill Williams**; Jerry Ambler, **Jerry Ambler**; Television Announcer, **Walter Reed**; Rodeo Official, **Terry Frost**; Bartender, **Dick Curtis**

CREDITS: Director, **Budd Boetticher**; Producer, **Ted Richmond**; Story, **Peter B. Kyne**; Screenwriters, **Horace McCoy** and **Lillie Hayward**; Editor, **Edward Curtiss**; Technical Advisor, **Andy Jauregu**; Art Directors, **Bernard Herzbrun** and **Robert Boyle**; Set Decorators, **Russell A. Gausman** and **Joseph Kish**; Cinematographer, **Clifford Stine**; Gowns, **Bill Thomas**; Hair Stylist, **Joan St. Oegger**; Makeup, **Bud Westmore**; Sound, **Leslie I. Carey** and **Richard De Weese**; Music, **Joseph Gershenson**; Technicolor Color Consultant, **William Fritzsche**

LOCATION FILMING: At rodeos in Phoenix, Arizona; Pendleton, Oregon; Calgary, Alberta, Canada; and Cheyenne, Wyoming

STORY: World's champion rodeo performer Tom Moody (John Lund), recovering from an ankle injury, returns to the rodeo circuit. Brash Bart Eaton (Scott Brady) is the new up-and-coming rodeo star. Both men are romantically interested in Judy Bream (Joyce Holden). Lund decides to help Brady develop his rodeo skills. Brady's interest in Holden causes a riff between the two men. Brady's showboating causes circus clown Dan Bream (Chill Wills) to be seriously injured by a Brahma bull. From his hospital bed, Wills advises Brady to stop showing off, to straighten up and patch things up with Lund. Before Brady can do so, Lund challenges Brady to a contest where each man rides a Brahma

Bronco Buster (1952) scene card: Scott Brady (*left*) gets a lecture on how life should be lived from Chill Wills.

bull in the same corral at the same time. The winner is the man who stays on his animal the longest. Brady wins the contest but quick action from Lund saves Brady from being injured by one of the bulls. Brady is now able to apologize to Lund for his previous actions, which Lund now accepts. Holden decides that it's now time for Lund to marry her.

NOTES AND COMMENTARY: Budd Boetticher remembered *Bronco Buster* as a " fun picture" and especially liked working with John Lund, Chill Wills and Scott Brady. Peggy Dow was originally set to play the

femme lead in the picture but was not able to complete her starring role in the Samuel Goldwyn production, *I Want You* (RKO, 1952), in time to start work on *Bronco Buster*. Joyce Holden then replaced Dow.

Boetticher had the rodeo performers Casey Tibbs, Pete Crump, Bill Williams, Dan Pocre and Jerry Ambler stay at his house so he would have them available when he needed them. The Bill Williams in this film is the rodeo performer, not the movie actor as has been reported in some publications.

Bullfights were held every day at five o'clock on the Universal back lot. Boetticher, a bullfight aficion-ado, had an area especially prepared for this activity. John Lund and Scott Brady really couldn't ride like true rodeo cowboys.

The script was purposely written so John Lund's character would have a bad leg, Boetticher had Casey Tibbs perform, and the audience would then be told that Lund was a better rodeo performer than Tibbs.

The music played over the title credits and later during the film, was Raye and de Paul's "Ride 'Em Cowboy" (Universal, 1942) from the Abbott and Costello film of the same name.

REVIEWS: "Good action and thrills in story of rodeo, satisfying round of outdoor action thrills." *Variety*, 4/16/52; "Not bad but the rodeo sequences are superior to the plot." *Western Movies*, Pitts.

SUMMATION: This is a good outdoor action story with outstanding rodeo sequences. John Lund, Scott Brady, Joyce Holden and Chill Wills give good performances. Casey Tibbs, Pete Crump, Dan Poore, Bill Williams and Jerry Ambler add the proper authenticity to the proceedings. Budd Boetticher, adroitly interspersing actual rodeo footage with the story, nicely directs the film. Of particular interest is the scene with excellent camera work and film editing in which Wills is trampled by a Brahma bull.

FIGHTING! LOVING! LOOTING!
Branding their outlaw names
into the fiery fame of the WEST!

Calamity Jane and Sam Bass

Universal-International (July 1949); COLOR by Technicolor; RUNNING TIME: 85 min.

CAST: Calamity Jane, **Yvonne De Carlo**; Sam Bass, **Howard Duff**; Katherine Egan, **Dorothy Hart**; Sheriff Will Egan, **Willard Parker**; Jim Murphy, **Norman Lloyd**; Joel Collins, **Lloyd Bridges**; Dean, **Marc Lawrence**; Dakota, **Houseley Stevenson**; Abe Jones, **Milburn Stone**; Link, **Clifton Young**; Morgan, **John Rodney**; Marshal Peak, **Roy Roberts**; Mrs. Egan, **Ann Doran**; J. Wells, **Charles Cane**; Doc Purdy, **Walter Baldwin**; Stage Driver, **Jack Ingram**; Race Official, **Frances MacDonald**; Cowboy, **Stanley Blystone**; Deputy, **Pierce Lyden**; Cattleman, **I. Stanford Jolley**; Station Agent, **Harry Harvey**; Mr. Sherman, **George M. Carleton**; Underwood, **Paul Maxey**; Parsons, **Nedrick Young**; Baggage Man, **Russ Conway**

CREDITS: Director/Story, **George Sherman**; Producer, **Leonard Goldstein**; Associate Producer, **Aaron Rosenberg**; Screenwriters, **Maurice Geraghty** and **Melvin Levy**; Editor,

Edward Curtiss; Art Directors, **Bernard Herzbrun and Richard H. Riedel**; Set Decorators, **Russell A. Gausman** and **Al Fields**; Cinematographer, **Irving Glassberg**; Costumes, **Yvonne Wood**; Hair Stylist, **Carmen Dirigo**; Makeup, **Bud Westmore**; Sound, **Leslie I. Carey** and **Glenn E. Anderson**; Music, **Milton Schwarzwald**; Technicolor Color Director, **Natalie Kalmus**; Associate Technicolor Color Director, **Monroe W. Burbank**

LOCATION FILMING: Kanab, Utah; Red Rock Canyon and Iverson's Ranch, California

STORY: Sam Bass (Howard Duff) comes to Denton, Texas, the site of an annual horse race, to find work. The Denton mare is the favorite to win the race. Duff watches a blacksmith improperly shoe the mare and realizes that Calamity Jane's (Yvonne De Carlo) horse will win the race. As Duff knows the injury to the mare to be temporary, Duff bets on De Carlo's horse and wins enough money to purchase the Denton mare. Duff, then, joins Joel Collins' (Lloyd Bridges) cattle drive to Abilene, Kansas. In Abilene, Duff enters the mare in their annual horse race. Dean (Marc Lawrence) always enters a "ringer" to insure victory. De Carlo unwittingly tells Lawrence that Duff's horse is the Denton mare.

Calamity Jane and Sam Bass (1949) scene card: Houseley Stevenson (*center front*) counts the stolen money as Howard Duff (*left*), John Rodney, and Yvonne De Carlo keep guns on an unidentified actor.

Lawrence arranges to have the mare poisoned. Duff and his friends lose a substantial amount of money. Duff holds up Lawrence and only takes back the money he and his friends wagered. Branded an outlaw and realizing that he can't shake the outlaw brand, Duff forms a gang and begins a series of robberies. Duff is told that the Denton mare is alive and is stabled in Denton. This is really just a ruse to draw him out of hiding. A bank holdup goes awry and Duff is badly wounded. Still determined to see if the mare survived, Duff and De Carlo make it to Denton. Duff's wounds take their toll and he dies in De Carlo's arms.

NOTES AND COMMENTARY: Marc Lawrence enjoyed working with George Sherman. Lawrence commented, "He was somewhat of a pixie." Lawrence remembered Yvonne De Carlo from *Rainbow Island* (Paramount, 1944). He thought that film was somewhat at the beginning of her long film career. Howard Duff did not bring any fond memories to Marc Lawrence. Lawrence commented, "Howard Duff sort of stiff-armed me—very few likable qualities." The film was originally to be called *Adventures of Sam*

Bass. Interesting that the bank president is named George Sherman (see "Director/Story" credit).

REVIEWS: "Colorful production, plenty of action." *Hollywood Reporter*, 6/3/49; "Surprisingly good film, although mostly fiction." *Western Movies*, Pitts.

SUMMATION: This is a fast action-western that is briskly paced by director George Sherman. The film has good performances by Howard Duff, Dorothy Hart, Lloyd Bridges and especially Yvonne De Carlo, who is both attractive and properly tough as Calamity Jane. Duff is fortunate to have two lovely ladies, De Carlo and Hart, fighting over him. Don't expect historical fact in this whitewashed version of Sam Bass' outlaw career. Bass, in fact, died in the arms of a Texas Ranger and never knew Calamity Jane. This is the third Universal-International western in a row that De Carlo does not end up with the leading man. Dan Duryea is killed in *Black Bart* (Universal-International, 1948) and De Carlo loses out to Helena Carter for Rod Cameron's attentions in *River Lady* (Universal-International, 1948).

The Story of the Great Santa Fe Stampede!
A new hand is like a bronc ... he's got to be broken!
Wild black stallion ... that Mathews has sworn to ride!
To old hands the kid's a jinx!

Cattle Drive

Universal-International (August 1951); COLOR by Technicolor; RUNNING TIME: 77 min.

CAST: Dan Mathews, **Joel McCrea**; Chester Graham Jr., **Dean Stockwell**; Dallas, **Chill Wills**; Mr.

Graham, **Leon Ames**; Jim Currie, **Henry Brandon**; Cap, **Howard Petrie**; Careless, **Bob Steele**; Conductor O'Hara, **Griff Barnett**

CREDITS: Director, **Kurt Neumann**; Producer, **Aaron Rosenberg**; Screenwriters, **Jack Natteford** and **Lillie Hayward**; Editor, **Danny B. Landres**; Art Directors, **Bernard Herzbrun** and **Hilyard Brown**; Set Decorators, **Russell A. Gausman** and **Ruby R. Levitt**; Cinematographer, **Maury Gertsman**; Special Photography, **David S. Horsley**; Makeup, **Bud Westmore**; Sound, **Leslie I. Carey** and **Richard DeWeese**; Music Director, **Joseph Gershenson**; Technicolor Color Consultant, **William Fritzsche**

SONG: "Ten Thousand Cattle Gone Astray" (traditional)—sung by **Joel McCrea**. Frederick Herbert wrote special lyrics for this song.

LOCATION FILMING: Death Valley, California

STORY: Chester Graham Jr. (Dean Stockwell), a spoiled brat, is travelling west by rail with his father, Chester Sr. (Leon Ames), the owner and president of the railroad. When the train makes a stop to take on water, Stockwell gets off the train and is inadvertently left behind. Instead of staying at the water stop, Stockwell decides to walk to the nearest town. Dan Mathews (Joel McCrea) is trying to capture a beautiful black stallion, which he needs to start his own ranch where he plans to raise horses. McCrea has the stallion cornered but Stockwell's interference allows the stallion to escape. McCrea is on a cattle drive and decides to take Stockwell back to the camp where he persuades trail boss Cap (Howard Petrie) to take Stockwell to Santa Fe. Cowhand Currie (Henry Brandon) thinks Stockwell will be a jinx and doesn't want him on the drive. Stockwell gains the cowboys' respect when he is almost able to ride a mean half-broken horse. McCrea takes a liking to Stockwell and begins to make a better person out of him. Brandon and McCrea both think that they have the fastest horse and agree to a race to end the dispute. McCrea wins the race but finds Stockwell had tired Brandon's horse by riding him through most of the night. All bets are called off, Brandon is angry with Stockwell, but most importantly Stockwell has learned a lesson on good sportsmanship. The black stallion has followed the trail drive and drives the remuda off. The cowboys catch up to the horses but the black stallion again gets away. Brandon wants to shoot the stallion but McCrea asks for one more chance to capture him. McCrea with Stockwell's help is able to bring the stallion back to the camp. McCrea is determined to break the stallion. Stockwell wants to help McCrea and when he loosens the rope, the stallion breaks away. Brandon sees the stallion running through the cattle and fires a shot at the horse. The shot causes the cattle to stampede. The cowboys finally stop the stampede and discover that Stockwell is missing. Fearing the worst, McCrea returns to the camp where he finds Stockwell unharmed. Brandon admits that it was his shot that started

Cattle Drive (1951) scene card: Chill Wills, Joel McCrea, and Dean Stockwell arrive in Santa Fe after an arduous trail drive.

the stampede but Petrie states the stampede helped make up for time that had been lost. McCrea brings Stockwell to Ames in Santa Fe. Stockwell wants to stay out West and help McCrea catch the wild stallion. Ames decides to join McCrea and Stockwell in their quest so he can begin to really become acquainted with his son.

NOTES AND COMMENTARY: The picture that Joel McCrea shows Dean Stockwell of his sweetheart who waits for him in Santa Fe is of his real-life wife, actress Frances Dee.

Some sources, Rutherford and Smith's *More Cowboy Shooting Stars* (Empire, 1992) and Rainey's *The Shoot-Em-Ups Ride Again* (Scarecrow, 1990), indicate that Harry Carey Jr. appeared in this film. In a letter from Mr. Carey, he stated, "Thank you for your letter, but I never made a movie called *Cattle Drive*." On careful viewing you will find that Mr. Carey is correct.

Footage of the black stallion with the herd of horses was seen earlier in *Red Canyon* (1949) and *Sierra* (1950).

Some of the cattle stampede footage would be utilized in *Untamed Frontier* (1952).

The interesting script owes more than a little to the classic film *Captains Courageous* (Metro-Goldwyn-Mayer, 1937).

REVIEWS: "Pleasant family entertainment." *The Universal Story*, Hirschhorn; "Solid 77 minutes of action entertainment." *Variety*, 7/18/51.

SUMMATION: *Cattle Drive* is a good family western that stresses the finer values of life. Dean Stockwell delivers a nice performance as the spoiled brat who finally learns how he should act in society. Joel McCrea matches Stockwell with his easygoing, authoritative depiction as a savvy cowpoke. Chill Wills, Henry Brandon, Howard Petrie, Bob Steele, Leon Ames and Griff Barnett provide able support. This western saga is well-directed by Kurt Neumann from a fine script provided by Jack Natteford and Lillie Hayward.

THE MYSTERY OF THE GREAT WELLS FARGO ROBBERY!
Seven men hunted the Golden Secret of the Cave ...
but only ONE lived to Find it!

Cave of Outlaws

Universal-International (November 1951); COLOR by Technicolor; RUNNING TIME: 75 min.

CAST: Pete Carver, **Macdonald Carey**; Liz Trent, **Alexis Smith**; Dobbs, **Edgar Buchanan**; Ben Cross, **Victor Jory**; Garth, **Hugh O'Brian**; Cooley, **Houseley Stevenson**; Sheriff, **Hugh Sanders**; Doctor, **Raymond Bond**; Saloon Owner, **Robert Osterloh**; Deputy, **Johnny Carpenter**; Pete Carver (as a boy), **Russ Tamblyn**; Card Players, **Jack Ingram** and **Kenneth MacDonald**; Whitey, **Clem Fuller**; Jones, **Tim Graham**; Job Delancey, **Charles Horvath**; Jed Delancey, **James Van Horn**

CREDITS: Director, **William Castle**; Producer, **Leonard Goldstein**; Associate Producer, **William Alland**; Story/Screenwriter, **Elizabeth Wilson**; Editor, **Edward Curtiss**; Art Directors, **Bernard Herzbrun** and **Nathan Juran**; Set Decorators, **Russell A. Gausman and Oliver Emert**; Cinematographer, **Irving Glassberg**; Gowns, **Bill Thomas**; Hair Stylist, **Joan St. Oegger**; Makeup, **Bud Westmore**; Sound, **Leslie I. Carey** and **Glenn E. Anderson**; Music, **Joseph Gershenson**; Technicolor Color Consultant, **William Fritzsche**

LOCATION FILMING: Carlsbad Caverns, New Mexico; Vasquez Rocks and Iverson's Ranch, California

STORY: A train is held up in the Arizona territory and the robbers are chased to a huge underground cavern near the mining town of Copper Bend. All the outlaws are killed by the posse except the youngest member who receives a fifteen-year prison term. The money is not recovered. Fifteen years later, Pete Carver (Macdonald Carey) is released from prison and is followed by Wells Fargo agent Dobbs (Edgar Buchanan) to Copper Bend. Carey meets Liz (Alexis Smith) and decides to help her reopen her newspaper. Carey goes to the cave and is unable to find the money. Ben Cross (Victor Jory), the most powerful man in the town, offers to help Carey find the money. Carey and Buchanan go back to the cave and this time find the money. The money was found with the body of Smith's husband, who had been shot by Jory. Buchanan's leg is injured in the search and the money is left in the cave as Carey helps Buchanan back to town. Carey accuses Jory of murder in the headlines of the newspaper. Jory wounds Carey in a pistol duel. Carey has an unanswered shot but Jory persuades Carey not to take it until after he goes to trial to prove his innocence. Buchanan and Carey go back to the cave and recover the gold. Buchanan takes the gold since all Carey wants is the bullet that killed Smith's husband to prove Jory a murderer. Smith follows Carey to the cave. Jory gets the drop on both Smith and Carey and is about to kill Carey when a shot rings out. Buchanan shoots Jory. Carey will receive the reward for finding the money and will settle down with Smith.

NOTES AND COMMENTARY: The opening train robbery scene was lifted intact from *Wyoming Mail* (Universal-International, 1950). A close look will reveal James Arness, Gene Evans, Frankie Darro, Richard Jaeckel and Felipe Turich. Turich is obviously in Mexican garb, but in the new footage during the chase of the robbers by the posse, no such person appears. Oh yes, five men rob the train but only four are chased. A case of sloppy continuity that the producers apparently thought patrons would not notice.

Interestingly, most cast listings in various reference books (e.g. *The Shoot-Em-Ups* (Arlington House, 1978) and its sequel *The Shoot-Em-Ups Ride Again* (Scarecrow, 1990), and Lentz' *Western and Frontier Film and Television Credits: 1903–1995* (McFarland, 1996) fail to list Hugh Sanders, Raymond Bond and Robert Osterloh. The three actors receive on-screen billing.

The working title for this film was *The Cave*.

Howard Duff was originally signed to star but had to withdraw from the film because his broken leg was not sufficiently healed to take care of the strenuous action called for in the script. Macdonald Carey was signed to replace Duff.

Cave of Outlaws was Hugh O'Brian's first assignment for Universal-International under a long-term contract that was signed in March 1951.

REVIEWS: "An implausible plot haunts this B-western." *The Motion Picture Guide*, Nash and Ross; "Mediocre oater which should have been a lot better considering its fairly interesting plot and cast." *Western Movies*, Pitts.

SUMMATION: The story starts out promisingly with good elements of suspense. A good cast headed by Macdonald Carey, Alexis Smith, Edgar Buchanan and Victor Jory

Cave of Outlaws (1951) scene card: Macdonald Carey (*center*) plays poker with an unidentified actor (*left*) and Jack Ingram (*right*). Saloon owner Robert Osterloh looks over Carey's right shoulder.

handle the acting chores admirably. Director William Castle keeps things moving. The problem lies in the script and the character motivation of Carey. From the beginning, everything points to a vindictive Carey wanting the stolen money for his own use. Then, out of the blue, Carey is now the typical hero trying to return the money to its rightful owner. Unless you can buy this change in Carey, you will have a problem with this picture.

A Fighting Legend Lives Again...
The Saga of the Man Who Smashed Custer!
He was the greatest of all the Sioux and this is
the story of his life, his genius and his courage ...
and the love that made him what he was!

Chief Crazy Horse

ALTERNATE TITLE: *Valley of Fury*; Universal-International (April 1955); PRINT by Technicolor; FILMED in Cinemascope; RUNNING TIME: 86 min.

CAST: Crazy Horse, **Victor**

Mature; Black Shawl, **Suzan Ball**; Major Twist, **John Lund**; Little Big Man, **Ray Danton**; Flying Hawk, **Keith Larsen**; Worni, **Paul Guilfoyle**; Lt. Colin Cartwright, **David Janssen**; Spotted Tail, **Robert Warwick**; General Crook, **James Millican**; Red Cloud, **Morris Ankrum**; Aaron Cartwright, **Donald Randolph**; Jeff Mantz, **Robert F. Simon**; Caleb Mantz, **James Westerfield**; Old Man Afraid, **Stuart Randall**; Dull Knife, **Pat Hogan**; Major Carlisle, **Dennis Weaver**; Sergeant Guthrie, **John Peters**; He Dog, **Henry Wills**; Indian in the Sky, **Fred Carson**; Hardy, **Charles Horvath**

CREDITS: Director, **George Sherman**; Assistant Director, **Marshall Green**; Producer, **William Alland**; Co-Producer, **Leonard Goldstein**; Story, **Gerald Drayson Adams**; Screenwriters, **Franklin Coen** and **Gerald Drayson Adams**; Editor, **Al Clark**; Art Directors, **Alexander Golitzen** and **Robert Boyle**; Set Decorators, **Russell A. Gausman** and **Ray Jeffers**; Cinematographer, **Harold Lipstein**; Costumes, **Rosemary Odell**; Hair Stylist, **Joan St. Oegger**; Makeup, **Bud Westmore**; Sound, **Leslie I. Carey** and **Corson Jowett**; Music, **Frank Skinner**; Music Supervisor, **Joseph Gershenson**; Technical Advisor, **David Miller**; Technicolor Color Consultant, **William Fritzsche**

LOCATION FILMING: Badlands National Monument (along the Little Bighorn River), South Dakota

STORY: On his deathbed, Lakota chief Red Cloud (Morris Ankrum) prophesies that a great warrior will unite the tribes and lead them to victory over the whites until the warrior's death at the hands of one of his own tribesmen. In later years, wounded by Shoshones, Major Twist (John Lund) is cared for by Crazy Horse (Victor Mature) and Black Shawl (Suzan Ball), who are in love with each other. Lund gives Mature enough gifts to win Ball in marriage. Little Big Man (Ray Danton), who also wants to marry Ball, is enraged and offers a challenge to Mature. The two men fight with Mature emerging victorious and Danton banished from the tribe. Danton follows Lund to Fort Laramie. In the general store, owners Jeff (Robert F. Simon) and Caleb Mantz (James Westerfield) see that Danton has gold nuggets and learn the location of the gold, which is on Sioux lands. Gold brings settlers, and a new fort is built to protect the newcomers. Mature assumes command of all the warriors of the Lakota Sioux tribes and in their first skirmish defeats the cavalry. General Crook (James Millican) attempts to forge a treaty but Mature refuses to participate. Millican decides to capture Mature and Lund goes to warn Mature. As Lund approaches the Sioux village, he is shot by one of the Indians. Lund learns that Mature will carry the fight to the cavalry. Lund tries to return to the cavalry, even though it means fighting his friend Mature, but his wounds have not healed sufficiently to allow him to do so. Mature is successful in his encounters with the army and is able to defeat the forces at the Little Bighorn.

Chief Crazy Horse (1955) scene card: Victor Mature (*right*) receives permission from James Millican (*standing right*) for the Lakotas to leave the reservation and hunt buffalo. Dennis Weaver (*left*) and John Lund are witnesses to Millican's decision.

The various tribes now think that since they have defeated the cavalry they no longer need to band together. Mature warns them that by this action the tribes will be hunted down and placed on reservations. In short order, all the tribes have been placed on the reservation with the exception of Mature and his followers. Cold and starvation finally force Mature to surrender. At the fort, Danton seizes the opportunity to kill Mature and fulfill the prophecy.

NOTES AND COMMENTARY: *Chief Crazy Horse* received a certifi-

cate of outstanding merit from the Southern California Motion Picture Council. In the ending credits, Morris Ankrum's character name is listed as Red Cloud. Ankrum played Conquering Bear, the dying Lakota Sioux Chief who relates the prophecy of the coming of the great warrior to lead the Sioux nation. Stuntman Fred Carson was the rider of the horse as the rider and horse come down from the sky at the beginning of the picture. Then at the end when Victor Mature is dying, Carson again is the rider as the rider and the horse go back into the sky. Footage from *Can't Help Singing* (Universal, 1944) and *Tumbleweed* (Universal-International, 1953) can be seen in montage sequences in the film. The newspaper ads, but not the credits, gave Ray Danton an "and introducing" billing.

REVIEWS: "Told from the Indians' side of the fighting with a sympathetic treatment that comes off okay with enough action for the general outdoor trade." *Variety*, 2/23/55; "Its sympathetic treatment of the Indians notwithstanding, *Chief Crazy Horse* is one of the weaker films in the fifties cycle of Indian films." *The Western*, Hardy.

SUMMATION: *Chief Crazy Horse* is a valiant, somewhat entertaining but ultimately failed attempt to be the definitive film of the Indians' view of the hostilities with the cavalry. Vic-

tor Mature is not totally effective as a man beset with doubts over fulfilling his destiny. Mature's acting range is not sufficient to give the rounded characterization needed for this film. Suzan Ball is adequate as the woman Mature loves. John Lund is fine as the white man who becomes a friend of Mature and who understands the plight of the Indian. The film seems to be beyond director George Sherman's usually sure grasp. At times, the film seems a little stilted. The lack of an adequate budget hurts the action scenes, for which Sherman is famous, as the battle at the Little Bighorn is primarily fought off-camera. The ending is forced with Danton's murder of Mature. The script focuses on the fulfillment of the prophecy with no thought of recrimination about Danton's deed.

THE GUN BLAZING STORY OF THE LAST GREAT OUTLAW RAIDS!
The Columbia Roundhouse Ambush!

The Cimarron Kid

Universal-International (January 1952); COLOR by Technicolor; RUNNING TIME: 84 min.

CAST: Bill Doolin, **Audie Murphy**; Carrie Roberts, **Beverly Tyler**; Bitter Creek, **James Best**; Cimarron Rose, **Yvette Dugay**; Dynamite Dick, **John Hudson**; Red Buck, **Hugh O'Brian**; Pat Roberts, **Roy Roberts**; Swanson, **David Wolfe**; Bob Dalton, **Noah Beery**; Marshal John Sutton, **Leif Erickson**; George

Weber, **John Hubbard**; Stacey Marshall, **Frank Silvera**; Warden, **Frank Ferguson**; Train Passenger, **Jack Ingram**; Lawyer, **Wheaton Chambers**; Tulsa Jack, **John Bromfield**; Grat Dalton, **Palmer Lee**; Emmett Dalton, **Rand Brooks**; Will Dalton, **William Reynolds**; Big Jim, **Richard Garland**; Tilden, **Eugene Baxter**; Railroad Detective, **Eddie Dew**; Storekeeper, **Harry Harvey**; Charlie, **Davy Sharpe**; Silk

Conrad, **Tris Coffin**; Deputy, **Rory Mallison**

CREDITS: Director, **Budd Boetticher**; Producer, **Ted Richmond**; Story, **Louis Stevens** and **Kay Lenard**; Screenwriter, **Louis Stevens**; Editor, **Frank Gross**; Art Directors, **Bernard Herzbrun** and **Emrich Nicholson**; Set Decorators, **Russell A. Gausman** and **Joe Kish**; Cinematographer, **Charles P. Boyle**; Costumes, **Bill Thomas**; Hair Stylist, **Joan St. Oegger**; Makeup, **Bud Westmore**; Sound, **Leslie I. Carey** and **Corson Jowett**; Music, **Joseph Gershenson**; Technicolor Color Consultant, **William Fritzsche**

SONG: "Red River Valley" (traditional)

LOCATION FILMING: Sonora area, California, and Columbia, California

STORY: Bill Doolin (Audie Murphy) is paroled from prison. On returning home, the train on which Murphy is travelling is held up and Murphy is greeted by name by one of the holdup men. Although innocent, Murphy is accused of being an accessory in the robbery committed by Bob Dalton (Noah Beery) and his gang. Murphy is taken into custody by Swanson (David Wolfe) but escapes and joins Beery's gang. In a daring simultaneous holdup of two banks, Beery is killed and Murphy assumes leadership of the outlaws. Murphy and his gang begin a successful crime spree. Marshal Sutton (Leif Erickson) and his posse ambush the gang at their hideout and Murphy is wounded. Webber (John Hubbard) and Dynamite Dick (John Hudson) talk Murphy into one last robbery, which is really a trap to apprehend or kill Murphy and the remaining gang members. Murphy is alerted to the plan and escapes to Pat Roberts' (Roy Roberts) ranch. Roberts' daughter, Carrie (Beverly Tyler), is in love with Murphy and knows Murphy will have to pay his debt to society before they can settle down together. Tyler arranges to have Erickson arrest Murphy.

NOTES AND COMMENTARY: *The Cimarron Kid* is a favorite film of James Best. As Best summed it up, "I got a leading lady (Yvette Dugay) and I didn't get killed so soon."

In the early fifties, actors could put full loads into their guns and carry them around with them on the set. Hugh O'Brian began to play around with his revolver. Yvette Dugay, Audie Murphy and James Best were sitting on their horses at a hitching rack when O'Brian fired a shot into the nose of Dugay's horse. The horse went crazy and plunged out into the street. Unfortunately, it was a paved street layered with about two inches of dirt. The horse's feet flew out from under him and fell. Dugay was knocked out, lying between two sets of the thrashing horse's feet, and was in danger of being critically injured. Murphy and Best leapt from their saddles, grabbed Dugay and pulled her free before the horse could kick her to death. The film's crew became so angry with O'Brian for pulling such a stunt that they gave him the silent treatment for a time.

In the early stages of his career, it's been told that Hugh O'Brian

The Cimarron Kid (1952) scene card: A wounded Audie Murphy (*second left*) is visited by Beverly Tyler. Watching the reunion are William Reynolds (*far left*), Yvette Dugay, Frank Silvera, and James Best.

would do anything to get ahead. O'Brian would even page himself in airports to get attention. During the filming of *The Cimarron Kid*, James Best and O'Brian would be roommates. Best addressed O'Brian's penchant of doing anything to get ahead in a film and warned him not to get in his way or he would beat the "pudding" out of him. Best states "pudding" was not exactly the phrase used in that conversation.

Take a good look at the scene in which the posse attacks Murphy's camp. John Hudson tries to escape. Enter Davy Sharpe, doubling for Hudson. Sharpe was to run a horse down a little trail, fall off the horse down a

steep incline and hit a four or five inch mattress. If Sharpe missed that mattress, it would mean certain injury and perhaps death. Sharpe hit that mattress perfectly, rolled about fifteen feet into the water and then held his breath as long as he could. Director Budd Boetticher warned the cast and crew not to run into the water after Sharpe, no matter what happened. Boetticher was screaming, "No one go in there, no one go in there." Everyone thought Sharpe had been killed because of the length of time he remained under the water. All of a sudden, Sharpe poped up out of the water and everybody cheered. Another spectacular stunt for Davy Sharpe!

Universal-International made arrangements to use the entire town of Columbia, a mining community, for *The Cimarron Kid*. This included all 27 buildings, all 6 streets and the entire population of 52 inhabitants. Columbia is located in the Sonora area of California.

The Cimarron Kid was the first film assigned to Budd Boetticher after a long-term contract was signed.

Noah Beery was usually billed as Noah Beery Jr. Palmer Lee was later billed as Gregg Palmer.

REVIEWS: "Standard tinted outdoor action feature." *Variety*, 12/19/51; "A minor, but entertaining film." *The Western*, Hardy.

SUMMATION: This is a solid, above-average western that relies heavily on its many good action scenes to make the grade. Audie Murphy, who now adds Bill Doolin to his growing list of notorious outlaws, and Yvette Dugay contribute fine performances in an effective cast. Boetticher's direction adroitly paces the story and adds to the charm of this film.

THE COURAGE OF THE U.S. CAVALRY!
THE VENGEANCE OF THE WAR-CRAZED NAVAJO!
THE LAST FLAMING STAND AT FORT UNION!

Column South

Universal-International (June 1953); COLOR by Technicolor; RUNNING TIME: 84½ min.

CAST: Lt. Jed Sayre, **Audie Murphy**; Marcy Whitlock, **Joan Evans**; Capt. Lee Whitlock, **Robert Sterling**; Brig. Gen. Storey, **Ray Collins**; Chalmers, **Palmer Lee**; Menguito, **Dennis Weaver**; Corp. Biddle, **Russell Johnson**; Trooper Vaness, **Jack Kelly**; Lt. Posick, **Johnny Downs**; Sgt. McAfee, **Bob Steele**; Primrose, **James Best**; Joe Copper Face, **Ralph Moody**; Trooper Chavez, **Rico Alaniz**; Wagon Driver, **Monte Montague**; Jed, **Steve Darrell**; Prospector, **Britt Wood**; Bartender, **Frank Ellis**; Lt.

Fry, **Richard Garland**; Confederate Spy, **Denver Pyle**; Sabbath, **Edwin Rand**

CREDITS: Director, **Frederick de Cordova**; Assistant Director, **Fred Frank**; Producer, **Ted Richmond**; Story/Screenwriter, **William Sackheim**; Editor, **Milton Carruth**; Art Directors, **Alexander Golitzen** and **Hilyard Brown**; Set Decorators, **Russell A. Gausman** and **Ruby Levitt**; Cinematographer, **Charles P. Boyle**; Costumes, **Rosemary Odell**; Hair Stylist, **Joan St. Oegger**; Makeup, **Bud Westmore**; Sound, **Leslie I. Carey** and **Glenn E. Anderson**; Musical Director, **Joseph Gershenson**; Technical Director,

Col. Paul R. Davison; Technicolor Color Consultant, **William Fritzsche**

LOCATION FILMING: Apple Valley area, California

STORY: Captain Whitlock (Robert Sterling), accompanied by his sister Marcy (Joan Evans), arrives at Fort Union to assume command. Sterling's troops are made up of both Northern and Southern sympathizers. Acting commander Sayre (Audie Murphy) tells Sterling the Navajo Indians are peaceful and he is a childhood friend of Chief Menguito (Dennis Weaver). The peace is threatened when a prospector is scalped. Sterling thinks the Navajos have broken the peace but Murphy is certain the Indians are not to blame for the crime. With junior officer Chalmers' (Palmer Lee) assistance, Murphy is able to bring the real killer to justice and avert an Indian war. Brig. Gen. Storey (Ray Collins), a Copperhead, has a plan that will bring the southwest under Southern control but he needs Sterling's help to make his plan work. Even though Sterling is a Southerner, he is reluctant to join in the plan but eventually Collins convinces him to participate. Stolen army rifles have been planted in Weaver's camp, which forces Murphy to relocate the Indians on a

Column South (1953) scene card: Bob Steele (*center*) tells Audie Murphy (*left*) and Palmer Lee of an impending attack by the cavalry on the Navajo tribe.

less than desirable reservation site. Collins receives word of an Apache uprising, but this is actually a ruse to have Sterling lead his troops into Texas where Southerners will join the Confederate Army and Northerners will be made prisoners. Weaver and his men bolt the reservation. The Indians go on the warpath and capture Collins as he tries to return to Santa Fe. Murphy discovers the plot and the Union sympathizers get the drop on Sterling and the Southerners. Murphy and his men return to the fort giving Sterling and his men the chance to go on to Texas. Joan Evans, travelling with her brother, has fallen in love with Murphy. Evans elects to stay with Sterling because she is ashamed of her brother's actions. Murphy returns to find Weaver and the Navajos have taken over the fort. Sterling returns and helps Murphy retake the fort. Weaver and his band are allowed to return to the hills. Collins is arrested. Sterling and his men are allowed to join the Southern forces. Evans stays at the fort with Murphy.

NOTES AND COMMENTARY: Russell Johnson remembered working with Audie Murphy a number of times. Johnson thought Murphy was an interesting character. Johnson commented, "You can see why Audie was the most decorated soldier out of the Second World War. There was something dangerous about Audie. That sweet face of his. He was a mad man; he'd half kill you. He was a very, very tough

little bastard, Audie Murphy. He'd look like butter wouldn't melt in his mouth but he was an interesting star of the period. There was that spark behind that sweet little look of his. Once you saw it, you knew that man; there's a guy that could go berserk in a moment. He was absolutely an amazing fellow and having come out of the Second World War myself, I had a great admiration for his exploits during the war. If he'd decide he was going to do something, he was going to do it."

In the end credits, Ray Collins' character name is given as Storey but in the film Collins is called Stone in the dialogue and on a written title. Palmer Lee would shortly receive billing as Gregg Palmer and would be billed as such for the remainder of his long film career.

REVIEWS: "Fairly interesting Audie Murphy cavalry actioner." *Western Movies*, Pitts; "Familiar cavalry drama that owes its charm to the difficult-to-explain appeal of Murphy." *The Motion Picture Guide*, Nash and Ross.

SUMMATION: *Column South* is a satisfactory cavalry and Indians saga. Director Frederick de Cordova's direction keeps the audience's interest throughout by interspersing sufficient rugged action. Audie Murphy, Robert Sterling and Joan Evans deliver standard but adequate performances. Palmer Lee and Dennis Weaver stand out from the otherwise competent supporting cast.

Where a life was measured in minutes!
...And a gun, an arrow, or a knife was the LAW!

Comanche Territory

Universal-International (May 1950); COLOR by Technicolor; RUNNING TIME: 76 min.

CAST: Katie, **Maureen O'Hara**; James Bowie, **Macdonald Carey**; Dan'l Seeger, **Will Geer**; Stacey Howard, **Charles Drake**; Quisima, **Pedro de Cordoba**; Walsh, **Ian MacDonald**; Pakanah, **Rick Vallin**; Boozer, **Parley Baer**; Sam, **James Best**; Ed, **Edmund Cobb**; Big Joe, **Glenn Strange**; Indian Brave, **Iron Eyes Cody**; Card Player, **Guy Wilkerson**; Guest who encourages O'Hara to sing, **Harry Harvey**; Renegade Member, **Terry Frost**; Miners, **I. Stanford Jolley** and **John Cason**

CREDITS: Director, **George Sherman**; Producer, **Leonard Goldstein**; Story, **Lewis Meltzer**; Screenwriters, **Oscar Brodney** and **Lewis Meltzer**; Editor, **Frank Gross**; Choreographer, **Harold Belfer**; Art Directors, **Bernard Herzbrun** and **Richard H. Riedel**; Set Decorators, **Russell A. Gausman** and **Joseph Kish**; Cinematographer, **Maury Gertsman**; Costumes, **Yvonne Wood**; Hair Stylist, **Joan St. Oegger**; Makeup, **Bud Westmore**; Sound, **Leslie I. Carey** and **Richard De Weese**; Music, **Frank Skinner**; Technicolor Color Consultant, **William Fritzsche**; Special Photography, **David S. Horsley**

SONG: "The Bonny Shepherd Lad" (traditional)—sung by **Maureen O'Hara**

LOCATION FILMING: Yavapai County area (Red Rock Crossing, Little Park, Big Park), Arizona

STORY: The U.S. Government sends James Bowie (Macdonald Carey) to the Comanche territory to obtain the rights to mine silver on Indian lands. The renewal treaty has been stolen from Seeger (Will Geer). Without the treaty in effect, white settlers will move into the Comanche lands and take the silver for themselves. Carey finds Katie (Maureen O'Hara) and her brother, Stacey (Charles Drake), are behind the theft. O'Hara has the mistaken idea that if the white settlers can gain access to these lands the territory will grow and prosper. O'Hara hadn't considered the fact that a bloody Indian war would ensue. Drake just wants the silver for himself and has gathered a bunch of renegades to help him accomplish his objective. Drake submits the treaty to Quisima (Pedro de Cordoba), chief of the Comanches. Drake has added a clause that forces the Comanches to relinquish their firearms. This move will give Drake and his men a decided advantage when they move in to claim the silver rights for themselves. When Drake realizes his scheme is out in the open, he moves to wipe out the Indian tribe. O'Hara commandeers the wagon with

Comanche Territory (1950) scene card: Ian MacDonald (*far left*) tells I. Stanford Jolley (*second left*), John Cason (*left center*), Maureen O'Hara, unidentified actor, and Macdonald Carey about a bounty on wolves.

the Indians' firearms from Drake's outlaw band and arrives at the Indian village in time for Carey, Geer and the Indian tribe to defeat the renegades. Drake tries to escape but Carey rides him down and brings him to justice. Carey promises to return to O'Hara after he goes down to Texas to see what Sam Houston wants with him.

NOTES AND COMMENTARY: This was probably James Best's first film and an added pleasure for him was working with Maureen O'Hara. Best remarked, "Being Irish, I always wanted to meet her."

At the time he was signed for the film, he was not a good rider. To obtain the part, Best said that he could ride. The stuntman in charge of judging the actor's riding ability quickly found out Best could not ride. Best pleaded with the stuntman to let him stay in the film, and the stuntman relented on the promise that Best would work hard to improve his riding ability. Ed Cobb and Glenn Strange befriended James Best. To make certain Best would stay in the saddle, Cobb and Strange would ride on either side of him. So, whenever Best would start to fall out of the saddle, Cobb and Strange would reach over and pull him back. Later Best did learn to ride well. Because of Edmund Cobb's influence, James Best got married right after the completion of this film. Best and Cobb were sitting in a room having a few drinks. Cobb was telling Best how much he missed his wife, how much he loved her and so forth. Best began to get homesick for a lady he'd been dating in New York. Without Universal Studios knowing about it, he flew to New York and was married.

REVIEWS: "The film is a routine western with pretty Technicolor pictures." *The Motion Picture Guide,* Nash and Ross; "A polite ugh is the most to be said for this shoot-'em-up epic." *New York Times,* 4/8/50.

SUMMATION: This is only an average western enhanced by the beautiful scenic backgrounds. Maureen O'Hara and Macdonald Carey are adequate in their roles but the needed chemistry between the two stars just isn't there. Will Geer is given the role of a "B" western comic sidekick. The scene of Geer sniffing around the saloon patrons to find out who wore perfume when he was ambushed is unbelievable; something best left to a poverty row western of the forties. A saloon brawl fails in its attempt to add humor to the action. The film is at its best when its lets O'Hara show her action side as in the scene where she hi-jacks the wagon from the renegades and even beats veteran film bad man, Terry Frost, in a brief scuffle.

HIS BODY IS AN EMPTY SHELL THAT HIDES A LUSTFUL FIEND...

Curse of the Undead

ALTERNATE TITLE: *Mark of the West;* Universal-International (July 1959); RUNNING TIME: 79 min.

CAST: Preacher Dan, **Eric Fleming**; Drake Robey, **Michael Pate**; Dolores Carter, **Kathleen Crowley**; Dr. Carter, **John Hoyt**; Buffer, **Bruce Gordon**; Sheriff, **Edward Binns**; Tim Carter, **Jimmy Murphy**; Dora, **Helen Kleeb**; Bartender, **Jay Adler**; Henchmen, **Edwin Parker, John Truax, Frankie Van** and **Rush Williams**

CREDITS: Director, **Edward Dein**; Assistant Director, **James Welch**; Producer, **Joseph Gershenson**; Writers, **Edward Dein** and **Mildred Dein**; Editor, **George Gittens**; Art Directors, **Alexander Golitzen** and **Robert Clatworthy**; Set Decorators, **Russell A. Gausman** and **William P. Tapp**; Cinematographer, **Ellis W. Carter**; Costumes, **Bill Thomas**; Hair Stylist, **Larry Germain**; Makeup, **Bud Westmore**; Sound, **Leslie I. Carey** and **Joe Lapis**; Music, **Irving Gertz**; Music Supervisor, **Milton Rosen**

STORY: A small western town is beset with the mysterious deaths of young girls. The only clue is two puncture wounds on each victim's neck. The local doctor, Carter (John Hoyt) and Preacher Dan (Eric Fleming) try to find what's behind these tragedies. Greedy rancher Buffer (Bruce Gordon) is trying to force Hoyt to sell his ranch to him. Robey (Michael Pate) is behind the deaths in the community. Pate, a gunslinger, is also a vampire who needs the blood of living beings to subsist. Pate murders Hoyt to force Hoyt's son, Tim (Jimmy Murphy), to face Gordon in a gunfight, which he knows Gordon will win. With the ranch in the hands of Hoyt's daughter, Dolores (Kathleen Crowley), Pate answers her ad for a gunman to kill Gordon. Crowley hires Pate over her fiancé Fleming's objections. Pate begins drawing blood out of Crowley's neck to put Crowley under his control. Fleming finds an old journal, which proves Pate is a vampire. Pate makes an unsuccessful attempt to kill Fleming and steal the journal. Pate is able to steal a picture of himself that would verify Fleming's findings to Crowley. When Pate finds Fleming is going to obtain a court order to open the coffins, Pate knows he has to gun Fleming down. Fleming has been warned and he affixes a cross on the tip of a bullet that destroys the vampire and his menace to the community.

NOTES AND COMMENTARY: Michael Pate has fond memories of *Curse of the Undead*, "Kath [Kathleen Crowley] and I had a very interesting and testing time while making the film when we simply had to keep a straight face about certain scenes we found ourselves doing. I can't speak for Kath but I never thought it would become the cult film it became. A clue for you about how we approached the film, albeit our artistic integrity always remained unsullied, the original title for the script, which might have caused any number of people at Universal to swallow very hard was, wait for it, *Eat Me Gently*! I knew for sure that we were going to have a ball doing the film and it certainly proved to be just that. Kath was a brilliant actress but she also had a wicked sense of humor and she and I always found something quite often hilarious about various situations in the film, as me biting her neck—as any good vampire should do! We brought a tremendous energy and sense of delight to the way we played our parts in the film which conveyed itself to the audience—and so it was logical in the ensuing years that *Curse of the Undead* should become the cult Western vampire film it has."

Michael Pate went to Universal Studios to talk to Joe Gershenson about a picture. Gershenson had been receiving a musical supervisor credit on Universal-International productions but on this particular film would be the producer. The film was to be called *Curse of the Vampire*. Edward Dein, who wrote the script with his wife Mildred and

Written wishes to Gene

Kathleen Crowley

Curse of the Undead (1959): Michael Pate prepared to deliver the vampire's kiss to Kathleen Crowley.

who would direct the picture, was also present. Gershenson told Pate that Dein wanted him to play the part of a vampire. Pate recalled, "That was great but Ed must have seen a slight shadow slip across my face." Pate was then told the part would be that of a western vampire. Pate continues, "I was sold right away. Then when Eddie and Joe told me it looked as if they'd have Kathleen Crowley playing the girl in it and Eric Fleming the preacher—well, I just couldn't wait to start filming. I'd first met Kath Crowley way back in early '53 and pretty well fallen in love with her right on the spot."

The role of this western vampire pleased Michael Pate who commented, "I rather liked my raunchy hidalgo vampire and I'm certain Kath did. She knew for sure that only she and the Deins and me had any kind of idea what kind of film we were making. She used to talk with the others of the cast and be so serious about the film, merely to confirm how the others were in la-la land or merely waiting for knock-off time to roll around."

Asked to comment about the eroticism in scenes in which the vampire would bite the lovely heroine's neck, Pate responded, "Your descriptions of my and Kath's foreplay is revelatory. I guess we both did it all naturally. Our idea was most likely that really except for a few unimportant factors, vampires weren't all that different. Incidentally, it was all very enjoyable for the both of us, I recall, and there is a beautiful photograph extant of me circling the back of Kath's neck. It really is quite orgasmic as a photograph and should have won a thousand contests." Michael Pate made this comment of his other co-star, Eric Fleming, "Eric was Eric—hardworking, well-meaning, a little pedantic and pedestrian, bless him, but always worthwhile and genuine."

Kathleen Crowley talked about *Curse of the Undead*, "I was a leading lady at the time. I had starred with virtually the top leading men. They wanted to get good people because it was an unusual story. They had to have a strong actress in it. And they wanted someone who could be sympathetic at the same time. I thought I had the gift of two leading men at the same time. I just loved it because it was an unusual thing. We enjoyed shooting it. We thought it was a very good film because it was unusual. It qualifies as a chiller type thing and it qualifies as a western. It wears two hats."

REVIEWS: "This is a crude mixing of the Horror and Western genres." *The Western*, Hardy; "Lower-berth horror film, uninspired production." *Variety*, 7/1/59.

NOTES AND COMMENTS: *Curse of the Undead* attempts to be an eerie, atmospheric horror western. For the most part, the film succeeds thanks to strong performances by Michael Pate as a cowboy vampire and Kathleen Crowley as the woman in peril. Eric Fleming is effective as the stoic hero. In this telling of the vampire story, Pate plays his vampire as a whiskey-drinking, cigar-smoking fiend with a tendency for erotic foreplay in his neck-biting technique. This would have been a purely routine entry without the western setting and Pate's slightly different handling of the age-old vampire legend.

Great Guns! Great Fun!
When those rootin', tootin' troupers move in ...
the West moves out—even the Badmen run for cover!

Curtain Call at Cactus Creek

ALTERNATE TITLE: *Take the Stage*; Universal-International (June 1950); COLOR by Technicolor; RUNNING TIME: 86 min.

CAST: Edward Timmons, **Donald O'Connor**; Julie Martin, **Gale Storm**; Rimrock Thomas, **Walter Brennan**; Tracy Holland, **Vincent Price**; Lily Martin, **Eve Arden**; Ralph, **Chick Chandler**; Jake, **Joe Sawyer**; Marshall Clay, **Harry Shannon**; Yellowstone, **Rex Lease**; Pecos, **I. Stanford Jolley**; Jailer, **Eddy Waller**; Gang Members, **Edmund Cobb, Terry Frost** and **Lane Bradford**; Townsmen, **Hank Worden** and **Ralph Sanford**

CREDITS: Director, **Charles Lamont**; Producer, **Robert Arthur**; Story, **Stanley Roberts** and **Howard Dimsdale**; Screenwriter, **Howard Dimsdale**; Editor, **Frank Gross**; Choreographer, **Louis DaPron**; Art Directors, **Bernard Herzbrun** and **John F. DeCuir**; Set Decorators, **Russell A. Gausman** and **Ruby R. Levitt**; Cinematographer, **Russell Metty**; Costumes, **Rosemary Odell**; Hair Stylist, **Joan St. Oegger**; Makeup, **Bud Westmore**; Sound, **Leslie I. Carey** and **Richard De Weese**; Music, **Walter Scharf**; Technicolor Color Consultant, **Robert Brower**

SONGS: "Sweet Betsy from Pike" (traditional)—sung by **Walter Brennan**; "Waiting at the Church" (Pether and Leigh)—sung by **Eve Arden**; "Home Sweet Home" (Payne and Bishop)—sung by **Gale Storm**; "Be My Little Bumble Bee" (Murphy and Marshall)—sung by **Donald O'Connor** and **Gale Storm**; "Nola" (Arndt)—danced by **Donald O'Connor** and **Gale Storm**; and "Are You from Dixie" (Cobb and Yellen)—sung by **Donald O'Connor** and **Gale Storm**

STORY: Tracy Holland's (Vincent Price) theatrical troupe arrives in Cactus Creek at the same time Rimrock Thomas (Walter Brennan) and his outlaw gang show up. Brennan decides to delay holding up the bank until he can see the troupe, especially Lily (Eve Arden), perform. The bank is held up and, in the melee, Brennan hides in Edward Timmons' (Donald O'Connor) show wagon. Discovered by O'Connor, Brennan decides to join the troupe as a cover-up for his outlaw activities. When the bank is held up in the next town, O'Connor is accused of being a member of the gang and jailed. Brennan breaks him out of jail so O'Connor can succeed him as the gang leader. O'Connor accepts his fate and returns to town to tell his girlfriend, Julie (Gale Storm). O'Connor is spotted and Marshal Clay (Harry Shannon) leads a posse after him. In trying to get away, O'Connor inadvertently leads the posse to the outlaw camp. Brennan feels that O'Connor is like a son to him and allows O'Connor to capture him, thus clearing O'Connor's name. With the reward for Brennan, O'Connor is able to headline his own troupe and settle down with Storm. Brennan is paroled and one of the conditions of his parole is that he must now perform with O'Connor and Storm in the show.

NOTES AND COMMENTARY: Gale Storm loved the musical numbers in the film. Donald O'Connor still will call Storm and sing "Be My Little

Bumble Bee" to her. The final musical number "Are You From Dixie" would be in blackface. The makeup man had a difficult time trying to decide what kind of makeup to use. He finally made the decision and Donald O'Connor, Gale Storm and Walter Brennan were made up for the scene. Storm remembers that the makeup would not come off for two days and commented, "The makeup was really hard, like something that went into the skin."

REVIEWS: "Slick entertainment." *Variety* 5/24/50; "An engaging account of the travails of a theatrical troupe out West." *The Western,* Hardy.

Curtain Call at Cactus Creek **(1950) portrait card: Walter Brennan (*left*), Eve Arden and Vincent Price; left border shows Donald O'Connor and Gale Storm.**

SUMMATION: This is a sprightly, energetic musical comedy-western. The multi-talented Donald O'Connor sets the pace with his acrobatic ability, exceptional dancing skill, pleasant way with a song and comedic talent. Gale Storm does a fine job as O'Connor's love interest. Vincent Price is properly hammy as the show's thespian. Eve Arden registers strongly with both comedy and song. Walter Brennan does well as the bad man with a heart of gold. The performances of the theatrical troupe in the show-within-the-show, along with O'Connor's antics behind the scenes, elevate this film to an above average status.

THE STORY OF THE NOTORIOUS BRETT WADE
LAST OF THE FRONTIER GAMBLERS!
HIS NAME WAS ON THE LIPS OF EVERY WOMAN IN TOWN!
...AND ON EVERY BULLET IN THE TERRITORY!

Dawn at Socorro

Universal-International (September 1954); COLOR by Technicolor; RUNNING TIME: 80½ min.

CAST: Brett Wade, **Rory Calhoun**; Rannah Hayes, **Piper Laurie**; Dick Braden, **David Brian**; Clare, **Kathleen Hughes**; Jimmy Rapp, **Alex Nichol**; Sheriff Cauthen, **Edgar Buchanan**; Letty Diamond, **Mara Corday**; Doc Jameson, **Roy Roberts**; Buddy Ferris, **Skip Homeier**; Harry McNair, **James Millican**; Earl Ferris, **Lee Van Cleef**; Old Man Ferris, **Stanley Andrews**; Tom Ferris, **Richard Garland**; Vince McNair, **Scott Lee**; Desk Clerk, **Paul Brinegar**; Rancher, **Philo McCullough**; Jebb Hayes, **Forrest Taylor**; Way Station Manager, **William Fawcett**; Saloon Patrons at Table, **Dick Curtis**, **Tristram Coffin** and **Ray Bennett**; Observer at Gambling Table, **Frank Ellis**; Saloon Manager, **Terry Frost**

CREDITS: Director, **George Sherman**; Assistant Director, **Ronnie Rondell**; Producer, **William Alland**; Screenwriter, **George Zuckerman**; Editor, **Edward Curtiss**; Art Directors, **Alexander Golitzen** and **Robert Clatworthy**; Set Decorators, **Russell A. Gausman** and **Ruby R. Levitt**; Cinematographer, **Carl Guthrie**; Costumes, **Jay Morley Jr.**; Hair Stylist, **Joan St. Oegger**; Makeup, **Bud Westmore**; Sound, **Leslie I. Carey** and **Glenn E. Anderson**; Music Supervisor, **Joseph Gershenson**; Technicolor Color Consultant, **William Fritzsche**

LOCATION FILMING: Victorville, California

STORY: A drunken Buddy Ferris (Skip Homeier) gets into an argument with Marshal McNair (James Millican) and is killed. Rannah (Piper Laurie) is driven into

Dawn at Socorro (1954) portrait card: Rory Calhoun (*left*) and Lee Van Cleef struggle.

town by her father, Jebb Hayes (Forrest Taylor), and is told she is no longer his daughter. Taylor has falsely accused Laurie of making love to all his ranch hands. Saloon owner Dick Braden (David Brian) offers Laurie employment in Socorro. Homeier's father, Ferris (Stanley Andrews), and his sons, Tom (Richard Garland) and Earl (Lee Van Cleef), want revenge and set up a time to shoot it out with Millican and his son, Vince McNair (Scott Lee), and their good friend gambler/gunman Brett Wade (Rory Calhoun). From her hotel window,

Laurie sees the gunfight in which Andrews and Garland are slain by Calhoun. Discovering a medical problem is caused by an old wound that has not healed completely, Calhoun decides to go to Colorado Springs to recover. Taking a stagecoach on the first leg of the journey, Calhoun's fellow passengers are Laurie and Jimmy Rapp (Alex Nichol), a friend of Andrews who hates Calhoun. Calhoun and Laurie strike up a relationship and Laurie tells Calhoun she is travelling to Socorro to get married. In reality, she has accepted employment as a dance hall girl at Brian's saloon. When Calhoun discovers this, he decides to delay his train trip to Colorado Springs to try to persuade Laurie not to work for Brian. Brian plans to give Laurie a big rush and then replace her with another girl when he tires of her. Knowing this, Calhoun makes an unsuccessful attempt to win Brian's saloon in a card game. As Calhoun makes a final try to convince Laurie not to stay with Brian, Brian interrupts the conversation. A fight starts between Calhoun and Brian in which Calhoun emerges victorious. Enraged Brian hires Nichol to kill Calhoun. Calhoun proves to be the fastest on the draw and Nichol is killed. Brian and two of his men attempt to finish the job. Calhoun is able to shoot the three men. Then Calhoun takes the train to Colorado Springs and finds that Laurie is travelling with him.

NOTES AND COMMENTARY: Appearing in this film deprived Kathleen Hughes of the chance to audition for the part of Edie Doyle in *On the Waterfront* (Columbia, 1954). Hughes had to decline because Universal-International had assigned her to appear in *Dawn at Socorro*. Eva Marie Saint was given this plum role in *On the Waterfront*.

One of the Universal-International standby songs, "True Love," is played during a sequence with Rory Calhoun and Piper Laurie in the saloon in Socorro.

There was a nice exchange of dialogue between the stationmaster and Rory Calhoun when Calhoun finds that he's being forced into a

Dawn at Socorro (1954): **Kathleen Hughes as dance hall girl Clare.**

gunfight. *Bit player:* "Who's coming after you?" *Rory Calhoun:* "My past. Every dark, miserable day of it."

REVIEWS: "Decent, fast paced western with a strong supporting cast." *The Motion Picture Guide*, Nash and Ross; "For those who like Western pictures devoid the element of surprise, but otherwise sleek and efficient, this one should thoroughly satisfy." *New York Times*, 8/28/54.

SUMMATION: *Dawn at Socorro* is a solid western feature with good action and suspense. The film is buoyed by good characterizations by Rory Calhoun as a gambler/gunman who wants to outlive his past and Piper Laurie as a young woman falsely accused of being a loose woman. David Brian, one of the screen's best handsome, smiling villains, and Edgar Buchanan head a good supporting cast. George Sherman directs the fine screenplay, provided by George Zuckerman, with a knowing hand.

...this was the day of the Rope ... and the Ravager!
...this was A DAY OF FURY ... when JAGADE—
last of the maverick killers—
rode back to the town that had cast him out ...
to the woman who had spurned him ... to face a vengeance showdown!

A Day of Fury

Universal-International (May 1956); PRINT by Technicolor; RUNNING TIME: 78 min.

CAST: Jagade, **Dale Robertson**; Marshal Allan Burnett, **Jock Mahoney**; Sharman Fulton, **Mara Corday**; Judge J. McLean, **Carl Benton Reid**; Billy Brand, **Jan Merlin**; Preacher Jason, **John Dehner**; Miss Timmons, **Dee Carroll**; Marie, **Sheila Bromley**; Doc Logan, **James Bell**; Claire, **Dani Crayne**; Vanryzin, **Howard Wendell**; Duggen, **Charles Cane**; Burson, **Phil Chambers**; Beemans, **Sydney Mason**; Mrs. McLean, **Helen Kleeb**; Railroad Worker, **Terry Frost**; Charlie, **Harry Tyler**

CREDITS: Director, **Harmon Jones**; Assistant Director, **Joseph E. Kenny**; Producer, **Robert Arthur**; Story, **James Edmiston**; Screenwriters, **James Edmiston** and **Oscar Broadney**; Editor, **Sherman Todd**; Art Directors, **Alexander Golitzen** and **Robert Boyle**; Set Decorators, **Russell A. Gausman** and **Ray Jeffers**; Cinematographer, **Ellis W. Carter**; Costumes, **Rosemary Odell**; Hair Stylist, **Joan St. Oegger**; Makeup, **Bud Westmore**; Sound, **Leslie I. Carey** and **Stephen Bass**; Music Supervisor, **Joseph Gershenson**; Technicolor Color Consultant, **William Fritzsche**

SONG: "Take Me to Town" (Lee and Shapiro)—sung by **Dani Crayne**

STORY: After saving Marshal Burnett's (Jock Mahoney's) life, gunfighter Jagade (Dale Robertson) stops at the town of West Bend. Robertson's arrival disrupts the impending marriage between Mahoney and Sharman (Mara Corday), Robertson's old flame. Robertson further disrupts town activities by opening up the saloon, which is usually closed on Sundays. Corday tells Mahoney that if Robertson stays he will destroy the town. Corday takes it upon herself to visit Robertson at the saloon and offers to go with Robertson if he would leave town. Robertson refuses and Corday is seen leaving the saloon. Thinking Corday has returned to her old ways, Judge McLean (Carl Benton Reid) throws Corday out of his house, where she had been living. Reid decides to face Robertson in a gunfight. Mahoney shoots Reid in his gun arm to prevent his death at Robertson's hands. Misunderstanding, Reid retaliates by having Mahoney arrested. Knowing Mahoney is the only person he has to fear, Robertson sends cocky teenager Billy (Jan Merlin) to the town meeting at the church to stir up the townsmen to lynch Mahoney. When preacher Jason (John Dehner) bars Merlin's entry to the church, Merlin mortally wounds the preacher. As he is dying, Dehner tells Reid that Robertson fears Mahoney and Reid reinstates Mahoney as marshal. Corday makes another attempt to make Robertson leave town. Robertson will not leave as long as Mahoney is alive. Corday pulls a gun and is about to shoot Robertson when Mahoney shoots the gun out of Corday's hand. Mahoney tells Robertson to leave town. Robertson refuses and as Robertson is about to draw, the church bells ring causing enough of a distraction to allow Mahoney to shoot Robertson. Mahoney and Corday are now able to make a life for themselves.

NOTES AND COMMENTARY: Dale Robertson liked the original script called *Jagade*. Robertson mused, "It was an interesting story. After I finished it, I read it again. I figured this guy [Jagade] was the Devil. He, himself, never did anything wrong. He merely set things up to show the weakness of other people. Bob Arthur rewrote the story that touched on it and he took away a lot of the little subtle things that were so wonderful in that original script. It came out another western really. I enjoyed the picture very much. It would have been better had Bob Arthur not rewritten the script." Some interesting comments were made by Dale Robertson on the ending of the picture with the church bells that sounded during the face-off between Robertson and Jock Mahoney. Robertson remembered, "Nobody knew how to end it. They couldn't figure out what the hell to do. Going on the theory that he [Jagade] was the Devil, we established a little earlier about the church bells. He didn't like them. They bothered him. We set it up for the end, the way they built Jagade up, nobody was going to outdraw him really and they had to find a way where he could lose to Jock Mahoney. We came up with the idea that right at that split second that church bell rang, it would distract him for that split second. That was the reason for that.

In the original script, there were three old men at the train station. One of the men hit a chord on a banjo and said, "You all remember the day Jagade came through here."

A Day of Fury (1956) title card: Jack Mahoney (*left*), Mara Corday and Dale Robertson.

And he tells his portion of the story. The other says, "Yeah, that wasn't the best part." And he tells his portion of the story. The third man tells his portion. Dale Robertson said, "There were fights all the way in it, a lot of action. When you get through you cut back to the train station and the old man hits a chord on the banjo and says, 'Jagade, he could fight and fight some.' That was the way it originally ends, which I liked much better."

Dale Robertson commented on Jock Mahoney, " They were trying to push Jock Mahoney, trying to make a star out of him. And they did somewhat, he became a star but he was never a big box-office attraction. He was the most agile, one of the most fluid actors in the whole business. He was really wonderful, he was athletic, had great moves." Dale Robertson thought Mara Corday was a wonderful person. Robertson said, "She married Richard Long and I think they were the funniest couple that I'd ever been around in my life. He was always messing up and she was always on his ass for messing up. He drank a lot. He was drunk one night and she was driving and he was trying to cop a feel while she was driving the car. She was trying to fight him off and she was waggling all over the road and the police stopped her and arrested her because she was the driver and put her in jail. She was so mad at him."

A Day of Fury was Jan Merlin's first western. Merlin commented, "Typical of New York actors, whenever somebody asks them whether they can do anything, we automatically said, 'Of course.'" Merlin was asked by director Harmon Jones if he could ride, he said he could and was hired for the film. Merlin played a young, cocky kind of teenage kid looking for trouble. In his first scene, Merlin confronts a preacher (played by John Dehner) and after a few words, shoots the preacher. Merlin remembered, "We rehearsed the scene up to the point where I would run up and jump on the horse and run out of town. We proceeded to shoot the scene. I confronted the preacher and we had words together and I shot him dead. I ran to the horse, which was about fifty feet away tied to a rail. When I got to him I looked up and he was about ten feet tall. I couldn't climb aboard him.

A Day of Fury (1956): Jan Merlin realizes he has just shot John Dehner. Sydney Mason (*left*), unidentified actor, Mara Corday, and Carl Benton Reid are stunned by the violence (courtesy Jan Merlin).

The director said, 'Cut!' The back lot of Universal-International at night is very cold, so we were hoping to get the scene over with pretty quickly. The director talked to the wrangler and the wrangler lowered the stirrup a bit. We went through the scene again. I managed to struggle up on top of the saddle. We just sat there. We didn't go anywhere. I heard, 'Cut!' I didn't grab the reins and I didn't know how to get them off the rail. He [the director] had the wrangler show me how to tug one of the reins and it comes free of the rail. They had me confront the preacher and I shot him dead. I turned around and I ran towards the horse, jerked the reins off the rail and I clamored aboard the horse. When I got on all we did was turn in circles because I only had one rein. The other one was dragging on the ground. I heard, 'Cut!' At this point I was terribly embarrassed and unhappy. He [the director] talked to the wrangler and they arranged to have the reins already off the rail and over the horse's neck so that all I had to do was jump up on the saddle, grab the reins and away we could go. So, we did it all over again. I ran to my horse. The horse looked at me over his shoulder and he took off down the street and I chased him halfway out of town. That was the very first work that I did in a western. We had another fellow dressed in my clothes leap up on the horse and ride out of town." Merlin learned to ride later on for his western television series, *The Rough Riders* (ZIV, 1958-59).

Jan Merlin liked the scene he had with Mara Corday. Hiding in her room, Merlin has Corday call Robertson, who throws Merlin down the stairs. A frightened Merlin then races throughout the town until he is caught by Mahoney. Jan Merlin talked about the hanging sequence, "The situation was set up so well that it pretty much played itself. The mood of the lighting was fabulous. They had me running like crazy up and down the streets with the people pursuing me. Prior to my seeing the schoolteacher hanging, I played the scene we did with the sheriff Jock Mahoney. He was on the outside and I was inside not daring to come out. The buildup to that actual scene [the schoolteacher hanging] was wonderful preparation because we had been doing that from beginning to end. I think the effect of the scene was done with lighting and the situation. It was a good part for me."

Jan Merlin commented on Dale Robertson, "I liked Dale. He's an interesting actor to watch. He really changed his character for the role he played. He was playing a fellow called Jagade. He tried to give him kind of an odd pattern in the way he spoke his lines and it worked. It was different from the usual cowboy that he'd do. I thought he was a real good fellow to work with." Jan Merlin remarked that he had more fun with Jock Mahoney because "Jock is friendly as all get out." Merlin continued, "He liked to tease me about the horse bit. He showed me how he could leap on a horse with hardly touching it. He'd come up from behind and take a little run and leap right up in the air over his back and onto the saddle and I was astounded. But I didn't know at the time that Jock was a stuntman at one point. He was a heck of a wonderful guy." In the newspaper advertising, Jock Mahoney was mentioned as The "Range Rider" of television—in a great new role!

In talking about director Harmon Jones, Jan Merlin remembered, "Harmon was marvelous. First class fellow, always knew what he wanted from us. Very efficient, no wasted time, very patient. He was kind to me. Anybody else would have lost their temper after all I'd done. I lied about being able to ride. He forgave me for it. He was a real gentleman. I liked him."

The working title for *A Day of Fury* was *Jagade*.

Jock Mahoney received second billing and Mara Corday received third in the opening credits but the billings were reversed in the end credits.

The song "Take Me to Town" can be heard in *Wyoming Mail* (Universal-International, 1950), *Take Me to Town* (Universal-International, 1953) and *Showdown* (Universal-International, 1963).

REVIEWS: "Better characterization than is typical of westerns, offbeat action entry." *Variety*, 4/11/56; "A bit different plotline adds some interest to this oater." *Western Movies*, Pitts.

SUMMATION: *A Day of Fury* is an exceptional western with an excellent characterization by Dale Robertson of a gunfighter who knows the day of the gun is finished. Jock Mahoney, Mara Corday, Carl Benton Reid and Jan Merlin offer solid support. Harmon Jones directs knowingly, keeping an edge of suspense throughout. Only the ending as the tolling of the church bells is responsible for Robertson's death seems a little unlikely. Otherwise stellar entertainment is offered.

HE TURNED KILLER
the day he stood alone ... against the marauders!

Day of the Bad Man

Universal-International (April 1958); EASTMAN COLOR by Pathé; COLOR in Cinemascope; RUNNING TIME: 81 min.

CAST: Judge Jim Scott, **Fred MacMurray**; Myra Owens, **Joan Weldon**; Sheriff Barney Wiley, **John Ericson**; Charlie Hayes, **Robert Middleton**; Cora Johnson, **Marie Windsor**; Sam Wyckoff, **Edgar Buchanan**; Andrew Owens, **Edward Franz**; Howard Hayes, **Skip Homeier**; Mrs. Quary, **Peggy Converse**; Silas Mordigan, **Robert Foulk**; Mrs. Mordigan, **Ann Doran**; Jake Hayes, **Lee Van Cleef**; Mr. Slocum, **Eddy**

Waller; Rudy Hayes, **Christopher Dark**; Floyd, **Don Haggerty**; Monte Hayes, **Chris Alcaide**; George Foley, **Hank Patterson**; Townsmen, **Tom London, I. Stanford Jolley** and **Steve Darrell**; Fred Collins, **Kenneth MacDonald**; Dave, **Bill Henry**

CREDITS: Director, **Harry Keller**; Assistant Director, **Joseph E. Kenny**; Producer, **Gordon Kay**; Story, **John M. Cunningham**; Screenwriter, **Lawrence Roman**; Editor, **Sherman Todd**; Art Directors, **Alexander Golitzen** and **Alfred Sweeney**; Set Decorators, **Russell A. Gausman** and **Oliver Emert**; Cinematographer, **Irving Glassberg**; Costumes, **Bill Thomas**; Makeup, **Bud Westmore**; Sound, **Leslie I. Carey** and **Robert Pritchard**; Music, **Hans J. Salter**; Music Supervisor, **Joseph Gershenson**

STORY: On the day that convicted murderer Rudy Hayes (Christopher Dark) is to sentenced, family members Charlie (Robert Middleton), Howard (Skip Homeier), Jake (Lee Van Cleef) and Monte (Chris Alcaide) ride into town. Since Middleton thinks Judge Scott (Fred MacMurray) will sentence Dark to hang, Middleton makes an unsuccessful attempt to intimidate MacMurray. MacMurray asks Sheriff Wiley (John Ericson) to relieve Middleton and his family members of their guns. Ericson is not successful and is easily intimidated by Middleton. Middleton and his family visit the local townsmen and persuade them to ask MacMurray to punish Dark by banishing him from

the town. MacMurray's life is complicated when he finds that fiancée Myra (Joan Weldon) has fallen in love with Ericson. Middleton tells MacMurray that if he sentences Dark to hang, MacMurray will be killed. Unafraid, MacMurray sentences Dark to hang at a site away from the town. MacMurray then goes to his ranch to await the arrival of Middleton and his family. Weldon pleads to Ericson not to go with the prisoner but to stay and help MacMurray. Ericson shows his cowardly side by refusing to stay in town. Only Wyckoff (Edgar Buchanan) goes to the ranch to help MacMurray. With Buchanan's assistance, the four outlaws are dispatched. Weldon has come to the ranch realizing that MacMurray is the man she truly loves.

NOTES AND COMMENTARY: On the AMC channel, mention was made that Marie Windsor had a bump on her nose removed after she'd completed filming *Day of the Bad Man*. Windsor commented, "That was a stupid mistake. I always regretted having anything done to my nose." The AMC channel added that the procedure was done to enable Windsor to play the heroine instead of the bad girl. Windsor said, "I tried but it didn't actually work, I still played heavies."

Marie Windsor liked working on this picture because it was "like old home week." Windsor remarked, "I had a lot of friends on that picture. John Ericson and Joan [Weldon]. Lee [Van Cleef] was an old friend from other westerns. Skip

RED MacMURRAY · JOAN WELDON · JOHN ERICSON **DAY OF THE BADMAN**

CO-STARRING
ROBERT
MIDDLETON

MARIE
WINDSOR

with
EDGAR BUCHANAN
EDUARD FRANZ
SKIP HOMEIER

Directed by HARRY KELLER
Screenplay by LAWRENCE ROMAN
Produced by GORDON KAY

CINEMASCOPE
in Eastman COLOR

Day of the Bad Man (1958) scene card: Skip Homeier (*center right*) hits John Er-Icson while Robert Middleton (*far right*) and Lee Van Cleef look on.

[Homeier], too. In addition, John Ericson met Weldon when he was doing the William Holden part in *Stalag 17* in San Francisco in 1953. Weldon was working in *Song of Norway* at the theater next door. Ericson would go next door during the second act of *Stalag 17*, in which he did not appear, and would watch Weldon perform. They subsequently dated a few times and became good friends. Windsor was a very good friend of Ericson's. Ericson said that both he and Windsor liked to paint "which made them kindred spirits." Windsor and Ericson had been out of touch over the years but the au-

thor was able to provide information so the two could resume their friendship.

John Ericson remarked that he was not at all like the character that he portrayed in this film. To give a good performance, Ericson said that he had to understand the character's viewpoint which would allow the townspeople's lives to be risked and for the bad men to have their way. Also, Ericson's character was basically that of a coward who was very afraid of these men.

John Ericson talked about the fight scene that he had at Windsor's camp in the picture: "Doubles were used in the fight. The studio tried to match doubles with the actors involved. Doubles were usually filmed with their back to the camera or at least three-quarters hidden. The master scene was set up, with a walk-through. As the fight is filmed, the stunt-man would throw a punch. The scene would be stopped and the actor would throw the punch for the close-up. The scene would continue with the stunt-men." The blow to Ericson's stomach by a piece of wood swung by Lee Van Cleef was choreographed like a ballet. The scene was performed by a number count; each actor would silently count a part of the action scene. Van Cleef knew just when to stop the board's movement, then Ericson would react accordingly.

REVIEWS: "Passable low budget entry." *Western Movies*, Pitts; "A more or less standard western." *New York Times*, 1/30/58.

SUMMATION: *Day of the Bad Man* is a good little picture in the *High Noon* (United Artists, 1952) tradition. Fred MacMurray and Joan Weldon are very effective as the leads. Robert Middleton and John Ericson steal the show; Middleton as the menacing bad man and Ericson as the cowardly sheriff. Marie Windsor and Edgar Buchanan chip in with good supporting performances. Director Harry Keller does a good job with the film, generating ample suspense.

From the Pages of Max Brand's Immortal Classic of the West!
He had a name to live up to ...
a reputation to fight down ...
in the town they said couldn't be tamed!

Destry

Universal-International (January 1955); PRINT by Technicolor; RUNNING TIME: 95 min.

CAST: Tom Destry, **Audie Murphy**; Brandy, **Mari Blanchard**; Decker, **Lyle Bettger**; Rags Barnaby, **Thomas Mitchell**; Mayor Sellers, **Edgar Buchanan**; Martha Phillips, **Lori Nelson**; Doc Curtis, **Wallace Ford**; Bessie Mae Curtis, **Mary Wickes**; Jack Larson, **Alan Hale Jr.**; Curly, **George Wallace**; Mac, **Richard Reeves**; Henry Skinner, **Walter Baldwin**; Eli Skinner, **Lee Aaker**; Professor, **Mitchell Lawrence**; Dummy, **Frank Richards**; Sheriff Bailey, **Trevor Bardette**; Bartender, **Ralph Peters**; Cowhand, **John Doucette**; Townsman, **Rex Lease**

CREDITS: Director, **George Marshall**; Assistant Director, **Frank Shaw**; Producer, **Stanley Rubin**; Story, **Felix Jackson**; Screenwriter, **Edmund H. North** and **D.D. Beauchamp**; Editor, **Ted**

J. Kent; Art Directors, **Alexander Golitzen** and **Alfred Sweeney**; Set Decorators, **Russell A. Gausman** and **John P. Austin**; Cinematographer, **George Robinson**; Costumes, **Rosemary Odell**; Hair Stylist, **Joan St. Oegger**; Makeup, **Bud Westmore**; Sound, **Leslie I. Carey** and **Glenn E. Anderson**; Music Supervisor, **Joseph Gershenson**; Choreographer, **Kenny Williams**; Technicolor Color Consultant, **William Fritzsche**

SONGS: "Bang! Bang!" (Herbert and Hughes)—sung by **Mari Blanchard**; "If You Can Can—

Can" (Herbert and Hughes)—sung by **Mari Blanchard**; "Empty Arms" (Herbert and Hughes)—sung by **Mari Blanchard**

LOCATION FILMING: Great Los Angeles area, California

SOURCE: Novel, *Destry Rides Again* by **Max Brand**

STORY: In the lawless town of Restful, Decker (Lyle Bettger), aided by Brandy (Mari Blanchard), wins the deed to Skinner's (Walter Baldwin) ranch in a crooked card game. With Baldwin's deed, Bettger now owns a strip of land that will allow him to charge trail

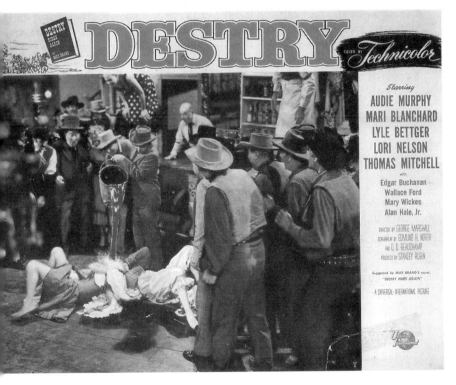

Destry (1955) scene card: Audie Murphy, with bucket in hand, pours water on Mari Blanchard (*left*) and Mary Wickes to break up their fight. Edgar Buchanan (*third actor to left of Murphy*) has an astonished expression on his face.

Destry (1955): Audie Murphy arrives in Restful carrying Lori Nelson's parasol and birdcage.

herders to drive their cattle over his property. While investigating Baldwin's claim that he was cheated, Sheriff Bailey (Trevor Bardette) is shot in the back by one of Bettger's henchmen, Curly (George Wallace). Mayor Sellers (Edgar Buchanan), in league with Bettger, appoints town drunk Rags (Thomas Mitchell) the new sheriff. Mitchell decides to quit drinking and sends for Tom Destry (Audie Murphy) to serve as his deputy. Instead of the rip-roaring, two-fisted lawman Mitchell expected, Mur- phy turns out to be a mild-man- nered individual who refuses to carry a gun. Murphy begins to question Bardette's death certifi- cate which states the late sheriff died of a heart attack. In a conver- sation with Murphy, Blanchard lets slip the fact that Bardette was killed. Murphy next finds that Doc- tor Curtis (Wallace Ford) falsified the death certificate at the point of a gun. By a ruse, Murphy gets bul- let samples from the guns of Bettger henchmen Wallace and Mac (Richard Reeves). With

Ford's help, Murphy finds that Bardette was shot in the back and Murphy is able to arrest Wallace. Blanchard diverts Murphy to her house so Wallace can be broken out of jail. In the breakout, Mitchell is killed. Incensed, Murphy straps on his late father's pistol and sets out to arrest Bettger. Warned by a henchman, Bettger sets up an ambush for Murphy when he enters the saloon. Blanchard, who has fallen in love with Murphy, tries to warn him. Murphy is able to gain access to the saloon through Blanchard's dressing room. In trying to arrest Bettger, a gunfight breaks out. In the gunfight, Murphy is able to shoot Bettger when Blanchard takes a bullet meant for Murphy. With the lawlessness ended, Murphy now finds time to romance Baldwin's niece, Martha (Lori Nelson).

NOTES AND COMMENTARY: *Destry* was a remake of *Destry Rides Again* (Universal, 1939) with Marlene Dietrich and James Stewart. Neither film had any resemblance to either the original story by Max Brand or to the first *Destry Rides Again* (Universal, 1932) with Tom Mix.

Robert Hoy was scheduled to double Audie Murphy in a stunt in the climactic shoot-out. Hoy told Murphy, "Murph, it's ridiculous me doing this. It's just jumping over the bar. Murph, you do it. It's your face. They'll have to shoot behind my head, just see a body."

Murphy replied, "Okay, I'll do it." And he did the stunt.

Lori Nelson commented about the film, "If you came from that generation of Jimmy Stewart and Marlene Dietrich, you probably liked that one better. The newer generation who were big fans of Audie Murphy and his generation and the fact that he was a war hero and all of that. I'm sure that colors how they feel about it." Lori Nelson thought that Mari Blanchard's singing was dubbed in *Destry* but she had no idea of who might have done the vocalizing.

The song "Empty Arms" can also be heard in *Imitation of Life* (Universal-International, 1959). George Marshall also directed the Dietrich-Stewart version in 1939.

REVIEWS: "Sure-fire western." *Hollywood Reporter*, 12/2/54; "Good remake of twice-filmed western." *Variety*, 12/8/54.

SUMMATION: *Destry* is a good, easygoing western with an ingratiating performance by Audie Murphy as a mild-mannered, gun-shy deputy sheriff. Thomas Mitchell delivers a fine performance as the town drunk who takes the responsibility of sheriff seriously. Mari Blanchard does a nice job as the saloon girl who falls for Audie Murphy. The film boasts a stellar supporting cast led by Lyle Bettger, Edgar Buchanan and Lori Nelson. George Marshall directs admirably, as well he should; for Marshall, it was the second time around.

A WILDERNESS OF DANGER...
AN EMPIRE OF SAVAGE HATE!

Drums Across the River

Universal-International (June 1954); COLOR by Technicolor; RUNNING TIME: 78 min.

CAST: Gary Brannon, **Audie Murphy**; Sam Brannon, **Walter Brennan**; Frank Walker, **Lyle Bettger**; Jennie, **Lisa Gaye**; Morgan, **Hugh O'Brian**; Sue, **Mara Corday**; Taos, **Jay Silverheels**; Nathan Marlowe, **Emile Meyer**; Sheriff Jim Beal, **Regis Toomey**; Chief Ouray, **Morris Ankrum**; Billy Costa, **Bob Steele**; Jed Walker, **James Anderson**; Les Walker, **George Wallace**; Ralph Costa, **Lane Bradford**; Stilwell, **Howard McNear**; Fallon, **Gregg Barton**; Indian, **Ken Terrell**; Medicine Man, **Chief Yowlachie**; Sheriff Ed Crockett, **Robert Bray**; Deputy, **Edmund Cobb**; Doctor, **John Alvin**

CREDITS: Director, **Nathan Juran**; Assistant Director, **Tom Shaw**; Producer, **Melville Tucker**; Story, **John K. Butler**; Screenwriters, **John K. Butler** and **Lawrence Roman**; Editor, **Virgil Vogel**; Art Directors, **Bernard Herzbrun** and **Richard H. Riedel**; Set Decorators, **Russell A. Gausman** and **Julia Heron**; Cinematographer, **Harold Lipstein**; Costumes, **Jay A. Morley Jr.**; Hair Stylist, **Joan St. Oegger**; Makeup, **Bud Westmore**; Sound, **Leslie I. Carey** and **Richard De Weese**; Music Director, **Joseph Gershenson**; Technicolor Color Consultant, **Monroe W. Burbank**

LOCATION FILMING: Kernville, Red Rock Canyon, and Burro Flats, California

STORY: Against the wishes of his father Sam Brannon (Walter Brennan), Gary (Audie Murphy) agrees to lead some of the townsmen of Crown City across the river to prospect for gold in the San Juan Mountains. Even though this is Ute Indian land, the prospectors think the Indians' high regard for Brennan will keep them from harm. Saloon owner Walker (Lyle Bettger) is manipulating the townspeople in order to start an Indian war. Bettger knows such a war will cause the Indians to be moved to a reservation. Bettger's Denver contacts will furnish supplies to the Indians and Bettger will gain rights to the gold. After the group crosses the river, the Utes take rancher Marlowe (Emile Meyer) captive and Indian gunfire pins down the rest of the party. Brennan joins the group and manages to have Meyer returned unharmed. Bettger spooks townsman Stilwell (Howard McNear) into shooting at the Utes, whereupon Bettger and his men join in. Most of the Indians are killed and the chief's son, Taos (Jay Silverheels), is wounded. Murphy takes Silverheels back to the Indian village and convinces the Utes not to

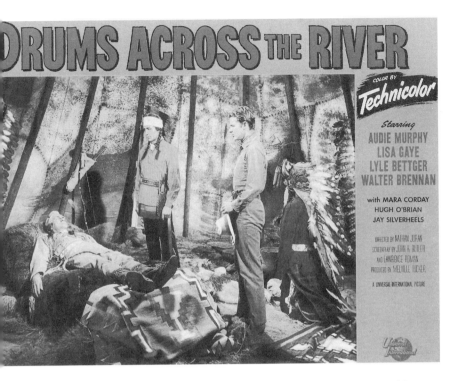

Drums Across the River (1954) scene card: Audie Murphy (*right*) talks peace with Ute chief Morris Ankrum (*left*) while Jay Silverheels watches.

start an Indian war. Murphy blames Bettger and his men for the trouble. Silverheels tells Murphy that there will be no war if their lands are not violated by the whites. Bettger now plots to have Murphy assist in a gold hijacking and have the blame placed on Murphy and the Utes. Bettger captures Murphy and Brennan, and Murphy is forced to participate in the robbery. The robbery is successful and gunman Morgan (Hugh O'Brian) is ordered to kill Murphy after the gold has been transferred to a safe hiding place. Murphy turns the tables on O'Brian and is able to hide the gold from the outlaws. Murphy is arrested and sentenced to hang. Murphy gets word to Bettger to rescue him if outlaws want the gold. Murphy is rescued and the outlaws make it look like Brennan was in charge of the rescue operation. Murphy tells Bettger that he hid the money on Indian lands. The Ute Indians attack the party and only Bettger is able to escape. Murphy catches up to Bettger and shoots him in an exchange of bullets, rescuing Brennan. The Utes will now allow the townsmen to mine gold on their land in exchange for hunting rights on the townsmen's side of the river.

NOTES AND COMMENTARY: Some of the footage of the Indians beating drums was previously seen in *Apache Drums* (Universal-International, 1951).

At one point in the picture, Lyle Bettger asked the motivation behind a line he was to deliver. Brennan retorted, "Just say the goddamn line." Bettger complied.

REVIEWS: "Actionful western." *Variety*, 5/19/54; "Fairly actionful Audie Murphy vehicle." *Western Movies*, Pitts.

SUMMATION: *Drums Across the River* is an action-filled western entry which highlights star Audie Murphy. In addition to delivering a neat performance, Audie is at his riding, fighting and shooting best. Walter Brennan is excellent as Murphy's farther and Lyle Bettger again is the consummate lead villain. Hugh O'Brian registers strongly as a ruthless gunman. On the distaff side, Lisa Gaye is no more than an attractive decoration but Mara Corday stands out as Bettger's mistress. Writers John K. Butler and Lawrence Roman deliver an exciting screenplay and director Nathan Juran keeps the proceedings moving along nicely.

SILVER CREEK ... THE MOST DANGEROUS CITY NORTH OF THE RIO GRANDE!
SILVER made it rich ... hot LEAD kept it poor ... and an Iron hand ruled its frightened people!

The Duel at Silver Creek

Universal-International (August 1952); COLOR by Technicolor; RUNNING TIME: 77 min.

CAST: The Silver Kid, **Audie Murphy**; Opal Lacy, **Faith Domergue**; Lightning Tyrone, **Stephen McNally**; Dusty Fargo, **Susan Cabot**; Rod Lacy, **Gerald Mohr**; Johnny Sombrero, **Eugene Iglesias**; Rat Face Blake, **Kyle James**; Pete Fargo, **Walter Sande**; Tinhorn Burgess, **Lee Marvin**; Jim Ryan, **George Eldredge**; The Silver Kid's Father, **Harry Harvey**; Outlaw, **Johnny Carpenter**; Army Physician, **Frank Wilcox**; Miner, **Steve Darrell**

CREDITS: Director, **Don Siegel**; Producer, **Leonard Goldstein**; Story, **Gerald Drayson Adams**; Screenwriters, **Gerald Drayson Adams** and **Joseph Hoffman**; Editor, **Russell Schoengarth**; Art Directors, **Bernard Herzbrun** and **Alexander Golitzen**; Set Decorators, **Russell A. Gausman** and **Joe Kish**; Cinematographer, **Irving Glassberg**; Costumes, **Bill Thomas**; Hair Stylist, **Joan St. Oegger**; Makeup, **Bud Westmore**; Sound, **Leslie I. Carey** and **Corson Jowett**; Music Director, **Joseph Gershenson**; Technicolor Color Consultant, **William Fritzsche**

LOCATION FILMING: Iverson's Ranch, California

STORY: The Silver Kid's (Audie Murphy) claim is jumped by a ruthless outlaw gang and his father is murdered. Murphy is able to shoot one of the gang and finds a unique medallion around the outlaw's neck. Marshal Tyrone (Stephen McNally) follows a lead to the gang's headquarters. In the posse's raid, McNally is wounded and the gang is able to get away. McNally is recuperating at an army post when a badly wounded miner is brought in. Stage passenger Opal Lacy (Faith Domergue) volunteers to assist the doctor in treating the wounded man. When she is alone, Domergue smothers the man and everyone thinks the man died due to his wounds. McNally falls for Domergue at first sight and tells her when he returns to Silver Creek, he will be camping on her doorstep. On returning to Silver Creek, McNally learns that his deputy has been murdered and Murphy is pointed out as a possible suspect. McNally believes Murphy to be innocent and makes him his new deputy. Murphy falls for Dusty Fargo (Susan Cabot), who is infatuated with McNally.

The Duel at Silver Creek (1952) scene card: Audie Murphy (*left*), Stephen McNally, Susan Cabot and Walter Sande have a quiet evening meal.

McNally begins courting Domergue. The claim jumpers try to ambush McNally when he leaves Domergue's house but Murphy intervenes and an outlaw is captured. The outlaw has a medallion that identifies him as a member of the claim jumpers. Domergue concocts a scheme in which she tells McNally that her brother, Rod (Gerald Mohr), has been kidnapped and the outlaws will trade him for the captured outlaw. Actually, Mohr is not her brother and is the leader of the claim jumpers. McNally finds out that Domergue is a member of the gang and offers Domergue her freedom if she will lead them to the outlaw hideout. Cabot takes it upon herself to make the hostage exchange and finds out the truth about Mohr. Mohr makes Cabot his captive. McNally and Murphy arrive at the outlaw camp. Domergue tries to warn Mohr but the posse had already been spotted and the outlaws are prepared to ambush the posse. Believing Domergue a traitor, Mohr shoots her. A gunfight breaks out between the posse and the outlaw gang. In the fight, Murphy rescues Cabot; McNally shoots Mohr and the posse rounds up the rest of the gang. Murphy and Cabot decide to get married.

NOTES AND COMMENTS: *The Duel at Silver Creek* was Audie Murphy's first picture after signing an exclusive contract with Universal-International in August 1951.

Claim Jumpers was the working title for this film. Kyle James was better known as James Anderson through most of his screen career.

When shown on cable TV, a comment is made that there is no duel in the film. In fact there is a challenge issued by Eugene Iglesias to Stephen McNally but the actual duel is between Audie Murphy and Inglesias. Under contract to RKO, Faith Domergue was on loanout to Universal-International for this picture. Faith Domergue was allowed to do her own riding stunts until her horse slipped and almost went down in a chase scene in the picture. After that close call, a double was used for her riding scenes.

REVIEWS: "Fast paced and lots of fun." *Western Movies*, Pitts; "A highly implausible, but nonetheless enjoyable, Western." *The Western*, Hardy.

SUMMATION: *The Duel at Silver Creek* is an exciting, well-made western with nonstop action from start to finish. The heroics are in the fine hands of Audie Murphy and Stephen McNally. Both men bring a sense of authority to their roles. Faith Domergue steals the acting honors with her portrayal of an amoral murderess. Susan Cabot is quite charming, as Murphy's love interest. Gerald Mohr handles the villainy in a capable manner. Don Siegel easily shows his command of the action film with a fast pace that holds interest throughout.

*JAMES STEWART, Memorable in The Glenn Miller Story and
Rear Window ... now ... as the Stranger with a Gun,
driven by restless longings, challenging the Klondike's snow
and sin and greed, where gold was the lure and
the fanciest woman in Dawson, his for the taking!*

The Far Country

Universal-International (February 1955); COLOR by Technicolor; RUNNING TIME: 97 min.

CAST: Jeff, **James Stewart**; Ronda, **Ruth Roman**; Renee, **Corinne Calvert**; Ben, **Walter Brennan**; Gannon, **John McIntire**; Rube, **Jay C. Flippen**; Ketchum, **Henry Morgan**; Ives, **Steve Brodie**; Hominy, **Connie Gilchrist**; Madden, **Robert Wilke**; Dusty, **Chubby Johnson**; Luke, **Royal Dano**; Newberry, **Jack Elam**; Grits, **Kathleen Freeman**; Molasses, **Connie Van**; Tom Kane, **Don Harvey**; Cowhand, **Terry Frost**; Carson, **Eddie Parker**; Captain Benson, **Stuart Randall**; Latigo, **Chuck Roberson**; Sheriff, **Paul Bryar**; Deputy, **Ted Mapes**; Second Mate, **Damian O'Flynn**; Miner, **Robert Bice**; Miner in Saloon, **John Doucette**; Tanana Pete, **Guy Wilkerson**; Yukon Sam, **Eddy Waller**; Rounds, **Gregg Barton**; Kingman, **Robert Foulk**; Doc Vallon, **Eugene Borden**; Bosun, **Allan Ray**; Saloon Girl, **Marjorie Stapp**

CREDITS: Director, **Anthony Mann**; Assistant Director, **John Sherwood**; Producer, **Aaron Rosenberg**; Story/Screenwriter, **Borden Chase**; Editor, **Russell Schoengarth**; Art Directors, **Bernard Herzbrun** and **Alexander Golitzen**; Set Decorators, **Russell A. Gausman and Oliver Emert**; Cinematographer, **William Daniels**; Costumes, **Joey Morley Jr.**; Hair Stylist. **Joan St. Oegger**; Makeup, **Bud Westmore**; Sound, **Leslie I. Carey** and **Robert Pritchard**; Music Direction, **Joseph E. Gershenson**; Technicolor Color Consultant, **William Fritzsche**

SONG: "Pretty Little Primrose" (Rosen and Herbert)—sung by **Connie Gilchrist, Kathleen Freeman** and **Connie Van**

LOCATION FILMING: Jasper National Park, Alberta, Canada

STORY: Jeff (James Stewart) and Ben (Walter Brennan) deliver a small herd of cattle to the Yukon. When the cattle cause a hanging to be interrupted, Gannon (John McIntire), the law in Skagway, confiscates Stewart's cattle. Stewart obtains a job guiding saloon owner Ronda's (Ruth Roman's) pack train to Dawson. Stewart, Brennan and Rube (Jay C. Flippen) return to Skagway and take back their cattle. Alerted to McIntire's pursuit by Renee (Corinne Calvert), Stewart is able to hold McIntire and his posse at bay long enough to have his cattle driven across the Canadian border. Stewart finds Dawson filled with

The Far Country (1955) scene card: James Stewart (*left*) and Walter Brennan (*right*) ride into Dawson.

a lawless element. Stewart refrains from helping out the decent people due to his philosophy of just looking out for himself. Stewart and Brennan buy a claim that earns them enough money to purchase a ranch in Utah. When they attempt to leave Dawson, outlaws ambush them and kill Brennan and wound Stewart. Stewart finds that McIntire's cutthroats are responsible for the nefarious doings and that Roman is in cahoots with McIntire. Stewart engages McIntire and his gunmen in a shoot-out. Roman, who loves Stewart, is killed when she tries to warn Stewart of McIntire's attempt to sneak up on Stewart. Stewart is wounded but manages to shoot McIntire. Calvert is around to nurse Stewart back to health.

NOTES AND COMMENTARY: James Stewart rode his favorite horse, Pie, in *The Far Country*. In one scene, Stewart says, "Pie picked up a rock." *The Far Country* received a Certificate of Outstanding Merit by the Southern California Motion Picture Council in February 1955. Marjorie Stapp remembered Walter Brennan as a character; a very nice and funny man who would like to tell jokes. Scenes of the pack train travelling over the Canadian wilderness would be used behind the opening title credits of *The Spoilers* (Universal-International, 1956).

REVIEWS: "Rugged outdoor actioner." *Variety*, 1/26/55; "Big budget and quite entertaining oater." *Western Movies*, Pitts.

SUMMATION: This is another good western from the collaboration of star James Stewart, director Anthony Mann and screenwriter Borden Chase. *The Far Country* is the fourth western saga (*Winchester '73*, Universal-International, 1950; *Bend of the River*, Universal-International, 1952; *The Naked Spur*, Metro-Goldwyn-Mayer, 1953, were the others) to come from this trio. It ranks as a top western but not up to the caliber of its predecessors. Stewart delivers a fine and moving performance as a man who is afraid to reach out and help his fellow man. It takes the death of his best friend, Walter Brennan, to convince him to make a change in his life. Ruth Roman and Corinne Calvert register well as the women in Stewart's life. Brennan is adequate in his "old man" routine. Cinematographer William Daniels' camera work is first-rate as he vividly shows the snow-capped mountains in Jasper National Park. Anthony Mann's direction and Borden Chase's script are not as taut as one would expect from their previous entries.

The West at its Wildest, Wackiest Best!!

Feudin', Fussin' and a-Fightin'

Universal-International (July 1948); RUNNING TIME: 78 min.

CAST: Wilbur McMurty, **Donald O'Connor**; Maribel Matthews, **Marjorie Main**; Billy Caswell, **Percy Kilbride**; Libby Matthews, **Penny Edwards**; Sharkey Dolan, **Joe Besser**; Chauncey, **Harry Shannon**; Emory Tuttle, **Fred Kohler Jr.**; Doc Overholt, **Howland Chamberlain**; Stage Driver, **Edmund Cobb**; Stage Passenger, **Joel Friedkin**; Guard, **I. Stanford Jolley**; **The Sportsmen Quartette**; Man in Tree, **Harry Brown**; Men in Café, **Roy Butler**, **Monte Montague** and **Bill Sundholm**; Checkers, **Tommy Coats** and **Francis Ford**; Judges, **Herbert Heywood** and **Kenneth MacDonald**; Citizen, **Charles Middleton**; Big Men, **Arthur Miles** and **Gene Roth**; Townsman, **Hank Worden**; Citizen at Dance, **Frances Williams**

CREDITS: Director, **George Sherman**; Assistant Director, **Horace Hough**; Producer, **Leonard Goldstein**; Associate Producer, **Aaron Rosenberg**; Screenwriter, **D.D. Beauchamp**; Editor, **Edward A. Curtiss**; Choreographer, **Louis DaPron**; Art Directors, **Bernard Herzbrun** and **Frank A. Richards**; Set Decoration, **Russell A. Gausman** and **Ray L. Jeffers**; Cinematographer, **Irving Glassberg**; Costumes,

Rosemary Odell; Hair Stylist, **Carmen Dirigo**; Makeup, **Bud Westmore**; Sound, **Leslie I. Carey** and **Richard De Weese**; Music, **Leith Stevens**.

SONGS: "Feudin' and Fightin'" (Lane and Dubin)—sung by **The Sportsmen Quartette**; "Me and My Shadow" (Dreyer, Jolson and Rose)—sung by **Donald O'Connor**; "S'-posin" (Denniker and Razaf)—sung by **Penny Edwards** and **Donald O'-Connor**

SOURCE: *Collier's* magazine story, "The Wonderful Race at Rimrock" by **D.D. Beauchamp**

STORY: The town of Rimrock has lost the annual footrace to the neighboring town of Big Bend for the past five years. It's race time again and Rimrock's pride, not to mention their money, is at stake. The townspeople are desperately trying to find a suitable entry. Traveling salesman Wilbur McMurty (Donald O'Connor) gets off the stagecoach for lunch as the horses are being changed. Trying to sell his wares in the local restaurant, the stage leaves without him. O'Connor, being fleet of foot, easily catches up to the stage. Maribel

Feudin', Fussin' and a-Fightin' (1948): **Marjorie Main** (*right*) wants Donald O'Connor (*left*) to represent Rimrock in the annual footrace. Percy Kilbride and Penny Edwards watch.

Feudin', Fussin' and a-Fightin' (1948): **Donald O'Connor and Penny Edwards (courtesy of Penny Edwards).**

Matthews (Marjorie Main), Billy Caswell (Percy Kilbride) and Sharkey Dolan (Joe Besser) quickly get over their amazement of O'Connor's speed and ride to stop the stage. O'Connor is arrested on trumped-up charges so he can be high pressured into running in the race for Rimrock. O'Connor is held captive in a barn with only Jasper, a horse, for company. Initially, O'Connor refuses to run but after falling for Libby Matthews (Penny Edwards) changes his mind. The Big Bend townsmen discover that they have a formidable foe and decide to stop O'Connor from running.

On the eve of the big race, O'Connor's drinking water in the barn is drugged but the water is consumed by Jasper instead. The veterinarian, in cahoots with the Big Ben townsmen, tells O'Connor the horse has a rare disease and someone must keep Jasper awake. O'Connor volunteers to walk Jasper in order to save his life. O'Connor is completely exhausted at race time. O'Connor races anyway and overcomes all obstacles to win the race. O'Connor becomes the town mayor and wins Edwards. Kilbride finally gets up the nerve to propose to Main, who accepts.

NOTES AND COMMENTARY: The working title for the picture was the same as the *Collier's* magazine story, "The Wonderful Race at Rimrock." The title change to *Feudin', Fussin' and a-Fightin'* was, obviously, to capitalize on the popularity of the song. The musical number, "S'posin'," was to be shot in the daylight with a tarp covering the whole street. This didn't work out so the number was finally shot at night. During the filming of the dance routine Edwards dislocated her shoulder going over a railing, which made it difficult to move her left arm. As the dance progresses, on some of the turns, you can see Edwards' left arm is lower than her right. Edwards commented that finishing the dance number was a painful experience for her, but fun.

Marjorie Main would come to the studio and bring a huge basket of food so she could continuously eat. In her scenes, she would repeatedly blow her lines 'til the person she was acting with was bad. Then Main would be letter perfect. She knew her lines and she wanted to dominate everything. Penny Edwards, Donald O'Connor and Donald's brother Jack would pass the time between scenes playing pinochle.

Penny Edwards called Donald O'Connor about fifteen years ago. O'Connor immediately started singing *S'posin'* and told Edwards that *Feudin', Fussin' and a-Fightin'* was his favorite movie.

O'Connor is still an outstanding entertainer. Penny Edwards said he had the ability to do opera and ballet. He is considered a great acrobat, singer and dancer; all of these talents O'Connor displayed in his long and still active film career. Penny Edwards thought George Sherman was fun to work with. Sherman was a short little guy. He arrived on the set one morning and said to the cast and crew, "My daughter said to me today, you're little and cute, just like I am."

REVIEWS: "Gay film fare that springs its laughs easily, making for lively, pleasant entertainment." *Variety*, 6/9/48; "A boisterous, good-natured backwoods musical that offered undemanding broad comedy and some fast and furious tap dancing." *The Universal Story*, Hirschhorn.

SUMMATION: The film's title is not an indication of the actual story line. In addition, some of the newspaper advertisements show players carrying rifles. The only firearms seen in the film are the pistols used to start the footraces. The picture could be dismissed as only average entertainment except for two musical numbers that elevate the film. The first is a solo effort for Donald O'Connor, "Me and My Shadow" and the second, "S'posin'," is a delightful duet for O'Connor and Penny Edwards. The cast carries out their roles capably. O'Connor is properly energetic. Marjorie Main and Percy Kilbride are really reprising their Ma and Pa Kettle roles, which is fine. Edwards shows that she is an extremely talented individual whose talents were never used to their full potential in Hollywood. Joe Besser adds good comic support.

...HE WAS FASTER THAN ANY MAN ALIVE!
HE HAD TO TAME A VIOLENT TOWN ...AND THREE HIRED KILLERS...
AND THE LAST ONE TO STAND IN HIS WAY WAS HIS KID BROTHER!

Four Fast Guns

Phoenix Film Studios / Universal-International (February 1960); Black and White; RUNNING TIME: 72 min.

CAST: Sabin, **James Craig**; Mary, **Martha Vickers**; Dipper, **Edgar Buchanan**; Johnny Naco, **Brett Halsey**; Hoag, **Paul Richards**; Quijano, **Richard Martin**; Farmer Brown, **Blu Wright**; Zodie, **John Swift**; Bartender, **Paul Raymond**; and **Jim Hurley**, **Grizzley Green**, **Roger Anderson**, **Joe Enna**, **H. Thomas Cain**, **Michael West**

CREDITS: Director/Producer, **William J. Hole Jr.**; Assistant Directors, **Lee Lukathen** and **Howard Haldeman**; Executive Producer, **Kenneth Altose**; Screenwriters, **James Edmiston** and **Dallas Gaultois**; Editors, **Reginald Brown**, **Harold Wooley** and **Henry F. Salerno**; Production Manager, **William Thomas**; Property Master, **Harold W. Johnson**; Cinematographer, **John M. Nickolaus Jr.**; Wardrobe, **Robert Wolf**; Makeup, **Ernest Parks**; Sound, **Dale Knight**; Sound by **West Coast**; Music Supervisor, **Alec Compinsky**; Gaffer, **Orlon French**; Production Secretary, **Patti Drake**; Script Supervisor, **Dwain Tolan**; Key Grip, **Richard Gibson**

LOCATION FILMING: Phoenix area, Arizona

STORY: The citizens of Purgatory mistake gunfighter Sabin (James Craig) for a town tamer. The citizens want to rid the town of Hoag (Paul Richards), a cripple who is responsible for the nefarious doings of the community. Richards has a degree of immunity due to an infirmity because no gunman wants the reputation of shooting a cripple. When Craig accepts the job, Richards enlists the services of various gunmen to kill Craig. The first three who try to kill Craig end up on Boot Hill. During this time, Richard's wife Mary (Martha Vickers) and Craig begin to fall in love but Vickers maintains that she will not leave her husband. A fourth gunfighter Johnny Naco (Brett Halsey) turns out to be Craig's younger brother. Craig is on the run from the law because he accepted responsibility for a murder Halsey committed. Vickers persuades Halsey not to kill Craig but just to run him out of town. Remorseful because of the shame that he brought on his brother, Halsey kills Richards. At the last moment Craig decides not to leave town. Craig and Halsey face each other in a showdown and Craig is victorious. Craig leaves Purgatory to start a new life in Tombstone and Vickers tells Craig that she will meet him there.

NOTES AND COMMENTARY: A number of the players do not seem to be Hollywood veterans. The author

Four Fast Guns (1960) scene card: Town tamer James Craig (*center*) starts a fight with bartender Paul Raymond. Edgar Buchanan is watching over the left door; right border shows James Craig.

could not find additional screen credits for Jim Hurley, Grizzley Green, Joe Enna and Michael West.

A Roger Anderson had western film credits for *Rancho Notorious* (RKO, 1952), *Cattle Queen* (United International, 1951) and *Gunfire* (Lippert, 1950). An H. Tom Cain was credited for his appearance in *The Broken Land* (20th Century–Fox, 1962). This was a Phoenix Film Studios production that was picked up for release by Universal-International.

REVIEWS: "Fair story, poorly told, picture is slow and downbeat."

Variety, 1/13/60; "Nothing special about this average oater." *Western Movies*, Pitts.

SUMMATION: This low-budget western has a few veteran cast members and a modicum of suspense at the climax, but for the most part scenes seem to be padded and drawn out to meet the film's brief running time. The performances of the primary cast members are adequate for this sagebrusher but the film is let down by inadequate direction and a script that is too measured to be fully effective.

*THEIR TRAIL WAS A GAUNTLET OF DESPERATE GUNS
THROUGH A DEVIL'S PLAYGROUND
OF APACHE HATE!*
*The story of the notorious Cully Gang and their last
reckless ride ... for the love-haunted girl who had promised her
lips to the one who got through—alive!*

Four Guns to the Border

Universal-International (November 1954); COLOR by Technicolor; RUNNING TIME: 82½ min.

CAST: Cully, **Rory Calhoun**; Lolly Bhumer, **Colleen Miller**; Bronco, **George Nader**; Simon Bhumer, **Walter Brennan**; Maggie Flannery, **Nina Foch**; Dutch, **John McIntire**; Jim Flannery, **Charles Drake**; Yaqui, **Jay Silverheels**; Greasy, **Nestor Paiva**; Mrs. Pritchard, **Mary Field**; Smitty, **Robert Hoy**; Evans, **Robert Herron**; Cashier, **Reg Parton**; Town Loafer, **Donald Kerr**; Barber, **Paul Brinegar**

CREDITS: Director, **Richard Carlson**; Assistant Director, **Tom Shaw**; Producer, **William Alland**; Screenwriters, **George Van Marter** and **Franklin Coen**; Editor, **Frank Gross**; Art Directors, **Alexander Golitzen** and **Eric Orbom**; Set Decorators, **Russell A. Gausman** and **Julia Heron**; Cinematographer, **Russell Metty**; Costumes, **Jay A. Morley Jr.**; Hair Stylist, **Joan St. Oegger**; Makeup, **Bud Westmore**; Sound, **Leslie I. Carey** and **Corson Jowett**; Music Supervision, **Joseph Gershenson**; Technicolor Color Consultant, **William Fritzsche**

LOCATION FILMING: Apple Valley, California

SOURCE: Novel by Louis L'Amour.

STORY: Simon Bhumer (Walter Brennan) and his daughter, Lolly (Colleen Miller), are heading for their ranch in Shadow Valley. On the trail they meet up with outlaw Cully (Rory Calhoun) and his gang (Dutch, John McIntire, Bronco, George Nader; and Yaqui, Jay Silverheels). Calhoun and his men plan to hold up the Cholla Bank. In Cholla, Calhoun picks a fight with Flannery (Charles Drake), the sheriff and an old friend. The fight is staged to decoy the townspeople away from the bank. The bank is held up and Calhoun's men make a successful getaway. Drake forms a posse to chase the robbers down and retrieve the money. Before they can reach Shadow Valley, Brennan and Miller are tracked and surrounded by hostile Indians. With the border an hour away, the outlaws go to Brennnan and Miller's rescue. In the fight, McIntire, Nader and Silverheels are killed and Calhoun is wounded. The posse's arrival causes the Indians to retreat. Miller, having fallen in love with Calhoun, convinces Brennan to take Calhoun to their ranch. Drake catches up with Calhoun and Calhoun challenges Drake to a gun duel

Miller finally convinces Calhoun not to fight and Calhoun surrenders to Drake. Miller promises to wait as Calhoun pays his debt to society.

NOTES AND COMMENTARY: On the Louis L'Amour web site, it is intimated that the original story or novel title was *Four Guns to the Border*. Also, it is mentioned that Mr. L'Amour had a hand in writing the screenplay but this is not verified by the screen credits. Reg Parton, the actor who played the cashier, also doubled Rory Calhoun in this and many other films. For the adult viewer there is a torrid love scene between Rory Calhoun and Colleen Miller who is clad only in a nightgown. The rain is beating down on the stable, the thunder roars, lightning cracks and then Walter Brennan breaks things up. Colleen Miller never thought of herself as being sensuous, but kind of naïve at the time because of her age. Look at Miller's reaction to the kiss. Miller commented, "The reaction you got on screen was that reaction because I was totally shocked." Completely unexpected by Miller, she was kissed by director Richard Carlson instead of Calhoun.

There is a scene where Walter Brennan brings Colleen Miller back to consciousness by pouring water

Four Guns to the Border (1954) scene card: The four outlaws, (*left to right*) George Nader, John McIntire, Rory Calhoun and Jay Silverheels, pause in their travels.

on her face; most of the water ends up on her blouse. Richard Carlson wanted to do Miller's part sexy. Miller said, "Every angle, every scene, he would see if there was something in there that would be sensuous."

The climactic scene as Colleen Miller begs and then berates Rory Calhoun for wanting to shoot it out with Charles Drake was done as a tracking shot. Miller had never done one of these before and Carlson was eager to film the scene in this manner. Miller said there were some timing things she had to master and she really hated doing this scene. Colleen Miller was friendly with Rory Calhoun's wife, Lita Baron. They both had been in the same ballet class together. Baron remarked to Miller that she didn't mind her kissing Calhoun as long as she didn't put any scratches on him. Colleen Miller thought "it would be a neat thing" to act in *Four Guns to the Border*.

Miller had learned to ride a horse and milk a cow in her childhood years in Yakima, Washington. Nina Foch played in the film as a favor to director Richard Carlson.

REVIEWS: "Western feature with s.a. [sex appeal] overtones, satisfactory fare for the outdoor trade." *Variety*, 9/22/54; "Slightly different story makes this oater acceptable entertainment." *Western Movies*, Pitts.

SUMMATION: *Four Guns to the Border* is a good, exciting western with finely honed tension in its climactic scene. Rory Calhoun handles himself nicely as an outlaw who reforms due to the love of a good woman. Shades of William S. Hart! Colleen Miller turns in a fine job as the woman who falls in love with a bad man. Walter Brennan, John McIntire and Charles Drake add good support. The above average script is well directed by Richard Carlson.

"I don't care what they say you are, or what your mother was—
I only know I love you ... and need to feel your arms around me!"
Anya Seton's daring best-seller flames to life on the screen!

Foxfire

Universal-International (July 1955); COLOR by Technicolor; RUNNING TIME: 91½ min.

CAST: Amanda, **Jane Russell**; Jonathan Dartland, **Jeff Chandler**; Hugh Slater, **Dan Duryea**; Maria, **Mara Corday**; Mr. Mablett, **Barton MacLane**; Mrs. Lawrence, **Frieda Inescort**; Saba, **Celia Lovsky**; Old Larky, **Eddy C. Waller**; Ernest Tyson, **Robert F. Simon**; Mrs. Mablett, **Charlotte Wynters**; Walt Whitman, **Robert Bice**; Foley, **Arthur Space**; Rev. Barton, **Guy Wilkerson**; Rose, **Grace Lenard**; Cleo, **Vici Raaf**; Mrs. Potter, **Lillian Bronson**; Bus Driver, **Dabbs Greer**; Man Tourist, **Hal K. Chester**

Foxfire (1955) scene card: Jeff Chandler holds Jane Russell (*left*) in a lighter moment with Dan Duryea and Mara Corday (*right*).

CREDITS: Director, **Joseph Pevney**; Assistant Director, **Ronnie Rondell**; Producer, **Aaron Rosenberg**; Screenwriter, **Ketti Frings**; Editor, **Ted J. Kent**, Art Directors, **Alexander Golitzen** and **Robert Clatworthy**; Set Decorators, **Russell A. Gausman** and **Ruby R. Levitt**; Cinematographer, **William H. Daniels**; Gowns, **Bill Thomas**; Hair Stylist, **Joan St. Oegger**; Jane Russell's Hair Stylist, **Stephanie McGrew**; Makeup, **Bud Westmore**; Jane Russell's Makeup, **Layne Britton**; Sound, **Leslie I. Carey** and **Robert Pritchard**; Music, **Frank Skinner**; Music Supervisor, **Joseph Gershenson**; Technicolor Color Consultant, **William Fritzsche**

SONG: "Foxfire" (Mancini and Chandler)—sung by **Jeff Chandler**

LOCATION FILMING: Apple Valley Inn, Apple Valley, California; and Oatman, Arizona

SOURCE: Novel, *Foxfire* by **Anya Seton**.

STORY: Socialite Amanda (Jane Russell) and mining engineer Jonathan Dartland (Jeff Chandler) marry after a whirlwind courtship. Chandler, who is half Apache, believes an abandoned mine still contains gold. Russell helps Chandler put over his proposal with mine owner Tyson (Robert F. Simon), who agrees to finance the operation. Russell, dejected that Chandler refuses to include her in all his interests, goes to see Chandler's mother Saba (Celia Lovsky). Lovsky returned to the Apache reservation after her husband's death. From Lovsky, Russell finds out much about the Apache heritage and beliefs. Russell tells Lovsky that she is pregnant but is unable to tell Chandler as he is upset about Russell's absence during the day. Chandler thought that Russell was having an affair with Chandler's friend Slater (Dan Duryea), the company physician. As Chandler buries himself in work, Russell miscarries and loses their baby. Russell believes that a separation is necessary to allow both to think their relationship over. Chandler still attempts to find gold and a large dynamite charge results in a cave-in. Chandler is injured but sees an opening in the shaft's floor. This opening leads to a lower shaft that is gold-laden. Chandler realizes he needs Russell and tries to reach her only to hear she has left on a plane that is taking her back east. Word reaches Russell before she boards the plane of Chandler's condition and she returns to Chandler. Russell and Chandler now realize their marriage will work.

NOTES AND COMMENTARY: The song "Foxfire" that was sung over the opening credits had lyrics written and sung by Jeff Chandler.

REVIEWS: "Foxfire is not so hot." *New York Times*, 7/14/55; "Average entertainment." *Variety*, 6/15/55.

SUMMATION: *Foxfire* is an okay soap opera with a western setting. Jane Russell and Jeff Chandler are effective as the romantic leads. Dan Duryea somewhat overdoes his drunken doctor routine. Celia Lovsky stands out in the otherwise routine supporting cast. Director Joseph Pevney is not able to raise the film above the ordinary.

He's Got a Gun in One Hand ...
and Lace-Trimmed Dynamite in the other!
The frontier's toughest Sheriff vs. the
West's bewitchiest gal—in the wildest town
that ever defied the law!

Frenchie

Universal-International (January 1951); COLOR by Technicolor; RUNNING TIME: 81 min.

CAST: Tom Banning, **Joel McCrea**; Frenchie Fontaine, **Shelley Winters**; Pete Lambert, **Paul Kelly**; Countess, **Elsa Lanchester**; Diane, **Marie Windsor**; Lance Cole, **John Russell**; Clyde Gorman, **John Emery**; Jeff Harding, **George Cleveland**;

Carter, **Regis Toomey**; Rednose, **Paul E. Burns**; Jim Dobbs, **Frank Ferguson**; Tony, **Vincent Renno**; Bartender, **Larry Dobkin**; Dealer, **Lucille Barkley**; Stage Driver, **Jack Ingram**; Drunk, **Chubby Johnson**; Patron at Bar, **Sam Flint**; Mr. Grady (Assayer), **Hank Worden**

CREDITS: Director, **Louis King**; Producer, **Michael Kraike**; Story/Screenwriter, **Oscar Brodney**; Editor, **Ted Kent**; Art Directors, **Bernard Herzbrun** and **Alexander Golit-zen**; Set Decorators, **Russell A. Gausman** and **Oliver Emert**; Cinematographer, **Maury Gerts-**man; Costumes, **Yvonne Wood**; Hair Stylist, **Joan St. Oegger**; Makeup, **Bud Westmore**; Sound, **Leslie I. Carey** and **Glenn E. Anderson**; Music, **Hans Salter**; Technicolor Color Consultant, **William Fritz-sche**

LOCATION FILMING: Bishop, California

STORY: Frenchie Fontaine (Shelley Winters) returns to Bottleneck to avenge her father's death. Two men, Lambert (Paul Kelly) and his unidentified partner, murdered Winter's father. Sheriff Banning (Joel McCrea) discovers the reason for

Frenchie (1951) scene card: John Emery (*left*) talks with Joel McCrea while Shelly Winters listens; left border features Joel McCrea and Shelly Winters.

Winters' return. Diane (Marie Windsor) and Winters are rivals for McCrea's affections. Winters finds out that Kelly's partner is Gorman (John Emery), Windsor's husband. When Emery is found murdered, the townspeople think McCrea killed Emery in order to marry Windsor and McCrea is arrested. Winters breaks McCrea out of jail and then decides to sell out to Kelly and leave town. McCrea discovers that Emery was Kelly's partner and now thinks that Winters killed Emery. Believing that McCrea is out of the way, Kelly decides to forcefully take over Winters' saloon. McCrea comes back to town and kills Kelly in a shoot-out. Windsor confesses that she killed Emery in self-defense. McCrea and Winters end up in each other arms.

NOTES AND COMMENTARY: The crew was really interested in the fight scene between Shelley Winters and Marie Windsor. Winters and Windsor agreed that they would film the scene without stunt people and agreed to go all out. The crew and the guys on the catwalk were all cheering first one and then the other actress, "Hit her one for me." After the scene had been completed, everybody applauded. Marie Windsor remembers Joel McCrea as "a sweetheart, really a lovely man." When asked to comment on director Louis King, Marie Windsor's reply was "I hate to admit that I forgot Louis King was the director. Are you sure it was Louis King?"

REVIEWS: "A warmed-over-lightly western." *The Universal Story*, Hirschhorn; "Mediocre western." *Western Movies*, Pitts.

SUMMATION: This is only a fair western, supposedly based on the classic picture *Destry Rides Again* (Universal, 1939) with Marlene Dietrich and James Stewart. Joel McCrea's character is patterned after that of Stewart's, a man who abhors violence and who will use a homespun story to illustrate a point. McCrea, who quite often portrayed easygoing men who only can be pushed to a point, is satisfactory in this role. Shelley Winters and Paul Kelly are adequate in their parts, while Elsa Lanchester, George Cleveland and Marie Windsor give the film some much-needed punch. *Frenchie* comes in with a roar and goes out with a whimper.

Lil was WANTED ... by the law and the lawless!
She was the gal who KISSES 'em first ... and asked questions afterwards!

The Gal Who Took the West

Universal-International (September 1949); COLOR by Technicolor; RUNNING TIME: 84 min.

CAST: Lillian Marlowe, **Yvonne De Carlo**; General Michael O'Hara, **Charles Coburn**; Lee O'Hara, **Scott Brady**; Grant O'Hara, **John Russell**; Nancy, **Myrna Dell**; Hawley (as an old timer), **Clem Bevans**; Ted (as an old timer), **Houseley Stevenson**; Bartender (as an old timer), **Russell Simpson**; Colonel Logan, **John Litel**; Hawley, **James Millican**; Ted, **Bob Stevenson**; Douglas Andrews, **James Todd**; Bartender, **Robin Short**; Mr. Nolan, **Edward Earle**; Lee's Men, **William Haade**, **Steve Darrell**, **Pierce Lyden**, **Francis McDonald**, **Glenn Strange** and **William Tannen**; Grant's Men, **Charles Cane**, **Ross Elliott**, **Jack Ingram**, **John James** and **Ethan Laidlaw**; Salesman, **Paul Brinegar**; Customer, **Charles Jordan**; Mrs. Logan, **Louise Lorimer**; Potkins, **Howard Negley**; Trooper, **House Peters Jr.**; Barber, **George Stern**; Servant, **Forrest Taylor**; Guest, **Forbes Murray**; Corporal Trooper, **Russ Whiteman**; Sue, **Audrey Young**; Dance Hall Girls, **Patricia Hall**, **Joan Fulton** and **Ann Pierce**; Cavalry Captain, **William Donnelly**; Sentry, **Fraser McWinn**; 2nd Bartender, **Harland Hoagland**

CREDITS: Director, **Frederick de Cordova**; Producer, **Robert Arthur**; Story and Screenplay, **William Bowers** and **Oscar Brodney**; Editor, **Milton Carruth**; Art Directors, **Bernard Herzbrun** and **Robert Boyle**; Set Decorators, **Russell A. Gausman** and **John Austin**; Cinematographer, **William Daniels**; Costumes, **Yvonne Wood**; Hair Stylist, **Joan St. Oegger**; Makeup, **Bud Westmore**; Sound, **Leslie I. Carey** and **Joe Lapis**; Music, **Frank Skinner**; Choreographer, **Harold Belfer**; Technicolor Color Consultant, **William Fritzsche**; Dialogue Director, **Jack Daniels**

SONGS: "Kellarney" (traditional) —sung by **Yvonne De Carlo**; "Clancy Lowered the Boom" (Heath and Lange)—sung by **Yvonne De Carlo**; "Frankie and Johnny" (traditional)—sung by **Yvonne De Carlo**

LOCATION FILMING: Arizona and Calabasas, California

STORY: A writer is gathering information for an article on the O'Hara family. Directed to three old-timers and finally to Lillian Marlowe (Yvonne De Carlo), now a grandmother, the writer gets his story. Lee (Scott Brady) and Grant (John Russell) are feuding cousins. Yvonne De Carlo is brought to Arizona to perform at the new opera house built by Gen. O'Hara (Charles Coburn). Coburn's power and authority is the only thing stopping open warfare between the two cousins. Quickly, both Brady and Russell fall head-over-heels in love with De Carlo. Realizing that De Carlo prefers Russell, Brady starts a knock-down, drag-out, no-holds-barred fistfight with Russell. Brady emerges victorious and demands that Russell marry De Carlo immediately. Brady is around to ensure that Russell's once wandering eye will wander no more.

NOTES AND COMMENTARY: Jack Brooks wrote special lyrics for "Kellarney" and "Frankie and Johnny." Universal Studios sent photographs of contract actress Donna Martell to newspapers around the country to publicize the picture. Interestingly enough, Martell was not in the film. In April of 1948, Deanna Durbin and Charles Coburn were announced as two of the four players who would star in *The Western Story*, the original shooting title of *The Gal Who Took the West*. As reported in *Box Office Barometer* in November 1948, in *The Western Story*, Durbin would play a New York singer who is brought to Phoenix by Coburn. While out West, Durbin meets three men in a home for the aged. Each man tells Durbin his own version of a famous incident of the Old West. The same characters are in each story with Durbin playing the young lady in a different manner in all three. The story would be rewritten to feature the fiery personality of Yvonne De Carlo.

When Myrna Dell reported for work on this film, she was told that she would have a temporary dressing room. There was an order put in for a better dressing room, but at the moment that was the best that could be done. Myrna accepted it without complaint. She found that the dressing room was made of canvas and had a little tear in it. So as a joke, Myrna put up a sign that said "5 cents a peek."

Myrna Dell enjoyed working with both Scott Brady and John Russell. She remembers Brady as sharp, very funny and a great friend. John Russell was very nice and very un-actorish. The only other screen personality she remembers as being un-actorish was Ronald Reagan. She also remembers Russell as being a little square but sweet. She liked to tease Russell by saying, "John dear, you look tired. Why don't you go to my dressing room and lie down?" At this, Brady would laugh and Russell would look a little shy.

Myrna Dell had worked with Yvonne De Carlo at Earl Carroll's. Myrna commented that De Carlo had always been a strange person. They had a quick conversation on the set. Yvonne told Myrna that she was taking drama lessons but not to tell director Fred de Cordova.

Yvonne De Carlo found romance on the set of the picture in the person of stuntman Jacques O'Mahoney (later known as Jock and Jack Mahoney in his long movie and television career). Mahoney was one of the stuntmen in the rugged fight between John Russell and Scott Brady.

Myrna Dell mentioned that she had appeared in 14 westerns and had hated every one of them. Then she relented about *The Gal Who Took the West* because, "I wasn't on a horse then."

REVIEWS: "Passably good entertainment," *Variety*, 9/14/49; "Scriocomedy Western is not good on either count; mediocre." *Western Movies*, Pitts.

SUMMATION: The film is an above average and very enjoyable western comedy, with the beautiful Yvonne De Carlo in fine fettle as the gal who brought peace to Arizona. De Carlo's musical numbers are a high point of the picture. Charles Coburn is in good form as the patriarch of the O'Hara clan and both Scott Brady and John Russell do well in their parts of the feuding cousins. The three old-timers, Clem Bevans, Russell Simpson and Houseley Stevenson, are on hand to add charm and humor to the proceedings.

ALL THE SAVAGE FURY OF THE GREAT PLAINS INDIAN WARS!
For the scarlet lips of a traitor's woman—
he stood alone—against the mighty Chief Red Cloud
and the scalp-hungry hordes at his command!

The Great Sioux Uprising

Universal-International (July 1953); COLOR by Technicolor; RUNNING TIME: 80 min.

CAST: Jonathan Westgate, **Jeff Chandler**; Joan Britton, **Faith Domergue**; Stephen Cook, **Lyle Bettger**; Ahab Jones, **Peter Whitney**; Uriah, **Stacy S. Harris**; Joe Baird, **Walter Sande**; Major McKay, **Stephen Chase**; Red Cloud, **John War Eagle**; Stand Watie, **Glenn Strange**; Gist, **Charles Arnt**; Heyoka, **Julia Montoya**; Sgt. Manners, **Ray Bennett**; Teo-Ka-Ha, **Dewey Drapeau**; Ray, **Boyd Red Morgan**; Lee, **Lane Bradford**; Sam, **Jack Ingram**; Jake, **Clem Fuller**; Small Ranchers, **Kermit Maynard** and **Edmund Cobb**; Bartender, **Ethan Laidlaw**

CREDITS: Director, **Lloyd Bacon**; Assistant Director, **Jesse Hibbs**; Producer, **Albert J. Cohen**; Co-Producer, **Leonard Goldstein**; Editor, **Edward Curtiss**; Art Directors, **Alexander Golitzen** and **Alfred Sweeney**; Set Decorators, **Russell A. Gausman** and **Joe Kish**; Cinematographer, **Maury Gertsman**; Costumes, **Bill Thomas**; Hair Stylist, **Joan St. Oegger**; Makeup, **Bud Westmore**; Sound, **Leslie I. Carey** and **Glenn E. Anderson**; Musical Director, **Joseph Gershenson**; Tecnicolor Color Consultant, **William Fritzsche**

LOCATION FILMING: Pendleton, Oregon

STORY: Rancher Cook (Lyle Bettger) wants to have a monopoly on supplying horses to the army. Bettger tolerates Joan Britton's (Faith Domergue) competition because he wants to marry her. Domergue travels into Sioux territory to try to persuade Chief Red Cloud (John War Eagle) to sell horses to her but War Eagle refuses. Bettger has followed Domergue and rustles the horses. The Indians try to overtake the rustlers. There is a fight in which one of the Sioux ponies is shot and an arrow hits an outlaw's horse. War Eagle's friend, Doctor Westgate (Jeff Chandler), rides into the Sioux village and is able to heal the injured pony. Chandler has been released from service as a Union surgeon because of an injury to his hand. Chandler has no confidence in his abilities as a physician and is content to earn a living as a veterinarian. Chandler promises to be on the lookout for the rustlers. Then Chandler has the opportunity to treat the outlaw's horse and finds an Indian arrow. Chandler decides to stay in the area to flush out the rustlers. Chandler suspects Bettger of being behind the rustling activities. Bettger becomes ill and Chandler's surgical ability saves his

The Great Sioux Uprising (1953) scene card: Standing—Jeff Chandler (*second from left*), Faith Domergue, and Peter Whitney; and (*seated center*) Sioux chief John War Eagle listens to Glenn Strange's attempt to align the Indian tribes with the Confederate forces against the cavalry and the white settlers.

life. In payment, Bettger gives Chandler a horse that turns out to be the one Chandler treated in the Indian village. Chandler goes to see War Eagle to have War Eagle identify the horse. Bettger discovers Chandler's plan and is able to destroy the horse in a fire. Domergue and Chandler's friend, Ahab Jones (Peter Whitney), meet Chandler and War Eagle and deliver the disappointing news. War Eagle imprisons Chandler, Domergue and Whitney. Again Bettger rustles Sioux horses and sends for help from the army by claiming the Sioux

are on the warpath and are trying to steal Bettger's horses. Chandler and Domergue are able to escape from the Sioux village. During a fight between the Sioux and the rustlers, Chandler is able to capture Bettger and reach the army before warfare can erupt between the cavalry and the Sioux. With his medical confidence restored, Chandler returns to duty in the Civil War, promising to return to Domergue at the war's end.

NOTES AND COMMENTARY: Stephen McNally was originally assigned to play the part of Stephen Cook. Because of his wife's illness and the long location filming planned for the film, McNally asked for his release. Lyle Bettger was signed as McNally's replacement.

This was Faith Domergue's first picture upon receiving her release from her RKO contract. Domergue signed a two-picture-a-year contract with Universal-International.

The working title for the film was *Sioux Uprising*.

REVIEWS: "Okay entry." *Variety*, 6/24/53; "Earnest performances, fetching Technicolor landscapes and some sturdy utterances on racial tolerance and understanding fail to lift *The Great Sioux Uprising* above standard level." *New York Times*, 7/18/53.

SUMMATION: *The Great Sioux Uprising* is only a routine cavalry verses Indians saga. To its credit, the film offers some fine scenic backgrounds; good acting by Jeff Chandler, Lyle Bettger and Faith Domergue and some well meaning dialogue on racial tolerance. On the negative side, Lloyd Bacon directs routinely and fails to add the needed punch to elevate the decidedly average script. The story has a drunken Peter Whitney, the hero's friend, let slip information that eventually puts Chandler and Domergue's life in peril and then happily gives his life to allow the two to escape from an Indian village. Pure hokum! The script is the real villain in this picture.

Come on ... get Lost in the LAUGHTER!
... a horse-shy movie cowboy takes a passing fancy
to a lady lawyer with some fancy passes!

The Groom Wore Spurs

Fidelity Pictures, Inc./Universal-International (March 1951); Black and White; RUNNING TIME: 80 min.

CAST: Abigail J. Furnival, **Ginger Rogers**; Ben Castle, **Jack Carson**; Alice Dean, **Joan Davis**; Harry Kallen, **Stanley Ridges**; Chief of Police, **John Litel**; Steve Hall, **James Brown**; Ignacio, **Victor Sen Yung**; Mrs. Forbes, **Myra McKinney**; Ricky, **Gordon Nelson**; Bellhop, **George Meader**; The Killer, Kemp Niver; Jake Harris, **Robert B. Williams**; Sam, **George Chesebro**; Reporter, **Douglas Evans**; J.N. Bergen, **George Eldredge**

CREDITS: Director, **Richard Whorf**; Assistant Director, **Tom Andre**; Airplane Sequence Director, **Ralph Ceder**; Producer, **Howard Welsch**; Screenwriters, **Robert Libott** and **Frank Burt**; Editor, **Otto Ludwig**; Set Decorator, **Julia Heron**; Production Designer, **Perry**

Ferguson; Production Supervisor, **Ben Hersh**; Cinematographer, **Peverell Marley**; Costumes for Ginger Rogers, **Jacie**; Hats for Ginger Rogers, **Rex, Inc**; Costumes for Joan Davis, **Eloise Jensson**; Hair Stylist, **Louise Mirhle**; Makeup, **Frank Westmore**; Sound, **Victor Appel** and **Mac Dalgleish**; Music, **Emil Newman** and **Arthur Lange**

SONGS: "The Groom Wore Spurs"; "No More Wand'ring Around" (Newman and Lange)

SOURCE: *Collier's* magazine story, "Legal Brides" by **Robert Carson**

STORY: Movie cowboy Ben Castle (Jack Carson) owes money to a Las Vegas gambler, Harry Kallen (Stanley Ridges). Carson hires lawyer Abigail Furnival (Ginger Rogers) to work out a settlement with Ridges. In Las Vegas Carson and Rogers fall in love and get married in a whirlwind courtship. Ridges knew Rogers' father and forgives the debt. Rogers realizes that was the reason she had been hired to represent Carson. Rogers leaves Carson but, at the prompting of her roommate, Alice Dean (Joan Davis), decides to live at Carson's ranch. Rogers finds that Carson, as a movie cowboy, dislikes horses and cannot play a guitar or sing. When the

The Groom Wore Spurs (1951) scene card: Killer Kemp Niver (*center*) demands that Jack Carson and Ginger Rogers fly him to safety; left border shows Jack Carson and Ginger Rogers.

marriage causes trouble for Carson at the studio, Rogers is able to renegotiate a new contract with a check to pay off his gambling debt. Carson tries to pay Ridges the money that he owes him, but Ridges burns the check. As Carson starts to leave, a killer (Kemp Niver) steps into the room and shoots Ridges. Carson is held for the crime but Rogers decides to defend him. Rogers persuades the chief of police (John Litel) to release Carson in her custody so they can bring in the killer. Acting on a tip, Rogers and Carson race to the airport where Niver has chartered a plane to Mexico. Using western tricks he learned in his movies, Carson catches Niver. Rogers and Carson decide to remain as man and wife.

NOTES AND COMMENTARY: This was a Fidelity Pictures production that was picked up for release by Universal-International.

REVIEWS: "Only mild comedy results." *Variety*, 2/7/51; "A jerky but mildly enjoyable satire on the life of a Hollywood cowboy." *The Western*, Hardy.

SUMMATION: *The Groom Wore Spurs* is a mildly entertaining comedy that promises more laughs than it actually delivers. Ginger Rogers and Jack Carson deliver some smiles but there are no real belly laughs. Joan Davis is largely wasted as Rogers' roommate. Only Victor Sen Yung is able to make anything out of a supporting role. Watch Sen Yung lip sync to a record played at the wrong speed. Director Richard Whorf is not able to elevate the routine script that he's saddled with.

CHALLENGE ONE ... YOU ANSWER TO ALL!
The saga of the Keough Brothers who fought together ...
faced death together ... till a red-lipped woman drove them apart!

Gun for a Coward

Universal-International (March 1957); FILMED in Eastman Color; FILMED in Cinemascope; RUNNING TIME: 88 min.

CAST: Will Keough, **Fred MacMurray**; Bless Keough, **Jeffrey Hunter**; Aud Niven, **Janice Rule**; Loving, **Chill Wills**; Hade (Harry) Keough, **Dean Stockwell**; Mrs. Keough, **Josephine Hutchinson**; Claire, **Betty Lynn**; Chief, **Iron Eyes Cody**; Danny, **Robert Hoy**; Marie, **Jane Howard**; Rose, **Marjorie Stapp**; Stringer, **John Larch**; Andy Niven, **Paul Birch**; Durkee, **Bob Steele**; Mrs. Anderson, **Frances Morris**; Nester, **Stanley Andrews**; Cattle Rustler, **Eddie Parker**

CREDITS: Director, **Abner Biberman**; Assistant Director, **William Holland**; Producer, **William Alland**; Screenwriter, **R. Wright Campbell**;

Gun for a Coward (1957) scene card:(*left to right*) **An unidentified actor, Marjorie Stapp, and Jane Howard watch as Dean Stockwell listens to Jeffrey Hunter tell him that they don't have time to spend with the ladies.**

Editor, **Edward Curtiss**; Art Directors, **Alexander Golitzen** and **Alfred Sweeney**; Set Decorators, **Russell A. Gausman** and **William Tapp**; Cinematographer, **George Robinson**; Costumes, **Jay A. Morley Jr.**; Hair Stylist, **Joan St. Oegger**; Makeup, **Bud Westmore**; Sound, **Leslie I. Carey** and **Robert Pritchard**; Music Supervision, **Joseph E. Gershenson**

LOCATION FILMING: Vasquez Rocks, California

STORY: Deathly afraid of snakes, Bless Keough (Jeffrey Hunter) is afraid to shoot a rattlesnake that is poised to strike at his younger brother

(Hade) Dean Stockwell. Their older brother Will (Fred MacMurray) steps in and kills the snake. Josephine Hutchinson, their mother, is overprotective of Hunter and wants him to leave the West and live in St. Louis with her. Hunter wants to stay at the ranch and finally gets up the courage to tell her that he's not ready to leave. Hutchinson then becomes ill and dies. MacMurray is in love with a neighboring rancher's daughter, Aud Niven (Janice Rule), but has never gotten around to setting a date. In the meantime, Rule and Hunter have fallen in love. MacMurray has to step in to defuse a tense encounter between Hunter and neighboring rancher Stringer (John Larch) over Hunter's interest in buying Larch's ranch. Larch does decide to sell and becomes a cowhand on MacMurray and Hunter's ranch. On a cattle drive, Hunter and Stockwell ride to a nearby town to purchase sugar. Larch and his brother Danny (Robert Hoy) leave the herd and go to town to drink. Stockwell gets into an argument with some toughs over two saloon girls, which results in the death of Hoy and one of the toughs. Back at the camp Hunter finally tells MacMurray that he and Rule are in love. MacMurray is hurt and angry. With only one day left on the drive, MacMurray leaves to make arrangements to sell the cattle in Abilene. The toughs decide to rustle the cattle and in the raid Stockwell is killed. The rustlers get away with the cattle and cowhand Durkee (Bob Steele) is told to follow the herd. Hunter is branded a coward because he wanted to engage the rustlers at the mouth of the canyon instead of at the cowboys' camp on the open range. MacMurray tells Hunter that he should have stayed with his brother. Larch goads Hunter into hitting him and then wants to engage Hunter in a gun duel. Again, MacMurray interferes by shooting Larch in the shoulder. Angry at his brother's continued interference in his life, Hunter begins a furious fistfight with MacMurray. Before the fight can be resolved, Steele returns with news of the cattle. MacMurray lets Hunter lead the men in pursuit of the outlaws and rides away leaving the ranch to Hunter and Rule.

NOTES AND COMMENTARY: Robert Hoy, a fine stuntman who played John Larch's brother, remembers that Al Wyatt doubled Fred MacMurray and Paul Baxley filled in for Jeffrey Hunter in their rugged fistfight.

Gun for a Coward was originally scheduled to be filmed by Warner Bros. with James Dean in the Jeffrey Hunter role. Dean's death ended that studio's interest in the story. Screenwriter R. Wright Campbell received an Academy Award nomination for his screenplay *Man of a Thousand Faces* (Universal-International, 1957).

Marjorie Stapp had no remembrances of her scene in the seedy saloon with fellow actors Dean Stockwell and Jeffrey Hunter. Later in her career when Stapp played in an episode of *Quantum Leap* (NBC) with Dean Stockwell, she told him that she remembered him in *The Boy with Green Hair* (RKO, 1949) and that he had been "a darling little boy." Marjorie Stapp and Director Abner Biberman had been in the same actors' group together. This was a group made up of some of the top character actors.

REVIEWS: "Story and characterization values make this above-average western." *Variety*, 1/16/57; "Direction is evenly paced, letting the action and story unfold naturally, ever sensitive to the relationships among characters." *The Motion Picture Guide*, Nash and Ross.

SUMMATION: *Gun for a Coward* is a very good western, rich in characterizations and story with enough action to satisfy the western fan. The acting is good throughout but special mention has to be made for the fine performances of Jeffrey Hunter and Janice Rule as the young lovers. Fred MacMurray, also, does a nice job as the older brother but does seem to be a little too old for the role. Director Abner Biberman keeps the proceedings moving nicely and the interest never wanes thanks to scriptwriter R. Wright Campbell's superior effort.

When the deadliest gun in the West
smashed the spoiler rule of
Montana's landlocked mountain empire!...
Alone through the lawless land—he drove a
maddened herd and mutinous men across
1000 dangerous miles to the Yellowstone!

Gunsmoke

Universal-International (March 1953); COLOR by Technicolor; RUNNING TIME: 79 min.

CAST: Reb Kittredge, **Audie Murphy**; Rita Saxon, **Susan Cabot**; Dan Saxon, **Paul Kelly**; Johnny Lake, **Charles Drake**; Cora Du-frayne, **Mary Castle**; Curley Mather, **Jack Kelly**; Professor, **Jesse White**; Matt Telford, **Donald Randolph**; Brazos, **William Reynolds**; Doc Ferrell, **Chubby Johnson**; Stage Driver, **Edmund Cobb**; Stage Passenger, **George Eldredge**; Station Master, **Forrest Taylor**; Hotel Clerk, **William Fawcett**; Telford Gang Member, **Mike Ragan**; Cowhand, **Denver Pyle**; O'Shea, **James F. Stone**; Bartender, **Bill Radovich**; Clay, **Jimmy Van Horn**; Two Dot, **Clem Fuller**

CREDITS: Director, **Nathan Juran**; Assistant Director, **William Holland**; Producer, **Aaron Rosenberg**; Screenwriter, **D.D. Beauchamp**; Editor, **Ted J. Kent**; Art Directors, **Alexander Golitzen** and **Robert F. Boyle**; Set Decorators, **Russell A. Gausman** and **Ray Jeffers**; Cinematographer, **Charles P. Boyle**; Costumes, **Rosemary Odell**; Hair Stylist, **Joan St. Oegger**; Makeup, **Bud Westmore**; Sound, **Leslie I. Carey** and **Robert Pritchard**; Music, **Joseph Gershenson**; Technicolor Color Consultant, **William Fritzsche**

SONG: "See What the Boys in the Back Room Will Have" (Hollander and Loesser)—sung by **Mary Castle**; "True Love" (Herbert and Hughes)—sung by **Mary Castle**

LOCATION FILMING: Big Bear, California

SOURCE: Novel, *Rough-shod* by **Norman A. Fox**

STORY: Hired gun Kittredge (Audie Murphy) is summoned to Montana by Telford (Donald Randolph) to help him obtain Dan Saxon's (Paul Kelly) ranch. Randolph

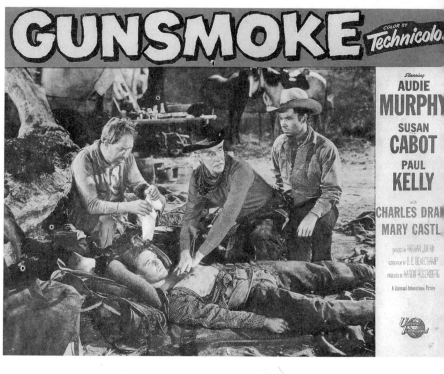

Gunsmoke (1953) scene card: A wounded William Reynolds is being cared for by (*left to right*) Jesse White, Paul Kelly and Audie Murphy.

doesn't offer Murphy enough money for the job. Murphy engages Kelly in a card game and wins Kelly's ranch. Murphy decides to drive the cattle to the Yellowstone and pay off all debts on the ranch. Randolph then hires Lake (Charles Drake), a friend of Murphy's, to stop the cattle drive. Drake starts a valley fire forcing Murphy to drive the cattle over the mountains. Murphy's cattle drive is successful and Murphy goes to Randolph to pay off the money owed. Randolph is going to shoot Murphy but Drake shoots Randolph instead. Murphy and Kelly's daughter Rita (Susan Cabot) are going to start life on the ranch together.

NOTES AND COMMENTARY: Working titles for *Gunsmoke* were *Roughshod*, the book title, and *A Man's Country*.

"See What the Boys in the Back Room Will Have" was previously sung by Marlene Dietrich in *Destry Rides Again* (Universal, 1939). Mary Castle sings the song in the Dietrich style.

Mary Castle's song, "True Love," would be heard again in *Law and Order* (Universal-International, 1953). In addition, other arrangements of the song can be heard in *Dawn at Socorro* (Universal-International, 1954), *War Arrow* (Universal-International, 1954) and *Quantez* (Universal-International, 1957).

Universal's production values slipped up in the scene in which Jesse White is told by Audie Murphy to turn his chuck wagon around. The actual driver's arms can be easily seen behind White.

The scene in which Murphy lures Drake and his men into a blind canyon was used previously in *Bend of the River* (Universal-International, 1952)

The screen sizzles when Cabot enters a room to find a half-clad Murphy with a gun in his hand. The following exchange occurs: *Cabot:* "You can put the gun away. I'm not dangerous." *Murphy:* "You could be. You have the right equipment for it."

Earlier in his career, Mike Ragan was billed as Holly Bane. John Dehner was initially signed for the lead heavy part that was eventually played by Donald Randolph.

REVIEWS: "Typical western action designed for two-fisted war hero Murphy." *The Motion Picture Guide*, Nash and Ross; "Somewhat offbeat and nicely done." *Western Movies*, Pitts.

SUMMATION: This is a nicely turned action western. The cast, Audie Murphy, Susan Cabot, Paul Kelly, Charles Drake, and Jack Kelly in particular, turn in good performances. The story moves nicely to the expected climax of Murphy settling down with the lovely Cabot. This was the second of three films in which Murphy is paired with Cabot. The others were *The Duel at Silver Creek* (Universal-International, 1952) and *Ride Clear of Diablo* (Universal-International, 1954)

He Baited His Trap with a Woman!!
The terror taut story of a man trapped in a vise between
a lynch-hungry mob and a murder hungry Marshal!

Hell Bent for Leather

Universal-International (February 1960); EASTMAN COLOR by Pathé; FILMED in Cinemascope; RUNNING TIME: 82 min.

CAST: Clay, **Audie Murphy**; Janet, **Felicia Farr**; Deckett, **Step-hen McNally**; Ambrose, **Robert Middleton**; Moon, **Rad Fulton**; Travers, **Jan Merlin**; Perrick, **Herbert Rudley**; Gamble, **Malcolm Atterbury**; Shad, **Joseph Ruskin**; Kelsey, **Allan Lane**; Old Ben, **John Qualen**; William, **Eddie Little Sky**; Grover, **Steve Graves**; Stone, **Beau Gentry**; Jared, **Bob Steele**; Cowboy at the Bar, **Kermit Maynard**; Drunken Cowboy, **Mike Ragan**

CREDITS: Director, **George Sherman**; Assistant Director, **Phil Bowles**; Producer, **Gordon Kay**;

Screenwriter, **Christopher Knopf**; Editor, **Milton Carruth**; Art Director, **Richard H. Riedel**; Set Decorators, **Russell A. Gausman** and **Julia Heron**; Cinematographer, **Clifford Stine**; Hair Stylist, **Larry Germain**; Makeup, **Bud Westmore**; Sound, **Waldon O. Watson** and **Joe Lapis**; Music, **William Lava and Irving Gertz**; Music Supervisor, **Joseph Gershenson**

LOCATION FILMING: Lone Pine, California

SOURCE: Novel, *Hell Bent for Leather* by **Ray Hogan**

STORY: Killer Travers (Jan Merlin), afoot in the desert, stumbles onto Clay's (Audie Murphy) camp. Merlin steals Murphy's horse but in the getaway, Murphy is able to wing Merlin in the shoulder causing him to drop his distinctive shotgun. When Murphy is finally able to walk to the nearest town carrying Merlin's shotgun, the townspeople, not having seen a picture of Merlin, mistake Murphy for the killer. Marshal Deckett (Stephen McNally) is summoned and McNally also identifies Murphy as the killer. Murphy thinks this just a ploy to get him out

Hell Bent for Leather (1960) scene card: (*left to right*) **The posse of Eddie Little Sky, an unidentified actor, Rad Fulton (*behind*), Herbert Rudley and Bob Steele rush toward Audie Murphy and Felicia Farr to sort out the deaths of Stephen McNally and Jan Merlin.**

of the clutches of the townspeople when McNally admits he knows Murphy is not the killer. McNally refuses to untie Murphy, intending to kill Murphy and claim the credit for bringing a well-known killer to justice. Murphy is able to escape to a nearby ranch where he makes Janet (Felicia Farr) a hostage until he can get away. In the chase, Farr finds Murphy is telling the truth. Now McNally wants to kill Farr as well as Murphy. Murphy finds where Merlin is recuperating and goes to apprehend him so he can clear his name. Merlin escapes to a rocky region with Murphy and Farr right behind him. McNally and his posse also show up. When McNally tries to capture Murphy, he suddenly comes face-to-face with Merlin. Merlin kills McNally and Murphy, in turn, is able to shoot Merlin. Murphy and Farr decide to make a life together.

NOTES AND COMMENTARY: Jan Merlin remembered being on location at Lone Pine, "That tiny little town had one movie theater and played the same movie over all the time we were there. So, after seeing the picture, there was nothing to do except do the picture [*Hell Bent for Leather*]. After you learned your lines at night, you just went to bed. I didn't have much to learn because I was just in the beginning of the picture and the end of the picture. They more or less talked about me all through the rest of it."

The part of Travers fit Merlin to a "T" and Merlin commented,

Hell Bent for Leather (1960): Portrait shot of Jan Merlin as Travers (courtesy of Jan Merlin).

"That was really kind of a fun part. That's the kind of part I really enjoyed most because he was totally rotten in that. It was kind of the thing they were casting me in a great deal. When I came out [to Hollywood], I was afraid that they might relegate me to playing real nice young fellows. Very few times did I not play a heavy."

Jan Merlin talked about Audie Murphy, "I think it was the second time I worked with Audie Murphy. Audie and I liked each other very much. A lot of people found Audie rather standoffish and sometimes mean. He had a marvelous sense of humor and he was a very quiet little guy. The best words for him were he was still. He would do things and accomplish a great deal while you were doing the picture. Yet, you were never aware he was really making a big noise about it all. He was a very quiet man, did his job well, he always came in very professional, knew all his words, knew exactly what he wanted. If he disagreed about something in the scene that he didn't think was right, he'd bring it up. I just felt he was a heck of a nice guy. We never discussed our war experiences. I think that's why we sort of hit it off. I never asked him about his war experiences and he never asked me about mine. We fought in different areas of the world. He was in Europe and I was in the South Pacific. We had an affinity for each other."

"He was another one of those great guys," was how Jan Merlin described director George Sherman. Merlin added. "He's one of those action people who knew their stuff. You never have a question about what it is he wants you to do or how. He was pretty good about letting you play it pretty much as you saw it. He was just easy to work with. Under those conditions there, up in those rocks and dust and whatnot, it was made very easy since there was never any wasted time."

For the scenes in which Audie Murphy and Felicia Farr were running around the Lone Pine rocks, most of the physical work was performed by stunt doubles Willard Willingham and Polly Burson. Willingham and Burson were high in the rocks, jumping and running. Burson remarked, "This was the one time in the picture business, I was so scared that I froze. Nothing else hit me like this did. We were up on this rock. It was like a point. I had a longhaired wig on, clear down to my neck. I was doubling Jack Lemmon's wife [Farr]. We jumped over several rocks and I had this long skirt on. Now the wind, it was 'a blowing. The wind flipped over my head and so did that wig. Willard had jumped from one rock to the other. I can't see anything hardly. I can hear Willard saying, 'Come on, Polly. Come on, take my hand. Come on and jump.' Well I finally got to where I could see where his hand was because I had all that hair in my face. If he hadn't jerked me I might have been standing there yet unless the wind hadn't blown me off. Willard, bless his heart, very calmly said, 'Come on'."

In another scene, Audie Murphy and Felicia Farr were fighting over a gun while travelling in a buckboard. Polly Burson remembers, "I think one of the Yrigoyens [a talented stuntman] was driving. We're fighting over this gun. I have to end up with the gun. He lets me have the gun and when he did, down I went. I went in the air because I was pulling on it so hard and I kinda lit on my head but I kept rolling. I kept hold of that gun. Someone behind the camera started to run out. Somebody grabbed him and stopped him. He thought I was hurt. I wasn't in the best of shape but I wasn't hurt bad. I made it to the bottom of the hill with the gun."

In his last scene in the picture,

Robert Middleton, makes reference to one of the brothers as a "fink," an informer. The word "fink" can mean an unpleasant or contemptible person; an informer; a detective and a strikebreaker. In 1888, "fink" was used as a corruption of "think" as "I don't fink I'll." From the Homestead strike of 1892, the Pinkerton detectives were called "Pink" which in turn became "fink." It wasn't until about 1925 that the term "fink" was defined as "to squeal or to inform on." The scriptwriter used a terminology that was greatly understood by the audiences of the fifties but that wouldn't have been comprehended in the era the film was depicting.

REVIEWS: "Action-filled." *The Universal Story*, Hirschhorn; "Better than average Audie Murphy vehicle." *Hollywood Reporter*, 1/12/60.

SUMMATION: *Hell Bent for Leather* is a neat well-crafted little action western. Audie Murphy again does his hero role well. Felicia Farr chips in with a fine performance as a heroine in the "Hitchcock tradition" who becomes destined to share the hero's adventures. The story benefits from a good supporting cast with plenty of tough stuff from Stephen McNally, Robert Middleton and Jan Merlin. George Sherman, with his usual competence, utilizes a good script and taut direction to keep this actioner on the move.

THEY BUILT THE GREATEST FRONTIER THE WEST HAS EVER KNOWN!
...and with his rabble army on his side—he defied the world to destroy it!
The law he needed—he made!
The land he wanted—he stole!
The woman he loved—he took!

Horizons West

Universal-International (October 1952); COLOR by Technicolor; RUNNING TIME: 81 min.

CAST: Dan Hammond, **Robert Ryan**; Lorna Hardin, **Julia Adams**; Neal Hammond, **Rock Hudson**; Sally Eaton, **Judith Braun**; Ira Hammond, **John McIntire**; Cord Hardin, **Raymond Burr**; Tiny McGilligan, **James Arness**; Dandy Taylor, **Dennis Weaver**; Martha Hammond, **Frances Bavier**; Frank Tarleton, **Tom Powers**; Sam Hunter, **John Hubbard**; General Escobar, **Rudolfo Acosta**; Tompkins, **Douglas Fowley**; Layton, **Walter Reed**; Eli Dodson, **Raymond Greenleaf**; Henchman, **Dan Poore**; Borden, **Frank Chase**; Mrs. Tarleton, **Mae Clarke**; Sentry with torch, **Edwin Parker**; Rancher, **Dan White**; Salazar, **Peter Mamakos**; Irate townsman, **Robert Bice**

CREDITS: Director, **Budd Boet-**

ticher; Assistant Director, **Joe Kenny**; Producer, **Albert J. Cohen**; Story/Screenwriter, **Louis Stevens**; Editor, **Ted J. Kent**; Art Directors, **Bernard Herzbrun** and **Robert Clatworthy**; Set Decorators, **Russell A. Gausman** and **Joe Kish**; Cinematographer, **Charles P. Boyle**; Costumes, **Rosemary Odell**; Hair Stylist, **Joan St. Oegger**; Makeup, **Bud Westmore**; Sound, **Leslie I. Carey** and **Robert Pritchard**; Music, **Joseph Gershenson**; Technicolor Color Consultant, **William Fritzsche**

SONG: "Alexis, Darlin' of Texas" (James and Miller)

LOCATION FILMING: Andy Jauregui Ranch, California

STORY: Dan Hammond (Robert Ryan), Neal Hammond (Rock Hudson) and Tiny McGilligan (James Arness), after fighting for the Confederacy, return to their native Texas. Ryan is embittered over the South's defeat. Arriving in Austin, he makes Lorna Hardin's (Julia Adams) acquaintance. Adams is married to Cord Hardin (Raymond Burr), a ruthless and cruel individual. Ryan gets himself invited to a high-stakes poker game with Burr. Ryan loses to Burr and is unable to immediately pay his debt. To repay his debt, Ryan enlists as his army, the "dregs of the war" led by Dandy Taylor (Dennis Weaver). By rustling Burr's cattle, Ryan is able to repay the money he owes Burr. Burr suspects Ryan rustled his cattle and kidnaps and tortures Hudson, Ryan's brother. Ryan rescues Hudson and in the process, shoots Burr in self-defense. Ryan begins to build his empire by a systematic land grab scheme. When the small ranchers go to Ira (John McIntire), Ryan's father, and Hudson for help, Hudson vows to stop Ryan. Ryan is blamed by the townspeople for a murder committed by Weaver. He is arrested but kills Arness and escapes. McIntire, Hudson and Deputy Layton (Walter Reed) go to Zona Libre to bring Ryan back to Texas for trial. When Ryan gets the drop on McIntire and Hudson, Reed shoots Ryan. Ryan dies in Adams' arms.

NOTES AND COMMENTARY: The working title for *Horizons West* was *The Texas Man*.

Some references credit Judith Braun as singing "Alexis, Darlin' of Texas" but it was actually sung by an unidentified actress in an early saloon sequence.

Budd Boetticher never thinks about *Horizons West*. Robert Ryan and Rock Hudson were two of his "favorite guys" of all time. When Boetticher worked with Hudson, he never realized Hudson was gay. He commented about Hudson, "I just loved him. And still would anyway." When asked about Judith Braun, Boetticher said that he only remembered Braun for a war film he directed, *The Red Ball Express* (Universal-International, 1952).

Boetticher, who really was not fond of the scripts he was handed at Universal-International, expressed his disappointment in that the script did not call for a final confrontation between Robert Ryan and Rock Hudson.

In a letter from Walter Reed, he said of the film's climactic ending, "They had to have someone other

Horizons West (1952) scene card: Confederate soldiers (*left to right*) James Arness, Rock Hudson and Robert Ryan return to Texas after the conclusion of the Civil War.

than his Dad (John McIntire) or Brother (Rock Hudson) kill him (Robert Ryan), so it was me."

Walter Reed worked about twelve shows with Budd Boetticher. Reed considered Boetticher a very fine director and a good friend. Reed said, "I was his (Boetticher's) good luck charm."

REVIEWS: "Ambitious but deeply flawed Boetticher Western." *The Western*, Hardy; "So-so oater which is well acted." *Western Movies*, Pitts.

SUMMATION: This is a two-fisted western that pits brother against brother. Robert Ryan's forceful performance is the driving force that propels the film to its violent conclusion. Julia Adams, Rock Hudson and John McIntire provide able support. Budd Boetticher capably directs. The script lets the performers down by avoiding a final climactic showdown between brothers Ryan and Hudson. This weakness keeps the film from attaining a higher rating.

HE HAD TO FIGHT THE WHOLE TOWN...
To Find the Ghost That Took His Name

Joe Dakota

Universal-International (September 1957); EASTMAN COLOR by Pathé; RUNNING TIME: 79 min.

CAST: The Stranger, **Jock Mahoney**; Jody Weaver, **Luana Patten**; Cal Moore, **Charles McGraw**; Myrna Weaver, **Barbara Lawrence**; Aaron Grant, **Claude Akins**; Adam Grant, **Lee Van Cleef**; Marcus Vizzini, **Anthony Caruso**; Frank Weaver, **Paul Birch**; Jim Baldwin, **George Dunn**; Sam Cook, **Steve Darrell**; Rosa Vizzini, **Rita Lynn**; Tom Jensen, **Gregg Barton**; Claude Henderson, **Anthony Jochim**; Bertha Jensen, **Jeane Wood**; Ethel Cook, **Juney Ellis**; Joe Dakota (the Indian), **Francis McDonald**

CREDITS: Director, **Richard Bartlett**; Assistant Director, **Frank Shaw**; Producer, **Howard Christie**; Screenwriters, **William Talman** and **Norman Jolley**; Editor, **Fred Mac-Dowell**; Art Directors, **Alexander Golitzen** and **Bill Newberry**; Set Decorators, **Russell A. Gausman** and **Ray Jeffers**; Cinematographer, **George Robinson**; Gowns, **Marilyn Sotto**; Makeup, **Bud Westmore**; Sound, **Leslie I. Carey** and **Joe Lapis**; Music Supervision, **Joseph E. Gershenson**

SONG: "The Flower of San Antone" (Ray and David)—sung by **Jock Mahoney**

LOCATION FILMING: Conejo Valley, California

STORY: A stranger (Jock Mahoney) rides into a small western town looking for his Indian friend, Joe Dakota (Francis McDonald). Mahoney finds his friend missing and Cal Moore (Charles McGraw) leading an oil-drilling expedition on land belonging to McDonald. McGraw insists McDonald sold the land to him prior to his disappearance. Mahoney tells the townspeople that he really owns the land, takes possession of the shack and stops all drilling. Finally, Jody Weaver (Luana Patten) tells Mahoney that a drunken McDonald molested her and was in turn hanged by the townspeople. By further questioning Patten, Mahoney discovers the assailant had whiskers, something the Indian McDonald did not have. Mahoney already knew the bill of sale possessed by McGraw was a forgery since it was signed with a mark instead of the only name he could write, Joe Dakota. Mahoney had taught McDonald to write his (Mahoney's) name and this is the name McDonald had been using. The oil well comes in and needs to be capped. Mahoney accuses McGraw of murder. A fight between the two breaks out with Mahoney the victor. Townsman Marcus Vizzini (Anthony Caruso) sets fire to the well so the people can have their town back. The townspeople had let greed overcome them and their true values.

Joe Dakota (1957) scene card: Jock Mahoney (*right*) fights brothers Lee Van Cleef (*left*) and Claude Akins in the local wine shop.

NOTES AND COMMENTARY: *Joe Dakota* received a Certificate of Outstanding Merit from the Southern California Motion Picture Council in September 1957.

In *Variety*'s review of the film, the reviewer states that no shots are fired. This is an error; Charles McGraw does fire the only shot.

REVIEWS: "Tense western." *Hollywood Reporter,* 8/27/57; "Though the film lacks the vigour of *Bad Day at Black Rock* with its attacks on racism and civic cowardice, it remains an unusually thoughtful movie." *The Western*, Phil Hardy.

SUMMATION: This is a good little western dealing with a town's decision to hide a deadly secret from outsiders. Although highly reminiscent of the classic *Bad Day at Black Rock* (Metro-Goldwyn-Mayer, 1955), this saga is definitely not in the same classic status but nonetheless is an effective film. The acting of the principals is good, led by a nice easygoing performance by Jock Mahoney. Claude Akins and Lee Van Cleef are fine in comedy support. Director Richard Bartlett manages to generate some legitimate suspense from William Talman and Norman Jolley's well-written screenplay.

---

*Thundering, Plundering Under the Black Flag of Quantrill's Guerrillas!
The West's most reckless Outlaws, turning their
deadly guns on Lawrence, Kansas, in their historic raid!*

Kansas Raiders

Universal-International (November 1950); COLOR by Technicolor; RUNNING TIME: 80 min.

CAST: Jesse James, **Audie Murphy**; William Quantrill, **Brian Donlevy**; Kate Clarke, **Marguerite Chapman**; Bill Anderson, **Scott Brady**; Kit Dalton, **Tony Curtis**; Union Captain; **Richard Arlen**; Frank James, **Richard Long**; Cole Younger, **James Best**; Red Leg Leader, **John Kellogg**; James Younger, **Dewey Martin**; Willie, **George Chandler**; Pell, **Charles Delaney**; 1st Lieutenant, **Richard Egan**; Tate, **David Wolfe**; Red Leg Member, **Buddy Roosevelt**; Bank President, **Sam Flint**; Woman, **Myra McKinney**; Bank Teller, **Edward Piel Sr.**

CREDITS: Director, **Ray Enright**; Producer, **Ted Richmond**; Story/Screenwriter, **Robert L. Richards**; Editor, **Milton Carruth**; Art Directors, **Bernard Herzbrun** and **Emrich Nicholson**; Set Decorators, **Russell A. Gausman** and **Ruby R. Levitt**; Cinematographer, **Irving Glassberg**; Costumes, **Bill Thomas**; Hair Stylist, **Joan St. Oegger**; Makeup, **Bud Westmore**; Sound, **Leslie I. Carey and Glenn E. Anderson**; Music, **Joseph Gershenson**; Technicolor Color Consultant, **William Fritzsche**

LOCATION FILMING: Kanab, Utah
STORY: At the close of the Civil War, Jesse James (Audie Murphy), Frank James (Richard Long), Kit Dalton (Tony Curtis), Cole Younger (James Best) and James Younger (Dewey Martin) join William Quantrill's (Brian Donlevy) guerrilla army to fight the Union forces. Murphy soon discovers that Donlevy is no more that a murderous bandit, but somehow remains loyal. When the Confederacy no longer sanctions Donlevy's actions, Donlevy's men desert with the exception of Murphy and his group. In a skirmish, Donlevy is blinded and he then relinquishes his command to Murphy. Union soldiers surround the group in a burned out cabin. Donlevy dies a hero's death as his actions allow Murphy and his friends to escape to a life of crime.

NOTES AND COMMENTARY: Some of the Civil War montage scenes were previously seen in *Tap Roots* (Universal-International, 1948).

James Best thought the most interesting scene in the picture came when Audie Murphy shoots Scott Brady. Murphy, Best and others were prepared to shoot their way out of town. Murphy has words with Brady, who hits him with a rope. Murphy retaliates by shooting Brady. Best related, "I turned and looked into Audie's eyes and I saw a man who went through World War II and had killed a lot of guys. He was killing

Scott Brady. His looks chilled me. The hair on the back of my neck stood up because I saw a man who enjoyed killing. He enjoyed reenacting that. I don't mean joy joy. He was really into it. I saw death in the man's eyes." Best also said that he and Audie were as good friends as it could be. It seems Murphy did not really make friends anymore since he had lost so many during the war.

REVIEWS: "Outdoor action with an unconvincing story." *Variety*, 11/8/50; "Action fans will be pleased but a fine potential was completely wasted." *The Motion Picture Guide*, Nash and Ross.

SUMMATION: This is only an average western drama. The acting is only adequate for the screenplay that was served up. If the audience can buy into the fact that Audie Murphy has total regard, admiration and respect for Brian Donlevy while being sickened at Donlevy's barbarism and brutality, a higher rating may be given. The action scenes are, for the most part, well-handled. It is disconcerting to see a tall cactus show up during a montage scene of guerrillas and troops racing over the Kansas countryside.

Kansas Raiders (1950) still: In a duel-to-the-death knife fight, Audie Murphy (*left*) and David Wolfe are watched intently by Marguerite Chapman (*on porch*) and James Best (*to left of Chapman*) (courtesy of Sue Gossett).

---

21 years old! 21 notches on his guns!
The true and savage story of the West's most notorious outlaw
... who smiled like an angel and killed like devil incarnate!

The Kid from Texas

ALTERNATE TITLE: *Texas Kid, Outlaw*; Universal-International (March 1950); COLOR by Technicolor; RUNNING TIME: 78 min.

CAST: Billy the Kid, **Audie Murphy**; Irene Kain, **Gale Storm**; Alexander Kain, **Albert Dekker**; Jameson, **Sheppard Strudwick**; O'Fallon, **Will Geer**; Minniger, **William Talman**; Morales, **Martin Garralaga**; General Wallace, **Robert H. Barrat**; Crowe, **Walter Sande**; Pat Garrett, **Frank Wilcox**; Major Harper, **Dennis Hoey**; Sheriff Rand, **Ray Teal**; Morgan, **Don Haggerty**; Copeland, **Paul Ford**; Sid Curtis, **John Phillips**; Matt Curtis, **Harold Goodwin**; Lucas, **Zon Murray**; Denby, **Tom Trout**; Marita, **Rosa Turich**; Lupita, **Dorita Pallais**; Margarita, **Pilar del Rey**; Hagen, **Pierce Lyden**; Wagon Driver, **Jack Ingram**; Line Cook, **William Fawcett**; Townsman, **Terry Frost**; Blacksmith, **Edward Gargen**; Mr. Hale, **Edmund Cobb**

CREDITS: Director, **Kurt Neumann**; Producer, **Paul Short**; Story, **Robert Hardy Andrews**; Screenwriters, **Robert Hardy Andrews** and **Karl Lamb**; Editor, **Frank Gross**; Art Directors, **Bernard Herzbrun** and **Emrich Nicholson**; Set Decorators, **Russell A. Gausman** and **Oliver Emert**; Cinematographer, **Charles Van Enger**; Gowns, **Rosemary Odell**; Hair Stylist, **Joan St. Oegger**; Makeup, **Bud Westmore**; Sound, **Leslie I. Carey** and **Robert Pritchard**; Music, **Milton Schwarzwald**; Technicolor Color Consultant, **William Fritzsche**

LOCATION FILMING: Idyllwild area, California

STORY: Lincoln County, New Mexico, is on the verge of a range war, with rancher Harper (Dennis Hoey) pitted against ranchers Kain (Albert Dekker) and Jameson (Sheppard Strudwick). Into this hostile environment comes Billy the Kid (Audie Murphy)—a young man on the run who is hired by Strudwick to work as a cowhand on his ranch—and Irene Kain (Gale Storm), Dekker's young bride. Strudwick convinces Murphy not to wear his guns. Storm visits the ranch of Dekker and Strudwick and meets Murphy. There is an immediate attraction between the two. Later, some of Hoey's men come to the ranch and one cowhand, a drunken Lucas (Zon Murray), kills Strudwick. Murphy straps on his guns and vows to get the men responsible. When Hoey has some of Dekker's cattle rustled, Dekker sees this as an opportunity to use Murphy and his guns and at the same time publicly deplore violence. General Wallace (Robert H. Barrat) brings an end to the

The Kid from Texas **(1950): Gale Storm tries to talk Audie Murphy out of participating in the range war stirred up by Albert Dekker and Dennis Joey (courtesy of Sue Gossett).**

Lincoln County War and offers a pardon to Murphy if he will lay down his guns. Since some of Strudwick's killers have not been brought to justice, Murphy declines. This action makes Murphy an outlaw and Dekker contributes to the reward money. Murphy is captured by Talman. When Murphy finds out Dekker has double-crossed him, he breaks jail, killing Talman in the process. Months later, when being chased by a posse, Murphy and his men take refuge in Dekker's house. During the siege, Storm finds out about Dekker's contribution to Murphy's reward and decides to leave him. The posse allows all the women to leave the house. When the posse tries to burn Murphy and his men out, Dekker attempts to shoot Murphy but is killed by O'Fallan (Will Geer). Only Murphy is able to get out of the burning house alive. Storm decides to leave New Mexico and Murphy makes a last attempt to see her. Marshal Pat Garrett (Frank Willcox) intuitively knows where Murphy will go and confronts and kills him.

NOTES AND COMMENTARY: Gale Storm remembers Audie Murphy as being very good to work with and very professional. He was always on time and knew his lines but Murphy was not a warm, friendly person to be with. Storm quickly added that this was not required. At the time this movie was filmed, Audie Murphy was newly married to actress Wanda Hendrix, who accompanied him on the location shooting. Ann Blyth was initially announced as Audie Murphy's co-star in *The Kid from Texas*.

Gale Storm professed a fear of horses. Although she hailed from Texas, Storm never really learned to ride. She only rode when required to in the making of western films.

Also, that is not Gale Storm playing the piano in the two scenes. Gale said she didn't play because she was not that good at it but she knew enough to make the scene look believable.

REVIEWS: "Despite an occasional bit of gunplay and the facts as supplied from the commentary, *The Kid from Texas* doesn't give special statue to a noted saga. Anyway, that saga isn't dead." *New York Times*, 6/2/50; "Not much history in the Audie Murphy vehicle but there is plenty of action." *Western Movies*, Pitts.

SUMMATION: This is a well-done western, with a good blend of action and characterization. Audie Murphy makes a good Billy the Kid, with his youthfulness belying his violent tendencies. Sheppard Strudwick is especially good as Billy's mentor. Gale Storm, Albert Dekker, Will Geer offer fine support.

HE HELD A KNIFE AT THE THROAT OF THE COMANCHE FRONTIER!

Kiss of Fire

Universal-International (October 1955); PRINT by Technicolor; RUNNING TIME: 87 min.

CAST: El Tigre, **Jack Palance**; Princess Lucia, **Barbara Rush**; Duke of Montera, **Rex Reason**; Felicia, **Martha Hyer**; Vega, **Leslie Bradley**; Diego, **Alan Reed**; Padre Domingo, **Lawrence Dobkin**; Victor, **Joseph Waring**; Pahvant, **Pat Hogan**; Shining Moon, **Karen Kadler**; Ship Captain, **Steven Geray**; Acosta, **Henry Rowland**

CREDITS: Director, **Joseph M. Newman**; Assistant Director, **Marshall Green**; Producer, **Samuel Marx**; Screenwriters, **Franklin Coen** and **Richard Collins**; Editor, **Arthur H. Nadel**; Art Directors, **Alexander Golitzen** and **Robert Boyle**; Set Decorators, **Russell A. Gausman** and **Julia Heron**; Cinematographer, **Carl Guthrie**; Costumes, **Jay A. Morley, Jr.**; Hair Stylist, **Joan St. Oegger**; Makeup, **Bud Westmore**; Sound, **Leslie I. Carey** and **Joe Lapis**; Music Supervisor, **Joseph Gershenson**; Technicolor Color Consultant, **William Fritzsche**

UNIVERSAL-INTERNATIONAL presents **JACK PALANCE BARBARA RUSH** *KISS OF FIRE*

PRINT BY **TECHNICOLOR**

CO-STARRING
**REX REASON
MARTHA HYER**
with ALAN REED
LESLIE BRADLEY

Directed by
JOSEPH M. NEWMAN
Screenplay by FRANKLIN COEN
and RICHARD COLLINS
Produced by SAMUEL MARX

Kiss of Fire (1955) scene card: Jack Palance (*kneeling*) defeats an identified actor after a short scuffle and finds the group was to be led into an ambush. (*Left to right*) Alan Reed, Joseph Waring, Martha Hyer, Barbara Rush, Leslie Bradley and Rex Reason observe.

SONG: "Kiss of Fire" (Allen and Hill)

LOCATION FILMING: The desert near Las Vegas, Nevada

SOURCE: Novel, *The Rose and the Flame* by **Jonreed Lauritzen**

STORY: With the impending death of the King of Spain, Princess Lucia (Barbara Rush) is commanded to leave New Mexico and return to California. There is opposition to Rush assuming the throne. The only route open to her to sail to Spain is to travel overland and leave from a California port. Fearing Rush's enemies, her guardian, the Duke of Montera (Rex Reason), enlists the help of the notorious renegade El Tigre (Jack Palance). Reason wants to marry Rush to become her consort. Rush, in turn, falls in love with Palance. As the group travels to California, they soon have Rush's Spanish enemies behind them and the deadly Paiutes in front. Palance devises a plan in which the group will split into two factions: One will attack the Spanish pretending to be Paiutes and the other attacking the Paiutes. If all works, the Spanish and Paiutes will engage each other and Rush will be able to slip behind the line of battle and escape. Reason is to lead one faction and Palance the other. Reason changes places with the soldier who was to care for Rush believing all will perish in the battle and he will be free to marry Rush. Palance survives the battle and learns of Reason's duplicity. Palance is able to gain access on the ship that will transport Rush to Spain. Palance defeats Reason in a rugged fight and Rush decides to stay with Palance and settle in California.

NOTES AND COMMENTARY: The working title for *Kiss of Fire* was *The Rose and the Flame*.

Asked about star Jack Palance, Actor/Stuntman Robert Hoy would only comment, "Oh, ho, ho, ho! That idiot, yeah!" Hoy remembered the lovely ladies who graced *Kiss of Fire* and said, "Barbara Rush was the girl. And the girl who married the big producer [Hal Wallis] in Hollywood, Martha Hyer."

Footage of the Paiutes beating the war drums was originally seen in *Apache Drums* (Universal-International, 1951).

REVIEWS: "Weak entry for the action market, a poorly motivated story that at times becomes completely unbelievable." *Variety*, 8/31/55; "*Kiss of Fire* was the kiss of death as far as its entertainment value was concerned." *The Universal Story*, Hirschhorn.

SUMMATION: In *Kiss of Fire*, the fire went out. Universal-International has fashioned a dull early western opus with outrageous acting by all concerned, especially Jack Palance. The dialogue is written to sound as if great literature is being presented but the work easily adds up to one big bore. The action, as it is, is undistinguished. To add insult to injury, the climactic battle scene between the Spaniards and the Paiutes is held completely offscreen. Instead of being titled *Kiss of Fire*, perhaps a better title should have been *Kiss of Mis-Fire*.

THE RANGE IS ROLLICKING WITH HAPPY LAUGHS
... straight from the heart of Texas!
The heartwarming adventures of that lovable Miz Birdie,
her wacky pets, her wonderful friends and her rip-roaring rancho!

The Lady from Texas

Universal-International (October 1951); COLOR by Technicolor; RUNNING TIME: 77½ min.

CAST: Dan Mason, **Howard Duff**; Bonnie Lee, **Mona Freeman**; Miss Birdie, **Josephine Hull**; Judge George Jeffers, **Gene Lockhart**; Cyril Guthrie, **Craig Stevens**; Sheriff, **Jay C. Flippen**; Dave Blodgett, **Ed Beg-** ley; Lawyer Haddon, **Morgan Farley**; Jose, **Chris-Pin Martin**; Mabel, **Barbara Knudson**; Lawyer Craig Toland, **Kenneth Patterson**; Townsman, **John Maxwell**; Mr. Smith, **William Fawcett**; Cowboy, **Lane Bradford**; Bailiff, **Dabbs Greer**; Justice of the Peace, **Edmund Cobb**

CREDITS: Director, **Joseph**

The Lady from Texas (1951) scene card: Josephine Hull (*center*) assures Mona Freeman and Howard Duff that her pet skunk, Annabelle, is a perfect lady unless she's frightened.

Pevney; Producer, **Leonard Goldstein**; Story, **Harold Shumate**; Screenwriters, **Gerald Drayson Adams** and **Connie Lee Bennett**; Editor, **Virgil Vogel**; Art Directors, **Bernard Herzbrun** and **Emrich H. Nicholson**; Set Decorators, **Russell A. Gausman** and **Joseph Kish**; Cinematographer, **Charles P. Boyle**; Gowns, **Rosemary Odell**; Hair Stylist, **Joan St. Oegger**; Makeup, **Bud Westmore**; Sound, **Leslie I. Carey** and **Joe Lapis**; Music Supervisor, **Joseph Gershenson**; Technicolor Color Consult, **William Fritzsche**

LOCATION FILMING: Andy Jauregui and Walker Ranches, California

STORY: Dave Blodgett's (Ed Begley) son-in-law, Cyril Guthrie (Craig Stevens), is managing Begley's ranch to the betterment of himself. Stevens is attempting to gain control of eccentric widow Miss Birdie's (Josephine Hull) ranch for a railroad right-of-way.

Wandering cowboy Dan Mason (Howard Duff) is maneuvered by Begley's cook, Bonnie Lee (Mona Freeman), into taking a job on Hull's ranch. Freeman and Hull's employee, Jose (Chris-Pin Martin), are trying to protect Hull from Stevens' schemes. Stevens takes Hull to court to prove she is not of sound mind and that Stevens should become Hull's guardian. Duff marries Freeman so they can also be considered as guardians. Despite all efforts by Stevens and his lawyer accomplice, Craig Toland (Kenneth Patterson), Judge Jeffers (Gene Lockhart) declares Hull to be of sound mind. The townspeople rally around Hull. Duff and Freeman plan to live at Hull's ranch and look after her interests.

NOTES AND COMMENTARY: This was Josephine Hull's last picture. Hull was an Academy Award–Winner for Best Supporting Actress in *Harvey* (Universal-International, 1950).

REVIEWS: "Delightful western comedy." *Western Movies*, Pitts; "Good outdoor comedy-drama." *Variety*, 9/26/51.

SUMMATION: *The Lady from Texas* is a delightful, heart-warming comedy-western anchored by Josephine Hull's deft portrayal of the slightly daft Miss Birdie. Hull is ably assisted by Howard Duff as a cowhand who refuses to be pushed around and Mona Freeman as a young woman who knows how to prod a stubborn man. The mild villainy is capably handled by Craig Stevens. Gene Lockhart, Chris-Pin Martin and Kenneth Patterson stand out in a fine supporting cast. Joseph Pevney directs with a knowing touch from an engaging script by Gerald Drayson Adams and Connie Lee Bennett.

HIS NAME WAS WRITTEN WITH BULLETS and
HE CARRIED A PRICE ON HIS HEAD....
THE MAN THEY CALLED ... THE LAST OF THE FAST GUNS

The Last of the Fast Guns

Universal-International (July 1958); EASTMAN COLOR by Pathé; FILMED in Cinemascope; RUNNING TIME: 82 min.

CAST: Brad Ellison, **Jock Mahoney**; Miles Lang, **Gilbert Roland**; Maria O'Reilly, **Linda Cristal**; Padre José, **Eduard Franz**; Michael O'Reilly, **Lorne Greene**; John Forbes, **Carl Benton Reid**; Sam Grypton, **Edward C. Platt**; Cordoba, **Eduardo Noriega**; Manuel, **Jorge Trevino**; Alcalde, **Rafael Alcayde**; Johnny Ringo, **Lee Morgan**; James Younger, **Milton Bernstein**; Ben Thompson, **Stillman Segar**; Garcia, **Jose Chavez Trone**; Pablo, **Francisco Reiguera**; Sheriff, **Richard Cutting**; Bartender, **Ralph Neff**

CREDITS: Director, **George Sherman**; Assistant Director, **Phil Bowles**; Producer, **Howard Christie**; Writer, **David P. Harmon**; Editor, **Patrick McCormack**; Art Directors, **Alexander Golitzen** and **Roberto Silva**; Set Decorators, **Russell A. Gausman** and **Rafael Suarez**; Cinematographer, **Alex Phillips**; Makeup, **Bud Westmore**; Sound, **Leslie I. Carey** and **Javier Mateos**; Music Supervisor, **Joseph Gershenson**

LOCATION FILMING: Northern Mexico

STORY: Brad Ellision (Jock Mahoney), last of the fast guns, is hired by John Forbes (Carl Benton Reid) to find Reid's brother to prevent an unscrupulous partner from inheriting Reid's fortune. Reid's brother was last known to have been in Mexico. Mahoney arrives at Michael O'Reilly's (Lorne Greene) ranch in Mexico and is told that Reid's brother is dead. Mahoney meets Miles Lang (Gilbert Roland), who works at Greene's ranch, and gets Roland to guide him through the mountainous area of Mexico. During an attempt on Mahoney's life, Roland is wounded as he exchanges shots with the assailant. Roland's shot kills the would-be murderer. Padre José (Eduard Franz) is called to attend to Roland's wounds and he then volunteers to help the men find Reid's brother. In their search, Mahoney and Roland use Franz's hut as their base of operations. Mahoney can only learn from the local countrymen that Reid's brother is dead. On their return to Franz' hut, Mahoney and Franz find evidence that Roland has been kidnapped. Franz goes to Greene's ranch for help in looking for Roland. Mahoney goes to a safe haven for gun fighters run by Edward C. Platt and is captured by Roland. In Franz' hut, Roland found evidence that Franz is Reid's brother. Roland is in the employ of

Reid's partner to make certain no one finds Franz. Since Franz' identity is known, Roland goes to Greene's ranch on the pretext of taking Franz to safety but in reality to murder him. The captive Mahoney is released by captor Eduardo Noreiga, when he finds that Franz' life is in danger. Franz is beloved by the Mexican people of the area for his good works. Mahoney arrives at Greene's ranch only to find that Roland has left the ranch with Franz. As Roland is about to kill Franz, the murder is prevented by the sudden arrival of the Mexican people. Franz allows Roland to ride away but Mahoney chases after Roland to bring him to justice. As Roland tries to get away, he falls from a high mountain to his death. Mahoney decides to settle down in Mexico to a new life without guns.

NOTES AND COMMENTARY: The working title for *Last of the Fast Guns* was *The Western Story*. Linda Cristal professed not to remember this film. Her work in *Last of the Fast Guns* inspired Universal-International to sign her to a long term contract.

The script has Jock Mahoney lamenting the fact that both Jesse James and Billy the Kid had been killed "this year." In actuality, Billy the Kid was shot by Pat Garrett on July 14, 1881, and Robert Ford killed Jesse James on April 3, 1882. If Mahoney meant they were killed the same year, he was incorrect but the statement would be correct if the meaning was within the past year.

REVIEWS: "Good entry, authentic Mexican locations give added

The Last of the Fast Guns (1958) scene card: Jock Mahoney and Linda Cristal discuss what he saw when she was bathing in the river, and his life as a gunfighter.

interest to this period oater." *Variety*, 6/25/58; "Largely photographed in the mountain region of New Mexico, the film looks far better than its traditional plot might suggest." *The Western*, Hardy (Mr. Hardy must have misread Northern Mexico for New Mexico—author)

SUMMATION: *Last of the Fast Guns* is an above average western story weakened by the familiar theme of the "best" friend turning out to be the hero's adversary. All the actors are effective in their roles with only Eduard Franz rising above the material. Cinematographer Alex Phillips captures the glorious Mexican countryside which gives the picture a needed boost. Veteran director George Sherman directs capably keeping the story moving along nicely.

WILD THEY FOUGHT! ... WILD THEY LOVED!
Each knowing that the day of passion would bring the day of vengeance!
One, loving the girl—but needing the woman!
The other, loving the woman—but needing revenge!

The Last Sunset

Byrnaprod S.A./Universal-International (July 1961); EASTMAN COLOR by Pathé; RUNNING TIME: 112 min.

CAST: Dana Stribling, **Rock Hudson**; Brendan O'Malley, **Kirk Douglas**; Belle Breckenridge, **Dorothy Malone**; John Breckenridge, **Joseph Cotten**; Missy Breckenridge, **Carol Lynley**; Frank Hobbs, **Neville Brand**; Milton Wing, **Regis Toomey**; Julesburg Kid, **Rad Fulton**; Calverton, **Adam Williams**; Ed Hobbs, **Jack Elam**; Bowman, **John Shay**; Rosario, **Margarita De Luna**; Jose, **José Torvay**

CREDITS: Director, **Robert Aldrich**; Assistant Director, **Thomas J. Connors, Jr.**; Producers, **Eugene Frenke** and **Edward Lewis**; Scree writer, **Dalton Trumbo**; Supervising Editor, **Edward Mann**; Editor, **Michael Luciano**; Art Directors, **Alexander Golitzen** and **Alfred Sweeney**; Set Decorator, **Oliver Emert**; Cinematographer, **Ernest Lazlo**; Costumes, **Norma Koch**; Hair Stylist, **Larry Germain**; Makeup, **Bud Westmore**; Sound, **Waldon O. Watson** and **Donald Cunliffe**; Music, **Ernest Gold**; Music Director, **Joseph Gershenson**

SONGS: "Pretty Little Girl in the Yellow Dress" (Tiomkin and Washington)—sung by **Kirk Douglas** and "La Paloma"—sung by **Kirk Douglas and chorus**

LOCATION FILMING: Caliente; Mexico City, Distrito Federal and Aquas Calientes, AGS, Mexico

SOURCE: Novel, *Sundown at Crazy Horse* by **Howard Rigsby**

STORY: Knowing that he's being trailed by lawman Dana Stribling (Rock Hudson), Brendan O'Malley (Kirk Douglas) makes his way to John Breckenridge's (Joseph Cotten) ranch. Hudson wants to bring Douglas back to Texas to stand trial for the murder of his brother-in-law. Hudson wants to rekindle a romantic flame between himself and Cotten's wife Belle Breckenridge (Dorothy Malone). Malone warns Douglas to keep his distance. Malone's daughter, Missy Breckenridge (Carol Lynley), is smitten with the charm of Douglas. Cotten needs men to help trail herd his cattle to Texas, and Douglas agrees to hire on as a gunman. Hudson arrives at the Cotten ranch where he is persuaded to sign on as trail boss for the drive. Hudson tells Douglas he will arrest him when they touch Texas soil. During the journey, Cotten goes into a tough Mexican town to hire additional vaqueros and is killed in a saloon altercation. With Cotten's death, both Douglas and Hudson declare their romantic inclinations to Malone. Malone favors Hudson which makes Douglas jealous until he sees Lynley in the same yellow dress that Malone wore years before. Douglas and Lynley have a romantic liaison and decide to live together. The trail drive reaches Texas and Douglas and Hudson decide to settle their differences in a gun duel at sunset. Malone breaks the news to Douglas that Lynley is his daughter. Douglas meets Hudson as planned and in the duel Hudson shoots Douglas. Then Hudson discovers that Douglas' gun is unloaded. Hudson and Malone decide to make their life together.

NOTES AND COMMENTARY: From many reports, Kirk Douglas and Robert Aldrich did not get along well at all during the filming of *The Last Sunset*. Also, Aldrich liked Rock Hudson's work ethics and enjoyed working with him. The world premier for *The Last Sunset* was held at Grauman's Chinese Theater in Hollywood, California.

Dalton Trumbo, accused of supposedly Communist leanings, was blacklisted in Hollywood because of his refusal to testify before the U.S. House on Un-American Activities Committee in 1947. In 1950, Trumbo spent 11 months in prison. Using the pseudonym Robert Rich, Trumbo won an Academy Award for his screenplay of *The Brave One* (Universal-International, 1956). Trumbo had written a screenplay for *The Last Sunset*. While working on this project, Otto Preminger promised Trumbo screen credit to write the screenplay for *Exodus* (United Artists, 1960). He would be the first blacklisted writer to overcome this stigma and opened the door for other writers who had received similar treatment. Trumbo subsequently received screen credit for *The Last Sunset*.

REVIEWS: "A routine combination of Hollywood and Western clichés." *New York Times*, 6/15/61; "A pretty routine western whose only novelty was a touch of incest." *The Universal Story*, Hirschhorn.

SUMMATION: *The Last Sunset* is an adult western with lust, incest, and murder at center screen. The film contains good acting from the principals and some magnificent photography of the Mexican countryside, but the screenplay is much too predictable for a film that wants attention as more than just entertainment. Kirk Douglas' role is straight out of Grecian tragedy, running the gamut of emotion from love to hate, with stops in between. Douglas even chimes in with two songs. Rock Hudson gives a straightforward performance as the lawman obsessed with gaining his revenge on Douglas. Dorothy Malone does the best she can with a part that has her knee-deep in love only days after she's laid her husband to rest. Joseph Cotten at first looks to be giving a send-up on the "old drunk" part, but redeems himself as he's being humiliated in a dirty Mexican saloon. Carol Lynley gives a credible performance as a teenager who fancies herself as a woman. But this is Douglas' show, first, last and always. Too bad Trumbo's script in the end lets the performers down. The film is interesting but not first-rate.

... His Guns Were the Only Law!
The story of Frame Johnson and the five days of fury
when he stood alone against the last of the Southwest's renegade rule!

Law and Order

Universal-International (May 1953); COLOR by Technicolor; RUNNING TIME: 80 min.

CAST: Frame Johnson, **Ronald Reagan**; Jeannie, **Dorothy Malone**; Kurt Durling, **Preston Foster**; Lute Johnson, **Alex Nicol**; Maria, **Ruth Hampton**; Jimmy Johnson, **Russell Johnson**; Fin Elder, **Barry Kelly**; Denver Cahoon, **Chubby Johnson**; Jed, **Jack Kelly**; Frank Durling, **Dennis Weaver**; Durango Kid, **Wally Cassell**; Judge Williams, **Richard Garrick**; Rider in Tombstone, **Lane Bradford**; Mayor, **Sam Flint**; Townsman, **Kermit Maynard**; Stable Boy, **Thor Holmes**; Dixon, **Thomas Browne Henry**; Parker, **Tristram Coffin**; Ben Wiley, **William O'Neill**; Johnny Benton, **Don Garner**; Martin, **James F. Stone**; Land Agent, **Harry Harvey**; Rider in Cottonwood, **Mike Ragan**; Blackjack Player, **William Tannen**; Cowboys, **Jack Ingram, Kenneth MacDonald** and **Edwin Parker**; Clarissa, **Valerie Jackson**; Cantina Owner, **Martin Garralaga**

CREDITS: Director, **Nathan Juran**; Assistant Director, **Fred Frank**; Producer, **John W. Rogers**; Screenwriters, **John Bagni, Gwen Bagni** and **D.D. Beauchamp**; Adaptation, **Inez Cocke**; Editor, **Ted J. Kent**; Art Directors, **Alexander Golitzen** and **Robert Clatworthy**; Set Decorators, **Russell A. Gaus-**man and **John Austin**; Cinematographer, **Clifford Stine**; Costumes, **Rosemary Odell**; Hair Stylist, **Joan St. Oegger**; Makeup, **Bud Westmore**; Sound, **Leslie I. Carey** and **Robert Pritchard**; Music, **Joseph Gershenson**; Technicolor Color Consultant, **William Fritzsche**

SONG: "True Love" (Herbert and Hughes)—sung by **Mary Castle**

LOCATION FILMING: Red Rock Canyon, California

SOURCE: Story, *Saint Johnson* by **William R. Burnett**

STORY: Frame Johnson (Ronald Reagan) decides to give up his life as a lawman in Tombstone and settle down on a ranch he has purchased in Cottonwood. Reagan finds an old enemy, Kurt Durling (Preston Foster), is running the town.

The townspeople want Reagan to be town marshal but he refuses. Lute Johnson (Alex Nicol), Reagan's brother, decides to accept the job instead. In a saloon argument, Frank Durling (Dennis Weaver) guns down Alex Nicol. This act makes Reagan decide to take over the job of town marshal. Jimmy (Russell Johnson), Reagan's younger brother, falls in love with Foster's sister, Maria (Ruth Hampton). Johnson goes to Foster's ranch to see Hampton. Weaver tries to stop Hampton from leaving with Johnson and in the struggle is shot by Johnson. Reagan makes Johnson turn himself in but Foster arranges a jailbreak to discredit Reagan. Foster starts a vicious hand-to-hand struggle with Reagan in the streets of Cottonwood which ends with Foster being run over by a stagecoach. Reagan goes after Johnson to bring him back for trial. Reagan confronts Johnson whereupon Johnson wounds Reagan in the shoulder. Johnson comes to his senses and decides to return to Cottonwood. Reagan is now free to marry Jeannie (Dorothy Malone) and Johnson will settle down with Hampton.

NOTES AND COMMENTARY: This was the fourth time Universal had used W.R. Burnett's story. The first version starred Walter Huston as Frame Johnson in 1932, the second was a Johnny Mack Brown serial, *Wild West Days* (Universal, 1937) and the third was a series "B" western for Johnny Mack Brown in 1940. Brown was given character names other than Frame Johnson in his outings. Mike Ragan was also billed as Holly Bane in his movie career. The song, "True Love," heard in the scene in which Russell Johnson visits Ruth Hampton at her brother's ranch, was lifted from the soundtrack of *Gunsmoke* (Universal-International, 1953). Clayton Moore, best known for his role as the Lone Ranger in television and the movies, was signed for the movie but never appeared in the film.

Johnny Carpenter remarked that Ronald Reagan was a personal friend. When interviewed he had little recollection of the movie, however. During the early to mid-fifties, Carpenter produced, starred in and sometime wrote a number of "B" westerns. Carpenter said, "I worked at Universal quite a bit. But mainly at the time I was producing my own [pictures] and I had to do a lot of work [at Universal] and they didn't pay much money. An actor, in those days, got maybe twenty-five dollars a day or something. I was more successful in producing my own."

Russell Johnson thought he had a good role in *Law and Order* and that it was an interesting film. Johnson commented on his role, "It was a nice shot for me as parts were concerned as an actor. That was a good part and I enjoyed it." Between takes Russell Johnson and Ronald Reagan had a few discussions in which they found out they were on the opposite ends of the political spectrum. It got to the point where Johnson only wanted to talk to Reagan when they were working. Johnson remarked, "He was very political. He couldn't spend a minute without being political. That was a pain in the ass." Reagan was president of the Screen Actors Guild around the time he made this film. In addition, Reagan had also turned from being a Democrat to a very conservative Republican. Reagan was starting to become active in politics. When it came to actually making the picture, Johnson felt that Reagan was an easy man to work with. The scene in the film that Russell Johnson remembered the

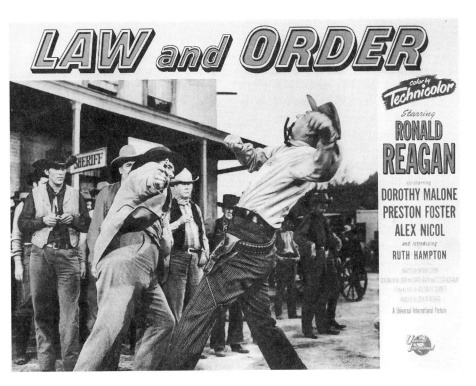

Law and Order (1953) scene card: Preston Foster strikes Ronald Reagan in their climactic fistfight.

most was the one in which he shot Reagan in the left shoulder. He said, "Interestingly, coincidentally, I shot him in the same shoulder that he was actually shot by that guy, Hinckley, except I didn't intend to kill him. I was trying to get away from him. I was sorry about it too, afterwards, as well as the character in the film was concerned." Johnson recalled that it was a rough day of filmmaking with he and Reagan climbing all over the rocks at Vasquez or either Red Rock Canyon. Johnson couldn't remember which location it actually was, but for the record, it was Red Rock Canyon.

Due to dental surgery, Ruth Hampton replaced Susan Cabot in the role of Maria. Ruth Hampton was an entrant in a Miss Universe contest, an annual activity sponsored by Universal studios. At the end of every contest, a number of the participants would be signed to 13-week contracts. The salaries offered by Universal weren't very much, but to willing aspirants like Hampton it was a chance to appear on the silver screen. After the 13 weeks, someone would make the decision whether to keep them or let them go. Hampton appeared in five other films at the studio: *Abbott and Costello Go to*

Mars (Universal-International, 1953); *Take Me to Town* (Universal-International, 1953); *Johnny Dark* (Universal-International, 1954); *Ricochet Romance* (Universal-International, 1954); and *The Glenn Miller Story* (Universal-International, 1954), then was never heard from again.

Russell Johnson enjoyed working with Preston Foster in this film. The fact that Foster had been in movies for many years impressed Johnson. Foster would tell stories about filmmaking in the thirties when he was just getting started and how it was to be under contract to the major studios at that time. Johnson said of Foster, "I had great admiration for him, great respect. He was a wonderful actor." Dennis Weaver and Russell Johnson knew each other from working together in theater groups in the late forties and early fifties. They were already good friends at the time this film was made. Johnson had this to say about Weaver, "Dennis is a wonderful man, a wonderful actor, an athletic guy. A guy who'd look great on a horse, a good sense of humor,

totally enjoyable." Russell Johnson had this comment on his western career, "I was never a fan of westerns or being in westerns. I never felt comfortable riding a horse, even though I had a western series years later in '59 and '60, when all the westerns were on the air. It was called *Black Saddle* (NBC, ABC). I co-starred with Peter Breck."

REVIEWS: "Good Technicolor western feature." *Variety*, 4/8/53; "Quite mediocre compared to the classic 1932 version." *Western Movies*, Pitts.

SUMMATION: This is a good western, perhaps not up to the standards of the 1932 classic, but certainly first class entertainment. The principal actors, Ronald Reagan, Preston Foster, Dorothy Malone, Alex Nicol and Chubby Johnson, acquit themselves well in their respective roles. Russell Johnson is handed the plumb role of Reagan's headstrong younger brother and makes the most of it. Nathan Juran's direction is on target and makes the most of a taut script.

FROM AUSTIN TO ABILENE ... THE MAN HUNTERS SWARMED!
From seven states they came to set the net to get the
hunted man they called the greatest gunfighter of them all!

The Lawless Breed

Universal-International (January 1953); COLOR by Technicolor; RUNNING TIME: 83 min.

CAST: John Wesley Hardin, **Rock Hudson**; Rosie McCoy, **Julia Adams**; Jane Brown, **Mary Castle**; J.C. Hardin/John Clements, **John McIntire**; Ike Haney, **Hugh O'Brian**; Jim Clements, **Dennis Weaver**; Zeke Clements, **Forrest Lewis**; Dirk Hanley, **Lee Van Cleef**; Chick Noonan, **Tom Fadden**; John Hardin, Jr., **Race Gentry**; Joe Clements, **Richard Garland**; Ben Hanley, **Glenn Strange**; Joe Hardin, **William Pullen**; Gus Hanley, **Michael Ansara**; Marv (Bartender), **Dick Wessel**; Card Player, **Stanley Blystone**; Lieutenant, **John Pickard**; Swamper, **Francis Ford**; Aunt Em, **Gertrude Granger**; Bartender in Abilene, **I. Stanford Jolley**; Wild Bill Hickok, **Robert Anderson**; Judge, **Stephen Chase**; Captain W.H. McNelly, **Thomas E. Jackson**; Henry Johnson, **Edward Earle**; Bartender in Polland, **Emory Parnell**; Bully, **George Wallace**

CREDITS: Director,   **Raoul Walsh**; Assistant Director, **William Holland**; Producer/Story, **William Alland**; Screenwriter, **Bernard Gordon**; Editor, **Frank Gross**; Art Directors, **Bernard Herzbrun** and **Richard Riedel**; Set Decorators, **Russell A. Gausman** and **Oliver Emert**; Cinematographer, **Irving Glassberg**; Costumes, **Rosemary Odell**; Hair Stylist, **Joan St. Oegger**; Makeup, **Bud Westmore**; Sound, **Leslie I. Carey** and **Corson Jowett**; Music, **Joseph Gershenson**; Technicolor Color Consultant, **William Fritzsche**

LOCATION FILMING: Vasquez Rocks, Andy Jauregui Ranch, California

The Lawless Breed (1952) scene card: **Julia Adams and Rock Hudson have a glass of beer between horse races.**

STORY: John Wesley Hardin (Rock Hudson) decides to obtain money to buy his own horse farm and marry Jane Brown (Mary Castle). In a card game, Hudson shoots crooked gambler Gus Hanley (Michael Ansara). Hudson runs away but later decides to stand trial for the Ansara killing. To raise sufficient money for his defense, Hudson enters his horse in two races and wins both. When Hudson goes to collect his winnings, the sheriff tries to arrest him. Hudson refuses to be arrested because a time has been set for him to surrender to the authorities and he walks away. The sheriff shoots Hudson in the back, wounding him, and Hudson returns fire killing the sheriff. The marshal goes to the farm of Hudson's father, J.C. (John McIntire), to arrest Hudson. Hudson is further wounded and bullets intended for Hudson kill Castle. Hudson takes up with Rosie McCoy (Julia Adams). They go to Alabama where they buy a farm and get married. A letter from Adams to McIntire telling him that she and Hudson are going to have a baby leads the Texas Rangers to Hudson. Hudson is arrested and sentenced to 25 years in prison. After 16 years, Hudson is pardoned. Hudson returns home and finds that his son, John, Jr. (Race Gentry), idolizes his gunfighting career. A quarrel erupts between the two and Gentry leaves the farm. Hudson goes after him and arrives in time to prevent his son from entering into a saloon gunfight with a bully (George Wallace). The two start to leave the saloon when Wallace shoots Hudson in the back, wounding him. Hudson prevents Gentry from taking any action and Gentry finally realizes the futility of settling arguments with a gun.

NOTES AND COMMENTARY: When the film was reissued, Hugh O'Brian, due to his popularity as Wyatt Earp on television, had been elevated to co-star billing. Before settling on *The Lawless Breed*, the film had working titles of *Bad Man with a Gun* and *Gun Hand*. Universal had used the title *The Lawless Breed* in 1946 for a Kirby Grant "B" western. The Grant western had its title changed for television showings to *The Lawless Clan* to avoid confusion with the Rock Hudson film. Montage footage of the Civil War included scenes from *Tap Roots* (Universal-International, 1948).

Robert Hoy, who played Joe the ranch foreman of *The High Chaparral* (NBC), thinks that the first western he worked on at Universal was *The Lawless Breed*.

During the filming of *The Lawless Breed*, director Raoul Walsh was continually bellowing at Rock Hudson, "Balls, Rock, Balls!!!" Obviously, Walsh was demanding Hudson to be at his most virile and it worked. It has been frequently documented that Hudson's performance in this film led to his starring roles in *Magnificent Obsession* (Universal-International, 1954) and *Giant* (Warner Bros., 1956).

Rock Hudson, Russell Johnson, Paul Birch and William Pullen were sitting in a cast trailer waiting for the next scene to shoot, when Hudson (as Pullen recalled his wording) asked the group, "Would you guys rather be under contract or work freelance?" Johnson, Birch and Pullen agreed that they preferred the security of a contract. They also assumed Hudson was being advised to demand more than the customary, at that time, $75 per week.

REVIEWS: "Good outdoor action feature." *Variety*, 12/3/52; "Well made, somewhat offbeat western loaded with rousing action and brimming with good performances." *Hollywood Reporter*, 11/28/52.

SUMMATION: This is a good, well-written, well-directed and acted western. Rock Hudson gives a strong performance that gave his career the boost he needed to become a major star. Julia Adams turns in one of the best performances of her career. Raoul Walsh guides the film steadily, emphasizing the dramatic aspects while not allowing the action scenes to be in any way diminished. This is easily one of the finest Universal-International westerns.

WHEN ONE MAN DARED THE TERROR THAT STALKED THE MOUNTAIN PASSES!
One by one their men had died, so they sent
Zack Hallet to do the job alone!
...even if his son came to fear him ... even if the woman
he loved learned to hate his name!

The Lone Hand

Universal-International (May 1953); COLOR by Technicolor; RUNNING TIME: 80 min.

CAST: Zachary Hallock, **Joel McCrea**; Sarah Jane Skaggs, **Barbara Hale**; Jonah Varden, **Alex Nicol**; George Hadley, **Charles Drake**; Joshua, **Jimmy Hunt**; Gus Varden, **Jim Arness**; Mr. Skaggs, **Roy Roberts**; Mr. Dunn, **Frank Ferguson**; Daniel Skaggs, **Wesley Morgan**; Pinkerton Man, **George Wallace**; Regulators, **Hugh Prosser** and **Denver Pyle**

CREDITS: Director, **George Sherman**; Assistant Director, **Jesse Hibbs**; Producer, **Howard Christie**;

Story, **Irving Ravetch**; Screenwriter, **Joseph Hoffman**; Editor, **Paul Weatherwax**; Art Directors, **Alexander Golitzen** and **Eric Orbom**; Set Decorators, **Russell A. Gausman** and **Oliver Emert**; Cinematographer, **Maury Gertsman**; Costumes, **Leah Rhodes**; Hair Stylist, **Joan St. Oegger**; Makeup, **Bud Westmore**; Sound, **Leslie I. Carey** and **Joe Lapis**; Music Director, **Joseph Gershenson**; Technicolor Color Consultant, **William Fritzsche**

LOCATION FILMING: Durango area, Colorado

STORY: Zachary (Joel McCrea) and his son, Joshua (Jimmy Hunt),

The Lone Hand (1953) scene card: On right, Joel McCrea and Jimmy Hunt, his son, are reunited after McCrea has whipped Charles Drake in a rugged fist-fight.

come to Timberline where McCrea buys a farm. During a bank robbery, Hunt notices that one of the robbers is wearing distinctive boots. Later Hunt sees the same outlaw as a Pinkerton man is killed. When rancher Hadley (Charles Drake), the leader of a vigilante group called the Regulators, questions McCrea and Hunt about the incident, McCrea refuses to get involved. Jonah Varden (Alex Nicol) and Gus Varden (Jim Arness), two members of the outlaw gang, try to recruit McCrea. Since McCrea is in debt, he decides to join the gang. Hunt follows McCrea and sees his father participate in a stage-coach robbery. McCrea weds Sarah Jane (Barbara Hale) because he needs someone to look after Hunt if he's killed in a robbery attempt. McCrea gradually falls in love with Hale. Hale asks McCrea to explain where he goes on the days the outlaws pull off a robbery. When McCrea refuses to answer, Hale leaves him. Finally a robbery is to be staged in which the big boss will participate. McCrea gives Hunt a message to take to the telegraph office and tells him to stay with Hale until he returns home. The message is intercepted by Charles Drake who then reveals to Hunt that he's the head of the outlaw gang and McCrea is a Pinkerton man. McCrea also goes to Hale and tells her what he's really been doing and where he's to meet the leader of the outlaws. Drake has taken Hunt captive to use as a hostage. McCrea is taken captive and the robbery is successful. The Regulators arrive before the outlaws can get away and Drake tries to escape but is captured by McCrea. Hale sought out the Regulators when Hunt did not show up.

NOTES AND COMMENTARY: *The Lone Hand* was to be Jimmy Hunt's last western feature. Hunt had previously appeared in *Saddle Tramp* (Universal-International, 1950), *Rock Island Trail* (Republic, 1950) and *The Capture* (RKO, 1950). Hunt appeared in *The All-American* (Universal-International, 1953) and retired from the screen unwilling to further pursue an acting career. Best known for his role in *Invaders from Mars* (20th Century–Fox, 1953), Hunt was coaxed out of acting

retirement to appear as the police chief in a remake of *Invaders from Mars* (Cannon, 1986). U-I has McCrea's character name as Hallet in the ads, but in the film it is Hallock.

REVIEWS: "Well-made program western feature." *Variety*, 4/1/53; "An above-average Technicolor western." *The Universal Story*, Hirschhorn.

SUMMATION: *The Lone Hand* is a good western adventure slightly marred by having a too obvious mystery villain. Joel McCrea delivers his usual steady performance as a man who has to hide secrets from his family. Barbara Hale registers strongly as McCrea's wife. Jimmy Hunt steals the movie, as McCrea's son who has to deal with the fact his father is an outlaw. The film's best scene involves Hunt being chased by a man he believes to be his father who has murderous intentions. Alex Nicol, Jim Arness and Charles Drake stand out among the fine supporting cast. George Sherman directs capably with well-staged action sequences.

LIFE CAN NEVER CAGE A MAN LIKE THIS!

Lonely Are the Brave

ALTERNATE TITLE: *Last Hero*, Joel Productions/Universal-International (June 1962); FILMED in Panavision; RUNNING TIME: 107 min.

CAST: Jack Burns, **Kirk Douglas**; Jerri Bondi, **Gena Rowlands**; Sheriff Johnson, **Walter Matthau**; Paul Bondi, **Michael Kane**; Hinton, **Carroll O'Connor**; Harry, **William** Schallert; Gutierrez, **George Kennedy**; Reverend Hoskins, **Karl Swenson**; First Deputy in Bar, **Bill Mimms**; Old Man, **Martin Garralaga**; Prisoner, **Lalo Rios**; "One Arm," **Bill Raisch**; Policeman, **Harry Lauter**; Airman in Helicopter, **Bill Bixby**

CREDITS: Director, **David Miller**;

Assistant Directors, **Tom Shaw** and **David Silver**; Producer, **Edward Lewis**; Screenwriter, **Dalton Trumbo**; Editor, **Leon Barsha**; Art Directors, **Alexander Golitzen** and **Robert Smith**; Set Decorator, **George Milo**; Cinematographer, **Philip Lathrop**; Hair Stylist, **Larry Germain**; Makeup, **Bud Westmore** and **Dave Grayson**; Sound, **Waldon O. Watson** and **Frank H. Wilkinson**; Music, **Jerry Goldsmith**; Music Supervisor, **Joseph Gershenson**

LOCATION FILMING: Albuquerque and the Sandia Mountains in Bernalillo County, New Mexico

SOURCE: Novel, "Brave Cowboy" by **Edward Abbey**

STORY: Cowboy Jack Burns (Kirk Douglas) travels by horseback to Albuquerque when he hears that close friend Paul Bondi (Michael Kane) has been sentenced to two years in prison for assisting illegal aliens. Douglas has himself thrown in jail where he plans a breakout with Kane. Kane refuses to go because he can't bear for his family to live on the run. Douglas goes through with the jailbreak and is able to ride to the foothills before a search gets underway. Sheriff Johnson

Lonely Are the Brave (1962) scene card: Kirk Douglas is spotted by an army helicopter; right border features Douglas.

(Walter Matthau) is in charge of capturing Douglas. As Douglas and his horse make their way up the side of the steep mountain, Matthau begins to admire Douglas' spirit. Douglas is even able to shoot an army helicopter out of the sky. As Douglas reaches the summit, police are closing in on two sides but Douglas is able to spur his horse to the safety of the woods. Douglas makes his way to the highway. Once he crosses, Douglas will quickly be in Mexico. The hard rain makes the highway slippery and the steady stream of traffic unnerves Douglas' horse. Unable to move across the highway, Douglas and his horse are hit by a truck carrying a load of toilets. Matthau arrives at the scene and refuses to identify Douglas as the fugitive. Douglas is taken to a hospital while his horse has to be destroyed.

NOTES AND COMMENTARY: William Schallert reminisced about his role of "Harry" in *Lonely are the Brave*, "I loved it. I felt that Dalton Trumbo had written a marvelous script. The characters were very well-drawn. It had an improvisational quality about it but we did the text exactly as written. It was written in a wonderful, wry, comic way. I like the character that I played a lot. He was a dolt but he was fun to play. Walter was wonderful to work with because he's really a terrifically funny guy. We got along very well and had a good time doing it. It was fun all around. A good experience."

In one scene Walter Matthau and William Schallert were scheduled to film a wild jeep ride in which Matthau would drive and Schallert would just hang on. Schallert commented on Matthau's driving ability "Walter came from New York and had not driven very much. I always had to help him when he was driving. It was always a little spooky." Since the scene would be filmed at a distance and a wild jeep ride was requested, the decision was made for one of the assistant directors to double Matthau. Schallert continued, "He put on a jacket that looked like Walter's and he and I drove together. He was a mad man. I was a little worried about how that [the scene] was going to work out. You know it's easy to roll a jeep over, especially if you are riding in an arroyo and you're not on a regular road. When we got to the end of the scene and the jeep stopped, I jumped out of the jeep and ran up the hill to the cameras screaming at them, 'I'm saying that I'm never going to do that again.' They got the shot and that's all that mattered."

Walter Matthau and William Schallert became good friends as the result of working together in *Lonely Are the Brave*. Schallert remembered, "We didn't know anything about each other but I ran into him, I think, in Albuquerque a day or so before we were going to start shooting. I had been riding around Albuquerque, listening to people talk. I went on a bus ride and listened to the bus driver and listened to the other people on the bus talking. I wanted to make sure I was getting the speech of the region approximately right. Then I ran into Walter. We sort of hung out that day together. During the course of the day a couple of things happened and we responded in similar fashion to them. We realized that we were kind of on the same wavelength. We got along very well. We liked working together. When the picture was over, we came back to L.A. and Walter came out to the house a few times. It turned out that my wife had worked in a television series [*Tallahassee 7000*, Syndicated, 1961] with him once. Eventually Walter bought a house right around the corner from where I lived. I've been living in the same house now for 37 years. He and I have been quite close. Walt's a great guy, a wonderful person."

REVIEWS: "This yesterday's versus today's values oater is a good one." *Western Movies*, Pitts; "Per-fectly swell little Western drama." *New York Times*, 6/28/62.

SUMMATION: *Lonely Are the Brave* is a very good contemporary western. Kirk Douglas gives one of his finest portrayals as a cowboy who refuses to give in to modern times and prefers to live under the code of the Old West. Walter Matthau also registers strongly as the sheriff who learns to respect the anachronistic cowboy. William Schallert does fine in the role of Matthau's assistant, adding some welcome humor to the proceedings. In roles that amount to little more than cameos, Gena Rowlands and Michael Parks are both quite good as Douglas' best friends. David Miller's direction is on the mark as he effectively crafts a story of a man trying to live in a world that no longer exists.

A COUPLA SQUARES IN THE ARTIC CIRCLE
BUD AND LOU AND BRAND NEW FUN
IN THE LAND OF THE MIDNIGHT SUN!

Lost in Alaska

ALTERNATE TITLE: *Abbott and Costello Lost in Alaska*; Universal-International (August, 1952); Black and White; RUNNING TIME: 76 min.

CAST: Tom Watson, **Bud Abbott**; George Bell, **Lou Costello**; Rosette, **Mitzi Green**; Nugget Joe McDermott, **Tom Ewell**; Jake Stillman, **Bruce Cabot**; Sherman, **Emory Parnell**; Henchman, **Jack Ingram**; Old-Timer, **Rex Lease**; Henchman, **Joseph Kirk**; Mrs. McGillicuddy, **Minerva Urecal**; Captain Chisholm, **Paul Newland**; Willie, **Michael Ross**; Higgins, **Howard Negley**; Croupier, **Billy Wayne**; Woman in Window, **Maudie Prickett**; Canook, **Iron Eyes Cody**; Eskimo Woman, **Julia Montoya**

Lost in Alaska (1952) scene card: Lou Costello (*second left*), Tom Ewell (*third left*) and Bud Abbott (*center*) are surrounded by greedy saloon owner Bruce Cabot (*second right*) and some greedy miners led by Emory Parnell (*third right*); right border shows Costello, Abbott, Mitzi Green and Ewell.

CREDITS: Director, **Jean Yarbrough**; Producer, **Howard Christie**; Story, **Elwood Ullman**; Screenwriters, **Martin A. Ragaway** and **Leonard Stern**; Editor, **Leonard Weiner**; Art Directors, **Bernard Herzbrun** and **Robert Boyle**; Set Decorators, **Russell A. Gausman** and **Ray Jeffers**; Cinematographer, **George Robinson**; Costumes, **Kara**; Hair Stylist, **Joan St. Oegger**; Makeup, **Bud Westmore**; Sound, **Leslie I. Carey** and **Harold Lewis**; Music Director, **Joseph Gershenson**; Choreographer, **Harold Belfer**

SONGS: "A Country Gal" (Mancini and Rosen)—sung by **Mitzi Green**; "There'll Be a Hot Time in the Igloo Tonight" (Mancini and Rosen)—sung by **Mitzi Green** and **Lou Costello**

STORY: Voluntary firemen Tom Watson (Bud Abbott) and George Bell (Lou Costello) rescue McDermott (Tom Ewell) from drowning. Ewell wants to die because his girlfriend, Rosette (Mitzi Green), wants nothing more to do with him even though Ewell owns a gold mine worth millions. Ewell receives a message that

Green wants to see him. Abbott and Costello accompany Ewell to Alaska because the police think Ewell is dead and Abbott and Costello are the culprits. It seems that saloon owner Stillman (Bruce Cabot) sent the note because he wants Ewell's gold. Cabot wants Green to marry Ewell. Then Cabot will make a widow out of Green so they can split the millions. To add to his problems, Ewell made a number of prospectors his beneficiary and it will be to their benefit to have Ewell dead. Ewell decides to move his gold so his map will have no value and his life will not be in jeopardy. Cabot and a couple of henchmen follow Ewell and Green. Abbott and Costello, after being lost in Alaska, catch up to Ewell at an Eskimo village. When Cabot comes near the village, Abbott and Costello delay Cabot so Ewell can move his gold. Abbott, Costello, Ewell and Green are caught between Cabot and the prospectors out in the middle of an ice field. Before anyone can retrieve the gold, the ice breaks and the gold is lost forever. Cabot promises to throw a big wedding for Ewell and Green.

NOTES AND COMMENTS: The working title for the film was *The Sourdoughs*. Jean Yarbrough directed this film as a favor to Lou Costello. Scenes from *Lost in Alaska* were used in *The World of Abbott and Costello* (Universal, 1965).

Mitzi Green, a former child star, came out of a retirement of fifteen years to appear in **Lost in Alaska**. Denise Darcell was originally scheduled to play the part of Rosette but bowed out. Green promptly retired after this film.

REVIEWS: "Slipshod Abbott and Costello, one of their poorer efforts for Universal." *Variety*, 7/30/52; "Tired Abbott and Costello vehicle, for their fans only." *Western Movies*, Pitts.

SUMMATION: *Lost in Alaska* is a far cry from Abbott and Costello's best efforts. Except for a rather funny opening when Lou Costello saves Tom Ewell from drowning, the laughs are few and far between. Poor production values also help mar any chance for the picture's success. Never at any time would anyone believe the actors were in Alaska and not on a Hollywood soundstage. Abbott and Costello dredge up some of their old comedy routines but, alas, in this retelling, they've lost the sparkle that once had audiences rolling in the aisles. The film doesn't give the other performers much to do but troopers Tom Ewell, Mitzi Green and Bruce Cabot do what they can with this tired script. Director Jean Yarbrough just goes through the motions of guiding the film to its tired conclusion.

THE ROAR OF DYNAMITE! THE THUNDER OF STAMPEDE!
The Great Mountain Wars Blaze With All Their Violence!
While one man's destiny was caught in their crossfire ...
and his love was trapped in a woman's arms!

The Man from Bitter Ridge

Universal-International (June 1955); FILMED in Eastman Color; RUNNING TIME: 80 min.

CAST: Jeff Carr, **Lex Barker**; Holly Kenton, **Mara Corday**; Alec Black, **Stephen McNally**; Ranse Jackman, **John Dehner**; Walter Dunham, **Trevor Bardette**; Shep Bascom, **Ray Teal**; Linc Jackman, **Warren Stevens**; Clem Jackman, **Myron Healey**; Norman Roberts, **John Harmon**; Wolf Landers, **John Cliff**; Jace Gordon, **Richard Garland**; Bundy, **Frank Sully**; Bender, **Dan White**; Hank Mains, **Jennings Miles**; Bartender, **Lee Morgan**; Sheepmen, **Lane Chandler** and **Dennis Moore**

CREDITS: Director, **Jack Arnold**; Assistant Director, **Marshall Green**; Producer, **Howard Pine**; Screenwriter, **Lawrence Roman**; Adaptation, **Teddi Sherman**; Editor, **Milton Carruth**; Art Directors, **Alexander Golitzen** and **Bill Newberry**; Set Decorators, **Russell A. Gausman** and **James M. Walters**; Cinematographer, **Russell Metty**; Costumes, **Jay A. Morley, Jr.**; Hair Stylist, **Joan St. Oegger**; Makeup, **Bud Westmore**; Sound, **Leslie I. Carey** and **Robert Pritchard**; Music Supervisor, **Joseph Gershenson**

LOCATION FILMING: Conejo Valley and Skeleton Canyon, California

SOURCE: Novel, *Justice Comes to Tomahawk* by **William MacLeod Raine**

STORY: Posse members accuse Carr (Lex Barker) of being a member of the gang responsible for the stagecoach robberies. When Barker is able to prove his innocence, Clem Jackman (Myron Healey), a brother of gang leader Ranse Jackman (John Dehner), tries to kill Barker. His attempt fails due to Holly Kenton's (Mara Corday) interference. Dehner is placing the blame for the rash of stagecoach holdups on the sheepmen led by Black (Stephen McNally). Barker reveals he has been sent by the stageline to investigate the robberies. Barker meets with McNally at the sheepmen's camp and believes McNally to be innocent of the crimes. Barker and McNally become rivals for Corday's affections. Barker and McNally track down Bascom (Ray Teal), a gang member. Linc Jackman (Warren Stevens), another brother of Dehner, and henchman Wolf Landers (John Cliff) ambush Teal, Barker and McNally. In the skirmish, Teal is wounded, Barker kills Stevens and Cliff escapes. Teal is taken to the sheepmen's camp. Healey leads an attack on the camp, dynamiting sheep and making a futile attempt on the lives

The Man from Bitter Ridge (1955) scene card: Racked with pneumonia in real life, Myron Healey menaces Lex Barker in this back-alley fight.

of Barker and Healey. Barker, Mc-Nally and the sheepmen ride into town and a pitched battle develops with the outlaw gang. In the battle, both Dehner and Healey are killed. Corday decides Barker is the man she loves.

NOTES AND COMMENTARY: *The Man from Bitter Ridge* was the first U-I western to be filmed in Eastman Color. Beginning with the studio's first 1957 release, *Gun for a Coward*, all medium-budgeted westerns to be filmed in color utilized this color process. *Justice Comes to Tomahawk* was the working title for the picture.

The only thing Warren Stevens could remember about the picture was a location scene in the west valley in Conejo or someplace. It was Stevens' first scene in the film and he was to ride down a hill. Stevens commented, "We were going lickety-split and the rein broke on my horse, the bridle. I had no way of controlling the horse at all. It took quite a while to calm him down. They got the shot but that's the only thing I remember about the whole picture."

Lex Barker and Warren Stevens were in three films together, *The Man from Bitter Ridge, Duel on the Mississippi* (Columbia, 1955) and *The Price of Fear* (Universal-International, 1956). Barker and Stevens became "pretty close friends." Stevens was shocked when Barker passed away. Stevens said, "We were the same age, almost exactly. A very nice man, I liked him very much."

Myron Healey remembered his back-alley fight scene with Lex Barker. Healey commented, "That was the one time in a half a century in films, it was the one time I got sick while I was on a show." Healey had pneumonia and a doctor would

The Man from Bitter Ridge (1955): **Mara Corday, Lex Barker and Corday's horse, Little Brown Jug.**

come to Healey's apartment each morning and give Healey a shot. The studio had people to help Healey get up and dressed. Healey would be driven to Universal in a limousine where he would check into the studio's hospital. A nurse would place Healey on a stretcher-type bed. Up on the back lot, director Jack Arnold, Lex Barker and a young man about Healey's height and build would run through the scene that would be shot. When Arnold was ready to shoot, Healey would be placed in an ambulance and be driven to the set. Healey would watch the final rehearsal. Healey remembered, "They'd get me all checked up, checked my makeup in the ambulance. They'd help me up and half-carry and half-walk me over into the set. The director would say, 'You got it, Myron?' I'd nod and he'd say, 'Action' and we'd go. We got the scene and I'd look over at the director and he'd say, 'Okay, get back.' So I'd head back to the ambulance and off I'd go to the hospital. This went on three days until the weekend. Finally the first part of the week I was able to work again."

The climactic shootout between Lex Barker and Myron Healey filmed at the barn and corral that was just off the Universal western street. Healey reminisced, "From the top roof, they had the fall to the other slanted roof. I did most of the stuff myself and for the final fall I came off the secondary thing and fell to the ground. I think I was doubled on that. You can't risk breaking your arm or something like that."

Lex Barker taught Mara Corday how to ride for *The Man from Bitter Ridge*. From the riding lessons, romance blossomed until Barker decided to go back to Lana Turner.

REVIEWS: "Snappy western. Arnold directs furiously, piling on the action while Metty gives the film the look of a movie with twice the budget." *The Western*, Phil Hardy; "Good western feature, stressing story and action." *Variety*, 4/20/55.

SUMMATION: This is a fast moving, well-paced action western. Director Jack Arnold, more noted for his science fiction films, proves that he's equally adept at guiding western stories to a successful conclusion. Lex Barker and Stephen McNally make virile and likable heroes. Mara Corday is fine as the love interest for both our heroes. The villainy is in good hands with John Dehner, Warren Stevens and especially Myron Healey. The expression on Healey's face, a maniacal smile, when he tries to knife Barker in a back-alley fight is worth the time to view the film in itself. Trevor Bardette does a fine job as the incumbent sheriff. A good film.

OUT OF TEXAS' BRAVEST HOUR ...
Came the Man They Called "The Coward!" From the Alamo's
flaming ruins he walked alone ... with a price on his life ...
a curse on his name ... and a pledge in his heart for revenge!

The Man from the Alamo

Universal-International (August 1953); COLOR by Technicolor; RUNNING TIME: 79 min.

CAST: John Stroud, **Glenn Ford**; Beth Anders, **Julia Adams**; John Gage, **Chill Wills**; Lt. Lamar, **Hugh O'Brian**; Jess Wade, **Victor Jory**; Dawes, **Neville Brand**; Cavish, **John Day**; Ma Anders, **Myra Marsh**; Kate Lamar, **Jeanne Cooper**; Carlos, **Marc Cavell**; Mapes, **Edward Norris**; Sergeant, **Guy Williams**; Texas Cabinet Member, **Frank Wilcox**; Sam Houston, **Howard Negley**; Colonel Travis, **Arthur Space**; Davy Crockett, **Trevor Bardette**; Tennessee Volunteer, **Dennis Weaver**; Texans at the Alamo, **Walter Reed** and **Davy Sharpe**; Franklin Sheriff, **George Eldredge**; Franklin Townsmen, **Kenneth MacDonald** and **Hugh Prosser**; Trooper, **Robert Hoy**

CREDITS: Director, **Budd Boetticher**; Assistant Director, **Tom Shaw**; Producer, **Aaron Rosenberg**; Story, **Niven Busch** and **Oliver Crawford**; Screenwriters, **Steve Fisher** and **D.D. Beauchamp**; Editor, **Virgil Vogel**; Art Directors, **Alexander Golitzen** and **Emrich Nicholson**; Set Decorators, **Russell A. Gausman** and **Ruby R. Levitt**; Cinematographer, **Russell Metty**; Costumes, **Bill Thomas**; Hair Stylist, **Joan St. Oegger**; Makeup, **Bud Westmore**; Sound, **Leslie I. Carey** and **Corson Jowett**; Music, **Frank Skinner**; Technicolor Color Consultant, **William Fritzsche**

LOCATION FILMING: greater Los Angeles area, California

STORY: John Stroud (Glenn Ford) is chosen by his friends to leave the Alamo prior to an all out assault by Santa Ana's forces. Ford plans to make certain all the families are safe in the face of an attack from other Mexican troops and then return to the Alamo. Ford arrives to find the ranches burned and Carlos (Marc Cavell), the son of a Mexican who worked for Ford, as the only survivor. Cavell tells Ford that white men dressed as Mexicans killed Ford's wife and child. Ford believes Jess Wade (Victor Jory) and his guerilla band were responsible. Sam Houston (Howard Negley) arrives in a nearby town to tell of the fall of the Alamo. Ford comes to town to find a temporary home for Cavell. Army lieutenant Lamar (Hugh O'Brian) recognizes Ford as the man who left the Alamo. The townspeople call Ford a coward and a traitor. Ford is about to leave town when Cavell recognizes a drunken cowboy, Dawes (Neville Brand), as one of the guerrilla band. Through Brand, Ford is able to join Jory's

The Man from the Alamo (1953) scene card: Julia Adams and Marc Cavell nurse an injured Glenn Ford back to health.

outfit. O'Brian leads a wagon train with the women, children and the elderly to a safer area. Jory realizes the wagon train carries the money that had been stored in the town's bank. Ford is able to warn the wagon train prior to the first attack but in a confrontation with Jory, slips down a steep embankment. Jory thinks Ford was killed in his fall. Cavell leaves the wagon train and finds the injured Ford. Ford is brought back to the camp where only Beth Anders (Julia Adams) will care for him. As Ford begins to recover, Adams starts to believe in Ford. Jory is waiting for a better opportunity to attack and finds it when O'Brian is ordered to report to

Negley. Ford tells O'Brian he will see that the wagon train gets through safely. Jory and his men attack but are no match for the sharp-shooting John Gage (Chill Wills) and the women. Jory tries to escape but Ford catches up to him. Ford engages Jory in a fight above a high waterfall and Ford knocks Jory to his death. Knowing the wagon train will be safe in Wills' hands, Ford leaves to join the Texas forces against the Mexican army. Cavell tells Adams that Ford will return to them.

NOTES AND COMMENTARY: Glenn Ford was injured while filming a chase scene. Ford suffered three broken ribs and was allowed to recuperate at his home following treatment at a hospital. Filming was shut down for five weeks. Director Budd Boetticher recounted the incident, "On the last day of *Man from the Alamo*, I wanted him [Ford] to stand up in the saddle and bulldog Victor Jory off his horse into the lake. That was all he was supposed to do and then I would cut to Davy Sharpe and the other double. Glenn always wanted to do everything himself. He went by the camera and decided that he would turn left and I always have my camera stay on the money. I have this on film. He ran into the woods and he came to a big tree. He was on Audie Murphy's gray quarter horse. He decided that he was going to turn left, the horse wanted to turn right and they had a tie. He and this tree, and you see all the Disney cartoons with the rabbit, he looked like one of those Disney cartoons. He hit the tree and he stayed there about five seconds, just spread-eagled. The horse was knocked cold, absolutely unconscious. Then he peeled off covered with bark. I ran over and turned him over and he was bleeding from the ears and the nose. Glenn opened his eyes just at that particular time when we thought he was dead anyway. He was supposed to do *Wings of the Hawk* (Universal-International, 1953)."

Budd Boetticher also had this to say about Glenn Ford, "I used to ride a horse on location with binoculars when we were shooting pictures like that. I would watch that sucker and would find out that he was on a horse, in front of seven or eight covered wagons, leading the stampede. I would have to ride out

and get him off. He wanted to do everything."

The World Premiere for *The Man from the Alamo* was held at the Majestic Theater in San Antonio, Texas. Stars Julia Adams, Chill Wills and Hugh O'Brian were in attendance.

In the cast listings, Chill Wills' character name is John Gage but other cast members in the film call him "Fred."

Horsewoman and former "B" western leading lady Evelyn Finley was Julia Adams' double in this film.

REVIEWS: "A superior B western from Boetticher." *The Western*, Hardy; "An absorbing, well made western filled with action." *Hollywood Reporter*, 7/10/53.

SUMMATION: *The Man from the Alamo* is a taut, well-done action-western film. A lot of the success for this film can be placed on the shoulders of star Glenn Ford and director Budd Boetticher. Ford delivers a finely delineated performance as a man torn by the fact others judge him as a coward and a deserter. The audience can look into Ford's face and feel his inner anguish. Boetticher has the story firmly in his grasp, showing why he is one of the most respected action directors. In the hands of a lesser director, not having someone tell why Ford is leaving the Alamo might have had been a fatal flaw in the script. Boetticher, wisely, focuses on the action and Ford's sturdy performance. From a very good supporting cast, Julia Adams, Chill Wills, Hugh O'Brian and Marc Cavell register strongly. Frank Skinner turns in an outstanding musical score.

THIS WAS THE NIGHT THE LAW TURNED LAWLESS
To win back the justice a town had betrayed!
...when the sheriff tore off his badge, forgot his
conscience and fought a force of evil with its own
ruthless weapons—of Violence, Fear and Murder!

Man in the Shadow

ALTERNATE TITLES: **Pay the Devil**; **Seeds of Wrath**; Universal-International (January 1958); FILMED in Cinemascope; RUNNING TIME: 80 min.

CAST: Ben Sadler, **Jeff Chandler**; Virgil Renchler, **Orson Welles**; Skippy Renchler, **Colleen Miller**; Ab Begley, **Ben Alexander**; Helen Sadler, **Barbara Lawrence**; Ed Yates, **John Larch**; Hank James, **James Gleason**; Aiken Clay, **Royal Dano**; Herb Parker, **Paul Fix**; Chet Hunaker, **Leo Gordon**; Jesus Cisneros, **Martin Garralaga**; Tony Santoro, **Mario Siletti**; Len Bookman, **Charles Horvath**; Jim Shaney, **William Schallert**; Harry Youngquist, **Joseph J. Greene**; Jake Kelley, **Forrest Lewis**; Dr. Creighton, **Harry Harvey, Sr**; Juan Martin, **Joe Schneider**; Gateman, **Mort Mills**; Renchler man, **Fred Graham**

CREDITS: Director, **Jack Arnold**; Assistant Director, **David Silver**; Producer, **Albert Zugsmith**; Screenwriter, **Gene L. Coon**; Editor, **Edward Curtiss**; Art Directors, **Alexander Golitzen** and **Alfred Sweeney**; Set Decorators, **Russell A. Gausman** and **John P. Austin**; Cinematographer, **Arthur E. Arling**; Gowns, **Bill Thomas**; Makeup, **Bud Westmore**; Sound, **Leslie I. Carey** and **Joe Lapis**; Music Supervision, **Joseph Gershenson**

LOCATION FILMING: Conejo Valley, California

STORY: At wealthy ranch owner Virgil Renchler's (Orson Welles) orders, Yates (John Larch) and Hunaker (Leo Gordon) beat up one of his Mexican hands, Martin (Joe Schneider). Schneider had been seen in the company of Welles' daughter, Skippy (Coleen Miller). The beating gets out of hand and Schneider is killed. The scene is witnessed by a fellow farmhand, Cisneros (Martin Garralaga), who reports the crime to sheriff Ben Sadler (Jeff Chandler). Chandler tries to investigate at the ranch but Welles refuses to cooperate. Gordon reports that Schneider was killed in an accident. Chandler gets a search warrant and finds evidence of a crime. An attempt is made on Chandler's life but fails. The townspeople, fearing economic blight if Welles declines to do business with the town, want Chandler to drop the investigation. Chandler is lured to an abandoned farmhouse where he is knocked out then dragged through town on the end of a rope from a truck. Chandler has had enough and goes to Welles' ranch to arrest the guilty parties. Chandler is captured and he is about to meet with a fatal accident of his own when the townspeople show up and help Chandler arrest Welles, Larch and Gordon.

NOTES AND COMMENTARY: All of Colleen Miller's scenes were filmed at night. Miller commented, "All the filming with me was done at 23 o'clock in the morning. It was a night shoot. Even in the daytime, I think it was nighttime." Between takes Orson Welles and Colleen Miller played gin. Welles told Miller to keep working and stay in the business. Miller had one more film to be released, *Step Down to Danger* (Uni-

versal-International, 1958) and then she retired from show business to be with her family. Miller did appear in the Audie Murphy western, *Gunfight at Comanche Creek* (Allied Artists, 1964) as a last hurrah.

Colleen Miller thought Orson Welles was not happy being in this film. He intimated he had to do the film because the studio let him do something else. That something else was *Touch of Evil* (Universal-International, 1958) in which Welles directed and starred.

William Schallert was in a wardrobe trailer on top of a hill on the Universal back lot when Orson

Man in the Shadow (1958) scene card: Harry Harvey, Sr., tends to an injured Jeff Chandler. Concerned townsmen Paul Fix, Ben Alexander, Forrest Lewis and Mario Siletti watch anxiously.

Welles came in. A pair of pants was hanging there and Welles asked whom the pants belonged to. The wardrobe man told Welles the pants were for his photo double. The pants were enormous. Welles then asked the size of the pants and when told, Welles began to chew the man out. "Here was Welles with his large stomach and the amount of weight he was carrying around acting like a child," Schallert thought, "something just bothered him about those pants hanging there and that was just a foible of Welles."

REVIEWS: "Fast modern day western, tough action and good story development." *Variety*, 11/27/57; "This Albert Zugsmith production is not a big picture. Just a good, blunt little one, ticking away with the steady matter-of-factness of an old fashioned alarm clock. And sounding off just as reliably." *New York Times*, 1/23/58.

SUMMATION: *Man in the Shadow* is a good, modern day western drama. Jeff Chandler as the small town sheriff turns in a fine performance but the film is dominated by the bravura acting of Orson Welles as the dominant power of the area. Colleen Miller, John Larch, Paul Fix and Mario Siletti are standouts in an impressive supporting cast. Jack Arnold directs with plenty of atmosphere and tension interspersed with some rugged action.

BARBED-WIRE SCARRED HIM ...
but couldn't stop him!
MEN FOUGHT HIM ...
but couldn't whip him!
WOMEN LOVED HIM ...
but couldn't hold him!
...except the one who made her bargain at the end of a loaded gun!

Man Without a Star

Universal-International (April 1955); COLOR by Technicolor; RUNNING TIME: 89 min.

CAST: Dempsey Rae, **Kirk Douglas**; Reed Bowman, **Jeanne Crain**; Idonee, **Claire Trevor**; Jeff Jimson, **William Campbell**; Steve Miles, **Richard Boone**; Strap Davis, **Jay C. Flippen**; Tess Cassidy, **Myrna Hansen**; Moccasin Mary, **Mara Corday**; Tom Cassidy, **Eddy C. Waller**; Latigo, **Sheb Wooley**; Tom Carter, **George Wallace**; Little Waco, **Frank Chase**; Mark Toliver, **Paul Birch**; Sheriff Olson, **Roy Barcroft**; Cookie, **Wm. "Bill" Phillips**; Brakeman, **Lee Roberts**; Hobo with a knife, **Jack Elam**; Ranch Owner, **Jack Ingram**; Drunken Cowboy, **Myron Healey**; Box Car Alice, **Millicent Patrick**; Hammer, **Casey MacGregor**; Johnson, **Ewing Mitchell**

CREDITS: Director, **King Vidor**; Assistant Director, **Frank Shaw**;

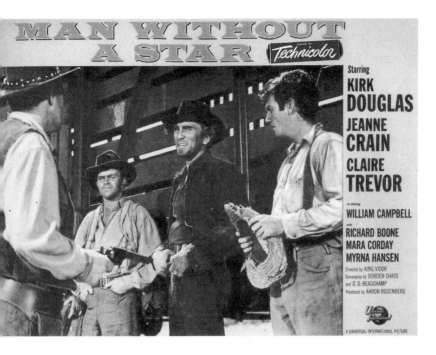

Man Without a Star (1955) scene card: Kirk Douglas (*center*) speaks up in William Campbell's defense (*right*) as George Wallace (*left*) accuses Campbell of murder.

Producer, **Aaron Rosenberg**; Screenwriters, **Borden Chase** and **D.D. Beauchamp**; Editor, **Virgil Vogel**; Art Directors, **Alexander Golitzen** and **Richard H. Riedel**; Set Decorators, **Russell A. Gausman** and **John Austin**; Cinematographer, **Russell Metty**; Costumes, **Rosemary Odell**; Hair Stylist, **Joan St. Oegger**; Makeup, **Bud Westmore**; Sound, **Leslie I. Carey** and **Joe Lapis**; Music Supervisor, **Joseph Gershenson**; Technicolor Color Consultant, **William Fritzsche**

SONGS: "Man Without a Star" (Hughes and Herbert)—sung by **Frankie Laine**; "And the Moon Grew Brighter and Brighter" (Singer and Kennedy)—sung by **Kirk Douglas**

LOCATION FILMING: Conejo Valley, California

SOURCE: Novel, *Man Without a Star* by **Dee Linford**

STORY: Wandering cowboy Rae (Kirk Douglas) takes young cowboy Jimson (William Campbell) under his wing. Both men are hired by foreman Davis (Jay C. Flippen) to work on the largest ranch in the area. Cattle from the large ranch and from all the small ranchers have been sharing the open range. The small ranchers want to use barbed wire to fence off enough grass to see their cattle through the winter. Douglas, who hates barbed wire because of injuries sustained from the wire, alienates himself from the small ranchers. Reed Bowman (Jeanne

Crain), the new owner of the large ranch, realizes Flippen is not man enough to crowd the small ranchers off the open range and turns to Douglas. Miles (Richard Boone), an old adversary of Douglas', brings more cattle to Crain's spread. When Boone and his men are hired to work on Crain's ranch, Douglas decides to quit. Crain seduces Douglas to entice him to stay but Douglas leaves in spite of her charms. Campbell kills a man in a gunfight causing a rift between he and Douglas. Douglas goes on a bender then decides to catch the next train out of town. He meets up with Boone and his men, who give Douglas a beating. Douglas then sides with the small ranchers. Boone decides to stampede cattle onto the range held by the small ranchers. Douglas and the ranchers are able to turn the cattle. Boone and Douglas have a vicious fistfight with Douglas emerging victorious. With the range war over, Douglas decides to move on while Campbell stays on to marry Tess Cassidy (Myrna Hansen), a rancher's daughter.

NOTES AND COMMENTARY: The novel, *Man Without a Star*, was purchased by Universal-International as a possible vehicle for Audie Murphy. Stuntman Fred Carson taught Kirk Douglas how to perform all of his gun-twirling tricks in this picture. Douglas also learned to play the banjo for his song in the picture.

The end credits give Eddy C. Waller's character name as Tom Cassidy but he introduces himself to Jeanne Crain as Bill Cassidy.

Man Without a Star was remade by Universal in 1969 as *A Man Called Gannon* with Tony Franciosa in the lead. The story was the basis for a *Virginian* (NBC) television episode, "Duel at Shiloh", in February 1963 with guest star Brian Keith.

REVIEWS: "Good western drama, highlighting action with sex and humor." *Variety*, 3/2/55; "A vigorous and solid entertainment with a healthy adult approach to its cast and story." *New York Times*, 3/25/55.

SUMMATION: *Man Without a Star* is a very good, exciting, well-acted and directed western. The cast performances are quite good with special mention of the acting of Kirk Douglas as the wandering cowboy with a dislike of barbed wire and William Campbell as the young cowboy befriended by Douglas. Director King Vidor brings humor and sexual tension to Borden Chase and D.D. Beauchamp's strong western screenplay.

He challenged the Outlaw Coast of Old California!
...To wrest Gold, Glory and a forbidden Love from
the plunder-mad Legions of a cut-throat's empire!

Mark of the Renegade

Universal-International (August 1951); COLOR by Technicolor; RUNNING TIME: 81 min.

CAST: Marcos, **Ricardo Montalban**; Manuella, **Cyd Charisse**; Luis, **J. Carrol Naish**; Don Pedro Garcia, **Gilbert Roland**; Anita Gonzales, **Andrea King**; Bardoso, **George Tobias**; Jose De Vasquez, **Antonio Moreno**; Duenna Concepcion, **Georgia Backus**; Colonel Vega, **Robert Warwick**; Miguel de Gandara, **Amando Silvestre**; Landlord, **David Wolfe**; Innkeeper, **Robert Cornthwaite**; Rosa, **Bridget Carr**; Paco, **Edward Rios**; Father Juan, **Renzo Cesana**; Cervera, **Alberto Morin**

CREDITS: Director, **Hugo Fregonese**; Producer, **Jack Gross**; Story, **Johnston McCulley**; Screenwriters, **Louis Solomon** and **Robert Hardy Andrews**; Editor, **Frank Gross**; Art Directors, **Bernard Herzbrun** and **Robert Boyle**; Set Decorators, **Russell A. Gausman and Ruby R. Levitt**; Cinematographer, **Charles P. Boyle**; Costumes, **Leah Rhodes**; Hair Stylist, **Joan St. Oegger**; Makeup, **Bud Westmore**; Sound, **Leslie I. Carey** and **Richard De Weese**; Music, **Frank Skinner**; Choreography, **Eugene Loring**; Technicolor Color Consultant, **William Fritzsche**

SONG: "La Amorita" danced by **Cyd Charisse** and **Ricardo Montalban**

STORY: Marcos (Ricardo Montalban) bears the mark of the renegade on his forehead. Pirates bring Montalban to California to meet Don Pedro (Gilbert Roland). Roland plans to wrest control of California from the Republic of Mexico. Only De Vasquez (Antonio Moreno) is powerful enough to block Roland's scheme. Roland wants Montalban to marry Moreno's daughter, Manuella (Cyd Charisse). Then Montalban will be revealed as a renegade. This fact will disgrace Moreno's family and render Moreno powerless to stop Roland. Montalban and Charisse fall in love. Roland plans to have Bardoso (George Tobias) and his pirates attack Los Angeles. Roland will repulse the pirates, reveal Montalban to be a renegade and become the savior of California. Montalban gets word to the California army about the pirate attack and the pirates are routed. Roland is exposed as a traitor and Montalban reveals that he is a secret agent sent by the Republic of Mexico to stop the uprising. Montalban dispatches Roland in a sword fight and now is free to marry Charisse.

NOTES AND COMMENTARY: The world premiere of *Mark of the Renegade* was held at the United Artists Theater in Hollywood, California.

Salvador Duhart, the consul general of Mexico, sponsored the event. The proceeds from this world premier went to local Mexican charities. The women's costumes in this film were heavy and uncomfortable. The actresses couldn't wait to get to the dressing rooms and change out of them.

Ricardo Montalban and Cyd Charisse played in six films together. The other five were *Fiesta* (Metro-Goldwyn-Mayer, 1947), *The Kissing Bandit* (Metro-Goldwyn-Mayer, 1948), *On an Island with You* (Metro-Goldwyn-Mayer, 1948), *Sombrero* (Metro-Goldwyn-Mayer, 1953)

and *Won Ton Ton, the Dog who Saved Hollywood* (Paramount, 1976). Andrea King remarked to the author on how well Montalban and Charisse danced together.

Andrea King remembered *Mark of the Renegade* as a wonderful adventure film played tongue-in-cheek. King said that Gilbert Roland was "a dashing man, a swashbuckler, a man of romance and just darling."

King said Montalban was marvelous in his role and that his role was "sort of a Douglas Fairbanks, Sr., remake of Zorro." Because of the way Montalban handled himself

Mark of the Renegade (1951) scene card: (*left to right*) Gilbert Roland, J. Carrol Naish, Amando Silvestre, Antonio Moreno, and Georgia Backus ask Cyd Charisse if there has been a visitor in her room.

in the film, it was thought this might be the beginning of a new career but Montalban's home studio, Metro-Goldwyn-Mayer, decided otherwise.

Andrea King had worked with George Tobias and J. Carrol Naish when she was under contract to Warner Bros. Tobias was "a hard working, working actor." King had worked with Naish in four previous films with her favorite being *The Beast with Five Fingers* (Warner Bros., 1946) in which King had the lead.

Director Hugo Fregonese was considered a kind, gentle man and an excellent director. Language was very hard for him, though, as he spoke a very broken English. The author asked Ms. King about her seduction scene with Montalban and she laughed and said, "I wish I'd done better." In the film she is quite unsuccessful as Montalban is pure in heart and knows that King is up to no good.

REVIEWS: "Early California costumer with enough action, about par." *Variety*, 7/25/51; "Swiftly paced romantic drama." *Hollywood Reporter*, 7/24/51.

SUMMATION: *Mark of the Renegade* is only an average, though somewhat entertaining, swashbuckling western set in old California. Ricardo Montalban and Cyd Charisse are attractive as the leads and acquit themselves well, Montalban especially as a virile action lead. Giving able support are Gilbert Roland, Andrea King and Antonio Moreno. George Tobias does not come off well as the pirate leader, appearing more as a buffoon than a fierce pirate leader. Hugo Fregonese directs capably enough with a script that could have supplied more action. The battle with the California army and the pirates is entirely offscreen. Perhaps as a tribute or reminder of their Metro-Goldwyn-Mayer days, Charisse and Montalban have a dance sequence that adds to the charm of this picture.

All the ACTION ... All the ROMANCE ... All the THRILLS!
...that made the Rex Beach
story an adventure classic!
...and all in blazing Cinecolor!

Michigan Kid

Universal (March 1947); FILMED in Cinecolor; RUNNING TIME: 69 min.

CAST: Michigan Kid (Jim Rowan), **Jon Hall**; Curley Davis, **Victor McLaglen**; Sue, **Rita Johnson**; Buster, **Andy Devine**; Soubrette, **Joan Fulton**; Steve, **William Brooks**; Sheriff, **Stanley Andrews**; Mr. Porter, **Byron Foulger**; Lanny, **Milburn Stone**; Dave, **Leonard East**; Mr. Nash, **Charles Trowbridge**; Pop Dawson, **Griff Barnett**; Bartender, **Dewey Robinson**; Sergeant, **Ray Teal**; Saloon Brawler, **Fred Graham**; Shotgun Guard, **Guy Wilkerson**; Outlaw, **Edmund Cobb**; Billiard Player,

Bob Wilke; Postmaster, **Eddy Waller**; Jeb, **Ernie Adams**

CREDITS: Director, **Ray Taylor**; Assistant Director, **Fritz Collings**; Producer, **Howard Welsch**; Story/Screenwriter; **Roy Chanslor**; Additional Dialogue, **Robert R. Presnell, Sr.**; Editor, **Paul Landres**; Art Directors, **Jack Otterson and Abraham Grossman**; Set Decorators, **Russell A. Gausman** and **Fred B. Martin**; Cinematographer, **Virgil Miller**; Special Photography, **D.S. Horsley**; Gowns, **Rosemary Odell**; Hair Stylist, **Carmen Dirigo**; Makeup, **Jack P. Pierce**; Sound, **Bernard B. Brown**; Sound Technician, **Robert Pritchard**; Music, **Hans J. Salter**; Cinecolor Supervisor, **Arthur F. Phelps**; Dialogue Director, **William Holland**

SONGS: "Whoops My Dear" (Brooks and Salter)—sung by **Joan Fulton**

LOCATION FILMING: Kernville, California

SOURCE: Novel, *Michigan Kid* by **Rex Beach**

STORY: Mustered out of the army, Jim Rowan (Jon Hall) makes his way west while his army buddies, Steve (William Brooks), Lanny (Milburn Stone) and Dave (Leonard East) go back to their homes in the east. An outlaw gang, led by Curley Davis (Victor McLaglen), attempts to hold up a stage to steal Pop Dawson's (Griff Barnett) money. In the melee, Barnett is shot but is able to fall out of the stagecoach, taking his money. Barnett hides the money and is able to leave clues to its hiding place as Hall comes upon the scene. The clues are in an envelope and in a watch. Barnett's niece, Sue (Rita Johnson), comes west and attempts to retrieve the watch alerting Porter (Byron Foulger) to its value. Foulger tips off McLaglen, who steals the watch and shoots bank president, Nash (Charles Trowbridge). Foulger throws suspicion on both Hall and Johnson and the sheriff (Stanley Andrews) arrests them. Hall has sent for his three army buddies. There is a series of escapes, chases and captures with Hall and Johnson being arrested again. Buster (Andy Devine) has been revealed as the gang leader. Devine and McLaglen find the money. With the aid of his friends, Hall breaks out of jail again and proves to Andrews that Devine, McLaglen and Foulger are the real culprits. Hall and Johnson decide to get married.

NOTES AND COMMENTARY: In late 1946, Universal had merged with International Pictures and the film was finally released under the auspices of Universal-International. As with *The Vigilantes Return* (Universal, 1947), this film did not meet the studio's new guidelines. The running time was a minute short, the film was lensed in Cinecolor rather than the preferred Technicolor and the director, Ray Taylor, had a long association with the "B" western.

This was Jon Hall's first western film since he had starred in Edward Small's *Kit Carson* (United Artists, 1940).

Most film historians omit Griff Barnett, Charles Trowbridge and Dewey Robinson from their cast

Michigan Kid (1947) title card: Left side—Jon Hall, Joan Fulton and Milburn Stone; right side—Jon Hall, Victor McLaglen, Rita Johnson, Andy Devine; Jon Hall hits an unidentified actor.

listings even though all three received on-screen billing. Actor William Brooks was later billed as William Ching.

Joan Fulton later used the last name Shawlee in her career.

The Michigan Kid was previously made as a silent film by Universal in 1928. This earlier film was a Northwest melodrama with a spectacular forest fire. It would seem that the only thing these two films have in common is the title.

REVIEWS: "Too much of an old-fashioned flavor for its own good."

Hollywood Reporter, 2/11/47; "Better than average cayuse carnival." *Variety*, 2/12/47.

SUMMATION: This is only a fair western with plenty of movement but does not have enough of the tough action needed to make this an above average sagebrush saga. The roundup of bad guys Victor McLaglen, Andy Devine and Byron Foulger is unexpectedly mild. Performances of the principals are generally okay with a special nod to the casting against type of Devine as the outlaw leader.

MEET THE FABULOUS MARK FALLON!
...his touch a wildfire temptation to every woman!
...his luck a challenge to every lusty river man!
...his life a reckless adventure from St. Louis to New Orleans!

The Mississippi Gambler

Universal-International (February 1953); COLOR by Technicolor; RUNNING TIME: 98½ min.

CAST: Mark Fallon, **Tyrone Power**; Angelique Dureau, **Piper Laurie**; Ann Conant, **Julia Adams**; Kansas John Polly, **John McIntire**; Edmond Dureau, **Paul Cavanaugh**; Laurent Dureau, **John Baer**; George Elwood, **Ron Randell**; Caldwell, **Ralph Dumke**; Paul O. Monet, **Robert Warwick**; Pierre, **William Reynolds**; Andre, **Guy Williams**; Spud, **King Donovan**; Julian Conant, **Dennis Weaver**; Kennerly, **Hugh Beaumont**; Judge, **Frank Wilcox**; Voodoo Dancer, **Gwen Verdon**; Girl, **Angela Stevens**; Bank Examiner, **George Eldredge**; Bridesmaids, **Anita Ekberg** and **Jackie Loughery**; Henchmen, **Al Wyatt** and **Dale Van Sickel**; Emile, **Fred Cavens**; Duroux Lawyer, **Edward Earle**; Gambler, **Paul Bradley**

CREDITS: Director, **Rudolph Mate**; Assistant Director, **John F. Sherwood**; Producer, **Ted Richmond**; Story/Screenwriter, **Seton I. Miller**; Editor, **Edward Curtiss**; Art Directors, **Alexander Golitzen** and **Richard Riedel**; Set Decorators, **Russell A. Gausman** and **Julia Heron**; Cinematographer, **Irving Glassberg**; Costumes, **Bill Thomas**; Hair Stylist, **Jean St. Oegger**; Makeup, **Bud Westmore**; Sound, **Leslie I. Carey** and **Richard De Weese**; Music, **Frank Skinner**; Choreographer, **Gwyneth Verdon**; Technicolor Color Consultant, **William Fritzsche**

SONGS: "De Lawd's Plan" (Mancini and Skinner)—sung by **LeRoi Antoine**; "Haitian Devil Song" (Antoine)—sung by **LeRoi Antoine** and **chorus** and danced by **Gwen Verdon**

LOCATION: Corriganville, California

STORY: Fallon (Tyrone Power) decides to become a Mississippi gambler so he teams up with Polly (John McIntire). On his first night as a gambler, Power is a big winner causing the enmity of Laurent Dureau (John Baer), a member of a prominent New Orleans family. Baer pays off his gambling debt by giving Power a necklace, a family heirloom treasured by his sister, Angelique (Piper Laurie). Power meets Laurie's father Edmond (Paul Cavanaugh) in New Orleans and is invited to his home. Power accepts primarily to see Laurie again but also to return the necklace. Laurie says she does not want to associate with a common gambler like Power. Elwood (Ron Randell), president of one of New Orleans' most prestigious banks, wants to marry Laurie. In a card game, Julian

The Mississippi Gambler (1953) scene card: Tyrone Power, Julia Adams and John McIntire have dinner in New Orleans.

Conant (Dennis Weaver), Ann Conant's (Julia Adams) brother, loses money that belonged to his employers and commits suicide. Power feels sorry for Adams and replaces the lost funds. Power tells Adams that Weaver was smart enough to place the firm's money in the riverboat's safe prior to gambling. Power and McIntire take Adams under their wing. Adams falls in love with Power and Baer falls in love with Adams. Adams turns down Baer's marriage proposal. Laurie decides to marry Randell. From this point, tragedy strikes Laurie. Baer dies by his own knife when he attempts to kill Power. Cavanaugh dies in a duel resulting from an unfounded slur on Adams

and Power's relationship. Randell absconds with money from his failing bank and disappears. Laurie becomes legally free from the marriage with Randell and realizes Power is the man who has truly loved her and goes to him.

NOTES AND COMMENTARY: *The Mississippi Gambler* held its World Premiere at the Fox Theater in St. Louis, Missouri, on January 13, 1953. A popular film, *The Mississippi Gambler* took in $3 million at the box office. This was a good for a tie for nineteenth place in 1953.

Jeff Chandler was originally slated for the lead role, but other commitments kept him from accepting the assignment. Rock Hudson was also considered. Tyrone Power was brought in at a whopping salary in his first production away from his home studio, Fox, since his disastrous loanout to MGM for *Marie Antoinette* (Metro-Goldwyn-Mayer, 1936). It's the only time he had worked on a non–Fox film since 1936. Power and producer Richmond became fast friends while working on this film and the two later formed a production company, Copa Productions, for independent filmmaking. Power and Richmond teamed up for *Abandon Ship!* (Columbia, 1957) and had begun production of *Solomon and Sheba* (United Artists, 1959) when Power died before the picture could be completed. Yul Brynner replaced Power. Many scenes had to be reshot, but Power can still be seen in long shots.

Leslie I. Carey and the Universal-International Sound Department were nominated for an Academy Award for Best Sound Recording in 1953. Carey finally took an Oscar home the next year for *The Glenn Miller Story* (Universal-International, 1954)

REVIEWS: "A rousing, colorful romantic film with lively action and moving drama." *Hollywood Reporter*, 1/9/53; "A robust, exciting tale." *The Motion Picture Guide*, Nash and Ross.

SUMMATION: This is good blend of adventure and romance on the Mississippi River with Tyrone Power still elegant and dashing in the lead. Piper Laurie delivers both fine acting and radiance in her performance as the woman whom Power loves. Lending able support to the proceedings are Julia Adams, John McIntire and Paul Cavanaugh. Rudolph Mate capably directs Seton I. Miller's script. The voodoo dance, while performed well, was quite unnecessary, as it tended to slow the otherwise fast moving story.

Land of ... EASY GOLD! EASY LIPS! EASY DEATH!
The glory-legend of the man with
six silver bullets ... and six men to search down!

Money, Women and Guns

Universal-International (January 1959); EASTMAN COLOR by Pathé; FILMED in Cinemascope; RUNNING TIME: 80 min.

CAST: "Silver" Ward Hogan, **Jock Mahoney**; Mary Kingman, **Kim Hunter**; Davy Kingman, **Tim Hovey**; Sheriff Crowley, **Gene Evans**; Jess Ryerson, **Tom Drake**; Art Birdwell, **Lon Chaney**; Clint Gunston, **William Campbell**; Johnny Bee, **Jeffrey Stone**; Henry Devers, **James Gleason**; Sally Gunston, **Judy Meredith**; Damion Bard, **Philip Terry**; Indian, **Richard Devon**; Nibbs, **Ian MacDonald**;

John Briggs, **Don Megowan**; Ben Merriweather, **Harry Tyler**; Old Prospector, **Tom London**; Job Kingman, **Nolan Leary**; Sheriff, **Steve Darrell**

CREDITS: Director, **Richard H. Bartlett**; Assistant Director, **Gordon McLean**; Producer, **Howie Horwitz**; Story, **Robert Blees** and **Harry Essex**; Screenwriter, **Montgomery Pittman**; Editor, **Patrick McCormack**; Art Directors, **Alexander Golitzen** and **Robert E. Smith**; Set Decorators, **Russell A. Gausman** and **William P. Tapp**; Cinematographer, **Philip Lathrop**; Costumes, **Morton Haack**; Makeup, **Bud Westmore**; Sound, **Leslie I. Carey**

and **Frank Wilkinson**; Music Supervisor, **Joseph Gershenson**

SONG: "Lonely is the Hunter" (Wakely)—sung by **Jimmy Wakely**

LOCATION FILMING: Lone Pine, California

STORY: Three claim jumpers attack Merriweather (Harry Tyler) and leave him mortally wounded. Tyler is able to shoot two of the three outlaws. Before Tyler dies, he writes the names of his beneficiaries, one of which is his killer. Famous detective "Silver" Ward Hogan (Jock Mahoney) is hired to seek out his heirs and also determine which one was the claim jumper. Mahoney is able to determine that heirs Davy Kingman

Money, Women and Guns (1959) scene card: Jock Mahoney introduces himself to Tim Hovey, Nolan Leary and Kim Hunter.

(Tim Hovey), Clint Gunston (William Campbell) and Henry Devers (James Gleason) are not responsible for Tyler's death. During his search, Mahoney and Hovey's mother begin to fall in love. The only heirs left to be further investigated are John Briggs (Don Megowan and someone known as Judas. Vying with Mahoney for the reward money for uncovering Tyler's murderer is bounty hunter Johnny Bee (Jeffrey Stone). Stone is riding with Mahoney as he's travelling to question Megowan. Mahoney has been using Tyler's mule to pack supplies. Stone lets it slip that the mule's name is Judas. Mahoney, then, realizes that Stone must be the third claim jumper and captures him. Stone tells Mahoney that the other claim jumpers shot Tyler and that he never fired a shot. Mahoney believes Stone's story because Stone had many chances to kill him. With the case solved, Mahoney forsakes his detective career to settle down with Mary Kingman (Hunter).

NOTES AND COMMENTARY: The working title for *Money, Women and Guns* was *Money, Women and Dreams*. Gene Evans commented about the movie, "I never saw it. I just did it. I don't remember what is was. I can remember how I came about doing it. It was a guy at Universal. He was a good friend to me. He was a good writer. (Note—Montgomery Pittman wrote the screenplay.) Anyway, Dick Bartlett directed it. Whoever produced it did some big things. (Note—Howie Horwitz was the producer.) I did it as a favor to Bartlett. They told me that they would get Kim Hunter to play. I got to work with Kim Hunter. (Note—Evans had no scenes in the film with Hunter.) I was crazy about her.

REVIEWS: "Pleasant oater with some good performances although a rather tame film." *Western Movies*, Pitts; "Pittman's script is clever but Bartlett's direction is oddly listless and accordingly the mystery unravels rather like a ball of wool instead of dramatically." *The Western*, Hardy.

NOTES AND COMMENTS: *Money, Women and Guns* is a pleasant little western. With the quality of the cast that was assembled, much more was expected both in story quality and depth of characterization. The title, itself, promises an action-packed saga. After the opening scene though, the film is almost devoid of action. Due to the episodic nature of the story, most of the performers don't have a chance to really make a big impression, although Kim Hunter, James Gleason, Lon Chaney, William Campbell and Tom Drake have their moments. Jock Mahoney is effective, as a detective, whose fictional exploits in the dime novels, has made him larger than life to most of the people that he meets. Neither Montgomery Pittman's script or Richard H. Bartlett's direction give that added punch to make this a memorable western story.

So Close Together ... only a bullet can separate them!
From Vera Cruz to Matamoros he rode ...
to take his vengeance with a loaded gun ...
to find the woman who waited in The Naked Dawn

The Naked Dawn

Universal-International (November 1955); PRINT by Technicolor; RUNNING TIME: 82 min.

CAST: Santiago, **Arthur Kennedy**; Maria, **Betta St. John**; Manuel Lopez, **Eugene Iglesias**; Tina, **Charlita**; Guntz, **Roy Engel**; Vincente, **Tony Martinez**; Railroad Guard, **Francis McDonald**

CREDITS: Director, **Edgar G. Ulmer**; Assistant Director, **Raoul Pagel**; Associate Producer, **James O. Radford**; Screenwriters, **Nina and Herman Schneider**; Editor, **Dan Milner**; Art Director, **Martin Lencer**; Set Decorator, **Harry Reif**; Cinematographer, **Frederick Gately**; Photographic Effects, **Jack R. Glass**; Makeup, **Steven Clensos**; Sound, **Robert Roderick**; Music Composer and Supervisor, **Herschel Burke Gilbert**

SONG: "Ai Hombre" (Copeland and Gilbert)—sung and danced by **Charlita**

LOCATION FILMING: Mexico

STORY: Two men, Santiago (Arthur Kennedy) and his friend Vincente (Tony Martinez), break into a freight car in the railroad yard and steal four boxes of merchandise. During the holdup, they are confronted by railroad guard Francis McDonald, who mortally wounds Martinez. To deliver the boxes to Guntz (Roy Engel), Kennedy enlists the aid of peasant farmer Lopez (Eugene Iglesias). When Engel refuses to hand over Martinez' share to Kennedy, Kennedy takes all but a few dollars from Engel's cash box. Kennedy decides to stay at Iglesias' farm for awhile. Kennedy desires Iglesias' wife Maria (Betta St. John) and St. John is enchanted by Kennedy's worldliness and wants to run away with Kennedy. Iglesias becomes greedy and wants all of Kennedy's money. Iglesias' attempts to kill Kennedy fail and Kennedy, in turn, plans to take St. John with him after all. As Kennedy and St. John leave, they see Engel and two men come to the farm and start to hang Iglesias. Kennedy prevents the hanging and shoots Engel. As Kennedy, St. John and Iglesias start to leave the farm, the wounded Engel and Kennedy exchange shots. Kennedy's shot kills Engel and Engel's shot mortally wounds Kennedy. Before he dies, Kennedy sends Iglesias and St. John off to start a new life together.

NOTES AND COMMENTARY: Screenwriter Julian Zimet used the pseudonym Nina and Herman Schneider. In his long career, Edgar G. Ulmer directed only one other

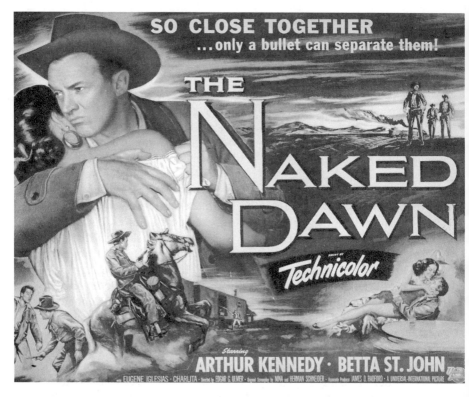

The Naked Dawn (1955) title card: Arthur Kennedy holds Betta St. John.

western, *Thunder Over Texas* (Beacon, 1934), the first of "Big Boy" Williams' short stint as a western hero in the mid-thirties. Ulmer used the pseudonym John Warner so Universal would not know that he was working elsewhere.

REVIEWS: "Mild programmer should prove passable." *Variety*, 7/27/55; "The Technicolor photography helped the familiar yarn along painlessly enough." *The Universal Story*, Hirschorn.

SUMMATION: Arthur Kennedy is basically the whole show in this film noir western filmed in Mexico. But try as hard as Kennedy, Betta St. John, Eugene Iglesias and director Edgar G. Ulmer can, this overly talkie film does not rise above the average.

*THIS WAS THE NIGHT WHEN NAKED FURY
FLAMED OUT ACROSS THE WEST!*

Night Passage

Universal-International (August 1957); COLOR by Technicolor; FILMED in Technirama; RUNNING TIME: 90 min.

CAST: Grant McLaine, **James Stewart**; The Utica Kid, **Audie Murphy**; Whitey Harbin, **Dan Duryea**; Charlotte Drew (Charlie), **Dianne Foster**; Verna Kimball, **Elaine Stewart**; Joey Adams, **Brandon de Wilde**; Ben Kimball, **Jay C. Flippen**; Will Renner, **Herbert Anderson**; Concho, **Robert J. Wilke**; Jeff Kurth, **Hugh Beaumont**; Shotgun, **Jack Elam**; Howdy Sladen, **Tommy Cook**; Mr. Feeney, **Paul Fix**; Miss Vittles, **Olive Carey**; Tim Riley, **James Flavin**; Jubilee, **Donald Curtis**; Mrs. Feeney, **Ellen Corby**; Latigo, **John Day**; O'Brien, **Kenny Williams**; Trinidad, **Frank Chase**; Pick Gannon, **Harold Goodwin**; Shannon, **Harold Tommy Hart**; Dusty, **Jack C. Williams**; Torgeson, **Boyd Stockman**; Pache, **Henry Wills**; Roan, **Chuck Roberson**; Click, **Willard Willingham**; Rosa, **Polly Burson**; Linda, **Patsy Novak**; Leary, **Ted Mapes**; Pete, **Ben Weldon**

CREDITS: Director, **James Neilson**; Assistant Director, **Marshall Green**; Second Unit Director, **James C. Havens**; Producer, **Aaron Rosenberg**; Screenwriter, **Borden Chase**; Editor, **Sherman Todd**; Art Directors, **Alexander Golitzen** and **Robert Clatworthy**; Set Decorators, **Russell A. Gausman** and **Oliver Emert**; Cinematographer, **William Daniels**; Special Photography, **Clifford Stine**; Costumes, **Bill Thomas**; Makeup, **Bud Westmore**; Sound, **Leslie I. Carey** and **Frank H. Wilkinson**; Music Composer and Conductor, **Dimitri Tiomkin**; Technicolor Color Consultant, **William Fritzsche**

SONGS: "Follow the River" (Washington and Tiomkin)—sung by **James Stewart**, and "You Can't Get Far Without a Railroad" (Washington and Tiomkin)—sung by **James Stewart**

LOCATION FILMING: Durango and Silverton, Colorado; SOURCE: Novel, *Night Passage* by **Norman A. Fox**

STORY: Grant McLaine (James Stewart), former troubleshooter for the railroad, has been summoned by his former boss, Kimball (Jay C. Flippen), to deliver the payroll money to end of track. En route, he sees a young boy, Joey (Brandon de Wilde), being mistreated by Concho (Robert J. Wilke). Stewart intervenes and de Wilde is allowed to go on his way. Stewart accepts the responsibility of delivering the payroll money. Harbin (Dan Duryea), leader of an outlaw gang, is responsible for the rash of payroll robberies. Duryea has been receiving information from railroad employee Renner (Herbert

Anderson). Flippen and his wife, Verna (Elaine Stewart), have their railroad car attached to the train going to end of track. Flippen wants to make certain Stewart delivers the payroll. Years earlier he was sent to apprehend the Utica Kid (Audie Murphy) who was stealing horses from the railroad. Stewart let Murphy escape because Murphy was his brother. Because of his failure to bring Murphy in, Stewart lost his job. Murphy is now a member of Duryea's gang and the only member of the gang not afraid of Duryea. Stewart allows de Wilde to join him on the ride to end of track and finds that de Wilde ran away from the gang and wants to work for the railroad. Duryea and his gang hold up the train but are unable to find the money. Stewart put the money in a box containing de Wilde's lunch. Wilke avenges himself on Stewart by knocking him out. Murphy takes de Wilde to the outlaw hideout. Duryea takes Elaine Stewart as hostage to force Flippen to send him the payroll money. James Stewart catches up to the gang and Duryea allows him to join up. Charlotte (Diane Foster), Murphy's girl friend, also comes to the outlaw camp to tell Murphy about J. Stewart and finds that Murphy is not planning to stop his life of crime. James Stewart also tells Murphy that he's really working for the railroad. Anderson finds the outlaw camp and tells Duryea that J. Stewart was delivering the payroll. A gunfight begins. Murphy takes de Wilde and the payroll and leaves on horseback. James Stewart, with Foster and Elaine Stewart chase after

Murphy. Duryea and his gang chase after J. Stewart. Duryea pins down J. Stewart and the women at an abandoned ore mill. James Stewart is able to get Elaine Stewart safely away in an ore car but Foster refuses to leave J. Stewart. With the odds hopelessly against J. Stewart, Murphy decides to help his brother. In the gunfight, Duryea kills Murphy and James Stewart shoots Duryea. James Stewart gets the payroll money to end of track and gets his old job back. James Stewart and Foster walk away together.

NOTES AND COMMENTARY: Dianne Foster had fond remembrances of her two co-stars, James Stewart and Audie Murphy. Stewart had the tendency to keep to himself and Murphy was an open individual. About Stewart, Foster remembered that "he [Stewart] seemed to be more comfortable with his close people, the production staff." Foster commented that Murphy was "so easygoing outwardly, open and friendly with the crew and other actors, mischievous at times." Murphy liked to tell stories and to gamble. The actors would have card games set up, break for a scene and then pick up where they left off if they had the time. For the most part, during the filming of *Night Passage*, Murphy displayed a relaxed, easygoing personality but there was an instance when Murphy showed his temper. Foster said, "He unleashed it and wow! He had his own horse brought to the location. He was a big, beautiful, very well trained animal. The horse decided to act up one day. He

Night Passage (1957) scene card: Bob Wilke is stopped by James Stewart from taking Brandon de Wilde back to the outlaw camp.

wasn't doing what Audie wanted him to do. He [Murphy] got off of him and he was really annoyed and on a short fuse. He was jerking the horse around and he hauled back and he smacked the horse with all the strength he had on the side of the jaw with his fist. The horse hardly blinked. The horse weighed a thousand pounds. Audie was lucky that he didn't break his hand. He had a powerful punch but the horse had a harder head. He just did it. He was mad enough and just ... Pow! He [Murphy] was just wonderful to be around. I think everybody felt that way too. He had a sweetness to him that was very,

very winning, a smile that could charm everybody." Foster felt that is was a dream to work with Stewart and loved the idea of working with Murphy and said, "It was nice to be wanted by two such exciting men."

Dianne Foster made this observation about Dan Duryea, "He was such a softy and so sweet and so charming. Quiet, amazingly quiet except when he picked up some funny thing to do. He was a real cutup."

The cast and crew went on location in late summer. Dianne Foster could not remember the exact month. Shooting continued through the fall and into the first snow of winter. A lot of back projection shots were filmed in case some scenes would have to be filmed at the studio. This turned out to be an excellent idea. On the last day on location, the snow began coming down. There was the thought that the threatening weather would blow over and the decision was made to go to work. Foster commented, "When it [the snow] came, it came so fast. Blankets of snow dropped on top of us on top of that mountain." The crew worked hard and fast to load all the equipment. There was a race against time to have everything loaded before the roads became impassable. When everything was packed the cast and crew began to make the descent, visibility was greatly reduced. The vehicles were slipping and sliding all over the road. Foster added, "It was a nightmare ride. I don't know how the drivers were able to control those huge trucks but they did. They got us down safely but we prayed all the way because that's a sheer drop into those gorges." Close-ups and a few scenes that need the background projection footage were filmed at the studio.

Stuntwoman Polly Burson became an actress for this film. An unnamed actress hired to play one of the camp followers was displeased with her performance. James Stewart stepped in and said, "Well, give it [the part] to Polly then." So Burson played the part and did not have to be doubled in the fight scene with Ellen Corby. Polly Burson doubled Elaine Stewart as she made her escape in the ore car and Burson also doubled 13-year-old Brandon de Wilde. Robert Wilke chases de Wilde across a rocky hill and de Wilde is roped by his feet and his feet are jerked out from under him. Except it was Burson who was roped. Burson remarked, "I'm the one that stuck my head in the ground." Burson said de Wilde made this comment, "It's bad enough being doubled, but by a girl!"

The actors and the crewmembers that were active physically had to rest and breathe oxygen to regain their energy. The altitude at Silverton was 10,000 feet. The air was very thin and the actors and crewmembers were easily tired. There were trailers set up like hospitals with cots, oxygen tents and masks.

Harold Goodwin's name was misspelled as Herold Goodwin in the cast listings.

REVIEWS: "Sock western, taut, well made and sometimes fascinating western." *Variety* 5/15/57; "Expansive and exceedingly well done entertainment." *Western Movies*, Pitts.

SUMMATION: *Night Passage* is another good western for James Stewart. Although not up to the standards of his previous Universal-International westerns (*Winchester '73*, 1950; *Bend of the River*, 1952, and *The Far Country*, 1955) which were directed by Anthony Mann, nonetheless the film still keeps Stewart on the right western trail.

Stewart delivers a fine performance as a man trying to regain his self-respect, as well as playing the accordion and singing a couple of tunes. Also turning in good performances are Audie Murphy, Dianne Foster and especially Dan Duryea as a laughing, psychotic killer. Screenwriter Borden Chase allows for sufficient characterization in his action-filled script. James Neilson directs competently and William Daniels and Clifford Stine take advantage of the colorful scenic Colorado backgrounds.

THE STRANGEST KILLER WHO EVER STALKED THE WEST!
Now a whole town was waiting for him ... and
the name on the bullet might be his!

No Name on the Bullet

Universal-International (February 1959); EASTMAN COLOR by Pathé; FILMED in Cinemascope; RUNNING TIME: 77 min.

CAST: John Gant, **Audie Murphy**; Luke Canfield, **Charles Drake**; Anne Benson, **Joan Evans**; Roseanne Fraden, **Virginia Grey**; Lou Fraden, **Warren Stevens**; Asa Canfield, **R.G. Armstrong**; Buck Hastings, **Willis Bouchey**; Judge Benson, **Edgar Stehli**; Reeger, **Simon Scott**; Stricker, **Karl Swenson**; Pierce, **Whit Bissell**; Sid, **Charles Watts**; Chaffee, **John Alderson**; Harold Miller, **Jerry Paris**; Storekeeper, **Russ Bender**; Hugo Mott, **Jim Ryland**; Farmer, **Guy Wilkinson**; Charlie (chess player), **Hank Patterson**; Wilson (bank teller), **Harold Goodwin**

CREDITS: Director, **Jack Arnold**; Assistant Director, **John Sherwood**; Producers, **Howard Christie** and **Jack Arnold**; Story, **Howard Amacker**; Screenwriter, **Gene L. Coon**; Editor, **Frank Gross**; Art Director, **Alexander Golitzen** and **Robert E. Smith**; Set Decorators, **Russell A. Gausman** and **Theodore Driscoll**; Cinematographer, **Harold Lipstein**; Costumes, **Bill Thomas**; Hair Stylist, **Larry Germain**; Makeup, **Bud Westmore**; Sound, **Leslie I. Carey** and **Frank Wilkerson**; Music, **Herman Stein**; Music Supervisor, **Joseph Gershenson**

LOCATION FILMING: Los Angeles area, California

STORY: Notorious gunman John Gant (Audie Murphy) rides into Lordsburg. A number of the townspeople wonder if they are the targets for Murphy's guns. Only local physician Luke Canfield (Charles Drake) and his blacksmith father, Asa (R.G. Armstrong), are not worried about Murphy's presence in town. The strain of Murphy's presence is too much for some of the townspeople. Banker Pierce (Whit

No Name on the Bullet (1959) scene card: Audie Murphy shoots Charles Drake in the shoulder.

Bissell), because of some shady dealings, commits suicide. Lou Fraden (Warren Stevens) thinks that Murphy is after him because he stole another man's wife. When Stevens faces Murphy, Murphy breaks Stevens down, showing him to be a coward. Finally it becomes evident that Murphy's target is a former judge, Benson (Edgar Stehli). Stehli is a sick man with not many months left to live. Stehli's daughter, Anne (Joan Evans), pleads with Murphy not to kill her father. Evans tells Murphy that her father will not defend himself and Murphy will have to murder Stehli. Murphy tears

Evans' blouse and when Murphy goes to see Stehli, goads him into picking up a gun. Stehli discharges one shot prior to succumbing to a fatal heart attack. Drake, who has been sent by Evans to save her father's life, thinks Murphy shot Stehli. Armed only with a blacksmith's hammer, Drake advances toward Murphy who then shoots Drake in the shoulder. As Murphy proceeds to his horse, Drake throws his hammer that shatters Murphy's gun arm. Murphy leaves Lordsburg knowing that the loss of his gun arm will eventually mean his death.

NOTES AND COMMENTARY: Warren Stevens could not remember much about the picture. Stevens had memories of Virginia Grey and commented, "Virginia Grey, a lovely woman. I don't remember much about it [the picture] but I remember her [Grey]. I had been a fan of hers before that. I saw Virginia a couple of years ago, not working or anything. She seemed okay. We never worked together before or since."

No Name on the Bullet found its way to television in 1969 as an episode on *The Virginian* (NBC). The segment was titled "Stopover" with guest star Herb Jeffries.

REVIEWS: "The film moves slowly, building with a nice feeling of eerieness and paranoia that was a minor staple of 1950s filmmaking."

The Motion Picture Guide, Nash and Ross; Okay action melodrama." *Western Movies*, Pitts.

SUMMATION: *No Name on the Bullet* is a well-acted, well-directed and well-scripted psychological western drama. Audie Murphy is quite good as the quiet gunman. Matching him as the force of good is Charles Drake. Joan Evans, R.G. Armstrong, Edgar Stehli and Warren Stevens head an outstanding supporting cast. Gene L. Coon's screenplay allows for some good characterizations as well as a good measure of suspense. Director Jack Arnold, who had three previous credits helming superior action-filled westerns, turns out his best western film.

Terrific on T.V. ... now a riot in the movies!

Once Upon a Horse

ALTERNATE TITLE: **Hot Horse**; Universal-International (September 1958); FILMED in Cinemascope

CAST: Dan Casey, **Dan Rowan**; Doc Logan, **Dick Martin**; Miss Amity Babb, **Martha Hyer**; Granville Dix, **Leif Erickson**; Miss Dovey Barnes, **Nita Talbot**; Postmaster, **James Gleason**; Mr. Tharp, **John McGiver**; Bruno de Gruen, **David Burns**; Henry Dick Coryell, **Dick Ryan**; Ben, **Max Baer**; Beulah's brother, **Buddy Baer**; Milligan, **Steve Pendleton**; Engineer, **Sydney Chatton**; Justice of the Peace, **Sam Hearn**; Beulah, **Ingrid Goude**; Small Boy, **Ricky Kelman**; Fireman, **Joe Oakie**; Tom Keene, **Tom Keene**; Robert Livingston, **Robert Livingston**; Kermit Maynard, **Kermit Maynard**; Bob Steele, **Bob Steele**; Blacksmith, **Paul Anderson**; Old Man at Wedding, **Tom London**; Saloon Patron, **Tom Kennedy**

CREDITS: Director, Producer and Screenwriter, **Hal Kanter**; Assistant Director, **Frank Shaw**; Assistant to the Director, **Wm. Watson**; Assistant to the Producer, **Dona**

Holloway; Editor, **Milton Carruth**; Art Directors, **Alexander Golitzen** and **Robert Clatworthy**; Set Decorators, **Russell A. Gausman** and **William P. Tapp**; Cinematographer, **Arthur E. Arling**; Special Photography, **Clifford Stine**; Costumes, **Bill Thomas**; Makeup, **Bud Westmore**; Sound, **Leslie I. Carey** and **Corson Jowett**; Music, **Frank Skinner**; Music Supervisor, **Joseph Gershenson**; Choreographer, **Kenny Williams**

SONG: "Once Upon a Horse" (Livingston and Evans)—sung by **Martha Hyer and chorus**

LOCATION FILMING: Conejo Valley, California

SOURCE: Story, *Why Rustlers Never Win* by **Henry Gregor Felsen**

STORY: Two would-be badmen, Casey (Dan Rowan) and Logan (Dick Martin), decide to try one more crooked episode before going to Chicago to live an honest life. They decide to rustle cattle and sell them in Empty Cup. The cattle buyer is Amity Babb (Martha Hyer), who happens to own the cattle that Rowan and Martin are attempting to sell. Cattle prices are down and feed prices are up, so there are no buyers for the cattle. Attempts to abandon the cattle are thwarted by Sheriff Dix (Leif Erickson) and his posse. To obtain money, Rowan romances Hyer while Martin steals the money from the bank's safe. The boys are unable to spend the money when Erickson tells them that the only people with money in the town are the bank robbers. Rowan and Martin are finally jailed and they make a last attempt to

escape. Hyer makes an arrangement to free them if they will sign the cattle over to Hyer. The cattle prices are now up and Hyer stands to make a small fortune. Hyer prevents Rowan and Martin from leaving town because she wants to marry Rowan. A mass wedding is being held with all the single women and men getting married. But one man wants a rich woman and a ruckus starts.

NOTES AND COMMENTARY: Universal-International released 32 prints of two screen tests to their exchanges for private showings. These prints were designed to stimulate interest in some of the studio's new faces. This 25-minute package included the first screen test of comedy team Dan Rowan and Dick Martin. Universal-International re-released this film as *Hot Horse* in 1963. The *New York Times* neglected to review this film on its first release but caught it on its reissue.

The four veteran cowboys had ended their starring "B" western careers years earlier. Tom Keene ended his starring western career with a series for Monogram Pictures in 1942. Keene, billed as Richard Powers, did have the lead in the Republic Pictures serial *Desperadoes of the West* (1950) and a guest-starring appearance in Roy Rogers' *Trail of Robin Hood* (Republic, 1950). Robert Livingston, with the release of *The Laramie Trail* (Republic, 1944), moved into supporting roles in pictures until a couple of sexploitation leads in the mid–70s. Kermit Maynard starred in mountie and standard rangeland sagas for Ambassador Pictures with his last

Once Upon a Horse (1958) title card: (*left to right*) **James Gleason, Dan Rowan, Dick Martin and Martha Hyer.**

starring ventures released in 1937. Bob Steele moved into supporting roles with the conclusion of his PRC western series in 1946.

REVIEWS: "A scatter-blast of laughs in this farce western, does not have a uniform gait, but it has some funny lines and situations." *Variety*, 8/6/58; "The plot is episodic, allowing more space for jokes than story, but, considering the low budget, Kanter's trick effects work well enough." *The Western*, Hardy.

SUMMATION: *Once Upon a Horse* is a fairly amusing satirical western. The gags, mostly of the sight

variety, fly fast and furious with a good portion of them hitting the mark. To the film's detriment, the jokes begin to run of out steam in the latter half of the film. The comedy team of Dan Rowan and Dick Martin try their best and give bright and spirited performances. Martha Hyer effectively portrays the glamorous businesswoman who falls in love with Rowan. It was nice to see the cameo appearances of veteran western stars Tom Keene, Robert Livingston, Kermit Maynard and Bob Steele. These range riders give a welcome boost to the proceedings.

Men gave her everything but a good name!
That Woman Tacey and Clint, the Gambling Man ...
he was her only weakness ... she was his greatest strength!

One Desire

Universal-International (August 1955); PRINT by Technicolor; RUNNING TIME: 94 min.

CAST: Tacey Cromwell, **Anne Baxter**; Clint Saunders, **Rock Hudson**; Judith Watrous, **Julie Adams**; Senator Watrous, **Carl Benton Reid**; Seely, **Natalie Wood**; MacBain, **William Hopper**; Mrs. O'Dell, **Betty Garde**; Nuggett, **Barry Curtis**; Marjorie Huggins, **Adrienne Marden**; Flo, **Fay Marley**; Kate, **Vici Raaf**; Bea, **Lynn Millan**; Sam, **Smoki Whitfield**; Judge Congrin, **Howard Wright**; Mr. Hathaway, **Edward Earle**; Mr. Wellington, **William Forrest**; Wagon Driver, **Edmund Cobb**; Marshal, **Guy Wilkerson**; Jack, **Terry Frost**; Firemen, **Robert Hoy** and **John Daheim**; Policeman, **Mike Ragan**

CREDITS: Director, **Jerry Hopper**; Assistant Director, **Tom Shaw**; Producer, **Ross Hunter**; Screenwriters, **Lawrence Roman** and **Robert Blees**; Editor, **Milton Carruth**; Art Directors, **Alexander Golitzen** and **Carroll Clark**; Set Decorators, **Russell A. Gausman** and **John P. Austin**; Cinematographer, **Maury Gertsman**; Costumes, **Bill Thomas**; Hair Stylist, **Joan St. Oegger**; Makeup, **Bud Westmore**; Sound, **Leslie I. Carey** and **Glenn E. Anderson**; Music, **Frank Skinner**; Music Supervisor, **Joseph Gershenson**; Technicolor Color Consultant, **William Fritzsche**

SOURCE: Novel, *Tacey Cromwell* by **Conrad Richter**

STORY: Running away from home, young Nugget (Barry Curtis) comes to The White Palace to find his older brother, gambler Clint Saunders (Rock Hudson). Hudson, who is having a romantic fling with part-owner Anne Baxter, is planning to go to Colorado to take advantage of a new silver strike. Hudson decides to take Curtis with him when Baxter tells Hudson she will come along to care for Curtis. As the trio relocates, Baxter attempts to become a respectable individual in the community. Hudson forsakes gambling to enter the banking business, especially since bank owner Watrous' (Carl Benton Reid) daughter is the lovely Judith (Julie Adams). A mining accident leaves Seely (Natalie Wood) an orphan and Baxter begins taking care of her. Adams wants Hudson for herself and, obtaining information about Baxter's tawdry past, is able to gain custody of Curtis and Wood. Baxter decides to return to The White Palace. Hudson tries to locate Baxter but Hudson is told that Baxter is not there. To make a home for the children, Hudson marries Adams. Unable to take the tyrannical rule of Adams, Wood runs away. Because Baxter maintained correspondence with her former neighbor Mrs. O'Dell (Betty Garde), Wood knows where Baxter is and goes to her. Baxter persuades Wood to let her take her home. Before Baxter can leave town, she is confronted by Adams and finds she was the cause of her losing the children and leaving town. Baxter decides to stay and open a gambling emporium across the street from Adams' home. Hudson and Baxter realize they still love each other but no more can come of their love because of Hudson's marriage to Adams. Realizing Hudson is still in love with Baxter,

Adams goes into a rage and knocks over a lamp that causes the draperies in her bedroom to catch fire. Adams is trapped and perishes in the flames. Sparks from the fire also destroy Baxter's gambling house. Hudson, Wood and Curtis rejoin Baxter to begin a new life together.

NOTES AND COMMENTARY: The film had working titles of *Tacey Cromwell* and *Tacey* before Universal-International decided on *One Desire*.

The scene was being filmed in which Rock Hudson would attempt to rescue Julie Adams from a burning room. Robert Hoy remembered,

One Desire (1955) scene card: Anne Baxter and Rock Hudson in a romantic moment.

"The special effects got out of control. And the set burned, caught on fire, the draperies. Then the whole stage caught on fire and somebody said, 'Open the barn doors.' Those are the big rolling doors on the stage. The first assistant director, a guy named Tom Shaw yelled. 'Nobody open the goddamn doors.' Had they done that, there would have been a rush of air and it would have been a blast furnace. Johnny Dahein, who played the other fireman with me, we grabbed Natalie [Wood]. She was fourteen or fifteen. I forget how old she was. We got her off that stage. The whole stage burnt to the ground on the show." The studio's fire department subdued the flames. Damage to the stage was estimated at several thousand dollars.

REVIEWS: "A plodding old-fashioned soap opera." *New York Times*, 9/3/55; "Ross Hunter's Technicolor production ensures that audiences got their money's worth in the way of gloss." *The Universal Story*, Hirschhorn.

SUMMATION: Despite all the production values lavished on *One Desire*, the result is only an average soap opera in a western setting. Anne Baxter gives it her all with a bravura performance as a woman trying to gain respectability. Rock Hudson is creditable as a selfish individual who finally realizes that riches only is not the way to true happiness. Hampered by an all too predictable script and Julie Adams' inability to pull off the part of a conniving, vindictive woman, director Jerry Hopper is unable to raise the film to anywhere above average. Betty Garde stands out among the effective supporting cast.

THIS WAS THE NIGHT OF THE TOMAHAWK ...
A Tattered Troupe of Heroes Who
Stemmed the Tide of Violent Redmen ...

Pillars of the Sky

ALTERNATE TITLE: *The Tomahawk and the Cross*; Universal-International (October 1956); PRINT by Technicolor; FILMED in Cinemascope; RUNNING TIME: 95 min.

CAST: First Sergeant Emmett Bell, **Jeff Chandler**; Calla Gaxton, **Dorothy Malone**; Doctor Joseph Holden, **Ward Bond**; Captain Tom Gaxton, **Keith Andes**; Sergeant Lloyd Carracart, **Lee Marvin**; Timothy, **Sydney Chaplin**; Colonel Edson Stedlow, **Willis Bouchey**; Kamiakin, **Michael Ansara**; Mrs. Anne Avery, **Olive Carey**; Sergeant Dutch Williams, **Charles Horvath**; Malachi, **Orlando Rodriguez**; Lieutenant Winston, **Glen Kramer**; Lieutenant Hammond, **Floyd Simmons**; Jacob, **Pat Hogan**; Lucas, **Felix Noriego**; Morgan, **Paul Smith**; Waco, **Martin Milner**;

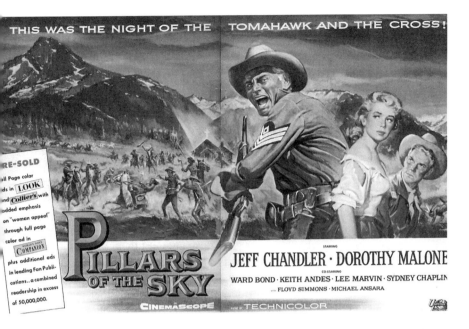

Pillars of the Sky (1956): Jeff Chandler, Dorothy Malone and Keith Andes.

Albie, **Robert Ellis**; Music, **Ralph J. Votrian**; Major Donahue, **Walter Coy**; Sgt. Major Frenchy Desmonds, **Alberto Morin**; Isaiah, **Richard Hale**; Zachariah, **Frank DeKova**; Captain Fanning, **Terry Wilson**; Major Randall, **Philip Kieffer**; Elijah, **Gilbert Conner**

CREDITS: Director, **George Marshall**; Assistant Director, **Marshall Green**; Producer, **Robert Arthur**; Screenwriter, **Sam Rolfe**; Editor, **Milton Carruth**; Art Directors, **Alexander Golitzen** and **Bill Newberry**; Set Decorators, **Russell A. Gausman** and **Oliver Emert**; Cinematographer, **Harold Lipstein**; Costumes, **Rosemary Odell**; Hair Stylist, **Joan St. Oegger**; Makeup, **Bud Westmore**; Sound, **Leslie I. Carey** and **Frank H. Wilkinson**; Music Supervisor, **Joseph**

Gershenson; Technicolor Color Consultant, **William Fritzsche**

LOCATION FILMING: LaGrande area, Oregon

SOURCE: Novel, *Frontier Fury* by **Will Henry**

STORY: Emmett Bell (Jeff Chandler) and his Indian police return from their patrol to find new commanding officer Colonel Stedlow (Willis Bouchey) has orders to build a road and a fort on Indian lands. Led by Chief Kamiakin (Michael Ansara), the Indian tribes unite to fight this threat to the Indian way of life. Missionary Joseph Holden (Ward Bond) Ward Bond brings both sides together to prevent a war but is not successful. Ansara holds two women as hostages to dissuade the cavalry to move onto

Indian lands. Chandler, Bond and two Indian policemen rescue the women. One turns out to be Calla Gaxton (Dorothy Malone), wife of Captain Gaxton (Keith Andes). Malone came to Oregon to be with Chandler, the man she loves. Ansara leads an Indian attack that wipes out most of the cavalry. The cavalry is able to reach temporary safety on the top of a butte. Because of the actions of Chandler and Andes during the skirmish, Malone realizes Andes is the man who really loves her. During the cover of night, the cavalry is able to leave the butte and reach Bond's mission house. Again, Ansara's forces attack and Bond rides out to talk with Ansara and the other chiefs. Ansara shoots Bond before he can plead his case. Chandler had followed Bond and tells the chiefs that Bond brought God into their lives. As Chandler is taking Bond's body back to the mission house, Ansara's attempt to kill Chandler is thwarted by Chief Zachariah (Frank DeKova). The war is ended and Chandler decides to carry on the work that Bond started.

NOTES AND COMMENTARY: Keith Andes vividly remembered a scene with Jeff Chandler. After a couple of rehearsals, everyone was ready to film the scene. Andes commented, "Mr. Marshall [the director] says, 'Okay, let's shoot the son of a bitch.' He was a gruff old guy. So we got ready, all the Indians and the wagons and all the crap you got to get going. Here we come. The wagons are going up hill, the horses are running and the Indians are yelling and Chandler and I are riding and shooting back. We ride up into the scene where we're supposed to get off. We get off. Now this is all in one shot. We have this conversation. Then he goes his way and I go mine. Marshall yells, 'Cut!' And I heard him say, 'Jesus Christ, Andes.' I thought, 'What the hell's the matter?' I look around and everybody's looking at me. I have a cigarette in my mouth. A cork-tipped cigarette. I could have crawled under a rock. Obviously we had to do it all over again. Cost them, in those days, another ten thousand dollars. Needless to say I checked my mouth before we went into another scene to see if I was smoking or not. Isn't that awful? What a habit-forming thing that is."

Some of the Indians were paid off on a Friday when the Pendleton Rodeo was going on and they did not show up for work on Monday. The scene required six Indians and only five stuntmen were available. Robert Hoy knew that stuntwoman Polly Burson was on the set and he recruited her. Hoy remembers, "I'm the first one to put a woman in as a man." Hoy knew Burson would have a wig on and she could horseback or trick ride so Burson rode with them. Burson commented, "I must have been a chief because I had pants and a top on. I said I'd go without a bottom but not a top. It was a fun show."

Robert Hoy and Henry Wills were in Indian outfits when they came to work and were told they hadn't shown up at Wardrobe. Hoy and Wills were told that they were supposed to be in the cavalry and work with caissons. This would require Castilian riding where one horse is ridden and a second horse is at the rider's right side that would be controlled by the rider's hand. The horses would pull a cannon. Hoy and Wills looked at each other and knew they were in trouble. All the Hollywood horses that were used to pull the cannon had been taken and local horses would have to be used. They had one wreck in the barnyard while trying to get out with the local horses. The run-through was fine and the scene was ready to be shot. Hoy remembered the scene, "So with this horse on my right, the one I'm hand-riding throws a fit, screams, reaches up over the traces, hits the ground and the horses start to run. Here we come. I had turned around, 'Henry, I'm quitting them.' Meaning I'm going to make a jump for it. We're going to get hurt. And I know he's [Wills] going to quit. Then we look down and see this young actor sitting on his horse, just frozen. This kid had stopped by the settler's ammunition box and cannon. The horse he was on was an old saddle falling-horse. The horse saw us coming and jumped up in the air over the ammunition box and fell in the cannon with the actor on top of him. Here we come. Coming right at this cannon. These horses hit it and my horse leaped up into the air. I had one foot on the cannon wheel and had each horse like that [Hoy was trying to hold both horses from coming down on the actor] and had

Henry's horse on top of us. We yelled, 'Someone get that actor out of there.' So I'm holding these horses. Some wrangler, thank God, pulled this actor out and all four horses fell in on top of Brownie [the actor's horse]. Brownie was an old falling-horse. Once Brownie was down, he just lay there. It's a wonder he didn't get hurt. But that was very close."

In another scene, an attempt was made to wreck a wagon about five times. John Hudson was driving the team and Polly Burson was doubling Dorothy Malone. The wagon was supposed to be rigged by cables so when the wagon reached a certain spot, the wagon would turn over. The wagon reached the spot and snapped but did not turn over. Hudson saw the wagon wasn't going to turn over and decided to stay but decided it would be best to push Burson off the wagon and out of harm's way. Burson remembered, "As it happened I wasn't prepared and I landed too much on my head." Burson was knocked out and Assistant Director Marshall Green wanted Robert Hoy to get in woman's clothes. Hoy commented, "I said no because I knew when Polly woke up and sees what happened, she'd be one mad lady." Burson continues, "I came to about the time I heard Marsh say that. I said, 'The Hell he will. If the thing ever works I can do it.' The darned thing didn't work three different times."

In the film, Robert Hoy was hurt doing a stunt. No one knew about Hoy's injury but Polly Burson.

Burson would come to Hoy's room and rub his back during the weekend. On Monday Hoy was ready to come back to work. Burson said, "Hoy had gotten hurt. I remember going to his room and rubbing him. We [stunt people] kind of had to watch out for each other."

REVIEWS: "Good cavalry-versus-Indians feature." *Variety*, 8/8/56; "It's a pleasure to watch a modest soldier vs. Indian picture shape into something respectable." *New York Times*, 10/13/56.

SUMMATION: *Pillars of the Sky* is a stirring and moving western with a religious theme. Jeff Chandler gives a powerful performance as a man who finally realizes his calling to serve God. Dorothy Malone, Ward Bond, Keith Andes, Sydney Chaplin and Willis Bouchey also contribute fine performances. Utilizing the scenic grandeur of the Oregon landscape, director George Marshall gives us a most unusual and satisfying motion picture.

Bold adventure in a wondrous era of flame and fury ...
With fighting men matching sabres for a beauty's lips!

Pirates of Monterey

Universal-International (December 1947); COLOR by Technicolor; RUNNING TIME: 77½ min.

CAST: Marguerita, **Maria Montez**; Phillip Kent, **Rod Cameron**; Pio, **Mikhail Rasumny**; Lt. Carlos Ortega, **Phillip Reed**; Major De Roja, **Gilbert Roland**; Senorita de Sola, **Gale Sondergard**; Filomena, **Tamara Shayne**; Governor, **Robert Warwick**; Sgt. Gomara, **Michael Raffetto**; Manuel, **Neyle Morrow**; Captain Cordova, **Victor Varconi**; Juan, **Charles Waggenheim**; Caretta Man, **Chris-Pin Martin**; Doctor, **Joe Bernard**; Pirate, **George J. Lewis**

CREDITS: Director, **Alfred Werker**; Assistant Director, **William Holland**; Executive Producer, **Joe Gershenson**; Producer, **Paul Malvern**; Story, **Edward T. Lowe** and **Bradford Ropes**; Screenwriters, **Sam Hellman** and **Margaret Buell Wilder**; Editor, **Russell Schoengarth**; Art Directors, **Jack Otterson** and **Richard H. Riedel**; Set Decorators, **Russell A. Gausman** and **Leigh Smith**; Cinematographers, **Hal Mohr**, **W. Howard Greene** and **Harry Hallenberger**; Costumes for Maria Montez, **Travis Banton**; Gown Supervisor, **Vera West**; Hair Stylist, **Carmen Dirigo**; Makeup, **Jack P. Pierce**; Sound, **Bernard B. Brown** and **Charles Carroll**; Music, **Milton Rosen**; Technicolor Color Director, **Natalie Kalmus**; Assistant Color Director, **William Fritzsche**

SONG: "Song of the Ladies Man" (Brooks)—sung by **Mikhail**

Pirates of Monterey (1947) scene card: Maria Montez and Rod Cameron realize they cannot live without each other.

Rasumny; LOCATION FILMING: Bronson Canyon, California

STORY: Phillip Kent (Rod Cameron) and Pio (Mikhail Rasumny) are on a secret mission to deliver new rifles to the governor of California. En route, they meet Marguerita (Maria Montez) and Filomena (Tamara Shayne). Cameron and Montez fall in love but when Montez leaves mysteriously, Cameron thinks she may be a spy. Cameron's caravan is ambushed on the final leg of the journey to Monterey but manages to escape to safety. In Monterey, Cameron is reunited with his old friend, Ortega (Phillip Reed), who is engaged to Montez. Cameron and Montez are willing to sacrifice

their love for their friendship of Reed. Senorita de Sola (Gale Sondergard) sends Montez after Cameron when he decides to leave Monterey. Cameron and Montez are captured by the pirates and find that Major De Roja (Gilbert Roland), a major in the Mexican army, is behind the plot to seize California from Mexico. Reed, learning of Cameron and Montez' love for each other, rides after Cameron in a jealous rage. Reed is also captured by the pirates. Rasumny discovers the plot and tells the governor (Robert Warwick). Meanwhile, Cameron and Reed are trying to fight their way free. Rasumny brings the troops to defeat the pirates. Cameron dispatches Roland in a sword fight and then marries Montez.

NOTES AND COMMENTARY: The ironies of Hollywood! Two years previously, Maria Montez turned down the lead for *Frontier Gal* (Universal, 1945). Some reasons given were that Montez no longer wanted to make films with co-stars named Jon Hall or Rod Cameron and she didn't relish the prospects of being cast as a spitfire. Yvonne De Carlo was given the lead in *Frontier Gal* and from there her stock was boosted at Universal and she soon replaced Montez as the studio's "Queen of Technicolor."

Pirates of Monterey was Montez' final film for Universal. With this film, Montez had reached the end of her contract. Montez' supporters said she decided not to renew in favor of freelancing. Other sources state Universal was still cleaning house of those contract players they felt would not enhance the new image the studio was trying to develop.

REVIEWS: "Escapist film, hot box office prospect." *Hollywood Reporter*, 11/12/47; "A beautiful Technicolor look to bolster its sagging screenplay." *The Motion Picture Guide*, Nash and Ross.

SUMMATION: This is a fair swashbuckling western of Old California partially saved by a rousing finale. The principals acquit themselves adequately with the script they were handed. The story is a bit too familiar. The hand-me-down screenplay needed more punch, more action than that was delivered. The most interesting scene has Gilbert Roland allowing his younger brother to be shot down in a jail-break attempt to cover up his (Roland's) activities in a plot against Mexico. If there had been more scenes of this caliber, we would have had a much better film.

ONLY A POSSE FROM HELL COULD STOP
THE GUN-MAD SPAWN OF THE DEVIL
FROM THE RUTHLESS TEARING APART OF THE WHOLE SOUTHWEST!

Posse from Hell

Universal-International (May 1961); EASTMAN COLOR by Pathé; RUNNING TIME: 89 min.

CAST: Banner Cole, **Audie Murphy**; Seymour Kern, **John Saxon**; Helen Caldwell, **Zohra Lampert**; Crip, **Vic Morrow**; Captain Brown, **Robert Keith**; Johnny Caddo, **Rudolph Acosta**; Uncle Billy Caldwell, **Royal Dano**; Burt Hogan, **Frank Overton**; Benson, **James Bell**; Jack Wiley, **Paul Carr**; Marshal Webb, **Ward Ramsey**; Leo, **Lee Van Cleef**; Larson, **Ray Teal**; Doctor Welles, **Forrest Taylor**; Hash, **Charles Horvath**; Russell, **Harry**

Lauter; Chunk, **Henry Wills**; Luke Gorman, **Stuart Randall**; Burl Hogan, **Allan Lane**; Townsmen, **Walter Reed**, **Kenneth MacDonald**, **Rand Brooks** and **Don C. Harvey**; Undertaker, **I. Stanford Jolley**; Livery Stable Owner, **Ralph Moody**; Cowhand, **Steve Darrell**; Brash Town Youngster, **Steve Terrell**

CREDITS: Director, **Herbert Coleman**; Assistant Director, **Ray Gosnell, Jr.**; Producer, **Gordon Kay**; Associate Producer, **Willard Willingham**; Executive Producer, **Edward Muhl**; Screenwriter, **Clair Huffaker**; Editor, **Frederic Knudt**-son; Art Directors, **Alexander Golitzen** and **Alfred Sweeney**; Set Decorator, **Oliver Emert**; Cinematographer, **Clifford Stine**; Hair Stylist, **Larry Germain**; Makeup, **Bud Westmore**; Sound, **Waldon O. Watson** and **Joe Lapis**; Music Supervisor, **Joseph Gershenson**

LOCATION FILMING: Lone Pine and the 20th Century–Fox Ranch (near Los Angeles), California

SOURCE: Novel, *Posse from Hell* by **Clair Huffaker**

STORY: Four desperadoes, led by Crip (Vic Morrow), ride into Paradise and take over the town. In one

Posse from Hell (1961) scene card: The posse listens to James Bell before chasing the outlaw gang—Audie Murphy (white shirt), Royal Dano (right of Murphy), Frank Overton (center), Robert Keith (third from right), and John Saxon (far right); right border shows Murphy and Saxon.

night, four townspeople are murdered, Marshal Webb (Ward Ramsey) is mortally wounded, the bank robbed, and a woman, Helen Caldwell (Zohra Lampert), abducted. The next day Banner Cole (Audie Murphy) rides into town to accept the job as Ramsey's deputy. Ramsey's last words to Murphy are to extract justice, not vengeance, by adhering to the law. Murphy is pressured into riding with a posse made up with men for whom Murphy has only contempt. Lampert is found abandoned after having been brutally raped by the killers. Murphy has Lampert's uncle, Billy Caldwell (Royal Dano), take Lampert back to town. Lampert does not want to go back to Paradise because she knows she will be ostracized by the townspeople. As the chase continues, Murphy finds himself with two posse members, Kern (John Saxon), an easterner who initially joined the posse to protect the interests of the bank, and Caddo (Rudolfo Acosta), who believes it is his duty to ride with the posse. Two of the outlaw gang have been killed in battles with Murphy and the posse. Acosta is killed when the desperadoes set up an ambush. Morrow and his one remaining henchman are riding back to Paradise. It is up to Murphy and Saxon to stop them. Murphy finds that Lampert and Dano went to their cabin outside of town instead of into Paradise. Morrow kills Dano and starts an attack on Murphy and Lampert in the cabin. Saxon exchanges shots with the henchman Hash (Charles Horvath), Saxon's shot

wounding Horvath and Horvath's shots killing Saxon's horse. The horse collapses, falling on Saxon's leg and breaking it. Horvath breaks into the cabin and is shot by Lampert. Murphy kills Morrow and then carries Saxon into town. The townspeople ask Murphy to be their new marshal. Because of Lampert and other worthwhile citizens, Murphy will accept the offer.

NOTES AND COMMENTARY: John Saxon commented on his role as Seymour Kern, "I liked that role a lot. Because it was something I felt I could identify with. I'm from New York and the character was supposed to be a city slicker who found himself in the circumstances of the Old West with gun-shooting and all that. He was discovering his capacity to do things that he didn't think he could do. He could shoot people and ride horses and stuff. It had both aspects, a kind of humanness, in the sense of rising to the occasion of something like courage and bravery."

The rattlesnake scene brought back memories to John Saxon, "We did have a snake. There was a rattlesnake out there. I don't mean one brought by a wrangler. I remember, one day, right in those rocks where we were shooting. A guy named Bill Donnelly, a prop man, suddenly discovered a snake under a rock. He collared it and didn't want to shoot it."

John Saxon recalled a story about Audie Murphy, "I remember hearing the story about Audie before I met him, Hugh O'Brian once liked to think, I guess, he was a fast draw. He put in a challenge; I think, in *The Hollywood Reporter*, a thousand dollars for who could draw the fastest. Or Audie said, 'Let's make it two thousand five hundred and use real bullets.'"

Producer Gordon Kay told author Boyd Magers that Zohra Lampert was a method actress. Lampert played around with her line deliveries, which threw Audie Murphy off in their scenes together. Initially Murphy did not know what to do with her. It has been reported that Murphy had a quiet conversation with Lampert, which cured her of these tendencies.

REVIEWS: "Stunning photography, strong characterizations, and well-paced action keep the inconsistencies of the plot in the background." *The Motion Picture Guide*, Nash and Ross; "The customers paid to see Murphy in action and they were more or less satisfied." *The Universal Story*, Hirschhorn.

SUMMATION: *Posse from Hell* is a good, although violent, western film featuring villains that have no redeeming characteristics and an off-camera rape incident. Audie Murphy and co-star John Saxon deliver good performances. Murphy plays a loner who finally realizes that there are worthwhile things in life. Saxon's character discovers what it takes to make a man, a man. Zohra Lampert is adequate as a woman who has to learn to live with the aftermath of rape. Rudolph Acosta chips in with a fine performance as a man scorned by the townspeople but more of man than his detractors. Director Herbert Coleman and screenwriter Clair Huffaker's script focuses primarily on Murphy and Saxon with good results.

A WOMAN TOO FREE WITH HER KISSES!
AND 4 MEN TOO FAST WITH THEIR GUNS!
...Each of them ready to buy her love for the price of the others' lives!

Quantez

Universal-International (October 1957); EASTMAN COLOR by Pathé; FILMED in Cinemascope; RUNNING TIME: 80 min.

CAST: Gentry/John Coventry, **Fred MacMurray**; Chaney, **Dorothy Malone**; Minstrel, **James Barton**; Gato, **Sydney Chaplin**; Teach, **John Gavin**; Heller, **John Larch**; Delgadito, **Michael Ansara**

CREDITS: Director, **Harry Keller**; Assistant Director, **George Lollier**; Producer, **Gordon Kay**; Story, **Anne Edwards** and **R. Wright Campbell**; Screenwriter, **R. Wright Campbell**; Editor, **Fred MacDowell**; Art Directors, **Alexander Golitzen** and **Alfred Ybarra**; Set Decorators, **Russell A. Gausman** and **Oliver Emert**; Cinematographer,

THEY RODE TO QUANTEZ TOWN...
half-way to freedom
but all the way to Hell!

QUANTEZ

CINEMASCOPE in *Eastman* COLOR

A Universal International Picture starring

Fred MacMURRAY · Dorothy MALONE · James BARTON

CO STARRING
SYDNEY CHAPLIN · JOHN GAVIN · JOHN LARCH

Quantez (1957) title card: Dorothy Malone and (*right, top to bottom*) Fred Mac-
Murray, Sydney Chaplin, John Gavin, and John Larch.

Carl E. Guthrie; Costumes, **Rose-mary Odell**; Hair Stylist, **Joan St. Oegger**; Makeup, **Bud Westmore**; Sound, **Leslie I. Carey** and **Corson Jowett**; Music, **Herman Stein**; Music Supervisor, **Joseph Gershenson**

SONGS: "The Lonely One" (Herbert and Hughes)—sung by **James Barton**; "True Love" (Herbert and Hughes)—sung by **Dorothy Malone**

STORY: Eluding a posse, gang leader Heller (John Larch) leads his group to Quantez, a town which turns out to be completely deserted. Larch's group consists of aging gunman Gentry (Fred MacMurray), young Teach (John Gavin), Indian-like Gato (Sydney Chaplin) and Larch's woman, Chaney (Dorothy Malone). Not being able to change horses, the group has to stay in Quantez overnight. Jealousy over Malone erupts with Gavin falling in love with her. Malone, who no longer wants to stay with Larch, also makes plays for Chaplin and Mac-Murray. Chaplin meets Indian chief Delgadito (Michael Ansara) and finds that the group will not be harmed if they leave before dawn.

Chaplin doesn't pass this information along since he wants the group killed. Chaplin plans to split the bank money with the Indians. As the tension mounts between the group members, a wandering minstrel (James Barton) comes to Quantez. Needing a horse, Larch plans to kill Barton but MacMurray allows Barton to get away. Barton recognized MacMurray as a notorious gunman, a fact not known by the rest of the group. In the morning, Larch tries to get Gavin to throw in with him to kill MacMurray and Chaplin. Gavin tells MacMurray about Larch's offer. This precipitates a gunfight in which MacMurray shoots Larch. Ansara and his Indians attack. Not trusting Chaplin, MacMurray sends Chaplin to his Indian friends and to his death. MacMurray, Malone and Gavin make a run for it with the Indians in pursuit. MacMurray sacrifices his life enabling Malone and Gavin to make a new start for themselves.

NOTES AND COMMENTARY: Again the song "True Love" can be heard in a Universal-International western. "True Love" was used in *Gunsmoke* (Universal-International, 1953), *Law and Order* (Universal-International, 1953) and *Dawn at Socorro* (Universal-International, 1954).

Producer Gordon Kay told author Boyd Magers that Universal was very high on making this film. The studio felt *Quantez* had a Shakespearean quality to it. Kay did agree that the film did not turn out very well. Gordon Kay brought director Harry Keller over from Republic Pictures. Kay and Keller had worked together on many Allan "Rocky" Lane films at Republic. Billed as Minstrel, James Barton clearly identifies himself as "Puritan."

REVIEWS: "This is a tedious and routine western, suffering from a repetitiveness in both scene and dialogue." *The Motion Picture Guide*, Nash and Ross; "An oddly listless film." *The Western*, Hardy.

SUMMATION: *Quantez* is an overly talkative western, which settles in around the average mark. Fred MacMurray, Dorothy Malone, James Barton and the rest of the cast try their best but the script clearly lets them down. Screenwriter R. Wright Campbell certainly tries his best but a plethora of words alone clearly doesn't elevate a film to classic or even above average status. Harry Keller, who cut his directorial teeth on Republic westerns and melodramas, handles nicely the opening and closing sequences, which stress action, but he is clearly out of his element in the dramatic sequences, which unfortunately occupy most of the story.

THE WILD SIERRAS THUNDER TO THE LAST GREAT GOLD MINE WARS!
For a woman's love he rode the lawless trail of the hunted!

The Raiders

ALTERNATE TITLE: *Riders of Vengeance*; Universal-International (November, 1952); COLOR by Technicolor; RUNNING TIME: 80 min.

CAST: Jan Morrell, **Richard Conte**; Elena Ortega, **Viveca Lindfors**; Elizabeth Ainsworth, **Barbara Britton**; Hank Purvis, **Hugh O'Brian**; Felipe Ortega, **Richard Martin**; Marty Smith, **Palmer Lee**; Frank Morrell, **William Reynolds**; Marshal Bill Henderson, **William Bishop**; Thomas Ainsworth, **Morris Ankrum**; Dick Logan, **Dennis Weaver**; Mary Morrell, **Margaret Field**; Welch, **John Kellogg**; Pete Robbins, **Lane Bradford**; Clark Leftus, **Riley Hill**; Juan Castillo, **Neyle Morrow**; Ramon Castillo, **Carlos Rivero**; Vicente, **George J. Lewis**; John Cummings, **Francis McDonald**

CREDITS: Director, **Lesley Selander**; Producer, **William Alland**; Story, **Lyn Crost Kennedy**; Screenwriters, **Polly James** and **Lillie Hayward**; Editor, **Paul Weatherwax**; Art Directors, **Bernard Herzbrun** and **Richard Riedel**; Set Decorators, **Russell A. Gausman** and **John Austin**; Cinematographer, **Carl Guthrie**; Costumes, **Bill Thomas**; Sound, **Leslie I. Carey** and **Glenn E. Anderson**; Music, **Joseph Gershenson**; Technicolor Color Consultant, **William Fritzsche**

STORY: Thomas Ainsworth (Morris Ankrum), leader of a land-grab scheme, is against statehood for California. Ankrum's men raid Morrell's (Richard Conte) cabin and kill his wife, Mary (Margaret Field), and his brother, Frank (William Reynolds). Conte swears vengeance and joins up with Ortego (Richard Martin) and other victims of Ankrum's ruthlessness. Conte and Martin lead their men on Ankrum, hoping to bankrupt him. Conte learns the identity of the men who murdered his wife and brother. Elena Ortega (Viveca Lindfors), Martin's sister, loves Conte and fails to stop him for exacting vengeance on the killers. Conte attempts to force Ankrum to write a confession but instead has to kill Ankrum in self-defense. Conte is arrested and found guilty. Before the execution can be carried out, California becomes a state and Conte is granted amnesty. Conte and Lindfors start a new life together.

NOTES AND COMMENTARY: The working title for the film was *The Riding Kid*.

Palmer Lee would soon receive billing as Gregg Palmer. Gregg Palmer remembered that *The Raiders* was filmed on the back lot of Universal. Palmer added, "That was before all the hotels. Now days we have to go to Kanab, Utah; Moab, Utah; Virginia; Arizona. They started to move away from Bell Ranch and Iverson's Ranch."

The Raiders (1952) scene card: *(left to right)* an unidentified actor, Neyle Morrow, Richard Martin, Richard Conte, and Palmer Lee.

The cast listing of *The Raiders* in one of the web sites includes Harry Carey, Jr., as Cheyenne Haney. *The Hollywood Reporter*, *Film Daily Yearbook of Motion Pictures* or the *New York Times* does not support this. Carey also states that he did not appear in this film but one with the same title which was released by Universal in 1964.

REVIEWS: "A fine, fast-moving western of the gold rush days." *Hollywood Reporter*, 10/8/52; "By handling a battered theme with a tidy minimum of nonsense, *The Raiders* emerges as an unstartling but rather respectable adventure drama of Old California." *New York Times*, 12/13/52.

SUMMATION: This is the only Universal-International western that I have not been able to view. I have seen seven favorable reviews and no negative ones. The reviewers liked the overall acting of the cast, especially the performances of Richard Conte, Viveca Lindfors, Barbara Britton, Hugh O'Brian, Richard Martin and William Bishop. Lesley Selander's direction was rated topnotch with his ability to keep the movie briskly paced.

THE STORY OF JEFF HARDER WHO BLAZED THE RECKLESS
TRAIL FOR THE IRON HORSE ACROSS THE WIDE FRONTIER!

Rails into Laramie

Universal-International (April 1954); COLOR by Technicolor; RUNNING TIME: 81 min.

CAST: Jefferson Harder, **John Payne**; Lou Carter, **Mari Blanchard**; Jim Shanessy, **Dan Duryea**; Helen Shanessy, **Joyce MacKenzie**; Lee Graham, **Barton MacLane**; Mayor Frank Logan, **Ralph Dumke**; Judge Pierce, **Harry Shannon**; Orrie Sommers, **James Griffith**; Ace Winton, **Lee Van Cleef**; Con Winton, **Myron Healey**; Pike Murphy, **Charles Horvath**; Grimes, **George Chandler**; Telegraph Operator, **Douglas Kennedy**; Higby, **Alexander Campbell**; Saloon Owner, **Kenneth MacDonald**; Saloon Patron, **Eddie Parker**; General Auger, **Stephen Chase**; Bartender, **Rex Lease**; Card Player, **John Harmon**; Stable Owner, **Forrest Taylor**; Railroad Worker, **Rusty Westcoatt**; Tough, **Dale Van Sickel**

CREDITS: Director, **Jesse Hibbs**; Assistant Director, **Tom Shaw**; Producer, **Ted Richmond**; Screenwriters, **D.D. Beauchamp** and **Joseph Hoffman**; Editor, **Ted J. Kent**; Art Directors, **Bernard Herzbrun** and **Robert Clatworthy**; Set Decorators, **Russell A. Gausman** and **Julia Heron**; Cinematographer, **Maury Gertsman**; Costumes, **Bill Thomas**; Hair Stylist, **Joan St. Oegger**; Makeup, **Bud Westmore**; Sound, **Leslie I. Carey** and **Richard De**

Weese; Music, **Joseph Gershenson**; Technicolor Color Consultant, **William Fritzsche**

SONG: "Laramie" (Herbert and Hughes)—sung by **Rex Allen**

LOCATION FILMING: Mojave area, California

STORY: Tough army sergeant Jefferson Harder (John Payne) is assigned the job of finding the reason for the railroad construction delay outside of Laramie. Shanessy (Dan Duryea), an old friend of Payne's, is the man behind the delay. Duryea wants the railroad stalled so he can milk the railroad workers dry. Payne shuts down construction until the workers will give an honest day's work for an honest day's pay. Duryea attempts to incite the railroad workers to sabotage the railroad. Payne arrests Duryea. Duryea has his men jump Payne. An unconscious Payne is placed in a railroad car that is leaving town. When Payne is late for Duryea's trial, Duryea is set free. The townsmen want to send a message to Payne's superior officer and town sheriff Sommers (James Griffith) volunteers to make the journey. Duryea has gunman Winton (Lee Van Cleef) kill Griffith. Lou Carter (Mari Blanchard), Duryea's partner, upset at Duryea's lawlessness, tips Payne off to Griffith's murderer. Payne has to shoot Van Cleef in a gun duel then arrests Duryea as the man who ordered the murder. Since male juries have been letting Duryea's men go free when arrested, Blanchard suggests an all-woman jury might be the answer. The all-woman jury with Blanchard as forewoman convicts Duryea. Duryea escapes and tries to kill Blanchard but only succeeds in wounding her. Duryea and henchman Winton (Myron Healey) attempt to escape on a stolen work train not knowing that they are headed for a head-on collision with an oncoming passenger train. Payne is able to reach the train, defeat the outlaws in hand-to-hand conflict and prevent the two trains from colliding. Payne plans to settle down with Blanchard when his army hitch is over in six months.

NOTES AND COMMENTARY: Myron Healey's girlfriend came to Mojave to visit. Healey tried to find a room for her with no results. Dan Duryea stepped in and told Healey that he could stay with him. Healey's girl could then use Healey's room. Duryea told Healey, "I've got the big king-sized bed and another double bed in there. You can make yourself at home and we'll sip some scotch." That night in Duryea's room Duryea said to Healey, "Now after we have a couple of drinks and everybody's settled in for the night, you can go and kiss your lady good night."

Mojave, California, is to this day a major railway center only 90 miles from Los Angeles. The Southern Pacific Railway designed the original townsite on its railroad line between Los Angeles and San Francisco. On August 8, 1876, the first passenger train made its stop and that date was established as the town's birthday. From Mojave, track was laid to Needles, California, and then on to the Arizona border in 1883. This latter part was sold to the Santa Fe Railway in 1898. The original rail line is part of the Burlington Northern Santa Fe Railway. With the railroad history and close proximity to Hollywood, Mojave was an ideal location for *Rails Into Laramie*.

The plot line of having an all-woman jury serve in an important trial with a western setting was seen earlier in *The Lady from Cheyenne* (Universal, 1941). A scene from *Wings of the Hawk* (Universal-International, 1953) was used in the montage sequence in which disgruntled workers sabotaged the railroad camp, supplies and trains.

The working title for this film was *Fort Laramie*.

REVIEWS: "Customers willing to settle for strictly formula-type westerns may derive some small satisfaction from this medium-budget entry." *New York Times*, 5/13/54

"A par-for-the course western." *The Universal Story*, Clive Hirschhorn.

SUMMATION: A below par script and leisurely direction is responsible for this slightly below average western saga. These conditions make it difficult for the performers to rise above the material with the exception of James Griffith. Griffith gives a sparkling performance as the

Rails Into Laramie (1954) scene card: Stephen Chase gives John Payne orders to clean up the trouble in Laramie.

town sheriff who tries to find his courage. Dan Duryea is more at home as his psychotic killer with an innate sense of humor but here he seems to be out of his element as a boss-heavy. The script has too many underdeveloped story lines to be a convincing motion picture. A few of these story lines include the fact that Duryea's wife and John Payne were once in love but nothing more is made of this secondary plotline. In another, Mari Blanchard suggests to Payne that the time is right for an all-woman jury. Payne dismisses this recommendation but suddenly an all-woman jury is now a fact. Myron Healey tries to intimidate the jury through one of the juror's spouses but this plotline is suddenly dropped. More action might have covered over the many holes in the script.

*IN THIS SAVAGE LAND ... a woman
belonged to the first man to claim her!
... this was the law of the tyrant
who ruled the frontier in 1842!*

Raw Edge

Universal-International (September 1956); PRINT by Technicolor; RUNNING TIME: 76 min.

CAST: Tex Kirby, **Rory Calhoun**; Hannah Montgomery, **Yvonne De Carlo**; Paca, **Mara Corday**; Tarp Penny, **Neville Brand**; John Randolph, **Rex Reason**; Pop Penny, **Emile Meyer**; Gerald Montgomery, **Herbert Rudley**; Sile Doty, **Robert J. Wilke**; Dan Kirby, **John Gilmore**; McKay, **Gregg Barton**; Whitey, **Ed Fury**; Missionary, **William Schallert**; Five Crows, **Robert Hoy**; Frenchy, **Paul Fiero**; Chief Kiyuva, **Francis McDonald**; Indian Woman, **Julia Montoya**; Clerk, **Richard James**

CREDITS: Director, **John F. Sherwood**; Assistant Director, **Joseph E. Kenny**; Producer, **Albert Zugsmith**; Story, **William Kozlenko** and **James Benson Nablo**; Screenwriters, **Harry Essex** and **Robert Hill**; Editor, **Russell Schoengarth**; Art Directors, **Alexander Golitzen** and **Alfred Sweeney**; Set Decorators, **Russell A. Gausman** and **Ruby R. Levitt**; Cinematographer, **Maury Gertsman**; Special Photography, **Clifford Stine**; Costumes, **Bill Thomas**; Hair Stylist, **Joan St. Oegger**; Makeup, **Bud Westmore**; Sound, **Leslie I. Carey** and **Frank H. Wilkinson**; Musical Supervisor, **Joseph Gershenson**; Technicolor Color Consultant, **William Fritzsche**

SONG: "Raw Edge" (Gilkyson)— sung by **Terry Gilkyson**

LOCATION FILMING: Mountains above Palm Springs and the Jack Garner Ranch, California

STORY: Tex Kirby (Rory Calhoun) comes to the Oregon Territory to visit his brother Dan (John Gilmore) only to find Dan has been hanged by Montgomery (Herbert Rudley) for assaulting his wife, Hannah (Yvonne De Carlo). Rudley is the law in the territory but Gilmore was innocent of the crime. Calhoun plans to take revenge on Rudley. Rudley made the law that any unmarried woman can be claimed by the first man to grab her. Thinking Calhoun will kill Rudley, Pop Penny (Emile Meyer) and his son Tarp (Neville Brand) decide to stay at Rudley's ranch to be close to De Carlo. Calhoun comes to the ranch to wait for Rudley to return. De Carlo leaves the ranch to go to Rudley. Brand catches up to De Carlo and offers to take her. When Brand and De Carlo stop at a stream for water, Brand assaults De Carlo and in the struggle De Carlo realizes Gilmore was hung for Brand's crime. Calhoun had followed and sends Brand on his way.

Raw Edge (1956) scene card: **Recently widowed Mara Corday is about to be claimed by Ed Fury. Robert Wilke (*right*) challenges Fury's claim.**

The Indians are on the warpath to gain revenge for the death of one of their tribal members. Paca (Mara Corday), Gilmore's widow, on the pretext of leading Rudley to safety, leads him to the Indian village to face Indian justice. When Rudley's body is delivered to Rudley's ranch, Brand seizes the opportunity to have De Carlo. Brand kills Meyer and engages in a gunfight and fistfight with Calhoun. Brand is killed in the fight. Calhoun plans to return to Texas with De Carlo at his side.

NOTES AND COMMENTARY: Robert Hoy did some stunt work and

played Five Crows. Hoy had a scene in which he was shot in the eye. Hoy remembered, "I said I'll come in there with a tomahawk and go 'One. Two. Kid, when I'm back like this, shoot me.' He was one of those Mr. Americas [Whitey played by Ed Fury] and had a break a way shirt on him—you know, for a fight scene later. I was a little leery about this guy, watching him." When it came time to film the scene, Fury didn't wait for Hoy to back up the necessary distance. Hoy continues, "He fired. The doctor said I was lucky. I closed my eyes before. They rushed me down the mountain. We were up in the mountains above Palm Springs way. I showed back up on the set with my eyeball all wrapped up. The doctor said, 'You lucky son of a bitch.' Wilke [Robert Wilke] got this Mr. America. He was playing one of the heavies and had to do some fights with the kid that shot me. Wilke was so mad that he'd shot me. Bob and I are old friends. He sashayed this guy's body up and down those rocks. He had streaks. You hate to have your body streaked." Fury's skin color was temporarily two-toned.

REVIEWS: "Standard outdoor action fare." *Variety*, 7/25/56; "Technicolor time-filler." *The Universal Story*, Hirschhorn.

SUMMATION: *Raw Edge* is a slightly above average western saga. Rory Calhoun makes a good western hero and Yvonne De Carlo does okay as the woman desired by all the men in the Oregon Territory. All the performances are standard and the action scenes are about par. There's nothing really too new in this picture but the film moves swiftly and it's easy to take.

The story of Ben Matthews ... THE GAMBLING MAN
... who followed his Luck ... his Love and killer's trail
from the brawling river ports to the golden glitter of Antoine's!

The Rawhide Years

Universal-International (July, 1956); PRINT by Technicolor; RUNNING TIME: 85 min.

CAST: Ben, **Tony Curtis**; Zoe, **Colleen Miller**; Rick Harper, **Arthur Kennedy**; Brand Comfort, **William Demarest**; Marshal Sommers, **William Gargan**; Andre Boucher, **Peter Van Eyck**; Matt Comfort, **Minor Watson**; Carrico, **Donald Randolph**; Neal, **Robert Wilke**; Captain, **Trevor Bardette**; Deputy Wade, **James Anderson**; Mate, **Robert Foulk**; Gif Lessing, **Chubby Johnson**; Miss Vanilla Bissell, **Leigh Snowden**; Frank Porter, **Don Beddoe**; Card Player, **Rex Lease**; Mob Leader, **I. Stanford Jolley**; Luke, **Malcolm Atterbury**; Chinese servant, **Clarence Lung**; Colonel Swope, **Charles Evans**; Miss Dal-Marie Smith, **Marlene Felton**; River Pirate, **Lane Bradford**; Crew member, **Mike Ragan**; Johnny, **Chuck Roberson**

CREDITS: Director, **Rudolph Mate**; Assistant Director, **John Sherwood**; Producer, **Stanley Rubin**; Screenwriter, **Earl Felton**; Adaptors, **Robert Presnell, Jr.**, and **D.D. Beauchamp**; Editor, **Russell Schoengarth**; Art Directors, **Alexander Golitzen** and **Richard H. Riedel**; Set Decorators, **Russell A. Gausman** and **Oliver Emert**; Cinema-tographer, **Irving Glassberg**;

Costumes, **Bill Thomas**; Hair Stylist, **Joan St. Oegger**; Makeup, **Bud Westmore**; Sound, **Leslie I. Carey** and **Robert Pritchard**; Music, **Frank Skinner** and **Hans J. Salter**; Music Supervision, **Joseph Gershenson**; Technicolor Color Consultant, **William Fritzsche**

SONGS: "The Gypsy with the Fire in His Shoes" (Lee and Almeida)—sung by **Colleen Miller**; "Happy Go Lucky" (Herbert and Hughes)—sung by **Colleen Miller**; "Give Me Your Love" (Herbert and Hughes)—sung by **Colleen Miller**

LOCATION FILMING: Lone Pine, California

SOURCE: Novel, *The Rawhide Years* by **Norman A. Fox**

STORY: Ben (Tony Curtis) is working with crooked gambler Carrico (Donald Randolph) to fleece card players on riverboats. Curtis has a change of heart when Porter (Don Beddoe) loses money he shouldn't have wagered. Curtis allows Matt Comfort (Minor Watson) to win the money back for Beddoe. Knowing Curtis is basically honest, Watson offers Curtis a job on his ranch. During the theft of a large wooden Indian, the river pirates kill Watson. Curtis fights one of the pirates but loses when the pirate uses

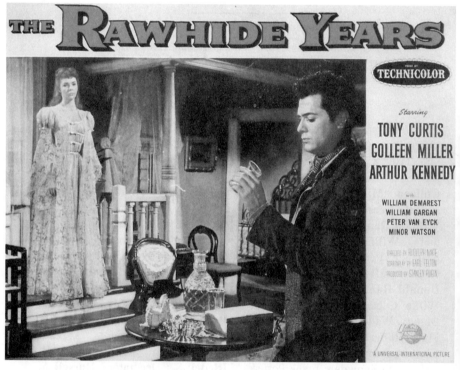

The Rawhide Years (1956) scene card: Colleen Miller tells Tony Curtis that she belongs to Peter Van Eyck.

a heavy studded belt as a weapon. Curtis and Randolph are accused of the murder. Curtis escapes and Randolph is lynched. After three years, Curtis returns with the larcenous Harper (Arthur Kennedy). Curtis finds out that his girlfriend Zoe (Colleen Miller) is now saloon owner Boucher's (Peter Van Eyck) girl. Before Curtis can leave town, he is beaten by Van Eyck who uses a heavy studded belt. Curtis recognizes the belt as the same one used by the river pirate. Curtis takes his discovery to Watson's brother, Brand (William Demarest). When Curtis sees the wooden Indian at the ranch, he realizes Demarest is in league with Van Eyck. Curtis is captured but Kennedy comes to the rescue, killing Demarest. Van Eyck and a posse chase Curtis and Kennedy. Curtis gets away but Kennedy is captured. Before Kennedy can be lynched, Curtis finds proof of Van Eyck and Demarest's guilt. Van Eyck is shot by a bullet meant for Curtis but lives long enough to verify Curtis' accusations. Curtis and Miller leave on the riverboat to begin a new life together.

NOTES AND COMMENTARY: Colleen Miller's songs were dubbed. Miller commented, "I think she sort of sounded like me if I could carry a tune." Colleen Miller remarked about her role in the picture, "I felt there something was missing. I have a feeling that was something missing, period. There really was. I think they felt they just needed to make the film. I don't think it was developed as well as it could have been. It was a showcase for the guys [Kennedy and Curtis] wrestling." Colleen Miller remembered that Tony Curtis was "A little flirty at the beginning but that was what he was supposed to be." Miller felt Curtis was "wild, untamed and natural, which was good for him." A stunt almost ended in tragedy. In one scene on a paddleboat, Tony Curtis was battling the leader of the river pirates and was to be tossed by the pirate from the back of the boat. Stuntman Davy Sharpe would then take over and dive between the rear of the boat and the moving paddlewheels. Only the paddlewheels would be moving, the boat was stationary. Sharpe would disappear into the water. Further out in the water stuntman Robert Hoy was waiting with weights attached to keep him submerged. This was a timing play; at the right moment, Hoy would loose the weights and pop up out of the water. Before the scene was filmed, Hoy went underwater to check things out and found planks had been pulled toward the paddlewheels a good eight or nine inches, which severely closed the gap between the boat and the paddlewheel. If Sharpe had performed the stunt, he would definitely have hit those planks, which would have probably resulted in a fatal injury. Hoy stopped the scene and instead of Sharpe diving into the water, a weighted dummy was used instead. The back lot lake where this scene was filmed is now the home for *Jaws* on the Universal tour.

REVIEWS: "Actionful western, good outdoor story." *Variety*, 6/6/56; "A good cast and fast-paced direction help to gloss over the inconsistencies in the plot." *The Motion Picture Guide*, Nash and Ross.

SUMMATION: *The Rawhide Years* is a fast, enjoyable western film. Tony Curtis gives a very engaging and athletic performance. Arthur Kennedy does a turn on the bad guy with a streak of decency. Colleen Miller is adequate as the girl loved by Curtis and Peter Van Eyck. Van Eyck puts a properly sinister and nasty touch to his part as leader of the river pirates. Minor Watson, William Gargan and Robert Wilke are the most notable of the supporting cast members. Rudolph Mate directs at a break-neck pace, which fortunately does not give the viewer the chance to notice inconsistencies in the story.

THE WEST'S MOST EXCITING ADVENTURE!
... from the Studio that gave you Canyon Passage!
The thunder of untamed hooves!
The roar of an outlaw's guns!
The drama of a woman whose reckless love tamed them both!

Red Canyon

Universal-International (April, 1949); COLOR by Technicolor; RUNNING TIME: 82 min.

CAST: Lucy Bostel, **Ann Blyth**; Lin Slone, **Howard Duff**; Mathew Bostel, **George Brent**; Jonah Johnson, **Edgar Buchanan**; Floyd Cordt, **John McIntire**; Brackton, **Chill Wills**; Aunt Jane, **Jane Darwell**; Virgil Cordt, **Lloyd Bridges**; Joel Creech, **James Seay**; Farlane, **Edmund MacDonald**; Sears, **David Clarke**; Hutch, **Denver Pyle**; Van, **Willard Willingham**; Townsman, **Hank Patterson**; Cowboys, **Edmund Cobb, Ethan Laidlaw** and **John Carpenter**; Charley, **Hank Worden**; Pronto, **Ray Bennett**

CREDITS: Director, **George Sherman**; Producer, **Leonard Goldstein**; Associate Producer, **Aaron Rosenberg**; Screenwriter, **Maurice Geraghty**; Editor, **Otto Ludwig**; Art Directors, **Bernard Herzbrun** and **Frank A. Richards**; Set Decorators, **Russell A. Gausman** and **Joseph Kish**; Cinematographer, **Irving Glassberg**; Costumes, **Rosemary Odell**, Hair Stylist, **Carmen Dirigo**; Makeup, **Bud Westmore**; Sound, **Leslie I. Carey** and **Vernon W. Kramer**; Music, **Walter Scharf**; Technicolor Color Director, **Natalie Kalmus**; Associate Technicolor Color Director, **William Fritzsche**

LOCATION FILMING: Kanab (Paria area), Utah

SOURCE: Novel, *Wildfire* by **Zane Grey**

STORY: Wandering cowboy Lin

Red Canyon (1949) scene card: Ann Blyth tends to her wounded father, George Brent; left border shows Howard Duff and Ann Blyth.

Slone (Howard Duff) wants to catch and ride Black Velvet, the famed leader of a wild horse herd. Joined by Johnson (Edgar Buchanan), they begin tracking the stallion. Duff finally catches Black Velvet. When travelling to an area where Duff can break and ride Black Velvet, he runs into Floyd Cordt (John McIntire) and Virgil (Lloyd Bridges), Duff's father and brother. McIntire is the leader of an outlaw gang and Bridges is his main confederate. Duff has been using an assumed name to distance himself from his outlaw family. McIntire wants Black Velvet but Duff refuses to give him up. Duff begins the process of breaking Black Velvet but is thrown and injured. Black Velvet is able to escape but the rope dangling from around his neck catches in some trees where Lucy Bostel (Ann Blyth) finds him. Since Duff has been injured, Blyth undertakes the process of breaking the stallion and training him to run in an upcoming race. Duff and Blyth begin to fall in love. Duff is hesitant to further the relationship since years earlier McIntire killed Blyth's mother while stealing horses from her father, Mathew (George Brent). Duff reveals his true identity to Blyth but she still rides Black Velvet to victory in the big race. McIntire reveals Duff's real name to Sheriff Brackton (Chill Wills). Brent tries to arrest Duff but he escapes. During the confusion, McIntire and his gang try to steal Black Velvet. Duff returns to confront McIntire and his gang. A gunfight ensues in which McIntire, Bridges and the other gang members are killed. Duff and Blyth are now free to continue their romance. They decide to let Black Velvet return to his wild horse herd.

NOTES AND COMMENTS: *Black Velvet* was the working title for *Red Canyon*.

Footage of the stallion and the wild horses was later utilized in *Sierra* (Universal-International, 1950), *Cattle Drive* (Universal-International, 1951), *Black Horse Canyon* (Universal-International, 1954) and *Mustang Country* (Universal, 1976).

REVIEWS: "A right smart sagebrush entry." *Hollywood Reporter*, 2/2/49; "The color photography of the Utah scenery, along with the footage of wild horses, adds a spark to the story of human conflict, giving it credence beyond that of a formula western." *The Motion Picture Guide*, Nash and Ross.

SUMMATION: *Red Canyon* is a good, solid western with fine scenic values, acting, directing and script. Howard Duff is quite good as the wandering cowboy who wants to sever ties with his outlaw family. Ann Blyth matches Duff as a young woman who wants to prove she's more than an attractive decoration. John McIntire and Lloyd Bridges capably handle the villainy. Edgar Buchanan, Chill Wills and Jane Darwell, in addition to presenting fine characterizations, add a bit of light comedy. Director George Sherman keeps this interesting story moving from start to finish.

DURANGO ... LAST LAWLESS OUTPOST OF THE WEST!
The town was a target and Alec Longmire
was the bull's-eye—but behind his badge was
an outlaw's brand and a gunfighter's skill on the draw!

Red Sundown

Universal-International (March 1956); PRINT by Technicolor; RUNNING TIME: 81 min.

CAST: Alec Longmire, **Rory Calhoun**; Caroline Murphy, **Martha Hyer**; Jade Murphy, **Dean Jagger**; Rufus Henshaw, **Robert Middleton**; Chet Swann, **Grant Williams**; Maria, **Lita Baron**; Purvis, **James Millican**; Sam Baldwin, **Trevor Bardette**; Rod Zellman, **Leo Gordon**; Hughie Clore, **David Kasday**; Zellman Brothers, **Lane Bradford** and **John Carpenter**; Henshaw Cowboys, **John Doucette** and **Eddie Parker**; Burt, **Steve Darrell**; Small

Rancher, **Dan White**; Townsman, **Ray Bennett**

CREDITS: Director, **Jack Arnold**; Assistant Director, **William Holland**; Producer, **Albert Zugsmith**; Screenwriter, **Martin Berkeley**; Editor, **Edward Curtiss**; Art Directors, **Alexander Golitzen** and **Eric Orbom**; Set Decorators, **Russell A. Gausman** and **John P. Austin**; Cinematographer, **William Snyder**; Costumes, **Jay A. Morley, Jr.**; Hair Stylist, **Joan St. Oegger**; Makeup, **Bud Westmore**; Sound, **Leslie I. Carey** and **Corson Jowett**; Music, **Hans J. Salter**; Music Supervisor, **Joseph Gershenson**; Technicolor Color Consultant, **William Fritzsche**

SONG: "Red Sundown" (Gilkyson)—sung by **Terry Gilkyson**

LOCATION FILMING: Conejo Valley, California

SOURCE: Novel, *Back Trail* by **Lewis B. Patten**

STORY: After a harrowing experience that almost resulted in his death, gunfighter Alec Longmire (Rory Calhoun) decides to try to hang up his guns and find honest work. In the town of Durango, Sheriff Murphy (Dean Jagger) offers Calhoun the job as his deputy. Calhoun accepts, knowing that the county is ripe for a range war

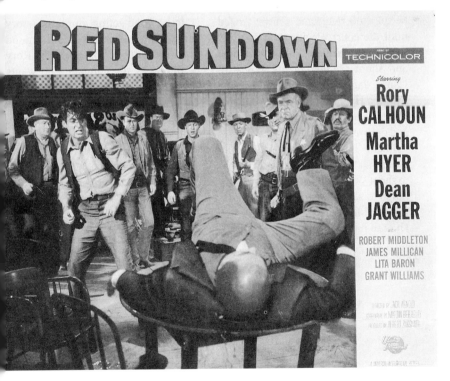

Red Sundown (1956) scene card: Rory Calhoun knocks Robert Middleton on a table in a rugged fistfight. Sheriff Dean Jagger (*second right*) watches anxiously.

between large rancher Henshaw (Robert Middleton) and the small ranchers led by Baldwin (Trevor Bardette) and Burt (Steve Darrell). When Middleton cannot buy Calhoun's services, he hires gunfighter Swann (Grant Williams). Williams terrorizes Bardette and his wife, demanding they leave the area. When Williams comes to Durango, Calhoun, at the point of a shotgun, orders Williams to leave town. Enraged, Middleton and his cowboys come to town and announce that the rangeland will be fenced in immediately. Calhoun and Middleton engage in a rugged fistfight with Calhoun emerging the victor. Middleton is arrested because no rangeland can be fenced until the courts decide who controls what range. Williams sneaks into town and shoots Jagger in his gun arm. Using Jagger's daughter Caroline (Martha Hyer) as a hostage, Williams forces Calhoun to drop his shotgun and only use his pistol to fight him. As Williams is sneaking up on Calhoun, a warning from Hyer enables Calhoun to shoot Williams. Calhoun leaves Durango to settle down and make something of himself before he can ask Hyer to marry him.

NOTES AND COMMENTARY: The working title for *Red Sundown* was *Decision at Durango*.

Footage from *Dawn at Socorro* (Universal-International, 1954) is used in Calhoun's flashback sequence. In this segment Calhoun dispatches Lee Van Cleef.

Rory Calhoun and Lita Baron were husband and wife at the time this movie was filmed.

REVIEWS: "Action and characterization are expertly blended in this fast-moving sagebrusher." *Variety*, 2/1/56; "Intriguing B Western." *The Western*, Hardy.

SUMMATION: *Red Sundown* is a superior minor "A" western containing good acting, directing, story and action. The cast is quite good with standout performances by Rory Calhoun as the gunman who wants to hang up his guns, James Millican as an aging gunman who finally realizes the futility of his profession and Grant Williams as a gunman who enjoys his work. Director Jack Arnold adroitly balances story and action and delivers some good entertainment.

She Had a Weapon for Every Kind of Man—
a loaded gun ... a ready kiss ... and
she knew how to use them both!
Outlaw queen of a renegade lair ... trading in
stolen cattle ... and hunted men!

The Redhead from Wyoming

Universal-International (January 1953); COLOR by Technicolor; RUNNING TIME: 80 min.

CAST: Kate Maxwell, **Maureen O'Hara**; Stan Blaine, **Alex Nicol**; Jim Averell, **William Bishop**; "Knuckles" Hogan, **Robert Strauss**; Reece Duncan, **Alexander Scourby**; Hal Jessup, **Palmer Lee**; Sandy, **Jack Kelly**; Myra, **Jeanne Cooper**; Matt Jessup, **Dennis Weaver**; Chet Jones, **Stacy Harris**; Wade, **Ray Bennett**; Cowhands, **Edmund Cobb** and **Davy Sharpe**; Outlaw, **Harold Goodwin**; Girl, **Claudette Thornton**; Jack, **Joe Bailey**; Ned, **Rush Williams**; Aldrich, **Philo McCullough**; Drunken Settler, **Syd Saylor**

CREDITS: Director, **Lee Sholem**; Assistant Director, **Jesse Hibbs**; Producer, **Leonard Goldstein**; Story, **Polly James**; Screenwriters, **Polly James** and **Herb Meadow**; Editor, **Milton Carruth**; Art Directors, **Bernard Herzbrun** and **Hilyard Brown**; Set Decorators, **Russell A. Gausman** and **Joseph Kish**; Cinematographer, **Winton Hoch**; Costumes, **Edward Stevens**; Hair Stylist, **Joan St. Oegger**; Makeup, **Bud Westmore**; Sound, **Leslie I. Carey** and **Corson Jowett**; Music, **Joseph Gershenson**; Technicolor Color Consultant, **William Fritzsche**

SONG: "Billy Boy" (traditional)—sung by **Maureen O'Hara, Palmer Lee, Jeanne Cooper and chorus**

LOCATION FILMING: Agoura, California

STORY: A range war is brewing in the Wyoming Territory with Duncan (Alexander Scourby), a large ranch owner, pitted against saloon owner Averell (William Bishop), leader of the small ranchers. Kate Maxwell (Maureen O'Hara) comes to Wyoming to run Bishop's saloon and finds out she also will be a cattle buyer for all the unbranded mavericks in the territory. In reality, O'Hara has become an unwitting accomplice in Bishop's cattle rustling activities. Sheriff Blane (Alex Nicol) is trying to capture the rustlers and has heard rumors of "strange faces" in the hills. O'Hara is framed by Bishop and is arrested on suspicion of murder and cattle rustling. Bishop prods Scourby into taking the fight to the small ranchers. Bishop's plan is to start the two factions fighting and then have his outlaw band take over. Nicol discovers Bishop's scheme. He convinces Scourby and the small ranchers to band together and prove Bishop's duplicity. The outlaws are duped into believing Bishop's plan has worked. Bishop's

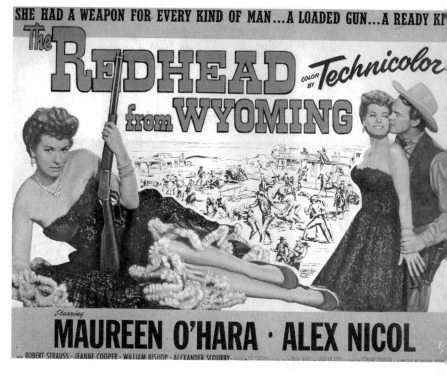

SHE HAD A WEAPON FOR EVERY KIND OF MAN...A LOADED GUN...A READY KN

The **REDHEAD** COLOR BY *Technicolor* *from* **WYOMING**

Starring
MAUREEN O'HARA · ALEX NICOL

ROBERT STRAUSS · JEANNE COOPER · WILLIAM BISHOP · ALEXANDER SCOURBY

The Redhead from Wyoming (1953) title card: Maureen O'Hara to left and again with Alex Nicol.

men find they are no match for the combined forces. Bishop tries to escape but is shot by O'Hara then finished off by Nicol. Nicol resigns as sheriff and prepares to settle down on a small ranch with O'Hara at his side.

NOTES AND COMMENTARY: The film's working title was *Cattle Kate*. Director Lee Sholem had this to say about the script, "It was conventional. It was a script. It wasn't anything fancy. It was a good show. It was entertaining." Hugh O'Brian had been slated for a role in the film. Universal-International switched O'Brian to a more important role in

The Great Companions with Dan Dailey. *The Great Companions* was released as *Meet Me at the Fair* (Universal-International, 1953). Some of the montage footage at the beginning of the film came from *Kansas Raiders* (Universal-International, 1950).

This is the film that Palmer Lee "fell in love" with Jeanne Cooper. Lee said, "She was fun to work with." Lee enjoyed her Irish accent and once told her, "You're not Irish, you're Scandinavian." Cooper replied, "What are you talking about?" Lee retorted, "Do you remember the Celts and the Saxon Wars? Those are the

Vikings that came down to you. The Black Irish came from the Spanish Armada." Cooper insisted, "I'm Irish. I'm Irish." Lee reiterated that Cooper was a delight. Palmer Lee would later in his career be billed as Gregg Palmer.

Lee Sholem though Maureen O'Hara was a lovely lady with a marvelous disposition. He noted that she was easy to handle and easy to work with. He felt it was nothing spectacular about working with her. Sholem also mentioned that O'Hara was a very nice lady. Sholem said, "I liked Maureen O'Hara." Lee Sholem said Alex Nicol was a good guy, who knew his business. Sholem mentioned that Nichol handled himself well but was no great star.

Lee Sholem thought William Bishop was a smooth easygoing guy who got along with everybody.

According to Lee Sholem, *The Redhead from Wyoming* was filmed in the San Fernando Valley on a large estate. It took about thirty days to film the movie.

Asked about Jack Kelly, Lee Sholem made this observation, "Jack Kelly was a much better actor that Jim Garner but he didn't have the sex appeal."

REVIEWS: "Tinted outdoor feature for general satisfaction." *Variety*, 12/24/52; "Exciting violence in handsome oater with lots of rousing action, good performances and gorgeous scenery. A natural for the action market." *Hollywood Reporter*, 12/19/52.

SUMMATION: Gunfights, fistic encounters and a cattle stampede are the main ingredients in this good, exciting western saga. The film is briskly directed by Lee Sholem. Maureen O'Hara is very good in her best Universal-International western. Alex Nicol registers strongly as a laconic sheriff who is not sure if he really wants to be the man in the middle of a range war. The skullduggery is in the capable hands of William Bishop, one of three men who I think make the perfect smiling, handsome villain. The other two actors are Lyle Bettger and David Brian. The climactic gun battle is well staged. One minor carp, why did they have to kill off Palmer Lee? Lee and Jeanne Cooper worked well together and it would have been nice to have a happy ending for those two, also.

EVERY GAL'S GOT A ROVING GUY ...
and SPRING is busting out LAUGHING!
The Ranch-House is a riot of romance and "careless kisses"...
cause that "MA KETTLE" gal's got a brand new fella!

Ricochet Romance

Universal-International (November 1954); RUNNING TIME: 80 min. CAST: Pansy Jones, **Marjorie Main**; Tom Williams, **Chill Wills**; Alfredo, **Alfonso Bedoya**; Manuel, **Pedro Gonzales-Gonzales**; Mr. Worthington Higgenmacher, **Rudy Vallee**; Angela Ann Mansfield, **Ruth Hampton**; Claire Renard, **Benay Venuta**; Dave King, **Darryl Hickman**; Betsy Williams, **Judith Ames**; Miss Clay, **Irene Ryan**; Mr. Webster, **Philip Tonge**; Timmy Williams, **Lee Aaker**; Mr. Harvey, **Charles Watts**; Mrs. Harvey, **Marjorie Bennett**; Mr. Daniels, **Phil Chamber**; Band, **The Guadalajara Trio**

CREDITS: Director, **Charles Lamont**; Producer, **Robert Arthur**, Story/Screenwriter, **Kay Lenard**; Editor, **Russell Schoengarth**; Art Directors, **Alexander Golitzen** and **Alfred Sweeney**; Set Decorators, **Russell A. Gausman** and **Ruby R. Levitt**; Cinematographer, **George Robinson**; Hair Stylist, **Joan St. Oegger**; Makeup, **Bud Westmore**; Sound, **Leslie I. Carey** and **Joe Lapis**; Music Supervisor, **Joseph Gershenson**

SONGS: "Un Tequila" (Lecuona and Gonzales)—sung by **Alfonso Bedoya, Pedro Gonzales-Gonzales** and **The Guadalajara Trio**; "Ricochet Romance" (Coleman, Darion and Gimbel)—sung by **Alfonso Bedoya**; "Para Vigo Me Voy" (Lecuona)—sung by **The Guadalajara Trio**; "Las Attenitas"—played by **The Guadalajara Trio**

STORY: Tom Williams (Chill Wills), the owner of a guest ranch out west, jeopardizes the ranch's chance for success with his continued obsession to become a master magician like Houdini. As new guests arrive, his latest attempt at a magic trick causes the cook to quit and the guests to decide to leave. Due to ranch hand Manuel's (Pedro Gonzales-Gonzales) quick thinking, the guests have to stay overnight. This gives Gonzales-Gonzales a chance to hire Pansy Jones (Marjorie Main) as the new cook. The other ranch hand, Alfonso Bedoya, thinks Wills needs a wife to settle him down. Bedoya hires actress Claire Renard (Benay Venuta) as a waitress but she was really hired to marry Wills. Other complications ensue when one of the guests (Ruth Hampton), decides neighboring rancher, Dave Kign (Darryl Hickman), is the man for her. Hickman is the boyfriend of Wills' daughter, Betsy (Judith Ames). Venuta wants Wills to sell his ranch and go with her to New York City. Bedoya, Gonzales-Gonzales and Main step in and help Ames win back Hickman and find a millionaire, Higgenmacher (Rudy Vallee), for

Ricochet Romance (1954) scene card: **Would-be magician Chill Wills shows a card trick to Ruth Hampton.**

Venuta. Wills is grateful because he really didn't want to leave his ranch anyway.

NOTES AND COMMENTARY: The working title for *Ricochet Romance* was *The Matchmakers*.

Later in her career, Judith Ames received screen credit as Rachel Ames.

REVIEWS: "Grassroots comedy, this entry boils down to another comedy in the 'Ma and Pa' Kettle series." *Variety*, 11/03/54; "The attempt at making a movie team of Marjorie Main and Chill Wills is a bit forced but Main fans will like it." *Western Movies*, Pitts.

SUMMATION: *Ricochet Romance* is a pleasant, likable comedy set in the modern west. Alfonso Bedoya and Pedro Gonzales-Gonzales easily steal the show from veterans Marjorie Main and Chill Wills with their singing, dancing and comedy antics. Main and Wills, however, strongly contribute to the film. Charles Lamont directed briskly, resulting in an entertaining movie. Like *Feudin', Fussin' and a-Fightin'* (1948), the film was given the title *Ricochet Romance* to capitalize on the song's popularity. Bedoya serenades Venuta and Vallee with this song until Gonzales-Gonzales points out its inappropriateness for the occasion.

ALONE ... HE FACED THE DEADLY CROSSFIRE
OF A KILLER-MOB ... AND A FEAR-CRAZED TOWN ...
His only love, another man's woman ... his only shield,
the marshal's star that covered his outlaw's heart!

Ride a Crooked Trail

Universal-International (September 1958); EASTMAN COLOR by Pathé; FILMED in Cinemascope; RUNNING TIME: 87 min.

CAST: Joe Maybe, **Audie Murphy**; Tessa Milotte, **Gia Scala**; Judge Kyle, **Walter Matthau**; Sam Teeler, **Henry Silva**; Little Brandy, **Joanna Moore**; Jimmy, **Eddie Little**; Mrs. Curtis, **Mary Field**; Sam Mason, **Leo Gordon**; Pecos, **Mort Mills**; Ben, **Frank Chase**; Jackson, **Bill Walker**; Attorney Clark, **Ned Wever**; Mr. Curtis, **Richard H. Cutting**; Durgen, **Morgan Woodward**; Townsman, **Eddie Parker**

CREDITS: Director, **Jesse Hibbs**; Assistant Director, **William Holland**; Producer, **Howard Pine**; Story, **George Bruce**; Screenwriter, **Borden Chase**; Editor, **Edward Curtiss**; Art Directors, **Alexander Golitzen** and **Bill Newberry**; Set Decorators, **Russell A. Gausman** and **Ray Jeffers**; Cinematographer, **Harold Lipstein**; Costumes, **Bill Thomas**; Makeup, **Bud Westmore**; Sound, **Leslie I. Carey** and **Donald McKay**; Music Supervisor, **Joseph Gershenson**

LOCATION FILMING: Ventura Canyon and Janns Conejo Ranch in the Los Angeles area, California

STORY: Bank robber Joe Maybe (Audie Murphy) rides into Webb City where Judge Kyle (Walter Matthau) mistakes Murphy as a United States Marshal. Matthau makes Murphy stay to maintain law and order. Arriving in town is Tessa Milotte (Gia Scala), girlfriend of gang leader Teeler (Henry Silva), to case the town to see how the bank can be robbed. Scala knows Murphy and Murphy tells Matthau that Scala is his wife. When Silva brings his gang to town, Murphy makes a deal with Silva to wait until money has arrived to purchase the trail herds that will be coming soon. Jimmy (Eddie Little), ward of the court, comes to live with Murphy and Scala and begins to learn of Murphy's past. Little has faith that Murphy is basically a decent person. Matthau overhears a conversation between Murphy and Little that confirms his feelings about Murphy. Little convinces Matthau to give Murphy a chance to show that he is a changed man. When the money arrives, Silva plans to double cross Murphy by robbing the bank and placing the blame on him. The bank is robbed and Matthau attempts to arrest Murphy. A well-placed shot by Little is enough of a diversion to allow Murphy to escape. Murphy is able to bring both Silva and the money back to Matthau. Matthau allows Murphy to remain as marshal. Little reminds Matthau that Murphy and Scala need to be married and Matthau decrees that the ceremony will be held that morning.

NOTES AND COMMENTARY: The working title for *Ride a Crooked Trail* was *Middle of the Street*. In Gia Scala's 11-year movie career, her only western was *Ride a Crooked Trail*. This was also to be her final film for Universal-International. For his role of attorney Clark, Ned Wever received screen credit as Ned Weaver.

REVIEWS: "Pleasant light treatment of a reformed gunfighter, an interesting presentation." *Variety*, 7/23/58; "Fairly good Audie Murphy vehicle." *Western Movies*, Pitts.

SUMMATION: *Ride a Crooked Trail* in lesser hands probably would be just an average western at best. Characterization and welcome humor combine to lift this yarn to an above average status. Audie Murphy and Gia Scala are engaging as bank robbers who finally are reformed primarily by a young boy who comes to live with them. Walter Matthau as a judge with a fondness for alcohol and tough justice, and Eddie Little as the young boy who changes Murphy and Scala's lives steal the show. Director Jesse Hibbs adroitly mixes humor, characterization and some good action to bring in an entertaining motion picture.

Ride a Crooked Trail (1958) scene card: Audie Murphy and Walter Matthau spring into action against some troublemakers.

DIABLO ... WHERE A LAUGHING KILLER WAITS ...
FOR THE VENGEANCE THAT RIDES WITH CLAY O'MARA!
The blazing story of the kid from Colorado ...
who faced a savage showdown with the West's last outlaw outpost ...
THE TOWN OF NO RETURN!

Ride Clear of Diablo

Universal-International (March 1954); COLOR by Technicolor; RUNNING TIME: 80½ min.

CAST: Clay O'Mara, **Audie Murphy**; Laurie Kenyon, **Susan Cabot**; Whitey Kincade, **Dan Duryea**; Kate, **Abbe Lane**; Jed Ringer, **Russell Johnson**; Fred Kenyon, **Paul Birch**; Tom Meredith, **William Pullen**; Tim Lowerie, **Jack Elam**; Reverend Moorehead, **Denver Pyle**; Bartender, **Harold Goodwin**; Blacksmith, **Ray Bennett**; Rancher, **Eddie Dew**; Lowerie Brothers, **Lane Bradford** and **Mike Ragan**; Gang Member, **Hank Patterson**; Railroad Conductor, **James Griffith**

CREDITS: Director, **Jesse Hibbs**; Assistant Director, **Fred Frank**; Producer, **John W. Rogers**; Story, **Ellis Marcus**; Screenwriter, **George Zuckerman**; Editor, **Edward Curtiss**; Art Directors, **Bernard Herzbrun** and **Robert Boyle**; Set Decorators, **Russell A. Gausman** and **Julia Heron**; Cinematographer, **Irving Glassberg**; Costumes, **Rosemary Odell**; Hair Stylist, **Joan St. Oegger**; Makeup, **Bud Westmore**; Sound, **Leslie I. Carey** and **Richard De Weese**; Musical Director, **Joseph Gershenson**; Technicolor Color Consultant, **William Fritzsche**

SONGS: "Wanted" (Hughes and Herbert)—sung by **Abbe Lane**; "Noche de Ronda" (Lara)—sung by **Abbe Lane**

LOCATION FILMING: Victorville area, California

STORY: Cattle rustlers kill Clay O'Mara's (Audie Murphy) father and brother and make a successful raid of their cattle. Lawyer Meredith (William Pullen), Sheriff Kenyon (Paul Birch) and Ringer (Russell Johnson) are the primary members of this gang operating around Santiago. Railroad surveyor Murphy comes to Santiago to find if the killers have been apprehended. When Murphy expresses a desire to talk to some cattle rustlers to see if he can get a lead on the killers, Birch makes him his deputy and suggests he go to Diablo and arrest Kincade (Dan Duryea). Birch intimates that Duryea might have information Murphy would like to hear. Birch really thinks that gunslinger Duryea will kill Murphy. To the town of Santiago's amazement, Murphy brings in Duryea to stand trial for murder. Murphy and Duryea begin to have a mutual regard for each other. Because of perjured testimony from Johnson, Duryea is acquitted. Then with Duryea's assistance, Murphy is able to retrieve a

Ride Clear of Diablo (1954) scene card: Audie Murphy talks to his prisoner Dan Duryea.

rancher's stolen stallion from Lowerie (Jack Elam) and his brothers. Pullen, Birch and Johnson plan to hijack silver ore. Johnson, resentful of the way he's been treated by Pullen and Birch, double-crosses his partners and keeps the silver for himself. Birch, in retaliation, tells Murphy that Johnson killed his kinfolks. With Duryea's help, Murphy obtains a tip on where Johnson is hiding. In a gunfight Murphy shoots Johnson but a stray bullet from Johnson's pistol hits Duryea, who tagged along with Murphy for the excitement. Murphy takes the wounded Duryea to a saloon in Diablo. Pullen, Birch and Elam arrive in Diablo to get rid of Murphy. Duryea tells Murphy that Pullen was the man who actually killed his father and brother. Because of his friendship with Murphy, Duryea is the first man through the saloon door. Duryea kills Birch before dying in a hail of bullets. Then Murphy shoots Elam and captures Pullen. Murphy then marries Birch's niece, Laurie (Susan Cabot).

NOTES AND COMMENTARY: William Pullen learned to ride because of this movie. A scene was to be shot in the late afternoon in which Pullen was to ride down a western street, turn left at the first corner, ride to a building, dismount and tie the horse to the hitch rail. The sun was setting and it was not a good time for a delay. Pullen commented, "I had only a little experience riding, and bareback at that." Pullen was able to get halfway down the street when the horse stopped and stood dead still. The head wrangler brought in another horse with the same result. The third horse was a charm as Pullen, very uncertainly, completed the scene to everyone's relief. Pullen then became determined to learn how to ride. Under the tutelage of wrangler Mickey Milrick, Pullen learned not only how to ride but how to make a running dismount and drive a carriage drawn by four horses. All of which cost Pullen nary a cent. For payment, Pullen had to unsaddle and wash the horse down after riding. Pullen remembered that this was a good experience and stated, "Sweet are the uses of adversity."

Russell Johnson loved working with Dan Duryea. He had these comments to make, "Oh, Dan, lovely guy, good actor, funny man, relaxed.

He was a hell of a good actor, a nice man, easy to work with. An actor's actor."

The song, "Noche de Ronda" can be heard in *Sombrero* (Metro-Goldwyn-Mayer, 1953), a Spanish language version of *Big Broadcast of 1938* (Paramount, 1938), *Masquerade in Mexico* (Paramount, 1945) and *Havana Rose* (Republic, 1951).

REVIEWS: "Good, standard western actioner." *Variety*, 2/3/54; "Fast moving, well directed oater." *Hollywood Reporter*, 2/3/54.

SUMMATION: *Ride Clear of Diablo* is a well-done action western bolstered by fine performances by Audie Murphy and Dan Duryea, who does a neat but believable turn on his laughing-killer role by showing a streak of honesty. The primary villainy is in good hands with fine performances by Paul Birch, William Pullen and Russell Johnson. Susan Cabot is pretty and makes a nice heroine and love interest for Murphy. Director Jesse Hibbs keeps the proceedings moving briskly despite a somewhat episodic screenplay.

Gambling mistress of the untamed Mississippi where men were as good as their fists and women as good as their kisses!

River Lady

Universal-International (June 1948); COLOR by Technicolor; RUNNING TIME: 78 min.

CAST: Sequin, **Yvonne De** Carlo; Beauvais, **Dan Duryea**; Dan Corrigan, **Rod Cameron**; Stephanie, **Helena Carter**; Mike, **Lloyd Gough**; Ma Dunnigan, **Florence**

Bates; Mr. Morrison, **John McIntire**; Swede, **Jack Lambert**; Mrs. Morrison, **Esther Somers**; Esther, **Anita Turner**; Rider, **Edmond Cobb**; Bouncer, **Dewey Robinson**; Hewitt, **Eddy C. Waller**; Limpy, **Milt Kibbee**; Dealer, **Billy Wayne**; Logger, **Jimmy Ames**; Executive, **Edward Earle**; Sands, **Frank Hagney**; McGee, **Jack Shutta**; Larson, **Harold Goodwin**; Card Player, **Robert Wilke**; Loggers, **Reed Howes**, **George Magrill** and **Dick Wessell**

CREDITS: Director, **George Sherman**; Assistant Director, **Joseph E. Kenny**; Producer, **Leonard Gold-** stein; Screenwriters, **D.D. Beauchamp** and **William Bowers**; Editor, **Otto Ludwig**; Art Directors, **Bernard Herzbrun** and **Emrich Nicholson**; Set Decorators, **Russell A. Gausman** and **Charles Wyrick**; Cinematographer, **Irving Glassberg**; Special Photography, **D.S. Horsley**; Costumes, **Yvonne Wood**; Hair Stylist, **Carmen Dirigo**; Makeup, **Bud Westmore**; Sound, **Leslie I. Carey** and **Jack A. Bolger, Jr.**; Music, **Paul Sawtell**; Orchestration, **David Tamkin**; Technicolor Color Director, **Natalie Kalmus**; Associate Technicolor Color Director, **Clemens Finley**

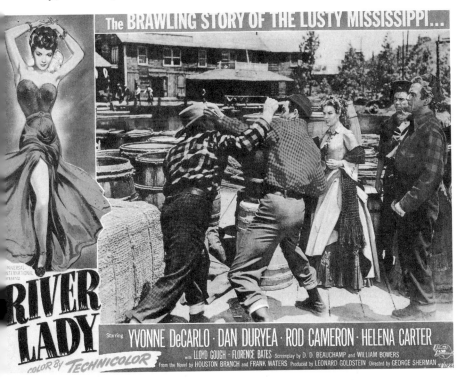

River Lady (1948) scene card: Jack Lambert is taught a lesson in manners by Rod Cameron as Helena Carter and Lloyd Gough watch; left border features Yvonne De Carlo.

SONG: "Louis Sands and Jim McGee" (Schumann and Brooks)—sung by **Yvonne De Carlo**; The melody was based on "O Tannenbaum"

SOURCE: Novel, *River Lady* by **Frank Waters** and **Houston Branch**

STORY: Beauvais (Dan Duryea) is the front man for Sequin's (Yvonne De Carlo) logging syndicate which is trying to force all the small loggers out of business in order to monopolize the logging industry. Logger Corrigan (Rod Cameron) and Duryea are rivals for De Carlo's affections but De Carlo prefers Cameron. To further Cameron's logging career, De Carlo is willing to let small logger Morrison (John McIntire) continue to operate on the condition that McIntire hire Cameron to run his business. Cameron becomes very successful and decides to marry De Carlo. Stephanie (Helena Carter), McIntire's daughter, is in love with Cameron and lets it slip that De Carlo bought the job for Cameron. In retaliation, Cameron marries Carter. Cameron finds buyers for the timber and convinces the smaller loggers to form a combine. Duryea hires all the loggers away from Cameron. Cameron thinks he's defeated until his friend Mike (Lloyd Gough) and Carter convince him to fight back. Cameron and Gough shanghai a logging crew and convince them that they should return to work for them. Duryea manages to start a log jam to stop Cameron from shipping the logs down river. When Cameron uses dynamite to break up the log jam, Duryea is killed in the explosion. Cameron realizes that Carter is the woman for him.

NOTES AND COMMENTARY: This was Rod Cameron's final film for Universal. Cameron then entered into motion picture contracts with Republic and Allied Artists and also appeared as the main villain in two George Montgomery westerns, *Belle Starr's Daughter* (20th Century–Fox, 1948) and *Dakota Lil* (20th Century–Fox, 1950). Interestingly, since this was Rod Cameron's last picture under his Universal contract, he now received third billing.

There were some interesting dialogue exchanges between Rod Cameron and Helena Carter:

> *Cameron:* "Come on if you want to, but behave yourself."
> *Carter:* "Isn't that what the girl says to the man."
> *Cameron:* "Behave yourself or I'll give you the worst spanking of your life."
> *Carter:* "I might even like that."

Reportedly, Yvonne De Carlo found *River Lady* physically demanding but not dramatically challenging.

REVIEWS: "Colorful, brawling action melodrama." *Western Movies*, Pitts; "Slim story is given a boost through some well-staged fistfights and the activities of the lumberjacks, the latter providing the tension the story lacks." *The Motion Picture Guide*, Nash and Ross.

SUMMATION: This is a good brawling logging saga highlighted by some exciting action scenes.

Director George Sherman moves surefooted through the story and gets good performances from his cast, especially Helena Carter as the woman with whom Rod Cameron eventually falls in love. Sherman wisely does not spend much time on Cameron's temporary despondency when he thinks he has been defeated by Yvonne De Carlo and Dan Duryea but moves quickly to more action. A musical highlight is De Carlo's rendition of "Louis Sands and Jim McGee."

A REBEL'S HATE ... A WOMAN'S UNDYING LOVE ...
tell the strange, exciting story of the Confederate soldier who
turned Sioux to wage a one-man war against the Yankees!

Run of the Arrow

ALTERNATE TITLE: *Hot Lead*; Globe Enterprises Production/RKO Radio; Pictures/Universal-International Release (September 1957); COLOR by Technicolor; FILMED in RKO-Scope; RUNNING TIME: 86 min.

CAST: O'Meara, **Rod Steiger**; Yellow Moccasin, **Sarita Montiel**; Captain Clark, **Brian Keith**; Lieutenant Driscoll, **Ralph Meeker**; Walking Coyote, **Jay C. Flippen**; Blue Buffalo, **Charles Bronson**; Mrs. O'Meara, **Olive Carey**; Crazy Wolf, **H.M. Wynant**; Lieutenant Stockwell, **Neyle Morrow**; Red Cloud, **Frank DeKova**; General Allen, **Colonel Tim McCoy**; Colonel Taylor, **Stuart Randall**; Ballad Singer, **Frank Warner**; Silent Tongue, **Billy Miller**; Corporal, **Chuck Hayward**; Sergeant, **Chuck Roberson**; Doctor, **Carleton Young**; Confederate Soldier, **Kermit Maynard**

CREDITS: Director/Producer/Screenwriter, **Samuel Fuller**; Assistant Director, **Ben Chapman**; Editor, **Gene Fowler, Jr.**; Art Directors, **Albert S. D'Agostino** and **Jack Okey**; Set Decorator, **Bert Granger**; Unit Manager, **Gene Bryant**; Cinematographer, **Joseph Biroc**; Hair Stylist, **Larry Germain**; Makeup Supervisor, **Harry Maret, Jr.**; Sound, **Virgil Smith** and **Terry Kellum**; Sound Effects Editor, **Bert Schoenfeld**; Music, **Victor Young**; Music Editor, **Audray Granville**

SONG: "Oh I'm a Good Old Rebel" (Randolph)—sung by **Frank Warner**

LOCATION FILMING: St. George, Utah

STORY: At the very close of the Civil War, Confederate soldier O'Meara (Rod Steiger) fires the last bullet that hits Union soldier Driscoll (Ralph Meeker). Finding that the bullet only wounded Meeker, Steiger brings Meeker to a Confederate field hospital for medical treatment. Steiger receives that bullet as a war trophy. Filled with hate, Steiger refuses to take an oath of allegiance and ventures to the

Run of the Arrow (1957) scene card: Neyle Morrow covers a dead cavalry soldier as Brian Keith and Ralph Meeker (*third from left*) watch.

West to live. Captured by the Sioux, Steiger's only hope for survival is to successfully elude pursuit in the "run of the arrow" ceremony. Aided by a Sioux woman, Yellow Moccasin (Sarita Montiel), Steiger becomes the first man to survive the run. Steiger becomes a member of the Sioux tribe, marries Montiel and adopts a young boy, Silent Tongue (Billy Miller). When the United States government wants to build a road and a fort on Sioux lands, permission is granted if the Sioux hunting lands are not violated and if Steiger can go with the troops to ensure the fort is built at the place specified in the treaty. The leader of the troops is Meeker, who Steiger recognizes immediately. Steiger tells Meeker that it was his bullet that wounded him at the war's end. Attacked by a renegade Sioux, Crazy Wolf (H.M. Wynant), and his followers, the leader of the expedition, Captain Clark (Brian Keith), is killed. Meeker takes the opportunity to build the fort on another site that violates the treaty with the Sioux. Steiger is sent to Meeker to give the soldiers a chance to leave peacefully. Meeker refuses the offer, spurring an attack by the Sioux, which virtually wipes out the cavalry forces. Meeker is captured and is to be tortured by being skinned alive. Steiger has compassion and uses his war trophy bullet to end Meeker's life. Montiel tells Steiger that he really is a United States citizen and not a Sioux. Steiger takes Montiel and Miller to live with his people.

NOTES AND COMMENTARY: The working title for *Run of the Arrow* was *The Last Bullet*. When this film was completed, all production at RKO Radio Pictures had been terminated. Universal-International became the distribution arm for the more important RKO features.

Civil War historian and author Shelby Foote noted the song "Oh I'm a Good Old Rebel" was written as a parody by Confederate Major Innes Randolph. The song was intended to elicit a humorous response in the wake of the stark conditions generated by the Reconstruction.

Rod Steiger hurt his foot and could not do the "run of the arrow" sequence. Director Sam Fuller then concentrated on the feet when it was filmed.

Sarita Montiel had a difficult time with the English language and no one could understand her. Angie Dickinson was brought in to dub all Montiel's lines in post-production. Samuel Fuller paid Dickinson back by giving her a lead part in *China Gate* (20th Century–Fox, 1957).

REVIEWS: "Rather strange psychological Western with solid performances to give it strength." *Western Movies*, Pitts; "Far from the standard Hollywood picture—this one makes you think—*Run of the Arrow* is an exemplary entry which shows Fuller in top form." *The Motion Picture Guide*, Nash and Ross.

SUMMATION: *Run of the Arrow* is an exceptional Western film. Rod Steiger gives a powerful performance as a man consumed with hate and how he learned to deal with life. Even though Steiger's performance carries the film, Brian Keith, Ralph Meeker and Charles Bronson offer sterling assistance in the fine supporting cast. Joseph Biroc captures the magnificence and grandeur of the St. George, Utah, area. Victor Young's impressive musical score adds to the effectiveness of this picture. Samuel Fuller's direction shows why he has earned the accolades heaped upon him.

HE TAMED THE TOUGHEST RANGE WAR IN THE WEST!

Saddle Tramp

Universal-International (September 1950); COLOR by Technicolor; RUNNING TIME: 77 min. CAST: Chuck Connor, **Joel McCrea**; Della, **Wanda Hendrix**; Rocky, **John Russell**; Jess Higgins, **John McIntire**; Ma Higgins, **Jeanette Nolan**; Pop, **Russell Simpson**; Mr.

Saddle Tramp (1950) scene card: Joel McCrea lifts Wanda Hendrix from her horse; left border—McCrea hits John Russell.

Hartnagle, **Ed Begley**; Robbie, **Jimmy Hunt**; Tommie, **Orley Lindgren**; Johnnie, **Gordon Gebert**; Butch, **Gregory Moffett**; Martinez, **Antonio Moreno**; Slim, **John Ridgely**; The Stranger, **Walter Coy**; Pancho, **Joaquin Garay**; Springer, **Peter Leeds**; Orvie, **Michael Steele**; Denver, **Paul Picerni**

CREDITS: Director, **Hugo Fregonese**; Producer, **Leonard Goldstein**; Story/Screenwriter, **Harold Shumate**; Editor, **Frank Gross**; Art Directors, **Bernard Herzbrun** and **Richard H. Riedel**; Set Decorators, **Russell A. Gausman** and **Oliver** Emert; Cinematographer, **Charles P. Boyle**; Costumes, **Bill Thomas**; Hair Stylist, **Joan St. Oegger**; Makeup, **Bud Westmore**; Sound, **Leslie I. Carey** and **Joe Lapis**; Music, **Joseph Gershenson**; Technicolor Color Consultant, **William Fritzche**

SONG: "The Cry of the Wild Goose" (Gilkyson)

LOCATION FILMING: Iverson Ranch, California

STORY: Footloose cowboy Connor (Joel McCrea) is riding through Nevada on his way to California. McCrea stops off at the ranch of his old friend, Slim (John Ridgely), and his four young sons. When Ridgely is thrown from McCrea's horse and killed, McCrea feels somewhat responsible for his friend's death and decides to care for the boys until a suitable home can be found. McCrea secures a job with Higgins (John McIntire), a rancher who dislikes children. McCrea hides the children in the brush and takes food from the ranch kitchen to feed them. Della (Wanda Hendrix), a 19-year-old girl who is running away from home, joins the boys and McCrea decides to take her under his wing also. Cattle are being rustled and there is bad blood between the McIntire ranch and neighboring rancher Martinez (Antonio Moreno). Each suspects the other of being the culprit. McIntire accuses McCrea of being in league with the rustlers but since there is no proof, just orders him off the ranch. With the children's help, McCrea is able to find the stolen cattle. The men actually responsible are Rocky (John Russell), McIntire's foreman; Springer (Peter Leeds), Moreno's foreman and Denver (Paul Picerni), a McIntire ranch hand. The rustlers capture McCrea but McCrea is able to free himself and start a rugged fistfight with Russell. McCrea wins the fight, the stolen cattle are recovered and McCrea settles down with Hendrix and the four boys.

NOTES AND COMMENTS: Paul Picerni's agent took him to Universal to see casting agent, Millie Gusse. Gusse interviewed Picerni and asked him if he could ride. Picerni, a veteran of World War II, said he could ride and he had been a member of the cavalry. Gusse was impressed and Picerni was cast in *Saddle Tramp*. On leaving the building, Picerni's agent remarked there was no cavalry in World War II, and even so, Picerni had been a member of the air force. Picerni remarked, "I know that, you know that, but she doesn't know that." In any event, Picerni quickly learned how to ride.

Paul Picerni remembers Joel McCrea as a "sweetheart of a guy." McCrea's character in person was similar to the character he usually portrayed on the movie screen.

Joel McCrea and Paul Picerni were riding in a limousine taking them out to location at Iverson's Ranch. They were travelling through San Fernando Valley, which at the time had nothing but farms, orange groves and chicken ranches. At the intersection of Woodland Hills and Topanga Canyon Boulevard, McCrea remarked that one day that area would be the center of Los Angeles. Picerni silently disagreed. Over the years a freeway was built, along with high-rise buildings. Harry Warner's ranch was sold to a development company and is the site of Warner Center, with high-rises, offices and department stores. Picerni commented, "McCrea wasn't far wrong when he said this would be the center of Los Angeles."

REVIEWS: "An enjoyable family western, thanks to McCrea's charm and a witty script." *The Motion Picture Guide*, Nash and Ross; "Kids provide fun in amusing yarn." *Hollywood Reporter*, 8/25/50.

SUMMATION: This is an easygoing family western with Joel McCrea in fine form as a footloose cowpuncher who doesn't want to take on any obligations but is forced to do so. The script focuses on McCrea's interactions with his four young charges and also with Wanda Hendrix. Jeanette Nolan as John McIntire wife, an Irish lass who believes in leprechauns, is an absolute delight and steals the show. McIntire, John Russell and Russell Simpson give good support. The rest of the cast is adequate. Hugo Fregonese directs with above average results.

He followed a violent trail of VENGEANCE!
Branded THIEF ... RENEGADE WOMAN KILLER ...
he had to win back honor, rank, love ... with a gunload of revenge!

The Saga of Hemp Brown

Universal-International (October 1958); EASTMAN COLOR by Pathé; FILMED in Cinemascope; RUNNING TIME: 80 min.

CAST: Hemp Brown, **Rory Calhoun**; Mona Langley, **Beverly Garland**; Jed Givens, **John Larch**; Hook, **Russell Johnson**; Serge Bolanos, **Fortunio Bonanova**; Sheriff, **Allan Lane**; Judge Rawlins, **Trevor Bardette**; Bo Slauter, **Morris Ankrum**; Colonel, **Addison Richards**; Mrs. Ford, **Marjorie Stapp**; Oldtimer, **Francis McDonald**; Amelia Smedley, **Yvette Vickers**; Alf Smedley, **Charles Boaz**; Gil Henry, **Hank Patterson**; Floyd Leacock, **Tom London**; Chang, **Victor Sen Yung**; Townsman, **I. Stanford Jolley**

CREDITS: Director, **Richard Carlson**; Assistant Director, **Gordon McLean**; Producer, **Gordon Kay**; Story, **Bernard Girard**; Screenwriter, **Bob Williams**; Editor, **Tony Martinelli**; Art Directors, **Alexander Golitzen** and **Robert Smith**; Set Decorators, **Russell A. Gausman** and **John P. Austin**; Cinematographer, **Philip Lathrop**; Costumes, **Bill Thomas**; Makeup, **Bud Westmore**; Sound, **Leslie I. Carey** and **Frank Wilkinson**; Music, **Joseph Gershenson**

LOCATION FILMING: Conejo Valley, California

STORY: Hemp Brown (Lt. Rory Calhoun) is in charge of a payroll detail and on the trail he meets an old cavalry sergeant Jed Givens (John Larch). Larch tells Calhoun he needs a lift to the fort to reenlist. In reality, Larch is the leader of the outlaw gang that ambushes the detail, steals the money and kills all the soldiers except Calhoun. Calhoun is left alive to take the responsibility for the massacre. The outlaws split up and plan to meet in a few weeks and divide the money. Calhoun is accused of cowardice by the army and given a dishonorable discharge. The army's records show that Larch died in an Indian skirmish. Calhoun vows to find Larch and clear his name. With Mona Langley's (Beverly Garland) help, Calhoun is able to make the connection between Larch and medicine show owner, Serge Bolanos (Fortunio Bonanova). Bonanova's show wagon transported the payroll to the rendezvous point. Calhoun captures Larch and forces Larch to clear his name. Calhoun and Garland have fallen in love with each other.

NOTES AND COMMENTARY: Beverly Garland remembered the showgirl costume she had to wear through most of her scenes in the picture. Garland wrote, "The costume, believe it or not, was very daring, especially when she put on her hose. My, we have come a long way from those straightlace days." Garland thought that Calhoun was the best looking actor around and wished she were much prettier so she could turn his head. She commented, "I am a good actress—not a beautiful one and I did not turn his head." She couldn't remember if Calhoun was a fine actor and said people were so busy looking at his eyes they didn't remember either. Beverly Garland was very impressed with John Larch. She wrote, "I did quite a few things with him and have always felt he was a fine actor."

In the fight sequence between Russell Johnson and Rory Calhoun, director Richard Carlson thought it would make a nice scene if Johnson would take a swing at Calhoun with his hook and take his hat off. Adding the hook added inches to Johnson's arm and changed his depth perception and he told Carlson, "I'm not going to swing that hook anywhere near his face." Calhoun added, "You're absolutely right. You're not going to." Johnson said that Calhoun was an adventurous kind of guy, a great personality and that he was easy to work with. He, also, commented, "There was no bullshit with him either."

The Saga of Hemp Brown was intended to be a television series. Producer Gordon Kay related this fact to author Boyd Magers. The story had a similar to *The Fugitive* (ABC, 1963–67) plot and episodes could be strung over many weeks as Calhoun searched for Larch.

Marjorie Stapp had previously worked with director Richard Carlson on the television program *I Led Three Lives* (ZIV, 1955-6). She appeared in three episodes.

REVIEWS: "Program oater with fair action, romance, production values." *Variety*, 8/13/58; "The medicine man character gives an unique touch to this otherwise gun-blazing western." *The Motion Picture Guide*, Nash and Ross.

SUMMATION: *The Saga of Hemp Brown* is a good, solid western with a suspenseful story and some rugged action. Director Richard Carlson keeps the story moving briskly along. There are good performances by Rory Calhoun as a man who is determined to clear his name and

Beverly Garland as the showgirl who is dissatisfied with the life that she's leading. John Larch has the plum role of the principal bad man and is allowed to stretch the gamut of emotion from nice guy to tough guy to a man afraid for his life. Russell Johnson as a vicious outlaw and Fortunio Bonanova as the medicine show owner give welcome support.

The Great Adventure ... The Mighty Conquest of Canada's Savage Mountain Empire

Saskatchewan

ALTERNATE TITLE: *O'Rourke of the Mounted*; Universal-International (March 1954); COLOR by Technicolor; RUNNING TIME: 87 min.

CAST: O'Rourke, **Alan Ladd**; Grace, **Shelley Winters**; Benton, **Robert Douglas**; Batouche, **J. Carrol Naish**; Smith, **Hugh O'Brian**; Abbott, **Richard Long**; Cajou, **Jay Silverheels**; Chief Dark Cloud, **Antonio Moreno**; Lawson, **George J. Lewis**; Banks, **Lowell Gilmore**; Spotted Eagle, **Anthony Caruso**; Keller, **Frank Chase**; Merrill, **Henry Wills**; Brill, **Robert D. Herron**; Cook, **John Cason**; Hassett, **Robert Hoy**

CREDITS: Director, **Raoul Walsh**; Assistant Director, **Frank Shaw**; Producer, **Aaron Rosenberg**; Story/Screenwriter, **Gil Doud**; Editor, **Frank Gross**; Art Directors, **Bernard Herzbrun** and **Richard H. Riedel**; Set Decorators, **Russell A. Gausman** and **John Austin**; Cinematographer, **John Seitz**; Costumes, **Bill Thomas**; Hair Stylist, **Joan St. Oegger**; Makeup, **Bud Westmore**; Sound, **Leslie I. Carey** and **Joe Lapis**; Music Direction, **Joseph Gershenson**; Technicolor Color Consultant, **William Fritzsche**

LOCATION FILMING: Banff National Park in Alberta, Canada, and the Canadian Rockies

STORY: Mountie Inspector O'Rourke (Alan Ladd) and his blood brother, Cree Indian Cajou (Jay Silverheels), come upon a wagon train that had been attacked by Sioux Indians. The sole survivor, Grace (Shelley Winters), does not want to return to the fort in Saskatchewan but is forced to do so when another party of Sioux attacks. At the fort Ladd meets the new commander, Benton (Robert Douglas), and finds that an order has been issued requiring the Cree to relinquish their rifles. Ladd is ordered to obtain Silverheels' weapon. Silverheels gives up his rifle but declares that he and Ladd are no longer friends. Ladd keeps Silverheels' rifle for himself. U.S. Marshal Smith (Hugh O'Brian) arrives at the fort looking for Winters who is wanted for the murder of O'Brian's brother in Montana. Douglas is ordered to vacate the fort and bring all troops, rifles and ammunition to Fort

Saskatchewan (1954) scene card: The Mounties, with Shelley Winters, Alan Ladd (*third*), and J. Carrol Naish (*fourth*), attempt to reach Fort Walsh.

Walsh. With the troops' departure, the Sioux Indians attempt to form an alliance with the Cree to fight the Mounties. The Sioux attack the Mounties and the Mounties are able to drive the Sioux off. Ladd realizes it would be suicide to stay on the wagon route and the party must take a mountainous route. Douglas disagrees and the men side with Ladd. Douglas vows Ladd and the men will be arrested and court martialed. During the trek, O'Brian tells Winters if she will go with him, she will not have to go back to Montana to stand trial. Winters and Ladd begin

to fall in love. O'Brian's jealousy emerges and he admits he killed his brother. When O'Brian levels a pistol at Ladd, Douglas shoots O'Brian. Through Ladd's ingenuity, the party is able to reach Fort Walsh safely. Ladd goes to the Cree camp and finds the Cree will remain peaceful if their weapons are returned. Ladd reaches Fort Walsh where Banks (Lowell Gilmore) ignores his findings. Since Gilmore thinks a treaty can be reached with the Sioux, Ladd is arrested. Silverheels sneaks into the fort and tells Ladd the Sioux are on the way to attack the fort and will encounter and wipe out Gilmore and his men. Silverheels breaks Ladd and his men out of the stockade. Ladd sees that the Cree receive rifles and ammunition. Ladd and the Cree arrive in time to save Gilmore and his men from annihilation and chase the Sioux across the border into the States. Douglas withdraws the charges against Ladd and his men. The Cree are allowed to keep their weapons. Ladd returns the rifle to Silverheels. Douglas orders Ladd to escort Winters to Montana to have the charges dropped against her.

NOTES AND COMMENTARY: Robert Hoy had a busy time in *Saskatchewan*. Not only did Hoy play the sergeant who arrested Ladd in the film, he doubled Anthony Caruso, Richard Long and Jay Silverheels and played some "non-descript Indians."

In the cast listings, Richard Long is billed as Abbott but early in the film Long introduces himself as Richard J. Scanlon and is called Scanlon throughout the picture.

REVIEWS: "The story doesn't amount to much but the scenic locales and fine photography make up for it." *Western Movies*, Pitts; "A big budget western with a tiny little plot." *The Universal Story*, Hirshhorn.

SUMMATION: *Saskatchewan* is an exciting, above average Mounties versus Indians adventure saga. The acting by Alan Ladd, Shelley Winters and the rest of the cast is adequate and the script is more or less routine. The magnificent Canadian vistas, Raoul Walsh's sure direction, which manages to generate some suspense, and some fine action scenes rescue the picture.

PITY THE SAILORS ON A NIGHT LIKE THIS!
ROXY'S in Port!
It's that ravishing riot from New Orleans ...
with lips no man could resist—and a right
hook no woman could dodge!

Scarlet Angel

Universal-International (June 1952); COLOR by Technicolor; RUNNING TIME: 80½ min.

CAST: Roxy McClanahan, **Yvonne De Carlo**; Frank Truscott, **Rock Hudson**; Malcolm Bradley, **Richard Denning**; Norton Wade, **Whitfield Connors**; Linda Caldwell, **Bodil Miller**; Susan Bradley, **Amanda Blake**; Morgan Caldwell, **Henry O'Neill**; Pierre, **Henry Brandon**; Eugenia Caldwell, **Maude Wallace**; Walter Frisby, **Dan Riss**; Phineas Calhoun, **Tol Avery**; Union Soldiers, **Eddie Dew** and **Fred Coby**; Pharmacist, **Nolan Leary**; Jason Mortimer, **Thomas Browne Henry**; Waiter at Scarlet

Scarlet Angel (1952) scene card: Yvonne De Carlo (*seated*) is accused by Dabbs Greer (*standing center*) of stealing his money. Leo Curley (*right in hat*) is poised to arrest her while Rock Hudson (*seated*) is about to start a free-for-all to allow DeCarlo to escape.

Angel, **Eddie Parker**; Sheriff Jasper, **Leo Curley**; Tinhorn Customer, **Dabbs Greer**; Bobbie Caldwell, **Mickey Pfleger**; Dr. Corbin, **Harry Harvey**; Crewman, **Charles Horvath**; Jeb, **Dale Van Sickel**; Bartender, **Bud Wolfe**; Waiter thrown from balcony, **Davy Sharpe**

CREDITS: Director, **Sidney Salkow**; Producer, **Leonard Goldstein**; Story/Screenwriter, **Oscar Brodney**; Editor, **Ted J. Kent**; Art Directors, **Bernard Herzbrun** and **Robert Clatworthy**; Set Decorators, **Russell A. Gausman** and **Julia Heron**; Cinematographer, **Russell Metty**; Choreography, **Harold Belfer**; Costumes, **Rosemary Odell**; Hair Stylist, **Joan St. Oegger**; Makeup, **Bud Westmore**; Sound, **Leslie I. Carey** and **Glenn E. Anderson**; Music Direction, **Joseph Gershenson**; Technicolor Color Consultant, **William Fritzsche**

STORY: Sea captain Frank Truscott (Rock Hudson) decides to make a night on the town in New Orleans and Roxy McClanahan (Yvonne De Carlo) plans to relieve him of his money. Hudson is aware of all De Carlo's tricks but hangs around because he finds De Carlo attractive. When De Carlo is about to be arrested for stealing a customer's money the previous night, Hudson starts a brawl that allows De Carlo to escape. De Carlo avoids Hudson's amorous intentions by deciding to help a sick woman, Linda Caldwell (Bodil Miller), and her baby. Needing to leave New Orleans, De Carlo steals money from Hudson and takes Miller and her baby to a house outside the city. Miller again becomes ill and dies. De Carlo decides to assume Miller's identity. A lawyer, Walter Frisby (Dan Riss), contacts De Carlo and tells her that her deceased husband's wealthy family wants her to come with the baby to San Francisco. De Carlo decides to continue with the impersonation and likes the idea of being wealthy. Even though "father-in-law" Morgan Caldwell (Henry O'Neill) welcomes her, Malcolm (Richard Denning) and Susan (Amanda Blake) resent De Carlo's presence. Denning and Blake see the baby as a threat to their inheritance. Denning is willing to marry De Carlo to ensure he will have money. De Carlo's life is complicated by the return of Hudson in her life. Hudson decides to allow De Carlo to continue her deception feeling that she will eventually realize that she should make a life with him.

De Carlo is about to tell O'Neill the truth when her old employer, Pierre (Henry Brandon), and a sleazy private investigator, Calhoun (Tol Avery), blackmail De Carlo. Brandon will state the baby is De Carlo's, depriving the baby of his rightful inheritance. De Carlo is about to marry Denning when De Carlo's "mother-in-law," Eugenia (Maude Wallace) sees a birthmark on the baby identical to a birthmark on her son. With the baby's inheritance assured, De Carlo is now free to marry Hudson.

NOTES AND COMMENTARY: *Scarlet Angel* was a remake and reworking of Marlene Dietrich's *The Flame of New Orleans* (Universal 1941).

REVIEWS: "Fair remake of *Flame of New Orleans*." *Western Movies*, Pitts; "A fetching Technicolor showcase for a lady (Yvonne De Carlo) who decidedly rates framing." *New York Times*, 6/21/52.

SUMMATION: *Scarlet Angel* is an enjoyable melodrama highlighted by Yvonne De Carlo's dynamic performance as a woman who finally realizes that money won't buy her happiness. Rock Hudson delivers a solid performance as De Carlo's love interest. Well-staged saloon brawls are interspersed through the film and add to the story's enjoyment. Director Sidney Salkow does a nice job of balancing the action with the melodramatics.

*THE SAGA OF THOSE HILARIOUS KANSAS BRAWLS SET
TO SINGIN' ... DANCIN' ... AND MAD, MAD MUSIC!*
The boys were after the girls!
The girls were after the boys!
And both of them were after the same darn thing!

The Second Greatest Sex

Universal-International (December 1955); COLOR by Technicolor; FILMED in Cinemascope; RUNNING TIME: 87 min.

CAST: Liza, **Jeanne Crain**; Matt, **George Nader**; Katy, **Kitty Kallen**; Job, **Bert Lahr**; Roscoe, **Paul Gilbert**; Reverend Maxwell, **Keith Andes**; Birdie, **Mamie Van Doren**; Alf, **Tommy Rall**; Tilda, **Kathleen Case**; Newt, **Jimmy Boyd**; Cassie, **Edna Skinner**; Cousin Emmy, **Cousin Emmy**; Zachary Bean, **Ward Ellis**; Sarah McClure, **Mary Marlo**; Jones City Leader, **Sheb Wooley**; Simon Clegghorn, **George Wallace**; "Doc" Grimshaw, **Harry Harvey**; Sally McClure, **Sharon Bell**; Square Dancers, **The Midwesterners**; Osawkie Townsman, **Ted Mapes**

CREDITS: Director, **George Marshall**; Assistant Director, **William Holland**; Producer, **Albert J. Cohen**; Screenwriter, **Charles Hoffman**; Editor, **Frank Gross**; Art Directors, **Alexander Golitzen** and **Robert Clatworthy**; Set Decorators, **Russell A. Gausman** and **John P. Austin**; Cinematographer, **Wilfrid M. Cline**; Special Photography, **Clifford Stine**; Costumes, **Jay A. Morley, Jr.**; Hair Stylist, **Joan St. Oegger**; Makeup, **Bud Westmore**;

Sound, **Leslie I. Carey** and **Glenn E. Anderson**; Music Supervisor, **Joseph Gershenson**; Choreographer, **Lee Scott**; Technicolor Color Consultant, **William Fritzsche**

SONGS: "What Good is a Woman Without a Man" (Sherrell and Moody)—sung by **Jeanne Crain, Kitty Kallen, Mamie Van Doren, Edna Skinner, Kathleen Case, Cousin Emmy** and **female chorus**; "Travelin' Man" (Sherrell and Moody)—sung and danced by **Paul Gilbert**; "My Love is Yours" (Sherrell and Moody)—sung by **George Nader**; "Down Yonder" (Gilbert)—danced by **The Midwesterners**; "What Good Is a Woman Without a Man"/"Travelin' Man" (Sherrell and Moody)—sung by **Edna Skinner** and **Paul Gilbert**; "There's Gonna Be a Wedding" (Sherrell and Moody)—sung by **Jimmy Boyd, Sharon Bell, Bert Lahr**; "How Lonely Can I Get" (Whitney and Kramer)—sung by **Kitty Kallen** and danced by **Tommy Rall**; "Send Us a Miracle" (Sherrell and Moody)—sung by **Keith Andes**; "Lysistrata" (Sherrell and Moody)—sung by **Jeanne Crain, Edna Skinner, Kitty Kallen, Mamie Van Doren, Cousin Emmy** and **female chorus**; "The

THE GIRLS ..... and ..... THE BOYS

JEANNE CRAIN	GEORGE NADER
KITTY KALLEN	BERT LAHR
MAMIE VAN DOREN	KEITH ANDES
KATHLEEN CASE	PAUL GILBERT

The SECOND GREATEST SEX

CINEMASCOPE
TECHNICOLOR

with TOMMY RALL · EDNA SKINNER
JIMMY BOYD · COUSIN EMMY
THE MIDWESTERNERS

DIRECTED BY GEORGE MARSHALL

WRITTEN FOR THE SCREEN BY
CHARLES HOFFMAN

PRODUCED BY ALBERT J. COHEN

A UNIVERSAL-INTERNATIONAL PICTURE

The Second Greatest Sex (1955) scene card: Bert Lahr (*center*) sings the title song; George Nader can be seen under Lahr's upraised arm.

Second Greatest Sex" (Livingston and Evans)—sung by **Bert Lahr** and **male chorus**; "The Second Greatest Sex" (reprise) (Livingston and Evans) sung by uncredited voices

SOURCE: Play, "Lysistrata" by **Aristophanes**

STORY: In Kansas, the men of three communities vie to have their township become the county seat. The township that possesses the safe with all the important records in a courthouse will receive this honor. The men of Osawkie have been away from home for two months to obtain the safe, leaving the women feeling very lonely. The men are successful but arrive home dead tired, which disappoints the women. When town leader Matt (George Nader) places the building of a court-house ahead of romancing Liza (Jeanne Crain), Crain becomes very angry. Nader quickly makes amends and the two are married. On their wedding night, the men of Mandaroon steal the safe and Nader has to organize the townsmen to once again go after the safe. Tired of all this fighting, schoolteacher Cassie (Edna Skinner) remembers the story of Lysistrata, and the women decide to go on strike until the fighting is stopped. Crain leads the townswomen to an abandoned fort where the women intend to stay until the men decide to stay home. Finally in a three-way battle between the men on Osawkie, Mandaroon and Jones City, the safe is lost forever. Crain suggests that the county seat be the equal responsibility of the three townships, to which the men readily agree. Now all the men and women are happily reunited.

NOTES AND COMMENTARY: Keith Andes had sung on Broadway but this was the only motion picture in which he was given the chance to sing. Keith Andes knew that George Nader was dubbed in his singing efforts but had no knowledge of whose voice was heard on the soundtrack. Jeanne Crain used the voice of Doreen Tryden in her vocal efforts.

At the studio Keith Andes used to "camp" it up a bit, talking like a homosexual and exaggerating the S's, with George Nader and Rock Hudson. Even though Nader and Hudson were gay, they had different reactions to the carrying-on. Nader though Andes' antics were hilarious but Hudson didn't think they were

funny at all. Edna Skinner had an outside scene in which large carbon arcs were used. The inside of Skinner's eyelids developed tiny blisters. Skinner was in agony for a few days.

REVIEWS: "Attractive cast in a gay musical with a western setting." *Variety*, 10/5/55; "It's fun—with some mighty fine, lively songs and dances all done up in Cinemascope and color." *New York Times*, 2/11/56.

SUMMATION: *The Second Greatest Sex* is a tuneful, toe-tapping, entertaining musical with a western setting. The stars, Jeanne Crain, George Nader, Kitty Kallen, and Mamie Van Doren acquit themselves well. Edna Skinner stands out in her comedic role as the old-maid schoolteacher. Bert Lahr, in addition to providing some good comedy, gives a nice turn to the title song. Broadway singer Keith Andes, with his rendition of *Send Us a Miracle*, makes one wonder why he was never cast in another musical film. Other show-stopping songs are "Lysistrata" and "Travelin' Man." Director George Marshall is to be commended for providing audiences a bright and sprightly time.

The flaming fury of the EVERGLADES INDIAN WARS!
The fighting story of the great chief OSCEOLA!

Seminole

Universal-International (March 1953); COLOR by Technicolor; RUNNING TIME: 87 min.

CAST: Lance Caldwell, **Rock Hudson**; Revere, **Barbara Hale**; Osceola, **Anthony Quinn**; Major Degan, **Richard Carlson**; Kajeck, **Hugh O'Brian**; Lt. Hamilton, **Russell Johnson**; Sgt. Magruder, **Lee Marvin**; Kulak, **Ralph Moody**; Zachary Taylor, **Fay Roope**; Corp. Gerard, **James Best**; Scott, **John Day**; Farmer, **Walter Reed**; Mattie Sue, **Soledad Jiminez**; Trooper Taft, **Robert Dane**; Indian, **Davy Sharpe**; Captain Sibley, **Robert Bray**; Trooper Scott, **Dan Poore**; Trooper, **Frank Chase**; Officer, **Alex Sharpe**; Hendricks, **Duane Thorson**

CREDITS: Director, **Budd Boetticher**; Assistant Director, **Tom Shaw**, Producer, **Howard Christie**; Story/Screenwriter, **Charles K. Peck, Jr.**; Editor, **Virgil Vogel**; Art Directors, **Alexander Golitzen** and **Emrich Nicholson**; Set Decorators, **Russell A. Gausman and Joseph Kish**; Cinematographer, **Russell Metty**; Costumes, **Rosemary Odell**; Hair Stylist, **Joan St. Oegger**; Makeup, **Bud Westmore**; Sound, **Leslie I. Carey** and **Glenn E. Anderson**; Music, **Joseph Gershenson**; Technicolor Color Consultant, **William Fritzsche**; Military Technical Advisor, **Col. Paul R. Davison**

LOCATION FILMING: Florida

STORY: Lance Caldwell (Rock Hudson), now a second lieutenant, returns to his native Florida to serve under Major Degan (Richard Carlson). Hudson finds the Seminoles are on the warpath because Carlson is trying to send the Indians to reservations out West. Hudson believes the Seminoles are embracing warfare only as a last resort and there must be a chance for peace. Osceola (Anthony Quinn), chief of the Seminoles and a boyhood friend of Hudson's, wants to meet with Hudson to discuss ways peace can be attained. Before Hudson and Quinn can meet, Carlson decides to enter the swamp and make a surprise attack on the Indian village. Carlson's raid is unsuccessful and the Seminoles virtually wipe out the soldiers. Only a wounded Carlson and two of his soldiers make it back to the fort. Hudson is also wounded but instead of being killed is captured by the Seminoles. Hudson finds that Quinn is the Seminole chieftain. Word is sent to Quinn that Carlson wants peace talks. This is a ruse and Quinn is captured, beaten and jailed. Hudson's anger at Quinn's treatment causes Carlson to have Hudson confined to quarters pending a court martial. During a heavy rain, Kajeck (Hugh O'Brian) sneaks into the fort to kill Quinn and thus become the

Seminole (1953) scene card: Hugh O'Brian (*left*) tells Fay Roope (*right*) that he is responsible for Anthony Quinn's death, which allows the army to drop the charges against Rock Hudson (*center*).

new chief of the Seminoles. Hudson foils O'Brian's attempt but in the struggle Quinn is knocked unconscious and his face goes beneath the rainwater that is filling up the cell and Quinn drowns. O'Brian escapes unseen from the fort and Hudson is accused of Quinn's death. Hudson is court martialed and is sentenced to be executed. O'Brian, now chief of the tribe, comes to the fort to exonerate Hudson and claim Quinn's body. There is hope for peace after time has healed the wounds between the two peoples.

NOTES AND COMMENTARY: The quicksand scene was filmed on a soundstage. A platform was filled with water. Powdered cork was placed on top of the water to simulate a quicksand bog. In trying to get the scene filmed James Best nearly drowned twice. The scene called for Best to stay underwater until Rock Hudson could rescue him. The first time someone forgot to turn on Best's air hose when he was underwater. Stuntmen were under the water with Best but they couldn't see him because the cork got in their eyes. Best was tied to the cannon but the ropes were loose. On the next take, the cannon sunk and Best came to the surface. Then the decision was made to put an aqualung under Best but the aqualung made Best rise to the surface. Finally the aqualung was secured. Best was tied down appropriately and now everything was finally ready to have Hudson come to the rescue. Hudson went under the water and grabbed Best in a "private part." Best, still underwater, started to laugh and nearly drowned. If you look closely at this scene as Best is pulled out of the "quicksand," you will see a trace of a smile on his face.

James Best remembers that a scene was filmed in which the Indians were ready to spear Rock Hudson. Best ran in front of Hudson and was run through with a spear. Unfortunately, this did not make the final cut. The scene that did make the final cut had a soldier, prior to the sneak attack on the Indian village, ask Carlson what should be done with Best. Carlson replies, "We'll pick him up after the skirmish." So, all the audience remembers is that the fever-ridden Best was left in the Everglades.

Budd Boetticher remembers that the company actually went to Florida to film the picture but that the Universal back lot made a better Seminole location.

In the film, stuntman Davy Sharpe played the part of a nondescript Indian who would be shot out of a tree and then fall onto the top of a straw hut. Sharpe had the tree tied off to give him a solid purchase as he fell. But as Sharpe pushed off, the wire broke that was holding the tree forward so that it wouldn't go backwards. This meant Sharpe would not hit the hut at the exact spot that had been planned. A cross had been painted on the roof of the hut to indicate the exact spot Sharpe should go through. Sharpe twisted his body in mid-air, gathered himself and made his entry into the hut. Sharpe had moved his body so that he almost hit the right spot. Instead of a clean entry, the back of Sharpe's neck, right at the shoulders, caught the crosspiece and it flipped him quick. The first thought was that Sharpe had been killed. Someone called, "Cut." The cast and crew rushed into the hut and Sharpe was lying in the catcher. A catcher, in those days, was made up of empty cardboard boxes built on top of 2x6s so the stuntman would have a little give when he hit and the boxes would collapse under him. There would be no thud when he hit and the stuntman would just slowly come to a stop. Everyone looked at Sharpe and not only were they stunned to see that he was alive but also that he had his traditional cigar in his mouth. No one ever figured how Sharpe had hid a cigar in his skimpy Indian wardrobe. Sharpe looked at the group and said, "Hi, guys. You know that would have killed an ordinary man."

Seminole was Barbara Hale's first freelance movie role after the completion of her contract with Columbia Pictures. Actor John Day is probably better known to movie buffs as stuntman-actor John Daheim. Russell Johnson liked Rock Hudson and thought that he was a great actor. He stated, "I knew him from the time I was under contract there at Universal. He was always very friendly, very nice and very open. He was a down to earth person. There was no bullshit with Rock."

Russell Johnson liked to work with Budd Boetticher. Boetticher always would be pleased with those actors who would try to do their own stunts. Johnson made these comments, " He was kind of a macho person. He considered himself a man's man. He had some of a half-assed love affair with bullfighting in his time, I think."

REVIEWS: "Regulation outdoor actioner, average entry." *Variety*, 2/25/53; "Though only about average for a Boetticher western, the film has some good action sequences." *The Motion Picture Guide*, Nash and Ross.

SUMMATION: This is a good action film bolstered by the intense, brooding and compelling performance by Anthony Quinn as the Seminole chief. Rock Hudson and Hugh O'Brian also give good accounts of themselves as the sympathetic Union officer and the war-minded Indian warrior. Richard Carlson's mannerisms remind you too much of those that Bogart's Captain Queeg in *The Caine Mutiny* (Columbia, 1954) would exhibit the following year but without the feelings of sympathy that Bogart was able to elicit. Two action scenes come off exceedingly well, Carlson's surprise attack on the Indian village and O'Brian's attempt to murder Quinn in the fort's jail. Boetticher directs well within the script's limitations that fail to define Carlson's part adequately.

THE MAN WHO SHOOK TEXAS LIKE A PAIR OF DICE ...
AND THE RANGER WHO HAD TO STOP HIM!!!

Seven Ways from Sundown

Universal-International (September 1960); EASTMAN COLOR by Pathé; RUNNING TIME: 87 min.

CAST: Seven Jones, **Audie Murphy**; Jim Flood, **Barry Sullivan**; Joy Karrington, **Venetia Stevenson**; Sergeant Hennessey, **John McIntire**; Lieutenant Herly, **Kenneth Tobey**; Ma Karrington, **Mary Field**; Graves, **Ken Lynch**; Lucinda, **Suzanne Lloyd**; Fogarty, **Ward Ramsey**; Duncan, **Don Collier**; Beeker, **Jack Kruschen**; Gilda, **Claudia Barrett**; Jody, **Teddy Rooney**; Dorton, **Don Haggerty**; Eavens, **Robert Burton**; Chief Wagoneer, **Fred Graham**; 2nd Wagoneer, **Dale Van Sickel**; Townsman, **Guy Wilkerson**

CREDITS: Director, **Harry Keller**;

Assistant Director, **Thomas J. Connor, Jr.**; Producer, **Gordon Kay**; Screenwriter, **Clair Huffaker**; Editor, **Tony Martinelli**; Art Directors, **Alexander Golitzen** and **William Newberry**; Set Decorator, **George Milo**; Cinematographer, **Ellis Carter**; Hair Stylist, **Larry Germain**; Makeup, **Bud Westmore**; Sound, **Waldon O. Watson** and **William Russell**; Music, **William Lava and Irving Gertz**; Music Supervisor, **Joseph Gershenson**

LOCATION FILMING: Las Vegas area, Nevada

SOURCE: Novel, *Seven Ways from Sundown* by **Clair Huffaker**

STORY: Raw ranger recruit Seven Jones (Audie Murphy) and veteran ranger Hennessey (John McIntire) are assigned to bring in Flood (Barry Sullivan), a notorious outlaw of considerable charm. Seeing that he's being followed, Sullivan sends a message to Murphy and McIntire to turn back. When Murphy and McIntire press on, Sullivan ambushes them, killing McIntire. Murphy continues to follow Sullivan and is able to arrest Sullivan. As Murphy brings Sullivan back to Texas to be tried for murder, Sullivan finds that he killed McIntire, a man who once saved his life. Murphy took up the life of a ranger because an older brother was killed in the line of duty. Sullivan killed Murphy's brother, a fact unknown to Murphy. Sullivan places the blame on a ranger companion who chose to hide rather than watch Murphy's brother's back. As the two men travel back to Texas, Murphy is able to thwart Sullivan's attempts to escape and all attempts to either free or kill Sullivan.

In the last encounter, Sullivan is able to hide a pistol under his shirt. After Sullivan is jailed, he begins to taunt ranger lieutenant Herly (Kenneth Tobey), the man who hid the night Murphy's brother was killed. Afraid that Sullivan will tell his story to Murphy, Tobey decides to stage a jailbreak and kill Sullivan. The plan backfires, Tobey is dispatched and Sullivan makes good his escape. Murphy has a chance to shoot Sullivan in the escape but cannot pull the trigger because of the friendship that has developed between the two. As he escapes Sullivan fires a wild shot that hits Joy (Venetia Stevenson), a girl with whom Murphy has fallen in love. Fortunately, Stevenson is just wounded but Murphy knows now that Sullivan must pay for his bloody past. Figuring that Sullivan will elude the posse, Murphy waits for Sullivan's return. Murphy tells Sullivan that he has to arrest him. Thinking about his shot that hit an innocent girl and his bullets that killed Murphy's brother, Sullivan lets Murphy beat him to the draw.

NOTES AND COMMENTARY: Teddy Rooney is Barry Sullivan's fishing companion in the film. Rooney was the son of the talented Mickey Rooney. The young Rooney's career was quite brief, spanning just a few years. George Sherman was the first director on this film. A violent argument between

Audie Murphy and Sherman led to Sherman's departure from the directorial helm. Harry Keller took over and received sole directorial-credit.

REVIEWS: "Well made oater." *Variety*, 9/14/60; "Suspenseful." *The Universal Story*, Hirschhorn.

SUMMATION: *Seven Ways from Sundown* is a neat western tale that emphasizes characterization and the resulting interaction between its two stars, Audie Murphy and Barry Sullivan. Murphy is the naïve young man who wants to believe in the best in everyone. Sullivan is the world-wizened hedonist who believes that the world exists for his pleasure and a simple "I'm sorry" is sufficient for friends he's hurt. The well-crafted script allows the two men from different backgrounds to grow to respect each other until Sullivan's behavior almost costs Murphy the girl he loves. The episodic nature of the script only allows John McIntire to shine in his all-too-brief role. Venetia Stevenson is pretty and competent which is all the script will allow her to be.

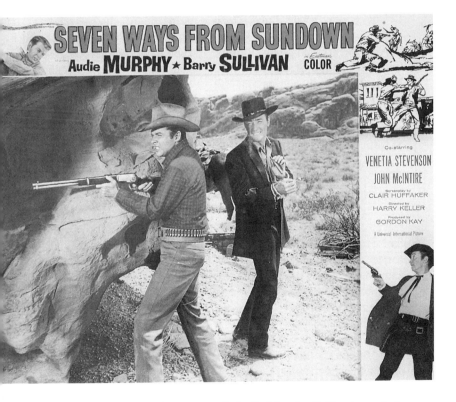

Seven Ways from Sundown (1960) scene card: Audie Murphy (*left*) gets ready to fend off an Indian attack as a concerned Barry Sullivan looks on; Sullivan in right border.

ENEMIES CHAINED TOGETHER LIKE MAD DOGS!

Showdown

Universal-International (May 1963); RUNNING TIME: 79 min.

CAST: Chris Foster, **Audie Murphy**; Estelle, **Kathleen Crowley**; Bert Pickett, **Charles Drake**; Lavalle, **Harold J. Stone**; Caslon, **Skip Homeier**; Foray, **L.Q. Jones**; Charlie Reeder, **Strother Martin**; Hebron, **Charles Horvath**; Marshal Beaudine, **John McKee**; Chaca, **Henry Wills**; Guard, **Joe Haworth**; Buster, **Kevin Brodie**; Smithy's wife, **Carol Thurston**; Express an, **Dabbs Greer**; Lloyd (Deputy), **William Phipps**; Card Player, **Bob Steele**; Bartender, **Harry Lauter**; Saloon patron, **Bill Henry**; Bouncer, **Dale Van Sickel**

CREDITS: Director, **R.G. Springsteen**; Assistant Director, **Terence Nelson**; Producer, **Gordon Kay**; Assistant to Producer, **Willard Willingham**; Executive Producer, **Edward Muhl**; Screenwriter, **Bronson Howitzer**; Editor, **Jerome Thoms**; Art Directors, **Alexander Golitzen** and **Alfred Sweeney**; Set Decorator, **Oliver Emert**; Cinematographer, **Ellis W. Carter**; Costumes, **Rosemary Odell**; Hair Stylist, **Larry Germain**; Makeup, **Bud Westmore**; Sound, **Waldon O. Watson** and **Frank H. Wilkinson**; Music, **Hans J. Salter**; Music Supervisor, **Joseph Gershenson**; Unit Production Manager, **Robert Larson**; Titles by **Pacific Title**

SONG: "Take Me to Town" (Lee and Shapiro)—sung by **Kathleen Crowley**

LOCATION FILMING: Lone Pine, California

STORY: Two cowhands, Chris (Audie Murphy) and Bert (Charles Drake), stop at a border town to cash their paychecks. Drake decides to enter a poker game. Drake, who has become drunk, is a big loser and starts an altercation that lands both Drake and Murphy in jail. The jail is a tall post with neck irons to contain the prisoners. Also, outlaw Lavelle (Harold J. Stone) and his men have been arrested. Stone initiates a jailbreak in which Murphy and Drake are forced to take part. The men take refuge in an express office. Stone breaks into a safe and steals all the ready cash before making a getaway. When Murphy and Drake see the sheriff and his men are shooting at all prisoners, they also decide to make a break for safety. Before they go, Drake takes some bonds marked pay to bearer. When Stone's men pick up Murphy and Drake, Drake uses the bonds to barter for his and Murphy's freedom. Drake is allowed to go to town to cash the bonds with Murphy held as a hostage. Drake sends the money to a former girlfriend, Estelle (Kathleen Crowley), before being brought back to Stone's camp. Murphy pleads for a chance to get the money from Crowley. Crowley doesn't want to part with the money but Murphy finally is

Showdown (1963) portrait card: Audie Murphy (*left*) and Harold J. Stone; right border (*top*) Murphy and Stone, (*bottom*) Murphy and Kathleen Crowley.

able to take the money from her. As Murphy is bargaining with Stone for Drake's freedom, henchman Caslon (Skip Homeier) brings Crowley as a captive. Drake starts a diversion that allows Murphy and Crowley to escape, while losing his life in the process. Murphy decides to take the money back to the express office. Stone heads Murphy off and arrives in town first. Stone plans to ambush Murphy but a warning saves his life and Murphy finally is able to dispatch Stone. Murphy and Crowley now plan a life together.

NOTES AND COMMENTARY: The beginning and end titles show that *Showdown* is a Universal-International picture. All the advertising, which includes posters and lobby cards, state that the film is a Universal picture. Audie Murphy was unhappy making *Showdown* in black and white and had no problem letting producer Gordon Kay know his displeasure. This was Murphy's first Universal-International western that was not filmed in color. Murphy had two previous westerns that had been filmed in black and white, *Red*

Badge of Courage (Metro-Goldwyn-Mayer, 1951) and *Cast a Long Shadow* (United Artists, 1959).

Kathleen Crowley's song "Take Me to Town" was used in three previous Universal-International westerns, *Wyoming Mail* (1950), *Take Me to Town* (1953) and *A Day of Fury* (1956).

The title *Showdown* had been used in a William Boyd "Hopalong Cassidy" western (Paramount, 1940), a William Elliott big budget western (Republic, 1950) and Universal reused the title for a Dean Martin/Rock Hudson western in 1973.

Showdown marked the last time Charles Drake played in a motion picture with Audie Murphy. The two also worked together in *Gunsmoke* (Universal-International, 1953), *To Hell and Back* (Universal-International, 1955), *Walk the Proud Land* (Universal-International, 1956) and *No Name on the Bullet* (Universal-International, 1959).

REVIEWS: "Routine oater, lack of color is no help." *Variety*, 4/3/63; "Another Audie Murphy western, aimed largely at the drive-in trade." *The Universal Story*, Hirschhorn.

SUMMATION: *Showdown* is a slightly better than average western strengthened by good performances from Audie Murphy, Kathleen Crowley and Charles Drake. For a change in a "B+ or A-" western, the heroine has some scenes in which she can emote and Crowley is up to the task. Murphy handles the hero role adequately and Drake does a fine job as Murphy's weakling friend. Veteran director. R.G. Springsteen keeps the story on the move but the lack of color is a decided detriment to the film.

NEITHER A WOMAN'S LOVE ... NOR A KILLER'S REPUTATION ...
Could make Jim Trask back up his badge with bullets!

Showdown at Abilene

Universal-International (October 1956); COLOR by Technicolor; RUNNING TIME: 80 min.

CAST: Jim Trask, **Jock Mahoney**; Peggy Bigelow, **Martha Hyer**; Dave Mosely, **Lyle Bettger**; Verne Ward, **David Janssen**; Chip Tomlin, **Grant Williams**; Dan Claudius, **Ted de Corsia**; Ross Bigelow, **Harry Harvey, Sr.**; Jack Bedford, **Dayton Lummis**; Nelson, **Richard H. Cutting**; Sprague, **Robert G. Anderson**; Frank Scovie, **John Maxwell**; Loop, **Lane Bradford**; Cattleman, **Kenneth MacDonald**

CREDITS: Director, **Charles Haas**; Assistant Director, **Phil Bowles**; Producer, **Howard Christie**; Screenwriter, **Berne Giler**; Editor, **Ray Snyder**; Art Directors, **Alexander Golitzen** and **Richard H. Riedel**;

Set Decorators, **Russell A. Gausman** and **Ruby R. Levitt**; Cinematographer, **Irving Glassberg**; Costumes, **Rosemary Odell**; Hair Stylist, **Joan St. Oegger**; Makeup, **Bud Westmore**; Sound, **Leslie I. Carey** and **Glenn E. Anderson**; Music Supervision, **Joseph Gershenson**; Technicolor Color Consultant, **William Fritzsche**

LOCATION FILMING: Morrison Ranch and Agoura, California

SOURCE: Novel, Gun Shy by Clarence Upson Young

STORY: Confederate soldier Jim Trash (Jock Mahoney) returns to Abilene where he finds the townspeople thought he had been killed in the war. In his absence, childhood friend Dave Mosely (Lyle Bettger) has become a prosperous cattle buyer and is now engaged to marry Mahoney's former girlfriend, Peggy (Martha Hyer). With more land being devoted to cattle, friction has developed between the farmers and the cattlemen. Sheriff Claudius (Ted de Corsia) is working for Bettger. Bettger wants to give Mahoney back his old job as sheriff. Mahoney takes the job as a favor to Bettger because of

Showdown at Abilene (1956) scene cord: Lyle Bettger (*left*) finds that Jock Mahoney killed his brother by accident in the Civil War and that his fiancée, Martha Hyer, is in love with Mahoney.

his involvement in a childhood accident resulting in the loss of Bettger's right hand. In reality, Mahoney takes the job because of his guilt feelings of mistakenly killing Bettger's brother in the Civil War. This is also the reason Mahoney does not try to win Hyer back. Ted de Corsia's violence and cruelty results in the death of farmer Tomlin (Grant Williams). Hyer breaks off her engagement to Bettger and Mahoney tells Bettger how his brother died. Hurt and angry, Bettger makes an unsuccessful attempt to kill Mahoney. Mahoney takes the bullets from Bettger's gun. With Williams' death, the farmers now band together to take revenge on Bettger and de Corsia. When de Corsia warns Bettger, an argument ensues with de Corsia shooting Bettger when the hammer on Bettger's gun falls on an empty chamber. Mahoney chases after de Corsia and meets him in a showdown in the dusty streets of Abilene. Although wounded, Mahoney is still able to kill de Corsia. Mahoney and Hyer are now free to settle down together.

NOTES AND COMMENTARY: *Showdown at Abilene* was remade as *Gunfight in Abilene* (Universal, 1967) with Bobby Darin as the lead. The working title for this film was *Gun Shy*.

REVIEWS: "Though the plot is routine, the direction is well paced and creates some intelligent sequences, lifting this film to a better level than the typical B western." *The Motion Picture Guide*, Nash and Ross; "Nicely entertaining Jock Mahoney vehicle." *Western Movies*, Pitts.

SUMMATION: This is a neat little western with the novel approach of having a hero who is afraid to fire a gun. Although Jock Mahoney and Martha Hyer deliver good performances as the leads, it is Lyle Bettger who steals the acting honors. Bettger is able to convey a range of emotions, both visually with his eyes and face and vocally with the changing timbre of his raspy voice, that add to the overall conviction of the story. Ted de Corsia makes a properly nasty villain who finally gets his just desserts. Director Charles Haas paces the story nicely. A special mention has to be made for the athleticism of Mahoney. In the course of the story's unfolding, Mahoney makes a couple of fantastic leaps to further facilitate the action.

ADVENTURE ... RAGING TO THE VERY PEAKS OF EXCITEMENT!
A hunted man ... a reckless girl ...
stalking the last of the wild horse herds!

Sierra

Universal-International (June 1950); COLOR by Technicolor; RUNNING TIME: 83 min.

CAST: Riley Martin, **Wanda Hendrix**; Ring Hassard, **Audie Murphy**; Lonesome, **Burl Ives**; Jeff Hassard, **Dean Jagger**; Big Matt, **Richard Rober**; Brent Coulter, **Anthony Curtis**; Sam Coulter, **Houseley Stevenson**; Duke Lafferty, **Elliot Reid**; Dr. Robbins, **Griff Barnett**; Aunt Susan, **Elizabeth Risdon**; Sheriff Knudsen, **Roy Roberts**; Hogan, **Gregg Martell**; Mrs. Jonas, **Sara Allgood**; Judge Prentiss, **Erskine Sanford**; Jed Coulter, **John Doucette**; Little Sam, **Jim Arness**; Jim Coulter, **Ted Jordan**; Snake Willens, **I. Stanford Jolley**; Al, **Jack Ingram**; Big Matt, **Richard Rober**

CREDITS: Director, **Alfred E. Green**; Producer, **Michael Kraike**; Screenwriter, **Edna Anhalt**; Additional Dialogue, **Milton Gunzberg**; Editor, **Ted J. Kent**; Art Directors, **Bernard Herzbrun** and **Robert F. Boyle**; Set Decorators, **Russell A. Gausman** and **John Austin**; Cinematographer, **Russell Metty**; Hair Stylist, **Joan St. Oegger**; Makeup, **Bud Westmore**; Sound, **Leslie I. Carey** and **Glenn E. Anderson**; Music, **Walter Scharf**; Technicolor Color Consultant, **William Fritzsche**

SONGS: "Hideaway" (Hughes and Herbert)—sung by **Burl Ives**; "End of the Road" (Hughes and Herbert)—sung by **Burl Ives**; "Black Angus McDougal" (Hughes and Herbert)—sung by **Burl Ives**; "Drift Along" (Hughes and Herbert)—sung by **Burl Ives**; "Sarah the Mule" (Ives)—sung by **Burl Ives**; "The Whale Song" (Ives)—sung by **Burl Ives**

LOCATION FILMING: Kanab, Utah

SOURCE: Novel, *Forbidden Valley* by **Stuart Hardy**

STORY: Jeff Hassard (Dean Jagger) is hiding out in the Sierras with his son, Ring (Audie Murphy), to avoid capture for a crime he did not commit. Their only friend is a hermit, Lonesome (Burl Ives). Into this setting comes lawyer Riley Martin (Wanda Hendrix), who is afoot with the loss of her horse. Hendrix believes Jagger to be innocent and is trying to find evidence to clear him. Hendrix' fiancé, Duke (Elliot Reid), wants Hendrix to stop her investigation. Murphy has some unbranded mustangs stolen by Reid's foreman, Big Matt (Richard Rober). When Sheriff Knudson (Roy Roberts) refuses to act against Rober, Murphy tries to take his horses back and is captured and arrested. At the trial, Murphy is revealed as Jagger's son and is placed back in jail. Ives breaks Murphy out of jail. Murphy hires out-

Sierra (1950) scene card: Dean Jagger blindfolds Wanda Hendrix as she rides double with Audie Murphy to a secret hideout; left border shows Hendrix and Murphy.

law Sam Coulter (Houseley Stevenson) and his family to assist him in rounding up a wild horse herd. Rober sees that the horses have been rounded up and run into a box canyon. Reid and Rober stampede the horses. Murphy is able to turn the horses back into the canyon and the horses trample Reid and Rober. Rober lives long enough to confess to the crimes of which Jagger has been accused. Stevenson and his gang are also innocent of any wrongdoing. Hendrix and Murphy will make a life together.

NOTES AND COMMENTARY: *Sierra* was a remake of *Forbidden Valley* (Universal, 1937) starring Noah Beery, Jr. This story was also the basis for a *Virginian* (NBC) television episode, "Hideout," in January 1965, featuring Roberta Shore with guest stars Forrest Tucker, Andrew Prine and Douglas Fowley.

Footage of the black stallion and the wild horse herd was previously seen in *Red Canyon* (Universal-International, 1949).

At the time this movie was

filmed, Wanda Hendrix and Audie Murphy were husband and wife.

Anthony Curtis and Jim Arness became major stars as Tony Curtis and James Arness, respectively.

REVIEWS: "Despite some nice color photography, this routine western was lowered several notches thanks to the flat direction and endless string of cliches." *The Motion Picture Guide*, Nash and Ross; "Cliché-ridden story." *Variety*, 4/26/50.

SUMMATION: *Sierra* is an average western bolstered by fine scenic values and good shots of beautiful wild horses running over the plains. Audie Murphy and Wanda Hendrix are adequate as the leads. Houseley Stevenson stands out among the supporting cast. The script is not fully convincing in the unfolding of the story. The scene in which Burl Ives sings deputy Gregg Martell to sleep so that Ives can break Murphy out of jail is best left to the lower grade western film.

ONE WAS A DEADLY DANGER TO THE OTHER TWO!
BEN LANE ... quiet, but ready like a waiting bullet!
FRANK JESSE ... determined, his gun always for hire!
KELLY ... explosive, plotting a strange revenge
that could destroy them all!

6 Black Horses

Universal-International (June 1962); EASTMAN COLOR by Pathé; RUNNING TIME: 80 min.

CAST: Ben Lane, **Audie Murphy**; Frank Jesse, **Dan Duryea**; Kelly, **Joan O'Brien**; Boone, **George Wallace**; Mustanger, **Roy Barcroft**; Joe (Puncher), **Bob Steele**; Indian Leader, **Henry Wills**; Undertaker, **Phil Chambers**; Mexican Girl, **Charlita Regis**; Kelly's Gunman, **Dale Van Sickel**; Charlie, **Richard Pasco**

CREDITS: Directed, **Harry Keller**; Assistant Director, **Ivan Volkman**; Producer, **Gordon Kay**; Executive Producer, **Edward Muhl**; Screenwriter, **Burt Kennedy**; Editor, **Aaron Stell**; Art Directors, **Alexander Golitzen** and **Robert Luthardt**; Set Decorator, **Oliver Emert**; Cinematographer, **Maury Gertsman**; Hair Stylist, **Larry Germain**; Makeup, **Bud Westmore**; Sound, **Waldon O. Watson** and **Frank H. Wilkinson**; Music Supervisor, **Joseph Gershenson**

LOCATION FILMING: Las Vegas area, Nevada

STORY: Drifting cowboy Ben Lane (Audie Murphy), afoot on the desert, lassoes a wild horse, unaware

6 Black Horses (1962) scene card: A lance thrown by an Apache hits Joan O'Brien in her shoulder as Audie Murphy comes to her aid; Dan Duryea behind Murphy; right border—Murphy, Duryea, O'Brien.

the horse is part of a herd claimed by mustangers. About to be hanged as a horse thief, the execution is stopped by Frank Jesse (Dan Duryea), a gunman temporarily earning honest money herding horses. In Perdido, the two men are hired by a mysterious woman, Kelly (Joan O'Brien), to guide her through Apache territory to her husband in Del Cobre. During the journey, after a skirmish with the Apaches, O'Brien confesses she wants to see Duryea killed because

Duryea killed her husband. As it becomes more dangerous to continue, Duryea insists on completing the journey to obtain the money he was promised for the job. When Murphy begins protesting against continuing, Duryea knocks Murphy out and continues on with O'Brien. Murphy catches up to Duryea. There is a faceoff in which Murphy outdraws and kills Duryea. Murphy's desire is to own his family's ranch in Montana and O'Brien decides to go with him.

NOTES AND COMMENTARY: When Audie Murphy tells Dan Duryea, "There's some things a man can't ride around," this comment should sound familiar to most western movie buffs. Screenwriter Burt Kennedy had Randolph Scott make the same statement in *The Tall T* (Columbia, 1957).

6 Black Horses was the third and final film that Dan Duryea made with Audie Murphy. The two worked well together. Since the two were protagonists, the box score was: *Ride Clear of Diablo* (Universal-International, 1954), Duryea died giving Murphy a chance to bring the true villains to justice; *Night Passage* (Universal-International, 1957), Murphy stops a Duryea bullet meant for James Stewart and in *6 Black Horses*, Duryea is beaten to the draw by Murphy. So their meetings ended in a tie.

REVIEWS: "Serviceable western, dramatically unstable but photographically appealing." *Variety*, 3/14/62; "*Six Black Horses* benefited from the sheer visual sweep of the scenery and relegated its puny story to the background." *The Universal Story*, Hirschhorn.

SUMMATION: *6 Black Horses* is a routine but entertaining western adventure thanks primarily to the workmanship of the two stars, Audie Murphy and Dan Duryea, and the fine location filming. Murphy does a good job as the honest member of the duo while Duryea is able to fine-tune his "nice" bad guy routine. In an interesting analogy, screenwriter Burt Kennedy has Duryea compare his gunfighter profession to the oldest profession. Duryea declares that in both instances you don't remember the faces of those who hire you. In the main though, Kennedy does not deliver a script that had the bite of those delivered for the Randolph Scott–Budd Boetticher films. It is beyond director Harry Keller's workmanlike abilities to raise the film to an above average picture.

NOT SINCE "MAJOR BENSON" SUCH A HEARTWARMING COMEDY!
You'll be rootin' for this cap-pistol shootin'
sawed-off orphan, who wins the West's biggest
movie star in a contest ... and then cuts him down to size!

Slim Carter

Universal-International (November 1957); EASTMAN COLOR by Pathé; RUNNING TIME: 82 min.

CAST: Slim Carter (Hughie Mack), **Jock Mahoney**; Clover Doyle, **Julie Adams**; Leo Gallaher, **Tim Hovey**; Joe Brewster, **William Hopper**; Montana Burriss, **Ben Johnson**;

Slim Carter (1957) title card: (*left to right*) Jock Mahoney, Joanna Moore, Mahoney, Julie Adams, and Tim Hovey.

Charlene Carroll, **Joanna Moore**; Richard L. Howard, **Walter Reed**; Hat Check Girl, **Maggie Mahoney**; Cigarette Girl, **Roxanne Arlen**; M.C., **Jim Healey**; Frank Hanneman, **Bill Williams**; Allie Hanneman, **Barbara Hale**; Nick (Stunt Indian), **Robert Hoy**

CREDITS: Director, **Richard H. Bartlett**; Assistant Director, **William Holland**; Producer, **Howie Horwitz**; Story, **David Bramson** and **Mary C. McCall, Jr.**; Screenwriter, **Montgomery Pittman**; Editor, **Fred MacDowell**; Art Directors, **Alexander Golitzen** and **Eric Orbom**; Set Decorators, **Russell A. Gausman** and **Ray Jeffers**; Cinematographer, **Ellis W. Carter**; Special Photography, **Clifford Stine**; Costumes, **Bill Thomas**; Makeup, **Bud Westmore**; Sound, **Leslie I. Carey** and **Corson Jowett**; Music, **Herman Stein**; Music Supervision, **Joseph Gershenson**

SONGS: "Ride Cowboy, Ride" (Wakely and Gershenson)—sung by **Jock Mahoney**; *Gold* (Freed and Smith)—sung by **Jock Mahoney**; and "Cowboy" (Wakely and Gershenson)—sung by **Jock Mahoney**

STORY: With the loss of their western star, Clover Doyle (Julie Adams) of Globe Studios finds a replacement in nightclub singer Slim Carter (Jock Mahoney). Knowing Mahoney's weakness for women, the studio signs Mahoney but makes Adams responsible for keeping him out of trouble. Mahoney becomes a top money-making star and to give him more publicity, the studio promotes a contest in which a youngster will come to Hollywood to live with Mahoney for a month. Orphan Leo Gallaher (Tim Hovey) wins the contest and his openness and honesty begin to change Mahoney's character. Mahoney even performs a dangerous stunt so Hovey will not be disappointed in him. Mahoney and Adams begin to fall in love, but a misunderstanding causes Adams to tell Mahoney that their relationship will have to remain on a business level. As Hovey is to return to the orphanage, Mahoney is pleading over the telephone to adopt Hovey. Finally, Adams discovers Mahoney is sincere and is not using Hovey in a cruel publicity stunt. Adams tells Mahoney she will marry him. Hovey is ecstatic to learn he is adopting a mother and father.

NOTES AND COMMENTARY: Walter Reed had these comments to make on Jock Mahoney, "Good guy. Great horseman and not a bad actor." Actress Maggie Mahoney had also received billing in other films as Margaret Field. Mahoney was the mother of Academy Award–winner Sally Field and later the wife of Jock Mahoney.

Slim Carter had its World Premier at the Joy Theater in New Orleans, Louisiana.

REVIEWS: "Surprising good satirical look at Hollywood and cowboy stars." *Western Movies*, Pitts; "A very enjoyable and pleasant romantic comedy." *Hollywood Reporter*, 9/27/57.

SUMMATION: *Slim Carter* is an enjoyable heartwarming comedy that tells of a western star who is humanized by a young boy. Jock Mahoney delivers a good performance as the western star and Julie Adams chips in with a nice job as the agent who discovers Mahoney. But it's little Tim Hovey who practically steals the show utilizing his naturalness that makes him one of the better child actors. Ben Johnson, William Hopper, Walter Reed, Bill Williams and Barbara Hale offer fine support. Richard H. Bartlett's direction is on target with this feel-good motion picture.

DOWN THE CHURNING FURY OF THE RIVER OF DEATH ...
PAST THE ARROWS OF SAVAGE UTES!
The story of four desperate people—their fate
in the hands of the man they had condemned to die!

Smoke Signal

Universal-International (March 1955); COLOR by Technicolor; RUNNING TIME: 88 min.

CAST: Brett Halliday, **Dana Andrews**; Laura Evans, **Piper Laurie**; Lieutenant Wayne Ford, **Rex Reason**; Captain Harper, **William Talman**; Sergeant Miles, **Milburn Stone**; Garode, **Douglas Spencer**; Corporal Rogers, **Gordon Jones**; Private Livingston, **William Schallert**; First Sergeant Daly, **Robert Wilke**; Private Porter, **Bill Phipps**; Delche, **Pat Hogan**; Ute Prisoner, **Peter Coe**

CREDITS: Director, **Jerry Hopper**; Assistant Director, **Joseph E. Kenny**; Producer, **Howard Christie**; Story/Screenwriters, **George F. Slavin** and **George W. George**; Editor, **Milton Carruth**; Art Directors, **Alexander Golitzen** and **Richard H. Riedel**; Set Decorators, **Russell A. Gausman** and **James M. Walters**; Cinematographer, **Clifford Stine**; Costumes, **Bill Thomas**; Hair Stylist, **Joan St. Oegger**; Makeup, **Bud Westmore**; Sound, **Leslie I. Carey** and **Robert Pritchard**; Music Supervisor, **Joseph Gershenson**; Technicolor Color Consultant, **William Fritzsche**

LOCATION FILMING: Moab area (Big Bend of the Colorado River, Professor Valley, Ida Gulch, San Juan River), Utah

STORY: An army company, led by Captain Harper (William Talman), and trapper Garode (Douglas Spencer) find a dead soldier who had been killed by a Ute arrow. Barely making it to the fort, Talman finds that Lieutenant Ford (Rex Reason) and his men are pinned down by the Utes. Also in the fort are Laura Evans (Piper Laurie), daughter of the deceased commander, and Brett Halliday (Dana Andrews), a former army officer wanted for desertion, treason and murder. Andrews tells Talman that he left the Utes and the Utes want to stop him from enlisting the Apache Indians' help in preventing an Indian war. Talman's hatred of Andrews stems from a battle with the cavalry against a band of Utes led by Andrews. With the situation looking hopeless, Andrews suggests that river travel is the only way to reach safety. Andrews shows his valor in the journey to the fort. Laurie finds that her father's hatred of the Indians resulted in unfair charges against Andrews and gradually falls in love with Andrews. Reason's jealousy of the romance between Andrews and Laurie causes Reason to attempt to kill Andrews. Laurie's shout saves Andrews' life but Reason falls from a high canyon wall to his death. As the survivors

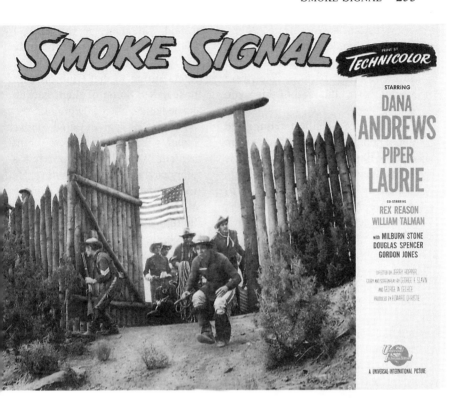

Smoke Signal (1955) scene card: Pat Hogan (*right*) leads the cavalry's escape to safety. (*Standing left to right*) **Milburn Stone, William Talman, Robert Wilke, Gordon Jones, Rex Reason,** and (*crouching*) **William Schallert.**

reach safety, Talman allows Andrews to escape so he can persuade the Apaches to stop the Indian war. Laurie knows Andrews will return.

NOTES AND COMMENTARY: William Schallert has fond memories of this film. Schallert hadn't been working much at the time and received the job on the day that his third son Mark came home from the hospital. Schallert commented, "We had been having a pretty slim time of it and it was good getting that job." *Smoke Signal* had an enjoyable part for William Schallert. Schallert said,

"It was really fun to play a character like that. I think I was blind in it. So that's a challenge. That's the kind of parts I used to get. I didn't fit in any of the usual categories in Hollywood. I wasn't a leading man. I obviously was going to be a character actor."

Bill Phipps and William Schallert decided to show off one day. They jumped into the river (probably the Big Bend of the Colorado River) and road the rapids past the point where a scene for the picture was being shot. The cast and crew began screaming at them. Schallert remembers, "They were afraid we were going to drown and screw up the picture. We were young. It was the kind of thing you do."

William Schallert reminisced about going on location, "You get on a shoot like that and everybody tells jokes. We were stuck in Moab, Utah, which is out in the middle of nowhere. Moab was at the time the sort of center of a uranium find. There were a lot of wildcat miners mining for uranium in the area. That was about all that was going on there. The town itself was quite little. There was a street with one turn, an L-shaped street. You turned to the left and you were outside town. They had something called the Club 66. We used to hang out there because there was no place else in town. Dana (Andrews) was drinking quite a bit at the time and once in a while he'd have a tough time getting up in the morning because of that. He got past that later on. You'd go crazy; it was like being in the army. We would sit around and tell jokes, mostly dirty jokes. I started to write a long, complex obscene poem. I don't remember any of this now, thank God. Each time we would get together, I would come in with another verse. And then Milburn [Stone] would add stuff to it. That was how we would kill time. It reminded me a lot of being in the army because it was such an out of the way place. Being on location has that feel to it anyway. The only difference is there are women around. Not many in this case, I think Piper [Laurie] was the only one in this picture. I spent a lot of nights sitting in that Club 66 with those guys. Some of them getting sloshed and some of them not."

Jerry Hopper directed *Smoke Signal*. William Schallert commented, "I liked him a lot. He's a funny guy. He had a funny story. He was a combat photographer during World War II. He'd gone into the Philippines and as he hit the beach something hit him in the leg and he didn't know what the hell it was. He thought he'd gotten shot. They took an x-ray. The guy said, 'This is crazy, but you've got an arrow in your leg.' It turned out it was a Parker pen clip that somehow or another had gotten blown off a pen and landed in his leg, pierced his skin and stuck in his calf or some place like that. It looked like an arrow because it was this bitty little thing."

Smoke Signal received a certificate of outstanding merit by the Southern California Motion Picture Council.

REVIEWS: "Standard outdoor actioner, visual qualities are better than the story values." *Variety*, 2/23/55; "Actionful and entertaining drama." *Western Movies*, Pitts.

SUMMATION: *Smoke Signal* is an above average cavalry versus Indians saga. Dana Andrews is effective as an army officer who wants peace with the Indians. Piper Laurie makes the most of her role of the daughter of an army officer who gradually falls in love with Andrews. William Talman is good in a role that allows his character to become a more sympathetic individual. Milburn Stone, Douglas Spencer, Gordon Jones and William Schallert offer fine support. Cinematographer Clifford Stine elegantly photographs the marvelous scenic vistas. Jerry Hopper's direction is able to add some much-needed suspense in the action western.

REX BEACH'S IMMORTAL SAGA OF THE YUKON!
The adventure—lusting saga of The Gold Seekers ...
who lived and loved by violence!

The Spoilers

Universal-International (January 1956); COLOR by Technicolor; RUNNING TIME: 84 min.

CAST: Cherry Malotte, **Anne Baxter**; Roy Glennister, **Jeff Chandler**; Alex McNamara, **Rory Calhoun**; Blackie, **Ray Danton**; Helen Chester, **Barbara Britton**; Dextry, **John McIntire**; Flapjack Simms, **Wallace Ford**; Banty Jones, **Forrest Lewis**; Judge Stillman, **Carl Benton Reid**; Mr. Skinner, **Raymond Walburn**; Duchess, **Ruth Donnelly**; Wheaton, **Dayton Lummis**; Jonathan Struve, **Willis Bouchey**; The Marshal, **Roy Barcroft**; Montrose, **Byron Foulger**; Bartender, **Robert Foulk**; Bank Manager, **Arthur Space**; Piano Player; **Harry Seymour**; Miner, **Bob Steele**; Berry, **Edwin Parker**; Deputy, **Lee Roberts**; Deputy, **John Close**; Miners, **Lane Bradford**, **Mike Ragan**, **Richard Alexander** and **Frank Sully**; Engineer, **John Harmon**; Deputy, **Terry Frost**

CREDITS: Director, **Jesse Hibbs**; Assistant Director, **Frank Shaw**; Producer, **Ross Hunter**; Screenwriters, **Oscar Brodney** and **Charles Hoffman**; Editor, **Paul Weatherwax**; Art Directors, **Alexander Golitzen** and **Alfred Sweeney**; Set Decorators, **Russell A. Gausman** and **John P. Austin**; Cinematographer, **Maury Gertsman**; Costumes, **Bill Thomas**; Hair Stylist, **Joan St. Oegger**; Makeup, **Bud Westmore**; Sound, **Leslie I. Carey** and **John A. Bolger, Jr.**; Music Supervisor, **Joseph Gershenson**; Technicolor Color Consultant, **William Fritzsche**

SONG: "Careless Love" (Hughes and Herbert)—sung by **Anne Baxter**

SOURCE: Novel, *The Spoilers* by **Rex Beach**

STORY: Mine owner Roy Glennister (Jeff Chandler) and his partner Dextry (John McIntire) return to Alaska from Seattle to find most of the smaller mine owners having their claims contested by newcomers. Chandler's girlfriend, saloon owner Cherry Malotte (Anne Baxter), becomes jealous when she sees Chandler being attentive to fellow passenger Helen Chester (Barbara Britton). A claim is filed against Chandler's mine and McIntire wants to repel the law by force. Britton helps convince Chandler to let the courts establish ownership. The divergent point of view causes Chandler and McIntire to split up. When the smaller mine owners have their claims restored, Chandler begins to have faith in the courts. Chandler's faith is short-lived as Judge Stillman (Carl Benton Reid) declares that it will be six months before a decision on ownership can be delivered. Gold Commissioner Alex McNamar (Rory Calhoun), his assistant Struve (Willis Bouchey), Reid and Britton are in league with each other to loot Chandler's mine of at least a quarter-of-a-million dollars in gold before the mine is returned to Chandler. To make it more difficult for Chandler to prove his case, the mine's safe, containing papers that will prove ownership, is moved to town and locked up in a bank vault. Chandler and McIntire resolve their differences and make an unsuccessful attempt to retrieve their safe. In the robbery attempt, Blackie (Ray Danton), who is in love with Baxter and wants his rival, Chandler, out of the way, murders the Marshal (Roy Barcroft). Chandler is arrested for the murder. Calhoun plans a phony jailbreak in which Chandler will be killed. Baxter finds out about the plan and is able to get Chandler out of jail unharmed. Gunfire has been heard in the vicinity of the jail and Calhoun thinks Chandler has been killed. Baxter acts grief-stricken and asks Calhoun to take her back to her apartment over her saloon. Chandler and McIntire retake their mine. In the bat-

tle, Danton is mortally wounded and confesses to the murder clearing Chandler. The miners arrest Reid and Bouchey before they can leave town. Chandler goes to Baxter's apartment and a knock-down, drag-out fight starts between Calhoun and Chandler that carries though the saloon and out to the muddy streets. Chandler emerges victorious and wins Baxter.

NOTES AND COMMENTARY: Reportedly, Rex Beach based his novel on actual claim-jumping activities in Nome, Alaska. There were four previous screen entries of Rex Beach's *The Spoilers*. The first two were silent films: in 1914 with William Farnum and Tom Santschi in a Selig release, and in a 1923 Goldwyn production with Milton Sills and Noah Beery, Sr. The first sound entry came from Paramount in 1930 with Gary Cooper and William Boyd. Not the Boyd of "Hopalong Cassidy" fame but an actor known as, but not billed as, William "Stage" Boyd. Universal was responsible for the 1942 version with John Wayne and Randolph Scott.

In the first three entries, the character of Cherry Malotte was the second feminine lead to the Helen Chester part. Chester ended up with Roy Glennister through the 1930 versions. When Universal decided to remake *The Spoilers* in 1941, the part of Cherry Malotte was upgraded to meet the talents of the now popular Marlene Dietrich and was the romantic interest for John Wayne.

The saga of Cherry Malotte continued in Rex Beach's *The Silver Horde* (Radio Pictures, 1930). Evelyn

Brent played Cherry and found true love in the arms of Boyd Emerson, played by a youthful Joel McCrea. Louis Wolheim, Jean Arthur and Raymond Hatton co-starred.

Former cowboy star Bob Steele receives 19th billing as a miner. To this author's eyes, he's probably the miner who drives the wagon in the bank holdup sequence.

This was the final motion picture appearance for Raymond Walburn. Walburn came out of retirement in 1962 to play the part of Erronious in the Broadway production, *A Funny Thing Happened on the Way to the Forum*.

Footage from *The Far Country* (Universal-International, 1955) was used behind the opening credits.

The scriptwriters came up with an interesting dialogue exchange between Anne Baxter and Forrest Lewis:

> *Baxter:* "When a man gets hot-under-the-collar, a drink is the second best thing to cool him off."
> *Lewis:* "What's the first best thing?"
> *Baxter:* "You're too young to know, Banty."

REVIEWS: "Good prospecting still." *Variety*, 12/7/55; "The basic ingredients in this tale of greed, gold and claim-jumping in an Alaskan boom town managed to retain its power to involve." *The Universal Story*, Clive Hirschhorn.

The Spoilers (1956) scene card: Jeff Chandler delivers a crushing blow to Rory Calhoun's jaw in another version of the famous fistfight.

SUMMATION: In the fifth telling of Rex Beach's adventure novel, *The Spoilers*, Universal-International has fashioned a handsomely mounted exciting production culminating in the now classic fistfight that allows good to triumph over evil. Combatants Jeff Chandler (good) and Rory Calhoun (evil) are perfect in their roles. Anne Baxter shines as Cherry Malotte, the object of both men's affections. John McIntire as Chandler's partner and Barbara Britton as the woman who momentarily distracts Chandler provide able support. Jesse Hibbs directs capably and keeps the story on the move and holds the audience's interest while awaiting the climactic fistfight.

ROOTIN' SHOOTING—BANG UP—WESTERN

Stagecoach to Dancers' Rock

A Gray-Mac Production/Universal-International (October 1962); RUNNING TIME: 72 min.

CAST: Jess Dollard, **Warren Stevens**; Dade Coleman, **Martin Landau**; Dr. Ann Thompson, **Jody Lawrence**; Major John Southern, **Don Wilbanks**; Hiram Best, **Del Moore**; Carl "Whip" Mott, **Bob Anderson**; Loi Yan Wu, **Judy Dan**; Quint Rucker, **Rand Brooks**; Jude, **Gene Roth**; Sheriff, **Charles Tannen**; Ben Wade, **Mike Ragan**; Roy, **Mauritz Hugo**; 1st Holster, **Tim Bolton**; 2nd Holster, **Milan Smith**; Mai Lei, **Alicia Li**; Ah Ling, **Cherrylene Lee**

CREDITS: Director/Producer, **Earl Bellamy**; Assistant Director, **Daniel J. McCauley**; Executive Producer, **Del Moore**; Story/Screenwriter, **Kenneth Darling**; Editor, **Budd Small**; Art Director, **Leslie Thomas**; Cinematographer, **Ed Fitzgerald**; Still Photographer, **Bob Coburn**; Makeup, **Larry Butterworth**; Sound, **William Bernds** and **Ryder Sound Services**; Property Master, **George W. McKinney**; Production Supervisor, **Harold Hourihan**; Music, **Franz Steininger**

SONGS: "Ballad of Dancers' Rock" (Steininger and Ackerman)—sung by **Bud Dashiell** and **The Kinsmen** and "Confucius Say" (Steininger and Ackerman)—sung by **Judy Dan**

LOCATION FILMING: Palm Dale and Lancaster areas, California

STORY: Five passengers, gambler Dade Coleman (Martin Landau), medical student Ann Thompson (Jody Lawrence), army major John Southern (Don Wilbanks), Indian agent Hiram Best (Del Moore), and librarian Loi Yan Wu (Judy Dan), leave Tucson on the stagecoach to Dancers' Rock through Apache country. Division agent Quint Rucker (Rand Brooks) decides to accompany stage driver Mott (Bob Anderson). Brooks is transporting a considerable sum of money. Road agent Dollard

Stagecoach to Dancers' Rock (1962) scene card: **Warren Stevens shoots a rattlesnake as Jody Lawrence looks on in disgust; right border—Martin Landau pointing a pistol, Stevens stands over Bob Anderson's body.**

(Warren Stevens) and his accomplice Wade (Mike Ragan) are working with Brooks to steal the money from the stage line. Stevens joins the stage as a passenger. Dan becomes ill and some of the passengers think she has smallpox. Ragan attempts to hold up the stage but becomes frightened and flees when he thinks the passengers have smallpox. When Anderson stops to rest the horses, Stevens, Landau, Lawrence, Wilbanks and Dan step down from the coach. Anderson and Brooks take this opportunity to drive off and strand the passengers. Walking through the desert to Dancers'

Rock, the passengers come upon the stagecoach. Apaches had attacked the coach and all occupants are dead and the horses run off. Stevens suggests that they stay with the coach. When Wilbanks discovers that Landau had found a canteen and refused to share the water with the others, Landau is told to stay on top of the coach. When everyone is asleep, Landau steals Stevens' pistol and Lawrence's knife then kills Wilbanks when he is discovered. Landau shoots Stevens in the leg to render him useless to overpower him. Landau rapes Lawrence and forces her to wait on him. Landau allows Dan to attend to Stevens and finally makes them move further out on the desert. Suddenly, Landau sees a stagecoach coming from Dancers' Rock to Tucson. Realizing that Lawrence's testimony would cost him his life, Landau shoots her. Landau tries to flag down the coach. The stagecoach driver, wounded and delirious from an Indian attack on the stage, mistakes Landau for an Apache and without slowing down, shoots him. Stevens is able to round up the stage horses that the Apaches had run off, and he and Dan start their journey to San Francisco.

NOTES AND COMMENTARY: Director Earl Bellamy was proud of *Stagecoach to Dancers' Rock* and made these comments, "It [the film] got a review and I have to say it was not a bad review. It gave me credit for the fact that it was shot in black and white, I enjoyed that. It was shot in black and white for the main reason we didn't have the money to put it in color. It turned out well. The people [the cast] were just great. I knew exactly who I wanted and I approached each one individually and they absolutely said they would do the show. I thought I had a pretty good cast. We shot the show in seven days." Bellamy spoke of the photography, "I thought we had very good camerawork, which I'm very conscious of. I lay out all my shots and work very hard with it. The cameraman and I are inseparable and I always get a cameraman I know and work well with. Consequently you get exactly what you want. I thought there were some good camera shots

on top of the stagecoach coming in the one station where they couldn't get the horses."

Earl Bellamy talked about the producing this film, "He [Del Moore] got the script from the writer, Kenny Darling, then he approached me to direct it. We went ahead, and had a little trouble with the money. The people that had originated it with Del, it was George Ray and one other, and they were going to put up the money. It turned out they didn't have a nickel. I ended up putting my own money in the show. Del wanted credit for coming up with the script. I took over from there. But I sold it. We independently made it and I ended up selling it a year to the day that we started. That worked out okay. Everybody was happy. We didn't make a dime but we got our money back."

In the film there is a scene where Martin Landau drops a rattlesnake at Warren Stevens' feet and Earl Bellamy remembered, "Warren said. 'Make sure when you drop it, get out of the way because I'm coming through.' That worked well, you have to do some of that stuff but you don't endanger anybody's life."

Warren Stevens remembers the picture and Earl Bellamy and reminisced, "There was not an interior in the whole thing. It was rough, with the wind machine and the desert. We did it with Earl Bellamy, a very good director, a fine director. On a low budget we did it. I don't know how he brought it in but he did. I had brought the script to him originally. [Note: Bellamy remembers receiving the story from Del Moore.] I thought it was a very good, nice little action picture. Half of it was stolen from *Lifeboat* [20th Century–Fox], the other half from *Stagecoach* [United Artists, 1939]. I can't say enough good things about him [Bellamy]. He was terrific and I had worked with him before [a *Wells Fargo* television show with Dale Robertson]. He and I understood each other very well, I think. That's why I brought the picture to him because I liked him as a director so much. I think he should have bigger breaks than he got. He was that fine a director as far as I'm concerned."

REVIEWS: "The low budget takes full advantage of the desert setting and the good performances to create a taut and ironic thriller." *The Motion Picture Guide*, Nash and Ross; "A low-budget, rather off-beat western." *The Universal Story*, Hirschhorn.

SUMMATION: *Stagecoach to Dancers' Rock* is a fascinating and impressive "B" western. The film begins like a poor man's *Stagecoach* (United Artists, 1939). Then about halfway through, Martin Landau takes over the film with an over-the-top performance as a crazed murderer that propels the story to its ironic climax. Landau gives the movie the presence it needs to be first-rate. The other performances range from satisfactory to good, with fine work by Warren Stevens, Jody Lawrence, Judy Dan and Rand Brooks. Earl Bellamy directs the proceedings with a loving hand and a deft touch, which results in a real western sleeper.

MIGHTY AS COCHISE!
DANGEROUS AS GERONIMO!
The story of Cara Blanca ... his last great raid and the 8 desperate souls who defied his howling hordes to save a frontier!

The Stand at Apache River

Universal-International (September 1953); COLOR by Technicolor; RUNNING TIME: 77 min.

CAST: Lane Dakota, **Stephen McNally**; Valerie Kendrick, **Julia Adams**; Colonel Morsby, **Hugh Marlowe**; Ann Kenyon, **Jaclynne Greene**; Tom Kenyon, **Hugh O'Brian**; Greiner, **Russell Johnson**; Hatcher, **Jack Kelly**; Cara Blanca, **Edgar Barrier**; Deadhorse, **Forrest Lewis**; Indians, **Duke Green** and **Davy Sharpe**

CREDITS: Director, **Lee Sholem**; Assistant Director, **Jesse Hibbs**; Producer, **William Alland**; Story/ Screenplay, **Arthur Ross**; Editor, **Leonard Weiner**; Art Directors, **Bernard Herzbrun** and **Hilyard Brown**; Set Decorators, **Russell A. Gausman** and **Oliver Emert**; Cinematographer, **Charles P. Boyle**; Costumes, **Bill**

The Stand at Apache River (1953) scene card: Jaclynne Greene (*left*) indulges in girl talk with Julia Adams.

Thomas; Hair Stylist, **Joan St. Oegger**; Makeup, **Bud Westmore**; Sound, **Leslie I. Carey** and **Richard De Weese**; Music, **Frank Skinner**; Technicolor Color Consultant, **William Fritzsche**

LOCATION FILMING: Red Rock Canyon and Victorville, California

SOURCE: Novel, *Apache Landing* by **Robert J. Hogan**

STORY: Marshal Dakota (Stephen McNally) brings his prisoner, Greiner (Russell Johnson), to the Apache River Station, a way station for a stage line. Johnson is an accused murderer who was able to hide his saddlebags containing bank money

before being wounded by Apaches. A stagecoach brings two more guests, Valerie Kendrick (Julia Adams), who is travelling to be married to a man she no longer loves, and the Indian-hating Colonel Morsby (Hugh Marlowe). Already at the station are Ann Kenyon (Jaclynn Green), who runs the station with her husband, guest Hatcher (Jack Kelly) and handyman Deadhorse (Forrest Lewis). The Apaches have escaped from a reservation. Led by Cara Blanca (Edgar Barrier), the Indians arrive at the station to trade trinkets for flour and salt. Barrier also explains that they want peace and have broken from the warring faction. When Barrier sees Marlowe, Barrier asks that the army not track them down and allow the Apaches to live in peace. When Marlowe refuses to grant Barrier's request, the Apaches surround the station. The Apaches are determined to take Marlowe as a hostage against cavalry troops. McNally takes the leadership role and makes a failed attempt to get Adams and Green through the Indian line to safety. Green's husband, Tom (Hugh O'Brian), is able to make it safely to the station only to find that Green is in love with Kelly. As the battle progresses, casualties are seen on both sides. Barrier is wounded and captured by McNally. Apaches kill Marlowe but are now determined to gain revenge against the other whites. Adams and McNally fall in love but Adams is unsure of a good life with McNally when she sees the hatred McNally has for Johnson. In the Apaches final attack, all the Indian warriors except Barrier have been killed. McNally, Adams, Johnson and Lewis are the only occupants of the station left alive. McNally no longer has his unrelenting hate for Johnson, and Adams and McNally will make a life together.

NOTES AND COMMENTARY: Universal-International was able to obtain the services of Hugh Marlowe for this picture when the Stanley Kramer production *Circle of Fire* with Barbara Stanwyck was postponed. *Circle of Fire* was never made.

Russell Johnson became upset with Stephen McNally in the film. There was a scene in which McNally had to slap Johnson. In Johnson's opinion the slap was much too hard and Johnson wanted to punch McNally. Cooler heads prevented Johnson from hitting McNally.

On American Movie Classics, a comment was made about frequent rewrites on *The Stand at Apache River* with a statement by Julia Adams, "You don't rewrite a script like that, you just reload it." In a conversation with director Lee Sholem, he said, "All the shows that I've done weren't rewritten that much."

Footage of the Indians' drumming was previously seen in *Apache Drums* (Universal-International, 1951). The working title for *The Stand at Apache River* was *Apache Landing*.

REVIEWS: "A fairly acceptable Technicolor western." *Hollywood Reporter*, 8/27/53; "A pleasing western." *The Motion Picture Guide*, Nash and Ross.

SUMMATION: *The Stand at Apache River* is a good western tale of whites trapped by hostile Indians. Director Lee Sholem does a good job of balancing characterizations of the cast members with some rugged action scenes. Sholem is almost able to capture the claustrophobia effect of the studio's earlier production *Apache Drums* (1951). Stephen McNally, Julia Adams and the entire supporting cast deliver fine performances.

*The legend of Bill Jordan who took the short end of the most
desperate gamble the West has ever known and staked
his courage against the fury of a town—to save it from itself!*

Star in the Dust

Universal-International (June 1956); COLOR by Technicolor; RUNNING TIME: 80 min.

CAST: Sheriff Bill Jordan, **John Agar**; Ellen Ballard, **Mamie Van Doren**; Sam Hall, **Richard Boone**; Nellie Mason, **Coleen Gray**; George Ballard, **Leif Erickson**; Orval Jones, **James Gleason**; Nan Hogan, **Randy Stuart**; The Music Man, **Terry Gilkyson**; Mike MacNamara, **Paul Fix**; Lew Hogan, **Harry Morgan**; Jess Ryman, **Stuart Randall**; Rigdon, **Robert Osterloh**; Ben Smith, **Stanley Andrews**; Jiggs Larribee, **John Day**; Leo Roos, **Stafford Repp**; Pastor Harris, **Lewis Martin**; Timothy Brown, **Renny McEvoy**; Ed Pardee, **Jesse Kirkpatrick**; Marv Tremain, **James Parnell**; Doc Quinn, **Anthony Jochim**; Carpenter's Helper, **Frank Sully**; Townsman, **Kenneth MacDonald**; Tom (Cowboy), **Clint Eastwood**; Farmers, **Jack Ingram** and **Kermit Maynard**

CREDITS: Director, **Charles Haas**; Assistant Director, **Frank Shaw**; Producer, **Albert Zugsmith**; Screenwriter, **Oscar Brodney**; Editor, **Ray Snyder**; Art Decorators, **Alexander Golitzen** and **Alfred Sweeney**; Set Decorators, **Russell A. Gausman** and **John P. Austin**; Cinematographer, **John L. Russell, Jr.**; Costumes, **Jay A. Morley, Jr.**; Hair Stylist, **Joan St. Oegger**; Makeup,

Bud Westmore; Sound, **Leslie I. Carey and Corson Jowett**; Music, **Frank Skinner**; Musical Director, **Joseph Gershenson**; Technicolor Color Consultant, **William Fritzsche**

SONG: "Sam Hall" (Gilkyson)—sung by **Terry Gilkyson** (Gilkyson revised both music and lyrics from the traditional original)

SOURCE: Novel, *Law Man* by **Lee Leighton**

STORY: Killer Sam Hall (Richard Boone) is scheduled to be executed at sundown. Boone was convicted of killing farmers who were trying to establish homesteads on cattlemen's land. Most of the townspeople think the hanging will not take place. The ranchers, led by banker George Ballard (Leif Erickson), want to break Boone out of jail. The farmers, with schoolmaster Rigdon (Robert Osterloh), at their head want Boone to hang. Sheriff Jordan (John Agar) is determined to see justice is carried out as prescribed by law. Erickson finds out that Boone's lover, Nellie (Coleen Gray), has letters to give Agar unless Boone is broken out of jail. Even though Erickson says he's not responsible for sending the letters to Boone, he convinces his sister, Ellen (Mamie Van Doren), to lure Agar away from the jail so Boone can be freed. Agar and Van Doren plan to wed. Erickson tells Nan Hogan (Randy Stuart) that

Star in the Dust (1956) scene card: Mamie Van Doren discusses Coleen Gray's visit with Leif Erickson.

her husband, Lew (Harry Morgan), sent the letters and it would be to her benefit to help in the jailbreak by getting a gun to Boone. Boone gets a gun and tries to make his escape when Agar is called away. Orval Jones (James Gleason) foils the jailbreak and captures Boone. Agar then makes Gleason one of his deputies. While waiting for Boone to escape, Gray tells Stuart that Erickson sent the letters. The women fight over the letters. Stuart is victorious and takes the letters to Agar. Agar feels that Van Doren betrayed him when he finds that Erickson may be the man behind the farmers' deaths. The ranchers come to town and demand Boone's

release and begin shooting at the jail. Stuart tells Van Doren that Erickson hired Boone to kill the farmers. The farmers arrive in town and a gun battle erupts between the two factions. Agar marches Boone out of the jail with the intention to hang him. Boone admits that the farmers were murdered on their own land and transported to land controlled by the cattlemen. Erickson tries to ambush Agar but is delayed long enough by Van Doren for Morgan to shoot Erickson. Boone is hanged and Agar and Van Doren are reunited.

NOTES AND COMMENTARY: The working title for *Star in the Dust* was *Law Man*.

In the film, Coleen Gray and Randy Stuart have a knock-down, drag-out fight. Gray and Stuart were good friends and their husbands were invited to the set to watch the filming of the fight. Gray and Stuart eschewed the use of doubles. Gray commented, "We did just fine. We used balsa wood and so forth, so no one got hurt. We finished the fight and got up and our husbands were both pale and clammy."

In talking about her role in the picture, Coleen Gray said, "I loved doing it. I was a plain person and a bouquet of poison ivy in the town."

The hanging scene stuck in Coleen Gray's memory. Gray remembered, "That kind of thing has a morbid fascination for people. And seeing Richard Boone on the horse and the rope around his neck, and then they cut. They didn't actually show it [the hanging]. Leading up to that time, it had such a horror to it. I think it's a dreadful way of executing people. But people watch. They come to see a hanging like in England. They would hang them first, then draw and quarter them. The poor victim will still be alive. But we don't need to go into that. Man's inhumanity to man."

Coleen Gray commented about Universal-International, "I always enjoyed working at Universal. The people were darn nice. It was a friendly studio. People were down to earth, the crew, the makeup men and wardrobe gals, the hairdressers and the grips and everybody. I felt very much at home there and comfortable. More so than when I worked at Fox.

Because I was younger and they always used to say that you'd better be good or you get fired kind of thing. They threatened me. Universal was friendly. I was freelancing, I think, at that time. So there was no nervousness about people saying if you're not good you would be let go. My favorite studio, I think."

Richard Boone was given a couple of good lines. One was "I'm a bad boy from a good family." The other was "When I leave your hotel, I'm going to squash you like a bug."

REVIEWS: "Good suspense western with well-motivated script, action and suspense are mixed in good proportion." *Variety*, 4/18/56; "A superior B western." *The Western*, Phil Hardy.

SUMMATION: *Star in the Dust* in an interesting, psychological western as two factions collide on the day gunman Richard Boone is to be executed. John Agar makes a properly heroic lawman. Mamie Van Doren gives an adequate performance as the sister of villain Leif Erickson who is forced to choose between her brother and her lover and almost ruins her chance at happiness. Boone gives the story an added punch with his excellent rendition of gunman Sam Hall. Coleen Gray, Randy Stuart, Paul Fix, James Gleason and Robert Osterloh shine in their supporting roles. Leif Erickson is a fine villain. Cinematographer John L. Russell, Jr., provides some refreshing camera angles in the style of Joseph H. Lewis. Director Charles Haas does a nice job of adroitly interspersing action with suspense.

THE RIP-ROARIN' HIP-SWINGIN' SAGA OF A LOGGING CAMP QUEEN...
...the Town She Tamed and the Men She Took!
The Tall, Tall Tale of Vermilion O'Toole!

Take Me to Town

Universal-International (June 1953); COLOR by Technicolor; RUNNING TIME: 81 min.

CAST: Vermilion O'Toole, **Ann Sheridan**; Will Hall, **Sterling Hayden**; Newton Cole, **Philip Reed**; Rose, **Lee Patrick**; Corney, **Lee Aaker**; Petey, **Harvey Grant**; Bucket, **Dusty Henley**; Ed Daggett, **Larry Gates**; Ed Higgins, **Forrest Lewis**; Mrs. Stoffer, **Phyllis Stanley**; Felice Pickett, **Dorothy Neumann**; Louise Pickett, **Ann Tyrrell**; Vendor on train, **Robert Easton**; Logger, **Fess Parker**; Sammy, **Frank Sully**; Mike, **Lane Chandler**; Chuck, **Robert Anderson**; Heroine, **Alice Kelley**; Hero, **Guy Williams**; Chorus Girls, **Anita Ekberg**, **Ruth Hampton**, **Valerie Jackson** and **Jackie Loughery**

CREDITS: Director, **Douglas Sirk**; Assistant Director, **Joseph E. Kenny**; Producer, **Ross Hunter**; Co-Producer, **Leonard Goldstein**; Story/Screenwriter, **Richard Morris**; Editor, **Milton Carruth**; Art Directors, **Alexander Golitzen** and **Hilyard Brown**; Set Decorators, **Russell A. Gausman** and **Julia Heron**; Cinematographer, **Russell Metty**; Costumes, **Bill Thomas**; Hair Stylist, **Joan St. Oegger**; Makeup, **Bud Westmore**; Sound, **Leslie I. Carey** and **Richard De Weese**; Music, **Joseph Gershenson**; Choreographer, **Hal Belfer**; Technicolor Color Consultant, **William Fritzsche**

SONGS: "The Tale of Vermilion O'Toole"—sung by **Dusty Walker**; "Oh, You Red-Head" (Herbert and Rosen)—sung by **Ann Sheridan**, **Lee Patrick and chorus**; "Take Me to Town" (Lee and Shapiro)—sung by **Dorothy Neumann**, **Ann Tyrrell** and **Ann Sheridan**

STORY: Marshal Daggett (Larry Gates) is escorting showgirl Vermilion O'Toole (Ann Sheridan) and con man Newton Cole (Philip Reed) to jail. Sheridan is really innocent of the charges placed against her. Both Sheridan and Reed manage to escape. Sheridan goes to Timberline where she is the star attraction for Rose's (Lee Patrick) show. Gates shows up in Timberline and Sheridan has to find a place to hide. Widower Will Hall's (Sterling Hayden) children are looking for a new mother and ask Sheridan to live with them. Hayden, who has left his children alone so he could work at a logging camp, comes home when he hears that Sheridan is living with his children. At first Hayden tells Sheridan she can't stay but allows her to remain when she saves one of his children from a bear. After Sheridan finds out Hayden is an ordained minister, she tells him of her past. Sheridan plans to leave but Hayden

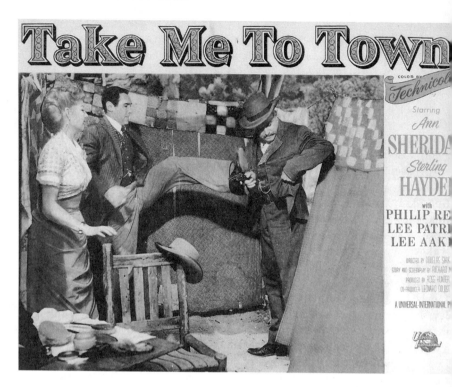

Take Me to Town (1953) scene card: Con man Philip Red kicks Larry Gates' gun hand to effect an escape as Ann Sheridan stands by.

convinces her to stay and help the ladies of the community raise money to build a church. Hayden and Sheridan have fallen in love to the delight of Hayden's children. Sheridan persuades the ladies to put on a show with musical and dramatic skits. Needing a piano, Sheridan gets Patrick to help out. With all the publicity, Reed and Gates come to the show. Gates attempts to arrest both Reed and Sheridan. Reed is able to turn the tables on Gates but Sheridan comes to Gates' assistance, forcing Reed to attempt to escape. Hayden catches up to Reed and is able to defeat him in a rugged fistfight.

Sheridan is happy to become a minister's wife.

NOTES AND COMMENTARY: The dangerous North American grizzly bear in this film is really a Malayan Sun Bear. This species is said to be the most easily tamed of all bears. The picture had two working titles, *Vermilion O'Toole* and *Flame of the Timberline*, before the studio settled on *Take Me to Town*.

The song, "Take Me to Town" was used by Universal-International in *Wyoming Mail* (1950), *A Day of Fury* (1956) and *Showdown* (1963).

REVIEWS: "Entertaining family

comedy drama." *Variety*, 5/20/53; "This is a delightful film, rendered all the more by Sirk's deft touch." *The Western*, Hardy.

SUMMARY: As "Bucket," the youngest of Hayden's children in the film, would say, "I like it." *Take Me to Town* is a bright, engaging slice of Americana with a western setting. Ann Sheridan is a delight, displaying a wide range of comedic and acting talents and throwing in a little singing and dancing for good measure. Sterling Hayden matches Sheridan as he plays a man of God with a decidedly humanistic touch. In addition, Hayden's children in the film, Lee Aaker, Harvey Grant and Dusty Henley, are wonderful scene-stealers. The film boasts a solid supporting cast with Forrest Lewis, Philip Reed, Lee Patrick, Larry Gates and Phyllis Stanley registering strongly. Douglas Sirk directs with a knowing touch. A delight!

ALL THE FLAMING FURY OF AMERICA'S MOST DANGEROUS DAYS!

Tap Roots

Walter Wanger Productions, Inc./Universal-International (August 1948); A George Marshall production; COLOR by Technicolor; RUNNING TIME: 109 min.

CAST: Keith Alexander, **Van Heflin**; Morna Dabney, **Susan Hayward**; Tishomingo, **Boris Karloff**; Aven Dabney, **Julie London**; Clay MacIvor, **Whitfield Connor**; Hoab Dabney, **Ward Bond**; Bruce Dabney, **Richard Long**; Reverend Kirkland, **Arthur Shields**; Dr. MacIntosh, **Griff Barnett**; Shellie, **Sondra Rogers**; Dabby, **Ruby Dandridge**; Sam Dabney, **Russell Simpson**; Jealous Husband, **Arthur Space**; Mob Leader, **William Haade**; General Johnson, **Jonathan Hale**; Valley Soldiers, **Harry Cording** and **Hank Worden**; Confederate Soldiers, **George J. Lewis** and **John James**; Confederate Lieutenant, **Keith Richards**

CREDITS: Director, **George Marshall**; Assistant Director, **Aaron Rosenberg**; Second Unit Director, **George Templeton**; Producer, **Walter Wanger**; Screenwriter, **Alan LeMay**; Additional Dialogue, **Lionel Wiggam**; Editor, **Milton Carruth**; Art Director, **Frank A. Richards**; Set Decorators, **Russell A. Gausman** and **Ruby R. Levitt**; Production Designer, **Alexander Golitzen**; Cinematographers, **Lionel Lindon** and **Winton C. Hoch**; Costumes, **Yvonne Wood**; Hair Stylist, **Carmen Dirigo**; Makeup, **Bud Westmore**; Sound, **Leslie I. Carey** and **Glenn E. Anderson**; Music, **Frank Skinner**, Orchestrations, **David Tamkin**; Technicolor Color Consultant, **Natalie Kalmus**; Associate Color Director, **Morgan Paddleford**

LOCATION FILMING: The Smoky Mountains of Tennessee and North

Tap Roots (1948) scene card: Whitfield Connor (*third right*) points a gun at Van Heflin (*behind tree*).

Carolina; SOURCE: Novel, *Tap Roots* by **James Street**

STORY: In Lebanon Valley, Mississippi, prior to the Civil War, Morna Daloney (Susan Hayward) and her sister Aven (Julie London) both have a romantic interest in Clay MacIvor (Whitfield Connor). Connor is planning to marry Hayward but has delayed the wedding because of a possible conflict between the North and South, and also Connor wants their house to be completed first. The patriarch of the valley, Sam Dabney (Russell Simpson), wants the valley to remain neutral in the event of war. Simpson's heart gives out and he passes this heritage on to his son, Hoab (Ward Bond). The wording of a newspaper article, actually a tribute to Simpson, inflames Simpson's grandson, Bruce (Richard Long). Long wants satisfaction from the author, Keith Alexander (Van Heflin). Simpson's long-time friend, Tishomingo (Boris Karloff), goes along to allay any possible conflict between Long and Heflin. Heflin, an ardent duelist, apologizes and goes back to the valley to meet the other family members, especially Susan Hayward. Heflin begins to court Hayward. Bond, Karloff and minister Kirkland

(Arthur Shields) make plans to keep the valley out of the war. Because he's attracted to Hayward, Heflin joins their cause even though he thinks the plan will not succeed. Hayward is paralyzed in a fall from her horse. In spite of this, Heflin professes his love to Hayward. Connor, not wanting to marry a cripple, eventually falls in love with London and marries her. With encouragement from Karloff and Heflin and medical treatment suggested by Karloff, Hayward overcomes her paralysis. The Civil War breaks out and Confederate soldiers led by Connor make plans to raid the valley. The inhabitants of the valley need time for Heflin to bring in much-needed guns. Hayward tries to buy that time by seducing Connor. Connor succumbs but is wise enough to know a surprise attack will now fail so he uses the time to bring in heavy artillery. The valley soldiers haven't a chance but carry the fight into the nearby swamp where Heflin is able to shoot Connor. The attack on the valley drives Bond to madness and he blames Hayward for selling out her friends and family to the enemy. During the battle Bond is gravely wounded. When Hayward is able to return, Bond condemns her but Heflin stands up to Bond and tells Bond that Hayward was the bravest among them. The strain of the day's events proves too much for Bond and he dies. Heflin and Hayward plan to start a new life for themselves in the valley much like Simpson did many years ago.

NOTES AND COMMENTS: Originally, the decision was made to release *Tap Roots* nationwide on a road show basis. Whitfield Connor received an "and introducing" billing. Connor's first show business role was as a cast member of *The Lone Ranger* radio program in the thirties. The script has dynamite being mentioned throughout the story. Unfortunately, it would take Alfred Nobel until 1865 to perfect a safer method of handling nitroglycerine by mixing the substance with silica to make what he called dynamite. This is the same Nobel who, in his will, left $31.5 million to establish prizes in physics, chemistry, physiology or medicine, literature, and peace. *Tap Roots* was one of the top 29 grossing films of 1947–48.

REVIEWS: "Exciting adventure cleverly produced." *Hollywood Reporter*, 6/24/48; "There's enough swash and buckle, it never reaches epic proportions, is too long and not always put together smoothly." *Variety*, 6/30/48.

SUMMATION: *Tap Roots* is a good, entertaining Civil War western though not in the class of *Gone with the Wind* (Selznick/Metro-Goldwyn-Mayer, 1939), which the producers thought this film might emulate. Van Heflin and Susan Hayward shine as the leads while providing the spark and sexual tension the picture needs. Boris Karloff, Ward Bond, Julie London and Richard Long provide fine support. The climactic battle scene is first rate with the necessary sweep and scope. Unfortunately, the overall story does not allow the final result to reach epic and possibly classic proportions by choosing not to delve deeper into the characterizations of its actors.

BY THE GUN ... THE ARROW ... THE KNIFE...
He led the Apache nation's wild revolt
against Geronimo's pillaging hordes!

Taza, Son of Cochise

Universal-International (February 1954); COLOR by Technicolor; FILMED in 3-D; RUNNING TIME: 79 min.

CAST: Taza, **Rock Hudson**; Oona, **Barbara Rush**; Captain Burnett, **Gregg Palmer**; Naiche, **Bart Roberts**; Grey Eagle, **Morris Ankrum**; Chato, **Gene Iglesias**; Cy Hagen, **Richard Cutting**; Geronimo, **Ian MacDonald**; General Crook, **Robert Burton**; Sgt. Hamma, **Joe Sawyer**; Lt. Willis, **Lance Fuller**; Lt. Richards, **Brad Jackson**; Skinya, **James Van Horn**; Kocha, **Charles Horvath**; Lobo, **Robert Hoy**; Mary, **Barbara Burck**; Tiswin Charlie, **Dan White**; Cochise, **Jeff Chandler**; Cavalry Soldiers, **Harold Cullen** and **Robert Hoy**

CREDITS: Director, **Douglas Sirk**; Assistant Director, **Tom Shaw**; Producer, **Ross Hunter**; Story/Adaptation, **Gerald Drayson Adams**; Screenwriter, **George Zuckerman**; Editor, **Milton Carruth**; Art Directors, **Bernard Herzbrun** and **Emrich Nicholson**; Set Decorators, **Russell A. Gausman** and **Oliver Emert**; Cinematographer, **Russell Metty**; Costume Designer, **Jay Morley, Jr.**; Hair Stylist, **Joan St. Oegger**; Makeup, **Bud Westmore**; Sound, **Leslie I. Carey** and **Glenn E. Anderson**; Music, **Frank Skinner**; Technicolor Color Consultant, **William Fritzsche**

LOCATION FILMING: Moab area (Arches National Park, Courthouse Wash, Ida Gulch, Professor Valley, Colorado River, Sand Flats), Utah

STORY: With the death of Cochise (Jeff Chandler), Taza (Rock Hudson) assumes the leadership of the Chiricahua Apache nation. His leadership is challenged by Geronimo (Ian MacDonald) who opposes Hudson's views of maintaining peace with the whites. Hudson's brother, Naiche (Bart Roberts), is a rival for Oona (Barbara Rush), who loves and is loved by Hudson. Roberts is also a follower of MacDonald and massacres the occupants of a single wagon travelling west. Roberts is captured and punished by Hudson but cavalry captain Burnett (Gregg Palmer) arrests the men to face army justice. This act displeases Hudson and the Apaches take Fort Apache and rescue his men. Hudson agrees to surrender the fort and take his people to the San Carlos Reservation if sufficient supplies will be provided and if the Apaches can police themselves. Hudson's demands are accepted and his new friend, Palmer, is assigned to help Hudson implement an Apache police force. MacDonald is captured by the army and sent to the reservation. MacDonald plans an assassination attempt on Palmer to force the

Taza, Son of Cochise (1954) scene card: A tense moment as Apache chief Rock Hudson dictates terms of peace to Robert Burton and Gregg Palmer. Army scout Richard Cutting (*second left*) advises the officers to listen.

Apaches to be policed by the cavalry. The attempt fails and MacDonald breaks out of the reservation and seeks to unite all Apache tribes against the whites. Hudson and his Apaches are confined to the reservation as the cavalry goes in pursuit of MacDonald. MacDonald's forces draw the cavalry into ambush. The situation looks grim for the cavalry until Hudson shows up with his Apache police. Hudson captures MacDonald. Roberts refuses to put down his weapon and is shot by one of the Apache policemen. Hudson is now able to marry Rush.

NOTES AND COMMENTARY:

Robert Hoy admired John Ford and the fact that Ford always revered the American flag in his films. Hoy came up with an idea that was incorporated in *Taza, Son of Cochise.* Hoy suggested that in a cavalry charge, fellow stuntman Harold Cullen would get shot and drop the American flag that he was carrying. Hoy would be right behind Cullen and reach down and pick up the colors. In the scene, you can see the American flag unfurl as it's plucked from the ground. Hoy said, "I thought I accomplished something that Mr. Ford would like."

In the film Robert Hoy played

Lobo. He has a scene in which he attempts to shoot Rock Hudson, misses and tries to get away. Hoy races to a corral, mounts a horse and the horse would jump over the corral fence. While in mid-air, in response to a shot from Hudson's rifle, Hoy would fall from the horse to the ground. There was a problem: the studio didn't have a jump horse available. There was a mare that Hoy could use but no one thought the horse could clear the fence. Hoy got an idea. The mare had a colt in the spring so they placed the colt on the other side of the fence out of camera range. When Hoy mounted the horse, the colt was given a dig in the ribs. The mother heard the colt's whinny; took off and cleared the fence without a problem. Hoy could tell by the horse's ears if the mare would make the jump. But Hoy was not about to take an unnecessary chance. Hoy tied off the top rail of the fence on one side only so if the mare couldn't clear the fence, the rail would go but wouldn't keep going and hit him as he made his fall.

Gregg Palmer remembered a scene that was shot on location in Moab, Utah. The cavalry were riding through a pass with hostile Indians trying to stop them. The Indians were real Indians from Arizona. The soldiers would fire at the Indians. The rifles were loaded so the carbon from the blanks would travel twenty feet and hit the Indians, which hurt.

Then the soldiers end up in a gorge and the Indians surround them. The Indians are up in the rocks and were told to shoot arrows right into the camera. The movie was being filmed in 3-D. The arrows began coming down among the actors. Palmer grabbed one of the arrows and hollered to stop the filming. The Indians were exacting their revenge for being hit with the "hot shots." The rubber tips had been removed from the arrows.

Bart Roberts gained greater fame billed as Rex Reason. The working title for this film was *Son of Cochise*. Although filmed in 3-D, most audiences saw the film in two-dimension.

REVIEWS: "Colorful Indian–U.S. Cavalry entry, beautifully photographed." *Variety*, 1/20/54; "It contained all the well-tried ingredients germane to the genre." *The Universal Story*, Hirschhorn.

SUMMATION: *Taza, Son of Cochise* is an exciting, well-done cavalry and Indians saga. Rock Hudson gives an authoritative and well-done portrayal of Taza. Barbara Rush, in addition to being very attractive, is quite good as the love interest. Gregg Palmer, Morris Ankrum, Gene Iglesias and Bart Roberts head a fine supporting cast. Douglas Sirk's direction is on the mark as he stresses some good action scenes throughout this most interesting story.

THE GLORY STORY OF THE GREAT SIOUX INDIAN UPRISING!
The war cry screams ... The war drums throb ...
and a howling horde of reckless redmen rides to vengeance!

Tomahawk

ALTERNATE TITLE: *Battle of Powder River*; Universal-International (February 1951); COLOR by Technicolor; RUNNING TIME: 82 min.

CAST: Bridger, **Van Heflin**; Julie Madden, **Yvonne De Carlo**; Lt. Rob Dancy, **Alex Nicol**; Col. Carrington, **Preston Foster**; Sol Beckworth, **Jack Oakie**; Dan Castello, **Tom Tully**; Red Cloud, **John War Eagle**; Burt Hanna, **Rock Hudson**; Monahseetah, **Susan Cabot**; Captain Fetterman, **Arthur Space**; Major Horton, **Russell Conway**; Mrs. Carrington, **Ann Doran**; Sergeant Newell, **Stuart Randall**; Private Parr, **Davy Sharpe**; Army Wife, **Sheila Darcy**; Blair Streeter, **Ray Montgomery**; Private Osborne, **John Peters**; Smith, **Regis Toomey**

CREDITS: Director, **George Sherman**; Producer, **Leonard Goldstein**; Story, **Daniel Jarrett**; Screenwriters, **Silvia Richards** and **Maurice Geraghty**; Editor, **Danny B. Landres**; Indian Technical Advisor, **David H. Miller**; Art Directors, **Bernard Herzbrun** and **Richard H. Riedel**; Set Decorators, **Russell A. Gausman** and **Oliver Emert**; Cinematographer, **Charles P. Boyle**; Additional Photography, **Marvin W. Spoor**; Costumes, **Bill Thomas**; Hair Stylist, **Joan St. Oegger**; Makeup, **Bud Westmore**; Sound, **Leslie I. Carey** and **Corson Jowett**; Music,

Hans J. Salter; Technicolor Color Consultant, **William Fritzsche**

LOCATION FILMING: Black Hills, South Dakota

STORY: Treaty negotiations between the Sioux Indian Nation and the United States break down when frontiersman Bridger (Van Heflin) announces that an Army fort is scheduled to be built on Sioux lands. Army Col. Carrington (Preston Foster) tries to recruit Heflin and his partner, Sol Beckworth (Jack Oakie), as scouts for the army. Heflin turns Foster down until he notices that Lt. Rob Dancy (Alex Nicol) is one of the soldiers assigned to Foster's command. Nicol leads the mail detail to the new fort and comes across a show wagon heading for Virginia City. Nicol decides to allow the wagon to accompany them when he finds that Julie Madden (Yvonne De Carlo) is a member of the troupe. During the journey, two Indian boys try to steal army horses and Nicol kills one of the boys. Because of the tense atmosphere, Nicol covers up the incident. The Sioux now want all white men to leave Sioux lands. Heflin knows major trouble is imminent. Heflin was once married to an Indian woman, who was killed in a massacre led by a fanatic. Nicol was a member of this group and was the

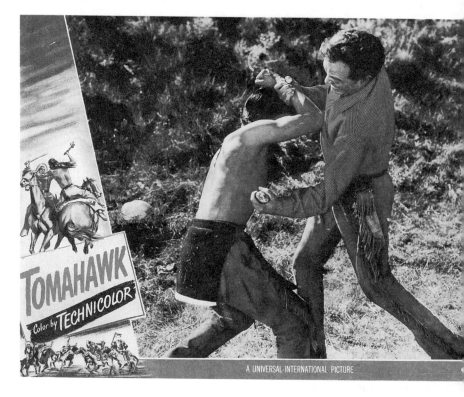

Tomahawk (1951) scene card: **Van Heflin (*right*) battles an unidentified actor to save Yvonne De Carlo's life.**

man who actually killed Heflin's wife. Heflin finally learns the truth about Nicol and is beating him in a hand-to-hand fight when Nicol is struck in the back by an Indian arrow. The other Indian boy, who tried to steal the horses, dispatched the arrow to avenge his friend's death. The Sioux finally mount an attack on the army forces. Oakie has brought a supply of new breech-loading rifles, and with Heflin's advice, the army annihilates the Indian warriors. The Sioux are able to obtain a new treaty with the United States in which the army leaves

Sioux lands. The Sioux then burn down the army fort.

NOTES AND COMMENTARY: *Tomahawk* was first announced to be filmed sometime after September 1, 1947. Then Universal-International placed the film on the production schedule in 1949.

Universal-International arranged to have six Sioux Indians make a ten-city tour to coincide with the world premiere of *Tomahawk* in Chicago on January 26, 1951. These Indians were members of the Sioux Tribe located in Pine Ridge, South Dakota, where Tomahawk was filmed, and also appeared in the picture.

Orange cardboard tomahawks, two feet in length, were given away at theaters as a part of the advance publicity campaign for *Tomahawk.* They had the title of the film and the star names on them.

The fort burning scene would be seen again in *The Battle at Apache Pass* (Universal-International, 1951). Sheila Darcy, who is seen in a scene with Susan Cabot and Ann Doran, was the wife of Preston Foster.

REVIEWS: "Nothing exceptional in the cavalry and Indians line, outside of its generous intimation of pro–Indian sentiment." *New York Times*, 2/19/51; "Weak plot detracts from the cast and use of color in this "A" drama." *Western Movies*, Pitts.

SUMMATION: *Tomahawk* is a decent though not outstanding western that tries to look at both sides of the war between Indians and the white man. Van Heflin makes a stalwart Jim Bridger. Yvonne De Carlo is okay in the thankless role of a wagon-show trouper. Alex Nicol overplays his part of an Indian-hating cavalry officer. George Sherman directs valiantly but has to deal with a crippled script, especially having the plot allow De Carlo to go riding alone in dangerous Indian territory. The beautiful scenic backgrounds are a major asset in this western saga.

The gallant, all-heart story of the making of a pair of champions!
IN THE BEST 4-H AND FFA TRADITION!

Tomboy and the Champ

Signal Pictures Corporation/ Universal-International (April 1961); EASTMAN COLOR by Pathé; RUNNING TIME: 92 min.

CAST: Tommy Jo Layne, **Candy Moore**; Jim Wilkins, **Ben Johnson**; Windy Skiles, **Jesse White**; Model T. Parson, **Jess Kirkpatrick**; Sarah Wilkins, **Christine Smith**; Fred Anderson, **John Carpenter**; Jasper Stockton, **Paul Bernath**; Fowler Stockton, **Norman Sherry**; Calf Scramblers, **Katy, Texas FFA**; Special Guest Stars, **Rex Allen, Casey Tibbs, Jerry Naill** and **Champy the Angus**; Hi Fi Club Announcer, **Wally Phillips**; 4-H Club President, **Ralph Fischer**; Curley Cone, **Larry Hickie**

CREDITS: Director, **Francis D. Lyon**; Assistant Directors, **Clem Beauchamp** and **Hal Polaire**; Producers/Story, **Tommy Reynolds** and **William Lightfoot**; Screenwriter, **Virginia M. Cooke**; Editor, **William B. Murphy**; Cinematographer, **William Clothier**; Sound, **Dale Knight**; Music, **Richard Shores**; Unit Manager, **Dallas Film Center**

Tomboy and the Champ (1961) scene card: Rex Allen sings "Who Says Animals Don't Cry" to a distraught Candy Moore and her pet Angus, Champy.

SONGS: "Barbecue Rock" (Wilkes); "Who Says Animals Don't Cry" (Reynolds and Lightfoot)—sung by **Rex Allen**; and "Get Ready with the Ribbon, Judge" (Reynolds and Lightfoot)—sung by **Jess Kirkpatrick, Larry Hickie, Paul Bernath and chorus**

LOCATION FILMING: Houston and Katy area, Texas, and Chicago, Illinois

STORY: Orphan Tommy Jo Layne (Candy Moore), who lives with her aunt and uncle, Sarah (Christine Smith) and Jim Wilkins (Ben Johnson), on a Texas ranch, wins Champy in a calf-scrambling contest. Moore wants to train Champy to be a Grand Champion steer. A storm blows open a gate which allows Champy to wander from the ranch. Discovering that Champy is missing, Moore starts after the missing calf and finds Champy mired in a mud bog. Unable to pull Champy from the bog, Moore stays in the cold muddy water keeping Champy's head above water. Johnson and preacher Parson (Jess Kirkpatrick) rescue the two but exposure to the bitter elements and the cold water causes Moore to contract polio. At first Moore wastes away her time in self-pity but finally is convinced to continue to train Champy. As Moore trains Champy, she gradually begins to shake off the effects of the polio. Champy is entered at a show in Houston and Moore is devastated when Champy does not win. Moore then enters Champy in the International Show in Chicago where Champy becomes the Grand Champion. Only then does Moore realize that when Champy is sold at auction, Champy will be slaughtered. Moore comes down with pneumonia and loses the will to fight the illness. Fred Anderson (John Carpenter), head of the meatpacking firm that bought Champy, decides to spare the steer. Champy is allowed to go to Moore's hospital bed, and the sight of Champy gives her the will to live.

NOTES AND COMMENTARY: Universal-International packaged *Tomboy and the Champ* with the featurette *Ole Rex* for most of its bookings around the country. The John Carpenter in this film is not the Johnny Carpenter who had a brief starring western career in the early to mid-fifties.

REVIEWS: "Standard programmer for the family trade." *Western Movies*, Pitts; "Okay for kids, but there's something strange about the whole premise." *The Motion Picture Guide*, Nash and Ross.

SUMMATION: *Tomboy and the Champ* tries hard to be a heartwarming family film. The basic premise of a young girl training an Angus calf to be Grand Champion is fine. The problem is with the execution. Tragedies abound until the attempt is made to have a heart-tugging ending. It is difficult to believe the young girl is totally unaware that when the steer is sold at auction a meatpacking company will slaughter it. And the ending has to be seen and still won't be believed in which a hospital and a physician will allow a live steer, with a tear in its eye no less, to visit the little girl in the hospital. The positive part of the film is showing the hard work the FFA and 4-H members perform to better themselves. Most of the acting is at best adequate with Ben Johnson trying hard to maintain his high professional standard. The usually reliable Jesse White was given a thankless role as a press agent with plenty of unfunny material. Filming at the actual locations in which the story takes place does add to the movie's enjoyment.

The most rousing ADVENTURE a man and a boy ever lived!
From the pen of the World's Master Storyteller
ROBERT LOUIS STEVENSON

The Treasure of Lost Canyon

Universal-International (March 1952); COLOR by Technicolor; RUNNING TIME: 81½ min.

CAST: Doc Homer Brown, **William Powell**; Myra Wade, **Julia Adams**; Jim Anderson, **Charles Drake**; Samuella Brown, **Rosemary De Camp**; David, **Tommy Ivo**; Lucius Cooke, **Henry Hull**; Baltimore Dan, **Chubby Johnson**; Gyppo, **John Doucette**; Paddy, **Marvin Press**; Judge Wade, **Griff Barnett**; Stagecoach Driver, **Paul Newland**; Guard, **Jimmy Ogg**; David's father, **Frank Wilcox**; Clem, **George Taylor**; Mrs. Crabtree, **Virginia Mullen**; Sheriff, **Jack Perrin**; Fire Captain, **Hugh Prosser**; Miners, **Philo McCullough** and **Ed Hinkle**

CREDITS: Director, **Ted Tetzlaff**; Producer, **Leonard Goldstein**; Associate Producer, **William Alland**; Screenwriters, **Brainerd Duffield** and **Emerson Crocker**; Editor, **Milton Carruth**; Art Directors, **Bernard Herzbrun** and **Alexander Golitzen**; Set Decorators, **Russell A. Gausman** and **John Austin**; Cinematographer, **Russell Metty**; Costumes, **Rosemary Odell**; Hair Stylist, **Joan St. Oegger**; Makeup, **Bud Westmore**; Sound, **Leslie I. Carey** and **Joe Lapis**; Music, **Joseph Gershenson**; Technicolor Color Consultant, **William Fritzsche**

SONG: "Lemuel, My Lark"— sung by Rosemary De Camp

LOCATION FILMING: McArthur-Burney Falls State Park, California

SOURCE: Story, "The Treasure of Franchard" by **Robert Louis Stevenson**

STORY: After Tommy Ivo's father dies, Lucius Cooke (Henry Hull) turns the boy over to a crooked medicine showman, Baltimore Dan (Chubby Johnson). Johnson, discovered by townspeople to be a thief, has a heart attack while attempting to escape and dies leaving Ivo homeless. Doc Homer (William Powell) and Samuella Brown (Rosemary De Camp) adopt Ivo. On a trip to Franchard Falls, Ivo and Powell discover the legendary treasure. The riches go to Powell's head and Ivo decides to return the treasure to the waters below Franchard Falls. An accidental fire destroys Powell's house and Powell, De Camp, and Ivo are now left homeless. Feeling responsible, Ivo goes to the falls and recovers the treasure. Meanwhile, Jim Anderson (Charles Drake) exposes Hull's duplicity. Hull had been bilking the financial holdings of both Powell and his deceased brother. Powell finds out Ivo is his nephew and this is worth more than the treasure.

NOTES AND COMMENTARY: The working title of the film, *The Treasure of Franchard*, came from

The Treasure of Lost Canyon (1952) scene card: Rosemary De Camp rushes to William Powell, who had been knocked in a stream by the kidnappers of young Tommy Ivo.

Stevenson's story. William Powell was borrowed from Metro-Goldwyn-Mayer to star in this film.

This was one of Rosemary De Camp's favorite pictures, primarily because it was based on a Robert Louis Stevenson story and she was able to work with William Powell. De Camp said of Powell, "He was one of the smoothest, best and coolest actors of the time. I had never met him before." Also, at the time of filming, De Camp was pregnant with her last child.

Rosemary De Camp commented on working with Julia Adams, "She

fiddled around and got the billing I was promised so—" (Author's comment: Adams has two short scenes while De Camp's part is instrumental both to the story and the charm of the picture.)

Rosemary De Camp thought Ted Tetzlaff was a great director and because he had once been a cameraman, "pictures meant more to him than words."

Asked whether she did her own singing in the picture, Rosemary De Camp replied, "No. I'm tone-deaf."

REVIEWS: "Top fare for family and neighborhood locations, story is warm and beguiling." *Hollywood Reporter*, 2/13/52; "Fairly good screen adaptation of Robert Louis Stevenson's 'The Treasure of Franchard.'" *Western Movies*, Pitts.

SUMMATION: This is an unusual, heart-warming western bolstered by William Powell's fine, engaging performance. Powell, known primarily throughout his career as an urban sophisticated gentleman, does a nice turn as the western philosopher and dreamer. Rosemary De Camp and Tommy Ivo give adequate support. Henry Hull is in fine fettle for the mild villainy. Chubby Johnson registers strongly as the unscrupulous medicine showman. This is a pleasant family film.

Outlawed by the town he tried to save ...
HE FACED THE SCREAMING FURY OF THE APACHE WARPATH ALONE!
THE LEGEND OF JIM HARVEY...
who fled a lynch-mad mob ... to clear his name!
fought the savage ambush ... to stay alive!
and won the lips of a woman ... he couldn't trust!

Tumbleweed

Universal-International (December 1953); COLOR by Technicolor; RUNNING TIME: 79 min.

CAST: Jim Harvey, **Audie Murphy**; Laura, **Lori Nelson**; Sheriff Murchoree, **Chill Wills**; Nick Buckley, **Roy Roberts**; Lam, **Russell Johnson**; Louella Buckley, **K.T. Stevens**; Sarah, **Madge Meredith**; Marv, **Lee Van Cleef**; Ted, **I. Stanford Jolley**; Seth, **Ross Elliott**; Aguila, **Ralph Moody**; Tigre, **Eugene Iglesias**; Trapper Ross, **Phil Chambers**; Weber, **Lyle Talbot**; Wrangler, **King Donovan**; Prospector, **Harry Harvey**; Townsman, **Lee Roberts**; Wagon Driver, **Ed Cobb**

CREDITS: Director, **Nathan Juran**; Assistant Director, **John Sherwood**; Producer, **Ross Hunter**; Screenwriter, **John Meredith Lucas**; Editor, **Virgil Vogel**; Art Directors, **Bernard Herzbrun** and **Richard H. Riedel**; Set Decorators, **Russell A. Gausman** and **John Austin**; Cinematographer, **Russell Metty**; Costumes, **Bill Thomas**; Hair Stylist, **Joan St. Oegger**; Makeup, **Bud Westmore**; Sound, **Leslie I. Carey** and **Glenn E. Anderson**; Musical Direction, **Joseph Gershenson**; Technicolor Color Consultant, **William Fritzsche**

LOCATION FILMING: Red Rock Canyon in Southern California

SOURCE: Novel, "Three Were Renegades" by **Kenneth Perkins**

STORY: Trail guide Jim Harvey (Audie Murphy) is hired to bring a wagon train safely to the town of Borax. Aguila (Ralph Moody) and his Yaqui Indians attack the wagon train. Murphy hides the women,

Laura (Lori Nelson) and Sarah (Madge Meredith), then under a flag of truce goes to see Moody. Murphy had been instrumental in saving his son Tigre's (Eugene Iglesias) life and, because of this, gambles Moody will let the wagon train pass. Instead, Moody captures Murphy and wipes out the wagon train. Iglesias' mother frees Murphy before Moody can return to torture him. On Murphy's arrival in Borax, he is branded a coward and a deserter. Only the women survived the attack and Meredith and her brother-in-law, Lam (Russell Johnson) want to see Murphy lynched. Sheriff Murchoree (Chill Wills) intervenes and jails Murphy until Murphy can be safely escorted out of town. Iglesias breaks Murphy out of jail and tells Murphy that a white man was behind the attack on the wagon train. As they try to get away, Iglesias is killed and Murphy is wounded. As he is dying, Iglesias gives Murphy his necklace to make it possible for Murphy to talk with Moody. Rancher Nick Buckley (Roy Roberts) helps Murphy by letting him take Tumbleweed, a sad-looking horse. Murphy thinks Roberts has played a cruel joke on him but finds the horse is very intelligent and helps Murphy in his quest to locate Moody. Moody and his renegade band trap Murphy, Wills and some posse members at a waterhole. Murphy devises a ruse to bring Moody out in the open. The Yaquis attack and as things look grim, Johnson, Nelson and Roberts arrive to frighten off the remaining Yaquis. Moody, mortally wounded, before

he dies, identifies Johnson as the man behind the wagon train raid. Johnson had found silver on his brother's land and wanted his brother killed so he would inherit the property. Johnson tries to escape but Murphy catches up to him. In a rugged fistfight, Johnson falls from a high precipice to his death. Roberts tells Murphy that Tumbleweed was his best horse, then gives the horse to Murphy and Nelson.

NOTES AND COMMENTARY: Russell Johnson remembered that this was the picture in which Audie Murphy hit him in the climactic fight at the picture's end. Johnson bobbed when he should have weaved and was hit in the mouth with the result that his lip was hung over an incisor tooth. Johnson commented, "That was the last time I wanted to get in the way of one of his punches."

Lori Nelson had this to say about Audie Murphy, "He was really a great guy to work with. He was nice. He was kind. He was very quiet and kind of reclusive. He didn't hang around people very much. He was very soft-spoken and kind of shy. He was a good actor, considering he had never taken an acting lesson in his life."

In the cast listings, Lyle Talbot's character name is Weber and King Donovan is listed as wrangler but Roy Roberts calls both of them Mac.

The working title for this vehicle was *Three Were Renegades*.

Faith Domergue was announced as Audie Murphy's co-star but the part was eventually given to Lori Nelson.

Tumbleweed (1953) scene card: Chill Wills is prepared to protect Audie Murphy while Lori Nelson and Russell Johnson observe.

REVIEWS: "Good outdoor feature." *Variety* 11/18/53; "This is a typical western outing for Murphy." *The Motion Picture Guide*, Nash and Ross.

SUMMATION: *Tumbleweed* is a neat little action western bolstered by Audie Murphy's competent performance and an interesting and talented horse that helps Murphy overcome disastrous odds to bring the true villain to justice. Lori Nelson is just fine as Murphy's love interest. Chill Wills, Roy Roberts and Russell Johnson stand out in a good supporting cast. Nathan Juran's brisk direction helps compensate for deficiencies in the script, notably how easy it is to spot the mystery villain.

The story of THE GREAT TEXAS RANGE WARS!
...the last flaming days of the cattle barons who held
their borders at gunpoint and defied a nation to cross!

Untamed Frontier

Universal-International (September 1952); COLOR by Technicolor; RUNNING TIME: 75 min.

CAST: Kirk Denbow, **Joseph Cotten**; Jane Stevens, **Shelley Winters**; Glenn Denbow, **Scott Brady**; Lottie, **Suzan Ball**; Matt Denbow, **Minor Watson**; Camilla Denbow, **Katherine Emery**; Bandera, **José Torvay**; Clayton Vance, **Douglas Spencer**; Max Wickersham, **John Alexander**; Dave Chittun, **Lee Van Cleef**; Charlie Fentress, **Richard Garland**; Ezra McCloud, **Robert Anderson**; Clem McCloud, **Fess Parker**; Sheriff Brogan, **Ray Bennett**; Doctor, **Forrest Taylor**; Man at Dance, **David Jansen**

CREDITS: Director, **Hugo Fregonese**; Producer, **Leonard Goldstein**; Story, **Houston Branch** and **Eugenia Night**; Screenwriters, **Gerald Drayson Adams, John** and **Gwen Bagni**; Additional Dialogue, **Polly James**; Editor, **Virgil Vogel**; Art Directors, **Bernard Herzbrun** and **Nathan Juran**; Set Decorators, **Russell A. Gausman** and **Ruby R. Levitt**; Cinematographer, **Charles P. Boyle**; Costumes, **Bill Thomas**; Hair Stylist, **Joan St. Oegger**; Makeup, **Bud Westmore**; Sound, **Leslie I. Carey** and **Richard De Weese**; Music, **Hans J. Salter**; Technicolor Color Consultant, **William Fritzsche**

SONG: "Cielito Lindo" (traditional)

LOCATION FILMING: Agoura, California

STORY: Cattle baron Matt Denbow (Minor Watson) refuses to allow settlers to cross his land to reach free government land. The proliferation of the small ranchers would reduce the amount of grazing land Watson would have for his cattle and would force him to reduce his herd. Watson's son, Glenn Denbow (Scott Brady), attends a dance in town and because he's late, dance-hall girl Lottie (Suzan Ball) refuses to dance with him. Brady makes a play for waitress Jane Stevens (Shelley Winters) to the displeasure of small rancher Charlie Fentress (Richard Garland). An altercation ensues in which Brady shoots Garland. Since Anderson was not carrying a gun, Brady is arrested for murder. Brady insists Anderson was going for his gun. Ball had, unknowing to Garland, lifted his gun from his holster. Since Winters is the only witness to the shooting, Brady's cousin, Kirk (Joseph Cotton), attempts to bribe Winters not to testify. Winters' refusal leaves Brady with only the option to marry Winters because Texas law will not allow a wife to testify against her husband. Through trickery, Brady convinces Winters to marry him.

Untamed Frontier (1952) scene card: Shelley Winters requests a hot branding iron from Joseph Cotten (*left*) to cauterize José Torvay's wound.

After the wedding, Winters finds out she was tricked and will have nothing to do with Brady. This suits Brady and he goes to town to be with Ball. Brady also knows Ball is in possession of Garland's gun and as long as Brady stays with Ball the gun will not be turned over to the sheriff. On the range, a bull gores vaquero Bandera (José Torvay). Winters gains respect from Cotten when she bravely cauterizes Torvay's wound with a white-hot branding iron, saving his life. Watson wants Brady back on the ranch and sends Cotten into town to get him. Brady senses Cotten and Winters have fallen in love and boasts that he will always be the fence that keeps them apart. Watson has a talk with Brady in an attempt to have Brady straighten out his life and work on the ranch. Brady refuses and leaves the ranch. There are now enough settlers to attempt to force their way across Watson's land to the government range. Watson sends the majority of his vaqueros to stop this attempt, leaving only a few men to watch the cattle. Ball and Brady's cohort, Dave Chittun (Lee Van Cleef), forces Brady to join in a scheme to rustle Watson's cattle. Brady and Van Cleef get away with a large herd but are soon followed by

Cotten and some of his men. In the confrontation between Cotten and his men with the rustlers, Brady and Van Cleef are killed. Meanwhile the settlers attempt to cross Watson's land. In an exchange of shots, Watson is mortally wounded. Cotten arrives on the scene and decides to allow the settlers to cross to avoid more bloodshed. With Brady dead, Cotten and Winters are free to begin their life together.

NOTES AND COMMENTS: The working title for this film was simply *Untamed*. This was the film debut of actress Suzan Ball. Scenes used in the cattle stampede were previously seen in *Cattle Drive* (1951).

REVIEWS: "Okay actioner carried along by good direction and performances." *Western Movies*, Pitts; "Surprisingly the picture is rather convincing in spite of the cut-and-dried format and garish predictability." *New York Times*, 8/23/52.

SUMMATION: Fine acting elevates this western from the run-of-the-mill sagebrush saga. Joseph Cotten, Shelley Winters, Scott Brady and Minor Watson deliver very good performances, which makes the viewer forget about the mostly routine script. Cotten, who is normally seen in modern-day dramas, looks the part of a working cowboy, which adds to the believability of the story. Mention has to be made regarding the exceptional cinematography of Charles P. Boyle. Boyle has the knack of making the night sequences almost seem like they were filmed in black and white. Hugo Fregonese directs with a steady hand, maintaining interest throughout.

THE THUNDERING AVENGERS RIDE AGAIN!
The Sweeping Saga of an Exciting Era...

The Vigilantes Return

ALTERNATE TITLE: **Return of the Vigilantes**; Universal (July 1947); FILMED in Cinecolor; RUNNING TIME: 67 min.

CAST: Johnnie Taggart, **Jon Hall**; Kitty, **Margaret Lindsay**, Andy, **Andy Devine**; Louise Holden, **Paula Drew**; Ben, **Jack Lambert**; Judge Holden, **Jonathan Hale**; Clay Curtwright, **Robert Wilcox**; Sheriff, **Arthur Hohl**; Ben's Girl, **Joan Fulton**; Messenger, **Lane Chandler**; Bartender, **Wallace Scott**; Stage Driver, **Fred Graham**; Gang Members, **John Hart**, **Monte Montague** and **Robert Wilke**

CREDITS: Director, **Ray Taylor**; Assistant Director, **William Tummel**; Producer, **Howard Welsch**; Screenwriter, **Roy Chanslor**; Dialogue Director, **William Holland**; Editor, **Paul Landres**; Art Directors, **Jack Otterson** and **Frank A. Richards**; Set Decorators, **Russell A. Gausman** and

The Vigilantes Return (1947) scene card: Margaret Lindsay hands Andy Devine the keys to the jail cell; left border—Andy Devine and Jon Hall.

Don Webb; Cinematographer, **Virgil Miller**; Gowns, **Rosemary Odell**; Makeup, **Jack P. Pierce**; Sound, **Bernard B. Brown** and **William Hedggog**; Music, **Paul Sawtell**; Cinecolor Supervisor, **Arthur F. Phelps**

SONG: "One Man Woman" (Brooks and Schwartzwald)—sung by **Margaret Lindsay**; LOCATION FILMING: Iverson Ranch, California

STORY: Lawman Taggart (Jon Hall) is assigned to work undercover to break up a lawless gang terrorizing the territory. Outlaw leader Clay Curtwright (Robert Wilcox) discovers Hall's true identity and allows Hall to join the gang. In his first venture with the gang, Wilcox knocks out Hall while Ben (Jack Lambert) shoots a bank guard. Hall is captured and accused of the murder. Andy (Andy Devine), with the help of Hall's ex-girlfriend Ritty (Margaret Lindsay), breaks Hall out of jail. Under the leadership of Hall, Devine, and Judge Holden (Jonathan Hale), the vigilantes ride again. A pitched battle in town between the vigilantes and the outlaw gang results in Wilcox's death, the restoration of law and order, and Hall and Lindsay getting back together.

NOTES AND COMMENTARY: *The Vigilantes Return*, according to trade journal *Boxoffice*, was scheduled to be a Universal-International release during the September 1946–November 1947 season. The picture could have been the first Universal-International western. Instead Abbott and Costello's *The Wistful Widow of Wagon Gap* (Universal-International, 1947) has that honor. The author's guess is *The Vigilantes Return* did not meet the new policy guidelines of a Universal-International picture. Although filmed in 1946, Universal held back the release of this film for over a year. The running time was three minutes short of the new standard. Even though the film is in color, it is Cinecolor rather than the preferred Technicolor. In addition, director Ray Taylor has long been associated with the "B" western, especially at Universal where he had directed numerous Buck Jones and Johnny Mack Brown entries.

This was John Hart's (television's other Lone Ranger) first film after five years in the army. Hart remembered that Jack Lambert was a mean guy but he had no problem getting along with him.

Jon Hall was a good friend of Hart's from World War II days. Through a member of the Bob Hope troupe who knew Frances Langford, Hall's wife, Hart would be invited to the Hall's for dinner and drinks.

Universal was not renewing contracts of some of their stalwart performers. This would be Jon Hall's final entry and Andy Devine would be seen only once more for Universal in the U-I August release, *Slave Girl* (Universal-International, 1947).

Beginning in the 50s, Joan Fulton was billed as Joan Shawlee.

The song, "One Man Woman" would be heard again in *South Sea Sinner* (Universal-International, 1949). Shelley Winters sang the song doing a Mae West impression. Since Margaret Lindsay was not known as a singer, she was probably dubbed.

REVIEWS: "A better than average modest budgeted outdoor opus." *Variety*, 7/9/47; "An effective, modest actioner." *The Western*, Hardy.

SUMMATION: This is a fast moving but familiar action western. The leads, Jon Hall, Margaret Lindsay and Andy Devine, acquit themselves ably. Jack Lambert makes a good impression as a vicious gunman. Director Ray Taylor paces matters nicely. Best action scene is when Hall and Devine ride their horses into the saloon then through a window to make their getaway from Lambert and other gang members.

Walk the Proud Land

ALTERNATE TITLE: *Apache Agent*; Universal-International (September 1956); COLOR by Technicolor; FILMED in Cinemascope; RUNNING TIME: 88 min.

CAST: John P. Clum, **Audie Murphy**; Tianay, **Anne Bancroft**, Mary Dennison, **Pat Crowley**; Tom Sweeney, **Charles Drake**; Taglito, **Tommy Rall**; Eskiminzin, **Robert Warwick**; Geronimo, **Jay Silverheels**; Tono, **Eugene Mazzola**; Disalin, **Anthony Caruso**; Santos, **Victor Millan**; Captain Larsen, **Ainslie Pryor**; Chato, **Eugene Iglesias**; General Wade, **Morris Ankrum**; Governor Safford, **Addison Richards**; Alchise, **Maurice Jara**; Stone, **Frank Chase**; Naylor, **Ed Hinton**; Pica, **Marty Carrizosa**; Medicine Man, **Francis McDonald**

CREDITS: Director, **Jesse Hibbs**; Assistant Director, **Phil Bowles**; Producer, **Aaron Rosenberg**; Screenwriters, **Gil Doud** and **Jack Sher**; Editor, **Sherman Todd**; Art Directors, **Alexander Golitzen and Bill Newberry**; Set Decorators, **Russell A. Gausman** and **Ray Jeffers**; Cinematographer, **Harold Lipstein**; Special Photography, **Clifford Stine**; Costumes, **Bill Thomas**; Hair Stylist, **Joan St. Oegger**; Makeup, **Bud Westmore**; Sound, **Leslie I. Carey** and **Frank H. Wilkinson**; Music Supervisor, **Joseph Gershenson**; Technicolor Color Consultant, **William Fritzsche**

LOCATION FILMING: Old Tucson, Arizona

SOURCE: Biography, *Apache Agent: The Story of John P. Clum* by **Woodworth Clum**

STORY: Easterner John Clum (Audie Murphy) travels to Arizona to become Indian agent for the San Carlos Apache Reservation. Noting the deplorable conditions under which the Apaches are living, Murphy orders the army off the reservation. Murphy forms an Apache police force to enforce the rules. Under an old Apache custom, Chief Eskininzin (Robert Warwick) allows Tianay (Anne Bancroft) to live and care for Murphy. This arrangement makes Murphy uneasy because he is betrothed to Mary (Pat Crowley). Nevertheless, Murphy allows Bancroft to stay so she won't lose face. Murphy obtains rifles so the warriors can hunt and the police can bear arms. Former soldier Sweeney (Charles Drake) is recruited to run the trading post and to train the police force. Crowley arrives to marry Murphy but is upset to find Bancroft living in Murphy's quarters and demands Murphy order Bancroft to leave. Geronimo (Jay Silverheels) comes to the reservation to gather warriors to fight the whites. Murphy decides to lead the Apache police to capture Silverheels. Crowley tries to convince Murphy such action will

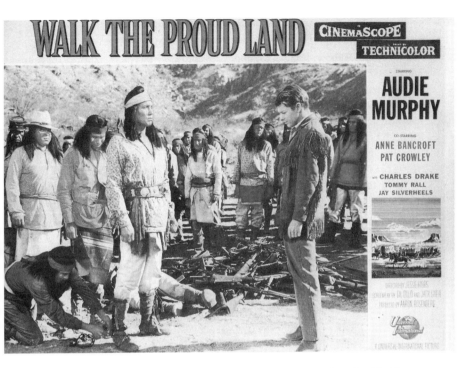

Walk the Proud Land (1956) scene card: Jay Silverheels is being shackled by an unidentified actor as Audie Murphy observes.

probably result in his death. When her pleas become futile, Crowley tells Murphy that she is returning home. Bancroft convinces Crowley to stay and be a source of strength for Murphy. By a ruse, Murphy is able to capture Silverheels and bring him back to the reservation. On his return, Murphy finds that the reservation is again under military control. Murphy starts to quit, but words from Crowley and his Apache friends convince him to stay.

NOTES AND COMMENTARY: Piper Laurie was assigned to co-star with Audie Murphy in this picture. Laurie then asked for and received a release from her Universal-Inter-national contract. Her contract had three more years to run. This agreement between Laurie and Universal was described by the *Hollywood Reporter* as "friendly." Pat Crowley was then cast as Murphy's co-star.

The working title for *Walk the Proud Land* was *Apache Agent*.

Walk the Proud Land was Audie Murphy's first western in Cinemascope.

Dancer Tommy Rall gets a chance to show his terpsichorean prowess in the Apache war dance scene.

Walk the Proud Land featured Jay Silverheels, again, as Geronimo.

Silverheels portrayed the Apache warrior in two other films, *Broken Arrow* (20th Century–Fox, 1950) and *The Battle at Apache Pass* (Universal-International, 1952).

REVIEWS: "Pretty good Audie Murphy actioner." *Western Movies*, Pitts; "A leisurely Western." *The Western*, Hardy.

SUMMATION: *Walk the Proud Land* is an interesting and unusual western for star Audie Murphy.

Playing the part of John P. Clum, Murphy imbues the part with more depth and characterization than he was usually allowed to do in his western career. Anne Bancroft is believable as the Apache woman who loves Murphy. Pat Crowley, Charles Drake and Robert Warwick deliver fine supporting performances. Director Jesse Hibbs paces the story nicely keeping the audience interested throughout.

---

*The Untold Story of Maj. Howell Brady ...
and the savage warriors who fought at his command!
They called them "Brady's Bunch" and their fighting
courage broke the raging might of the ruthless
Kiowa Indian Rebellion—to writ a magnificent
chapter in the history of the West.*

War Arrow

Universal-International (January 1954); COLOR by Technicolor; RUNNING TIME: 78 min.

CAST: Elaine Corwin, **Maureen O'Hara**; Major Howell Brady, **Jeff Chandler**; Avis, **Suzan Ball**; Col. Jackson Meade, **John McIntire**; Sgt. Agustus Wilks, **Noah Beery**; Sgt. Luke Schermerhorn, **Charles Drake**; Maygro, **Henry Brandon**; Pino, **Dennis Weaver**; Satanta, **Jay Silverheels**; Capt. Roger Corwin, **James Bannon**; Captain Neil, **Stephen Wyman**; Lieutenant, **Brad Jackson**

CREDITS: Director, **George Sherman**; Assistant Director, **Frank Shaw**; Producer, **John W. Rogers**; Screenwriter, **John Michael Hayes**; Editor, **Frank Gross**; Art Directors,

Bernard Herzbrun and **Alexander Golitzen**; Set Decorators, **Russell A. Gausman** and **Joseph Kish**; Cinematographer, **William H. Daniels**; Costumes, **Edward Stevenson**; Hair Stylist, **Joan St. Oegger**; Makeup, **Bud Westmore**; Sound, **Leslie I. Carey** and **Richard De Weese**; Musical Director, **Joseph Gershenson**; Technicolor Color Consultant, **William Fritzsche**

LOCATION FILMING: Agoura, California

STORY: Traveling west on special frontier duty, Major Howell Brady (Jeff Chandler) and his two sergeants, Schermerhorn (Charles Drake) and Wilks (Noah Beery), come upon a group of settlers who were massacred by the Kiowa

War Arrow (1954) scene card: Charles Drake, Noah Beery, and Jeff Chandler report for duty to John McIntire.

Indians. Chandler has come west to recruit Seminole Indians to fight the Kiowas. Colonel Meade (John McIntire) thinks Chandler's plan will fail because Seminoles are known to be cowards. At the fort, Chandler meets Elaine Corwin (Maureen O'Hara) whose husband was reported killed on a scouting expedition. Chandler persuades Seminole chief Maygro (Henry Brandon) to allow his braves to fight the Kiowas in exchange for fertile land on which to live. In combat, the Seminoles prove to be valiant warriors. In one skirmish, a white man is seen leading Kiowa forces, and a

sword bearing the name of O'Hara's husband is found at the scene. O'Hara tells Chandler that her husband was planning to desert. A captured Kiowa brave reveals that O'Hara's husband, Capt. Roger Corwin (James Bannon), is leading the Kiowa rebellion. Chandler learns Bannon will lead a Kiowa attack on the fort. O'Hara, who had previously rebuffed Chandler's romantic intentions, tells Chandler she loves him. The Kiowas attack and gain entrance to the fort. Assisted by the Seminoles, the cavalry is able to overcome the Kiowas. Bannon tries to escape but Chandler catches him and they engage each other in hand-to-hand combat. In the fight, a Kiowa brave kills Bannon. The Kiowa threat over, Chandler prepares to return to the East accompanied by O'Hara.

NOTES AND COMMENTARY: The working title for *War Arrow* was *Brady's Bunch*.

Robert Hoy doubled Noah Beery in his comic relief fall from a horse as he tries to show the Seminoles how to jump a horse.

The stagecoach holdup was previously seen in *Column South* (Universal-International, 1953).

"True Love," an often-used song at Universal-International can be heard at McIntire's birthday party.

Note the "dead Indian" who keeps flinching to avoid an explosion and other actors falling on him in the climactic battle scene.

The James Bannon in this film was usually billed as Jim Bannon and can be seen as Jack Packard in Columbia's *I Love a Mystery* series in the mid-forties and then as Red Ryder in four Cinecolor westerns for Eagle-Lion in 1949.

REVIEWS: "Formula cavalry and Indians actioner." *Variety*, 12/9/53; "Film is only average." *Western Movies*, Pitts.

SUMMATION: *War Arrow* is a better-than-average cavalry and Indians saga smartly directed by George Sherman. The film boasts good performances by Jeff Chandler, John McIntire, Charles Drake and Noah Beery. Maureen O'Hara is mainly decoration until the last reel when she shows her ability to handle action scenes. The Kiowa attack on the fort makes an exciting conclusion to the story.

A Kid from the Hills and a Barefoot Blonde
Fighting Their Way Through a Wild Frontier ...

The Wild and the Innocent

Universal-International (May 1959); EASTMAN COLOR by Pathé; FILMED in Cinemascope; RUNNING TIME: 84 min.

CAST: Yancey, **Audie Murphy**; Marcy, **Joanne Dru**; Paul, **Gilbert Roland**; Mr. Forbes, **Jim Backus**; Rosalie, **Sandra Dee**; Uncle Lije, **George Mitchell**; Chip, **Peter Breck**; Ben Stocker, **Strother Martin**; Ma Ransome, **Wesley Marie** Tackitt; Mrs. Forbes, **Betty Harford**; Pitchman, **Mel Leonard**; Kiri, **Lillian Adams**; Richie, **Val Benedict**; Henchmen, **Jim Sheppard, Ed Stroll, John Qualls** and **Frank Wolff**; Dance Hall Girls, **Rosemary Eliot, Barbara Morris** and **Louise Glenn**; Bouncer, **Stephen Roberts**; Townswoman, **Tammy Windsor**; Mountain Man, **William Fawcett**

CREDITS: Director, **Jack Sher**;

The Wild and the Innocent (1959) scene card: A pleasant interlude with Audie Murphy and Sandra Dee.

Assistant Directors, **William Holland** and **Frank Shaw**; Producer, **Sy Gomberg**; Story, **Sy Gomberg**; Screenwriters, **Sy Gomberg** and **Jack Sher**; Editor, **George Gittens**; Art Directors, **Alexander Golitzen** and **Robert Clatworthy**; Set Decorators, **Russell A. Gausman** and **William F. Taff**; Cinematographer, **Harold Lipstein**; Special Photography, **Clifford Stine**; Costumes, **Bill Thomas**; Hair Stylist, **Larry Germain**; Makeup, **Bud Westmore**; Sound, **Leslie I. Carey** and **Joe Lapis**; Music Supervisor, **Joseph Gershenson**; Original Music, **Hans J. Salter**

SONG: "A Touch of Pink" (Lampert and Loring)—sung by **George Mitchell** and **Audie Murphy**

LOCATION FILMING: Big Bear area, California

STORY: Mountain man Uncle Lije (George Mitchell) and his nephew Yancey (Audie Murphy) come down from the mountains to sell the fur pelts they have accumulated over the past two seasons. On making camp, a bear mauls Mitchell. Murphy now has to go on alone to sell the furs. Murphy arrives at the trading post only to find it has been destroyed by fire. At the post, a ne'er-do-well, Ben Stocker (Strother

Martin), attempts to steal Murphy's furs but is unsuccessful. Martin's daughter, Rosalie (Sandra Dee), stays behind to go with Murphy to the town of Casper. Murphy and Dee arrive during the Fourth of July celebration. Murphy is able to sell his pelts and finds a job for Dee at the "dance hall" owned by Sheriff Paul (Gilbert Roland). Dee falls in love with Murphy but Murphy likes dance-hall girl Marcy (Joanne Dru). Roland wants Dee for himself. Murphy takes Dru to the Fourth of July dance where he finds exactly what Dee's job will be at the dance hall. Murphy decides to take Dee from the dance hall. Roland warns Murphy that if he tries to take Dee away, he will kill him. Roland's shot misses but Murphy's return fire mortally wounds Roland. Murphy finally realizes Dee is the girl for him.

NOTES AND COMMENTARY: The working title for this film was *The Buckskin Kid and the Calico Gal.* Audie Murphy, Joanne Dru, Gilbert Roland and Sandra Dee had a major scene with considerable dialogue and a Fourth of July celebration in the background. There was concern on how to film this scene without the noise of the fireworks obliterating the actors' lines. The special effects department solved the problem. Noiseless firecrackers were produced. These firecrackers were plastic receptacles filled with a flammable powder instead of an explosive powder. When the filming had been completed, the sound of the exploding firecrackers was dubbed on the soundtrack in a manner so the audience could understand each actor's lines.

The Wild and the Innocent was Peter Breck's second film. Robert Mitchum brought Breck from Washington, D.C., to play a role in *Thunder Road* (United Artists, 1958). Breck felt his part in *The Wild and the Innocent* "was a good role for someone who was just starting out. It was a signature-heavy type of thing. I had a good time with it." Peter Breck talked about the scene in which Audie Murphy threw him in the horse trough, "I could have had the stuntman do that but I wanted to do it. I was always able to handle myself pretty well. I was a professional tumbler. In those days you could take [tumbling] classes in high school. I think I was very agile and was able to bounce off a wall or off the floor very easily." Stuntman and later director Hal Needham worked with Peter Breck and had doubled Breck in pickup work at Iverson's. Breck commented on the fight sequence with Audie Murphy at the dance in the film, "That again was a straight fight. He [Needham] taught me how to handle myself pretty much in a fight. He taught me everything there was to know. But I never did a stunt without some stuntman on the side being paid for it." Peter Breck enjoyed working with Joanne Dru and said, "That was my first introduction to what then was a glamour lady. Before that I was never involved in love scenes, or even lovely ladies. It was a breath of fresh air."

When the cast would break for

lunch on the back lot, Audie Murphy would work with his gun. Murphy would practice his fast draw and do some target shooting. Peter Breck remembered, "Tony Curtis really wanted to learn fast draw and he wanted to watch Audie because Audie was very fast. Tony kept on nagging him to draw. Audie was a very soft-spoken man, very easy but there was always that fire inside. He [Murphy] would put cans up on a fence, which backed on to a side of a mountain so nobody could get hurt. He would line up six cans and he had six bullets. Bam. One down. Bam. He hit five and that can would go down. Then he turned the gun on Tony and fired it. Bam. It was a blank. You would never see anyone who would go blanch white like he did. It scared the hell out of you. It did cure Tony of asking him to draw."

REVIEWS: "Another mild one from Universal." *Variety*, 3/11/59; "This comic western wanders aimlessly." *The Motion Picture Guide*, Nash and Ross.

SUMMATION: This is a slightly above average comedy western due to the deft casting of Audie Murphy and Sandra Dee as the naïve young lovers. Both performers handle their respective parts well and Joanne Dru as a dance hall girl and Gilbert Roland as the iron-fisted sheriff add adequate support. The script never realizes its potential and the spark needed to make this story more than just entertaining is not there. It's not the actors' fault, but the unsteady direction and the less than fully satisfactory script lets them down.

Born of lawless men and lusty women...
Theirs was a WILD HERITAGE

Wild Heritage

Universal-International (August 1958); EASTMAN COLOR by Pathé; RUNNING TIME: 78 min.

CAST: Judge Copeland, **Will Rogers, Jr.**; Emma Breslin, **Maureen O'Sullivan**; Dirk Breslin, **Rod McKuen**; Rusty, **Casey Tibbs**; Callie Bascomb, **Judy Meredith**; Jesse Bascomb, **Troy Donahue**; Talbot Breslin, **George Winslow**; Missouri Breslin, **Gigi Perreau**; Hugh, **Gary Gray**; Ma Bascomb, **Jeanette Nolan**; Jake Breslin, **Paul Birch**; Arn, **John Beradino**; Jud, **Phil Harvey**; Josh Burrage, **Lawrence Dobkin**; Bolivar Bascomb, **Steven Ellsworth**; Hilda Jansen, **Ingrid Goude**; Brazos, **Christopher Dark**; Chaco, **Guy Wilkerson**; Eastern Neighbors, **Johnny Carpenter** and **Beatrice Gray**

CREDITS: Director, **Charles Haas**; Assistant Director, **Sam Schneider**; Producer, **John E. Horton**; Screenwriters, **Paul King** and **Joseph Stone**; Editor, **Edward**

Wild Heritage (1959) scene card: Maureen O'Sullivan and her children George Winslow, Rod McKuen, Gary Gray, and Gigi Perreau sing "Abide with Me" in the wake of her husband's death.

Mann; Art Directors, **Alexander Golitzen and Robert Boyle**; Set Decorators, **Russell A. Gausman** and **John P. Austin**; Cinematographer, **Philip Lathrop**; Costumes, **Morton Haack**; Makeup, **Bud Westmore**; Sound, **Leslie I. Carey** and **Donald Cunliffe**; Music Supervisor, **Joseph Gershenson**

LOCATION FILMING: Lasky Mesa, California

SONG: "When Johnny Comes Marching Home" (Gilmore)—sung by Paul Birch, Rod McKuen, Gary Gray, Maureen O'Sullivan, Gigi Perreau and George Winslow; "Abide with Me" (Traditional)—

sung by Maureen O'Sullivan, Rod McKuen, Gigi Perreau, George Winslow and Gary Gray

STORY: Jake Breslin (Paul Birch) decides to move west with his wife, Emma (Maureen O'Sullivan) and his children, Dirk (Rod McKuen), Hugh (Gary Gray), Missouri (Gigi Perreau) and Talbot (George Winslow), to settle on larger farm land. At the first western settlement, Birch gets into an argument with bad man Arn (John Beradino) and is killed. Judge Copeland (Will Rogers, Jr.) helps the family decide to stay in the West. O'Sullivan's family meets another family that's decided to settle out west also. This family consists of Bolivar-Bascomb (Steven Ellsworth) and Ma (Jeanette Nolan) and their children, Callie (Judy Meredith) and Jesse (Troy Donahue). The children of both families have problems getting along until the accidental death of Ellsworth and the near fatal illness of O'Sullivan and Perreau help bond the families together. In addition, romance is starting to blossom between McKuen and Meredith, and Donahue and Perreau. Texan Rusty (Casey Tibbs) is trail-herding his cattle and stops to graze on O'Sullivan's land. Beradino and his partner, Jud (Phil Harvey), decide to rustle the cattle. In the raid, almost all the cattle are stolen and every Texan is killed except Tibbs. Since Tibbs owes his life to McKuen and Gray, he gives them the cattle the rustlers missed. McKuen gives half the cattle to Nolan's family in thanks for Nolan and Meredith pulling O'Sullivan and Perreau through their illnesses. Fearing a raid by Beradino and Harvey, the families band their herds together and take turns guarding them. The rustlers strike, wound Meredith and get away with the cattle. McKuen, Gray, Donahue and Winslow ride to the settlement figuring that is where the rustlers would take the herd. At the settlement, McKuen, Gray and Donahue face Beradino and Harvey. The outlaws are holding the upper hand and figure they can ride away with the cattle, when Winslow sneaks a gun to Gray. Gray and McKuen gun down Beradino and

Harvey. With the recovery of the herd, it looks like wedding bells are in store for the two couples and possibly O'Sullivan and Rogers.

NOTES AND COMMENTARY: In one scene Gary Gray helped Ingrid Goude down from a wagon. As Gray placed Goude on the ground, he looked down and couldn't help noticing her bosoms. As Gary put it, "She had been Miss Sweden ['57] and everything. I saw this beautiful girl and I forgot my lines."

An unusual thing was that no doubles were used for the lead actors in this film. Gray commented, "It was really unusual because normally you would have. Even in our fights we didn't. Nobody doubled us on that show at all." The most impressive thing that happened to Gary Gray on the film was to meet Casey Tibbs. Tibbs was one of the finest of all rodeo champions. After the filming of *Wild Heritage*, Gray took the opportunity to see Tibbs in action at a rodeo held at the Cow Palace in San Francisco.

In addition to having a small role as a well-wishing neighbor at the start of the film, Johnny Carpenter did some of the stunt work. Carpenter is most noted for his "B" westerns in the early to mid–50s.

In his long career, lead villain John Beradino first appeared in *Our Gang* comedies in the 30s. He was a professional baseball player and appeared in 912 major league games as a shortstop and second baseman with the St. Louis Browns, Cleveland Indians and Pittsburgh Pirates. Beradino reached his greatest fame as Dr. Steve Hardy on the soap opera *General Hospital* from 1963 to 1996.

The working title for *Wild Heritage* was *Death Rides This Trail*.

REVIEWS: "Mild frontier western" *Variety*, 6/25/58; "Mediocre entertainment" *The Universal Story*, Hirschhorn.

SUMMATION: *Wild Heritage* is a pleasant enough slice of Americana that just should have been better. The story gets off to a rocky start when the pioneer family has to travel through a muddy stretch of road, but all the ground around them looks nice and dry. Obviously the budget didn't allow an elaborate muddy setting. Then, when the family reaches the nearest settlement, Paul Birch, the husband and father of the family, steps into a saloon and pushes and shoves his way to the bar and is amazed when John Beradino takes exception to his actions. A convenient way for the screenwriters to have the Paul Birch character killed off. At least, it beats the bad guy saying, "I don't like your face." The ensemble does as much justice to the script as possible, but even so, no one rises above an adequate level of acting. Director Charles Haas does as well as he can with a script that could have used more care and a story that needed a much bigger budget to have been a memorable picture.

The Roaring Story of the Gun that Won the West!

Winchester '73

ALTERNATE TITLE: **Montana Winchester**; Universal-International (July 1950); RUNNING TIME: 92 min.

CAST: Lin McAdam, **James Stewart**; Lola Manners, **Shelley Winters**; Waco Johnny Dean, **Dan Duryea**; Dutch Henry Brown, **Stephen McNally**; High Spade, **Millard Mitchell**; Steve Miller, **Charles Drake**; Joe Lamont, **John McIntire**; Wyatt Earp, **Will Geer**; Sgt. Wilkes, **Jay C. Flippen**; Young Bull, **Rock Hudson**; Jack Riker, **John Alexander**; Wesley, **Steve Brodie**; Wheeler, **James Millican**; Latigo Means, **Abner Biberman**; Doan, **Tony Curtis**; Crator, **James Best**; Mossman, **Gregg Martell**; Cavalryman, **Frank Chase**; Long Tom, **Chuck Roberson**; Dudeen, **Carol Henry**; Marshal Noonan, **Ray Teal**; Mrs. Jameson, **Virginia Mullen**; Roan Daley, **John Doucette**; Bat Masterson, **Steve Darrell**; Indian with necklace; **Chief Yowlachie**; Clerk, **Frank Conlan**; Charles Bender, **Ray Bennett**; Virgil Earp, **Guy Wilkerson**; Bassett, **Bob Anderson**; Boys at rifle shoot, **Larry Olsen**, **Bill McKenzie** and **Jimmy Hawkins**; Target Watcher, **Edmund Cobb**; Target Clerk, **Forrest Taylor**; Station Master, **Ethan Laidlaw**; Townsman, **Bud Osborne**; Boy, **Tony Taylor**; Betty Jameson, **Bon-**

Winchester '73 (1950) scene card: James Stewart battles an unidentified actor; left border—Stewart.

nie **Kay Eddy**; Stagecoach Driver, **Jennings Miles**; Indian Interpreter, **John War Eagle**; Bartender (Dodge City), **Mel Archer**; Bartender (Tascosa), **Ted Mapes**

CREDITS: Director, **Anthony Mann**; Producer, **Aaron Rosenberg**; Story, **Stuart N. Lake**; Screenwriters, **Robert L. Richards** and **Borden Chase**; Editor, **Edward Curtiss**; Art Directors, **Bernard Herzbrun** and **Nathan Juran**; Set Decorators, **Russell A. Gausman** and **Roland A. Fields**; Cinematographer, **William Daniels**; Gowns, **Yvonne Wood**; Hair Stylist, **Joan St. Oegger**; Makeup, **Bud West-**more; Sound, **Leslie I. Carey** and **Richard De Weese**; Music, **Joseph E. Gershenson**

LOCATION FILMING: Tucson, Arizona

STORY: Lin McAdam (James Stewart) and High Spade (Millard Mitchell) ride into Dodge City looking for Dutch Henry Brown (Stephen McNally). Stewart wants to kill McNally for reasons known only to himself and Mitchell. They are certain McNally will be in Dodge City to enter the Fourth of July rifle shoot. The winner will receive a "one-of-a-kind" Winchester '73 rifle. Stewart also enters the contest and outshoots McNally to win the rifle. McNally and one of his men steal the rifle from Stewart. The rifle changes hands many times. Finally, McNally takes the rifle from gunman Dan Duryea. Since Duryea and McNally are planning to rob the Tascosa Bank, Duryea acquiesces for the time being. Stewart and Mitchell ride into Tascosa and find Shelley Winters, who they met earlier in their travels. Winters tells Stewart that Duryea knows where Stewart can find McNally. Stewart and Duryea scuffle, guns flash and Stewart kills Duryea. Other gang members start fighting with Stewart. Any chances for a successful holdup are ruined. McNally tries to get away but Stewart catches up with him. In a gun duel on a rocky mountainside, Stewart kills McNally. Mitchell tells Winters that McNally is Stewart's brother. Stewart wins both the rifle and Winters.

NOTES AND COMMENTARY: Producer Aaron Rosenberg had promised Tony Curtis that he would test him for one of the leads. James Best happened to be present and asked, since everything was already set up, if he, too, could be tested. Best figured Curtis already had the part but this way Rosenberg would know he would be suitable for one of the lesser roles. Best's screen test turned out well. Then instead of either Curtis or Best getting the part, Rosenberg decided he wanted to go with a star. Dan Duryea was given the part of Waco Johnny Dean.

The Indians were native to the Tucson area and had an animosity toward the Hollywood actors. In the scene where the Indians attacked the army camp, the Indians would shoot at the actors with full loads so the actors were constantly having to pick the powder burns out of their faces. James Best noticed one young man who was the Indian leader. Even though the Indian knew English, he pretended he didn't. Best told the Indian that he knew he understood English and not to ride close again and shoot with full loads. On the next shot, the Indians again used the full loads. Best vowed he would stop the Indians from hurting the actors. On the next take, Best not only used a full load but also added a handful of gravel. Best shot the leader in the leg and the Indian brave finally got the message. Afterwards, the Indians didn't really want to ride close to the actors. Best intimated that he was a little feisty in those days.

Rock Hudson played the Indian chief Young Bull, whom James Stewart shoots during the attack on the army camp. Hudson, performing his own stunts, had to do the scene three times, because Anthony Mann wanted him to fall exactly at one certain spot. Afterwards, co-workers told him he could collect additional monies because he was doing a stuntman's work.

Rock Hudson had been a mailman and had no training as an actor. Hudson was worried on how to play his part. James Best told him, "Don't play an Indian. Just read it dead straight. With your looks, you know." That's exactly what Hudson did and from there was cast in *The Iron Man* (Universal-International, 1951) with Jeff Chandler. Hudson's career began to take off.

In the credits James Best has the cast name of Crator but Jay C. Flippen calls him Coates on two separate occasions. Tony Curtis is listed as Doan but is never called by name in the film. Charles Drake makes a comment to Shelley Winters about wishing he'd had the wagon wheel greased at Doan's store. Steve Brodie and James Millican have cast listings as Wesley and Wheeler but they are introduced at two different times as Johnny and Ben. Many books that give a cast listing on this film list High Spade's given name as Johnny Williams, but in the scene in the Dodge City saloon Millard Mitchell states his name as Frankie Wilson.

Winchester '73 was scheduled to be filmed during the 1946-1947 production year. Joan Bennett was picked to star in this psychological western. Fritz Lang had been named to direct. The film was to have been produced by Walter Wanger and Fritz Lang, and would have been a Diana production.

Fritz Lang submitted a script to Humphrey Bogart. Bogart was to play the central character, Billy the Kid. Obviously, when the script was rewritten for James Stewart, the Billy the Kid character was omitted.

Walter Wanger again announced that *Winchester '73* would be made during the 1947-48 production year.

James Stewart agreed to appear in the film for a percentage of the profits in lieu of his usual salary. This turned out to be a good decision and led to other major stars negotiating similar contracts for their services.

Winchester '73 was remade as a television movie in 1967 by Universal with Tom Tyron in the lead. Needless to say, this film did not come up to the original entry.

REVIEWS: "A thoroughly enjoyable western, of superior quality." *Variety*, 6/7/50; "High grade and very entertaining class A western." *Western Movies*, Pitts.

SUMMATION: This taut, tense exciting western has deservedly earned its status as a classic.

James Stewart makes his second starring screen appearance in a western. *Broken Arrow* (20th Century–Fox, 1950) was made prior to *Winchester '73* but released afterwards. Stewart is not only convincing as a cowboy but gives an in-depth performance on the trials and anguish he is experiencing in his quest to avenge his father's death. Stewart is supported by a memorable cast, with special mention to Stephen McNally as Stewart's wastrel brother, Millard Mitchell as Stewart's best friend, and Charles Drake as a coward who is no match for the violence that he encounters. Duryea as Waco Johnny Dean begins his first of many portrayals of laughing psychotic killers. Later, Duryea would refine the part to the point that he would really give added punch to programmer productions. In this instance, he fills the part adequately. Usually a film episodic in nature will have slow spots, but none are experienced in this western. Anthony Mann's direction is able to heighten the tension of each episodic event, culminating in a tense shootout between the brothers. This is a most worthwhile film.

OUT OF THE THUNDER AND PLUNDER OF A NATION'S
MOST DANGEROUS DAYS ... COMES ITS MOST THRILLING STORY!
... of a gold-lusting adventurer and a fiery Bandit Queen ...
and the fighting revolt for an empire's richest prize!

Wings of the Hawk

Universal-International (September 1953); COLOR by Technicolor; FILMED in 3-Dimension; RUNNING TIME: 81 min.

CAST: Irish Gallager, **Van Heflin**; Raquel, **Julia Adams**; Elena, **Abbe Lane**; Colonel Ruiz, **George Dolenz**; Orozco, **Noah Beery**; Father Perez, **Antonio Moreno**; Tomas, **Pedro Gonzalez Gonzalez**; Arturo, **Rodolfo Acosta**; Carlos, **Paul Fierro**; Marco, **Mario Siletti**; Captain Gomez, **Rico Alaniz**; Ramon, **Ricardo Alba**; Capt. Rivera, **John Dahein**; Lita, **Nancy Westbrook**

CREDITS: Director, **Budd Boetticher**; Assistant Director, **Tom Shaw**; Producer, **Aaron Rosenberg**; Associate Producer, **David Johnson**; Screenwriter, **James E. Moser**; Adaptation, **Kay Lenard**; Editor, **Russell Schoengarth**; Art Directors, **Bernard Herzbrun** and **Robert Clatworthy**; Set Decorators, **Russell A. Gausman** and **Oliver Emert**; Cinematographer, **Clifford Stine**; Costumes, **Bill Thomas**; Hair Stylist, **Joan St. Oegger**; Makeup, **Bud Westmore**; Sound, **Leslie I. Carey** and **Joe Lapis**; Music, **Frank Skinner**; Technicolor Color Consultant, **William Fritzsche**

LOCATION FILMING: Corriganville and Burro Flats, California

SOURCE: Story, "Wings of the Vulture" by **Gerald Drayson Adams**

STORY: Mexican colonel Ruiz (George Dolenz) decides to take over Irish Gallager's (Van Heflin's) mine after a rich gold strike. Heflin attempts to get away from the Rurales but he needs help from the Insurrectors to accomplish this. Insurrector leader Arturo (Rodolfo Acosta) is not happy when Heflin is brought into the rebel's camp, but Heflin is needed to treat a wound Raquel (Julia Adams) received in the skirmish with the Rurales. After recovering from her wound, Adams takes Heflin to the nearest railroad station. Both Heflin and Adams are captured. Even though the rebels free Heflin and Adams from jail, it takes Heflin's bravery to turn the tables so all can escape. Adams learns of a plan to defeat the Mexican government but rifles are needed to be successful. Acosta doesn't want to get involved but Adams thinks the plan can be successful and takes over as leader of the Insurrectors. Heflin agrees to aid the rebels by helping them steal gold from his mine. Acosta goes to Dolenz and agrees to lead the Rurales to the rebel's camp in exchange for Adams' freedom. The Rurales attack the camp with Heflin, Adams and a few others escaping capture. Heflin leads a

Wings of the Hawk (1953) scene card: An unidentified actor fires a rifle at the Rurales to prevent Van Heflin from being captured.

successful raid on his mine and enough gold is taken to purchase rifles. Acosta has alerted Dolenz to Adams' intentions, and Heflin, Adams and Tomas (Pedro Gonzalez Gonzalez) are spotted bringing rifles into Mexico from Texas. Adams allows herself to be captured so the rifles can get through. Dolenz decides not to free Adams. Acosta protests and is mortally wounded but he is able to reach Heflin to tell him of Adams' fate. Knowing the route Dolenz must take, Heflin decides to dynamite his mine so Adams can be rescued. The armed rebels are too much for the Mexican soldiers.

Dolenz attempts to escape but is shot by Gonzalez Gonzalez to avenge the execution of his mother. Heflin plans to stay with Adams.

NOTES AND COMMENTARY: Glenn Ford signed a two-picture contract with Universal-International with *Wings of the Hawk* to be the first film under the pact. It was later decided to make *The Man from the Alamo* (Universal-International, 1953) first. Because of injuries sustained by Ford in the making of *The Man from the Alamo*, Van Heflin was signed for the role of Irish Gallag*er. Heflin and Boetticher became good friends.

Universal-International wanted the picture to be filmed in 3-D. All the directors had been invited to a big meeting at Warner Bros. with Jack Warner. Warner said, "Gentlemen, every man, woman and child in the United States will have their own personal 3-D glasses within a year." The directors knew 3-D pictures were a fad, something to tear people from their television sets. Boetticher refused to film *Wings of the Hawk* in 3-D. Boetticher commented, "So, I didn't do it. I thought this was absurd. They brought in another director after I left from Mexico and he shot ten days of 3-D stuff."

There was one scene that almost had tragic consequences. It comes at the end of the picture when Van Heflin jumps in a carriage with George Dolenz and Abbe Lane riding in it. The scene was first attempted on a Friday. None of the principals would be used in the scene. Joe Yrigoyen was driving the carriage, Robert Hoy was doubling Lane and Al Wyatt was doubling Heflin. The carriage had not been rigged properly to run up and down the hills. As Wyatt makes his jump to the carriage, the back left wheel loses its rim and the spokes are exposed. As Wyatt is in the air, Hoy reaches back and throws Wyatt away from the carriage to the ground. If Wyatt had landed on the spokes, they would have gone through him. Then the wheel was gone and the carriage turned over. The scene was finally shot the following Monday. Davy Sharpe replaced Wyatt be-

cause Wyatt had a prior commitment.

Budd Boetticher had directed nine films in two years without a day off. Boetticher told me, "So at the end of two years, I finagled my way out of there. I think they were glad to get rid of me." Boetticher asked the studio heads if he could be released from his contract. The studio heads agreed but released the news to the public that Universal-International was not picking up Boetticher's option, which was a kind way to say that he had been fired.

Stuntwoman Polly Burson doubled Julia Adams in this film. One shot became very dangerous for Burson. A herd of horses was moving fast and Burson was hanging down between them so she couldn't be seen. One of the horses knocked Burson's foot out of the strap that was keeping her on the horse. Burson fell to the ground among the running horses. Burson's husband, stuntman Jerry Gatlin, was the hero as he rushed to her rescue. Burson remarked, "I didn't get hurt too bad. Several of them hit me but nothing bad."

Polly Burson did Julia Adams' fast mounts and dismounts. A problem arose because Adams was dressed in tight Mexican pants. Burson commented, "They were as tight as your skin. I had to make a run at this old horse and get on him and the horse got mad because I couldn't get my leg up. When I turned around, he bit me in the 'you-know-where.'" There were zippers down the side to aid both Adams and Burson in getting into the outfit. Burson motioned that the zipper would have to be loosened. Burson's leg was painted black so they could unzip the pants.

Mario Siletti's character name is Marco in the closing credits but Heflin always calls him Marcus.

There was a neat bit of dialogue at the picture's end after Heflin has lost his gold mine. Julia Adams asks "Why did you do it, Irish? The mine was all you had." Van Heflin (looking directly at the beautiful Adams) replies, "It doesn't have to be, General. Know what I mean?"

REVIEWS: "A rousing action-packed adventure yarn." *Hollywood Reporter*, 8/27/53; "A pleasing western." *The Motion Picture Guide*, Nash and Ross.

SUMMATION: *Wings of the Hawk* is another well-done exciting western saga directed by Budd Boetticher. Boetticher directs with aplomb, showing again why he is well thought of in the western genre. The action begins almost immediately and doesn't let up until the picture's end. The fine running inserts lensed by cameraman Clifford Stine heighten the action scenes. Another asset is the good performances delivered by Van Heflin and Julia Adams. Heflin gives a measured performance as a man who wants to settle his differences peacefully but is not afraid to fight when there is no other recourse. Adams surprises by doing justice to her role as a Mexican revolutionary. Rodolfo Acosta and Pedro Gonzalez Gonzalez shine in support. Noah Beery can't pull off his role as a Mexican bandit. Beery probably should have studied his uncle Wallace Beery to see how to overact as a Mexican bandit and get away with it. Fortunately for the film, Beery's role is fleeting. Frank Skinner contributes another fine musical score.

THE MOST DARING DESPERADOS THAT EVER PANICKED THE WEST WITH LAUGHTER!

The Wistful Widow of Wagon Gap

ALTERNATE TITLE: *The Wistful Widow*; Universal-International (October 1947); Black and White; RUNNING TIME: 78 min.

CAST: Duke Egan, **Bud Abbott**; Chester Wooley, **Lou Costello**; Widow Hawkins, **Marjorie Main**; Juanita Hawkins, **Audrey Young**; Judge Benbow, **George Cleveland**; Jake Frame, **Gordon Jones**; Jim Simpson, **William Ching**; Phil, **Peter Thompson**; Matt Hawkins, **Bill Clauson**; Billy Hawkins, **Billy O'Leary**; Sarah Hawkins, **Pamela Wells**; Jefferson Hawkins, **Jimmie Bates**; Lincoln Hawkins, **Paul Dunn**; Sally Hawkins, **Diane Florentine**; Hank, **Rex Lease**; Lefty, **Glenn

The Wistful Widow of Wagon Gap (1947) scene card: Lou Costello turns the charm on Marjorie Main so she will assign him fewer duties; left border—Bud Abbott, Costello and Main.

Strange; Lem, **Edmund Cobb**; Squint, **Wade Crosby**; Miner, **Dewey Robinson**; Bartender, **Murray Leonard**; Shotgun Rider, **Lee "Lasses" White**; Cowboy at Hanging, **Zon Murray**; Dance Hall Hostess, **Iris Adrian**; Cowpuncher, **George J. Lewis**; Old Timer, **Emmett Lynn**; Tough Cowboy, **Charles King**; Bar Patron, **Frank Hagney**; Man thrown by widow, **Davy Sharpe**

CREDITS: Director, **Charles T. Barton**; Assistant Director, **Joseph E. Kenny**; Producer, **Robert Arthur**; Associate Producer, **Sebastian Cristillo**; Story, **D.D. Beauchamp** and

William Bowers; Screenwriters, **Robert Lees, Frederic I. Rinaldo** and **John Grant**; Editor, **Frank Gross**; Art Directors, **Bernard Herzbrun** and **Gabriel Scognamillo**; Set Decorators, **Russell A. Gausman** and **Charles Wyrick**; Cinematographer, **Charles Van Enger**; Costumes, **Rosemary Odell**, Hair Stylist, **Carmen Dirigo**; Makeup, **Bud Westmore**; Sound, **Charles Felstead** and **Robert Pritchard**; Music, **Walter Schumann**; Orchestrations, **David Tamkin**; Dialogue Director, **Norman Abbott**

SONG: "Set 'Em Up, Joe" (Fairchild and Brooks)—sung by **Audrey Young**

LOCATION FILMING: Iverson's Ranch, California

STORY: On their way to California, travelling salesmen Duke Egan (Abbott) and Chester Wooley (Costello) decide to sell their wares at the wide-open town of Wagon Gap, Montana. To show they are tough, Abbott has Costello fire his gun into the air. A dead man falls to the street behind the boys. Costello is accused of the killing and by Montana law becomes responsible for the dead man's family and debts. The family is headed by Widow Hawkins (Marjorie Main), who casts romantic designs on Costello. Costello turns down Main's marriage proposal and Main retaliates by making Costello do all the work on the ranch. The deceased's major debt was to gambling proprietor Jake Frame (Gordon Jones). Jones wants the oldest daughter, Juanita (Audrey Young), to sing in his saloon in order to pay back the money her father owed him. Main makes Costello work in the saloon at night instead. None of the tough cowboys want to tangle with Costello because they would have to take over the responsibility of supporting Main. Therefore, Costello is appointed sheriff and easily tames the town. Jones and his gang decide to hold up a stagecoach transporting a large payroll but Costello is able to thwart the outlaws. Since Jones' outlawry has been brought out into the open, Costello goes to arrest him. The gang is no longer afraid of Costello, since they believe Main is about to become a rich woman and all want to marry her. The gang begins shooting at Costello and a blazing gunfight ensues. Seeing the townspeople are getting the upper hand, Jones tries to escape but is captured by Jim Simpson (William Ching), the leader of the citizen's committee. Costello is cleared of the murder charge and both he and Abbott are allowed to travel on to California. Judge Benbow (George Cleveland) decides to marry Main, who actually will become the richest woman in Montana.

NOTES AND COMMENTARY: The story was written with the idea of having James Stewart as the star. This idea didn't work out and the script was rewritten to accommodate the talents of Abbott and Costello. Family ties are evident in this film. Associate producer Sebastian Cristillo is Lou's father, and dialogue director Norman Abbott is Bud's nephew. Abbott would later become producer/director of the television series, *The Jack Benny Show* (CBS, NBC) and *Sanford and Son* (NBC).

Patricia Alphin was announced as the ingenue in this film but when the film was released Alphin had the new screen name of Audrey Young.

Scenes from *The Wistful Widow of Wagon Gap* were used in *The World of Abbott and Costello* (Universal, 1965)

"Set 'Em Up, Joe" was sung by Yvonne De Carlo in the earlier Universal western, *Frontier Gal* (1945).

REVIEWS: "Abbott and Costello ride herd on plenty of laughs." *Variety*, 9/26/47; "A good plotline, Abbott and Costello and Marjorie Main, make this an amusing genre spoof." *Western Movies*, Pitts.

SUMMATION: This is good western comedy with Bud Abbott and, especially, Lou Costello in fine form. Costello, at this stage, still had not gotten old and tired-looking and therefore his mugging hits the target. Abbott and Costello rework their "oyster in the soup" routine from *Here Come the Co-Eds* (Universal, 1945). This time a frog is used with hilarious results. Marjorie Main adds her own brand of humor as a western version of Ma Kettle and is largely successful. William Ching, Gordon Jones, and George Cleveland add good support. Charles T. Barton directs briskly.

The West's Most Daring Train Robbery!
They're out to loot the U.S. Mail with Dynamite,
Bullets or a Woman's Wiles!

Wyoming Mail

Universal-International (October 1950); COLOR by Technicolor; RUNNING TIME: 87 min.

CAST: Steve Davis, **Stephen McNally**; Mary Williams, **Alexis Smith**; Cavanaugh, **Howard da Silva**; Haynes, **Ed Begley**; George Armstrong, **Dan Riss**; Charles De Haven, **Roy Roberts**; Indian Joe, **Armando Silvestre**; Sam, **Whit Bissell**; Russell, **James Arness**; Nate, **Richard Jaeckel**; Rufe, **Frankie Darro**; Pete, **Felipe Turich**; Beale, **Richard Eagan**; Shep, **Gene Evans**; Gilson, **Frank Fenton**; Ben, **Emerson Treacy**; Railroad Official, **Davy Sharpe**; Pat, **Harry Tyler**; Senator, **Charles Evans**; Townsmen, **Guy Wilkerson** and **Harold Goodwin**; Red, **John Cason**; Sheriff, **Ed Cassidy**; Waiter, **Chick Chandler**

CREDITS: Director, **Reginald Le Borg**, Producer, **Aubrey Schenck**; Story, **Robert Hardy Andrews**; Screenwriters, **Harry Essex** and **Leonard Lee**; Editor, **Edward A. Curtiss**; Art Directors, **Bernard Herzbrun** and **Hilyard A. Brown**; Set Decorators, **Russell A. Gausman** and **John Austin**; Cinematographer, **Russell Metty**; Costumes, **Bill Thomas**; Hair Stylist, **Joan St. Oegger**; Makeup, **Bud Westmore**; Sound, **Leslie I. Carey** and **Frank Moran**; Musical Direction, **Joseph Gershenson**; Technicolor Color Consultant, **William Fritzsche**

SONGS: "Take Me to Town" (Shapiro and Lee)—sung by chorus girls; "Endlessly" (Shapiro and Lee) —sung by **Alexis Smith**

LOCATION FILMING: Tuolumne County, California

STORY: A rash of unsolved train robberies, with the U.S. Mail the primary target, has resulted in an ultimatum to the postal department to

Wyoming Mail (1950) title card: Alexis Smith and Stephen McNally.

bring the gang to justice within three months. A new undercover man is needed to meet with the Wyoming Territory operative who has important information. George Armstrong (Dan Riss) is able to recruit Steve Davis (Stephen McNally). Haynes (Ed Begley), the territorial prison warden, murders the operative before McNally can talk to him. A clue leads McNally to the territorial prison where McNally arranges to be sent as a convicted bank robber. McNally meets Sam (Whit Bissell), a member of the train robbers, at the prison. Indian Joe (Armando Silvestre) helps McNally and Bissell break out of prison. During the

break, Bissell is mortally wounded. Before dying, Bissell gives McNally the name of a gang member. McNally is able to infiltrate the gang and discovers Mary Williams (Alexis Smith), the girl he loves, is also a member. When McNally's cover is blown, Smith refuses to reveal his identity to other gang members. McNally is able to bring the gang to justice and discovers the district commissioner, Roy Roberts, is the gang leader. Smith receives a pardon and settles down with McNally.

NOTES AND COMMENTARY: One scene has Davy Sharpe, doubling Stephen McNally, falling from the top of a telegraph pole overlooking a raging river. Gene Evans commented that this was a "helluva stunt," even though Davy fell into a net instead of the water. A dummy finished the fall into the river.

In the scene in which Gene Evans, James Arness and Frankie Darro had to ride straight down to the train, a problem emerged because Darro had been drinking. His co-workers could easily tell this because his face looked like a little prune. The first thing Darro said was, "What do we have to do, fellows?" Evans immediately knew they were in for a long day. Arness looks over to Darro and says, "Whoa, pardner." So, Evans and Arness rode on either side of Darro, each man keeping Darro in check. Darro started on the ride to the train, literally floating on top of his horse. If Darro hadn't been held in place, he would have fallen out of the saddle.

The studio paid for the ride home from the location setting (Evans thought the movie was filmed in Wyoming) for Gene Evans and James Arness. Both men had been drinking heavily when they got on the train. Evans had a half a bottle of whiskey left. Evans and Arness were feeling pretty good when the conductor appropriated the bottle. The conductor figured they had had enough to drink. Evans later commented, "Never mess with a man's bottle when that was all there is on the whole train and no matter how many hundreds of dollars you have in your pocket, you couldn't have bought a drink." They persuaded the conductor to return the bottle by holding the conductor outside the train. At the time the train was travelling about 40 to 45 miles an hour. The conductor wired ahead to Los Angeles, and Evans and Arness knew someone would be looking for them when the train pulled into Union Station. As soon as the train stopped, Evans and Arness took off. They went to Arness' house in Pacific Palisades. Evans was impressed, because at that stage in their careers, Arness had a house in such an exclusive section of town. As Evans walked into the living room, he saw a couch with an orange crate on either end, and there was a third orange crate in front of the couch with a rug or something on top of it. There was a lamp on one of the orange crates. In the bedroom, there was a mattress right on the floor. Such living conditions didn't bother Arness who had his place at Pacific Palisades where he could easily go surfing, an activity he loved to do.

Richard Eagan would gain fame as a leading man under the name, Richard Egan.

The train robbery sequence in which the engineer and the fireman are killed by thrown knives is used in its entirety in *Cave of Outlaws* (Universal-International, 1951).

The song, "Take Me to Town" can be heard in *Take Me to Town* (Universal-International, 1953), *A Day of Fury* (Universal-International, 1956) and *Showdown* (Universal-International, 1963)

REVIEWS: "Good early western." *Variety*, 10/4/50; "It may be set—a notch, say—above the rest of the ranbrush sagas." *New York Times*, 10/23/50.

SUMMATION: This is a good, well-paced action western. The cast is good, Stephen McNally properly tough as the undercover agent. The chemistry is there between McNally and the lovely Alexis Smith. The good supporting cast includes Howard da Silva, James Arness, Armando Silvestre and Gene Evans. A special mention has to be made for the superior stunt work by Davy Sharpe.

THEY BATTLED FOR THE GOLDEN HEART OF A FABULOUS MOUNTAIN!
...and a woman's unclaimed lips!

The Yellow Mountain

Universal-International (December 1954); PRINT by Technicolor; RUNNING TIME: 78 min.

CAST: Andy Martin, **Lex Barker**; Nevada Wray, **Mala Powers**; Pete Menlo, **Howard Duff**; Jackpot Wray, **William Demarest**; Bannon, **John McIntire**; Drake, **Leo Gordon**; Geraghty, **Dayton Lummis**; Sam Torrence, **Hal K. Dawson**; Old Prospector, **William Fawcett**; Joe, **James Parnell**; Wagon Driver, **Jack Ingram**; Saloon Bouncer, **Eddie Parker**; Bartender, **Kermit Maynard**; George Yost, **Denver Pyle**; Bannon Gunman, **Mike Ragan**

CREDITS: Director, **Jesse Hibbs**; Assistant Director, **Ronnie Rondell**; Producer, **Ross Hunter**; Story, **Harold Channing Wire**; Screenwriters, **George Zuckerman** and **Russell Hughes**; Adaptation, **Robert Blees**; Editor, **Edward Curtiss**; Art Directors, **Alexander Golitzen** and **Alfred Sweeney**; Set Decorators, **Russell A. Gausman** and **John Austin**; Cinematographer, **George Robinson**; Costumes, **Bill Thomas**; Hair Stylist, **Joan St. Oegger**; Makeup, **Bud Westmore**; Sound, **Leslie I. Carey** and **Joe Lapis**; Music Supervision, **Joseph Gershenson**; Technicolor Color Consultant, **William Fritzsche**

LOCATION FILMING: Mojave Desert area in Southern California

STORY: Andy Martin (Lex Barker) comes to Goldfield to collect money owed to him by saloon and mine owner Pete Menlo (Howard Duff), an old friend of Barker's. When Duff is threatened by rival mine owner Bannon (John McIntire) and his gunman Drake (Leo Gordon), Barker chooses to throw in with Duff. Duff and Barker decide to sink a mine. Barker discovers gold and assays show their mine is very valuable. McIntire attempts to stop Barker and Duff from making a success out of their mine by hiring all the miners in the area.

Wages escalate as both mines try to keep workers. Needing money to stay in the bidding war for miners, Barker tries to get two wagon loads of gold to the smelter. McIntire finds out about the attempt and sends Gordon to wreck the wagons. Gordon is successful and leaves an unconscious Barker in the desert to perish. A prospector (William Fawcett) rescues Barker and takes him back to town. Meanwhile, Duff enters into an agreement with McIntire to mine the gold. Barker and Duff have an argument and split up. In addition, Barker thinks assayer Nevada Wray (Mala Powers) is in love with Duff, not knowing Powers has turned down Duff's marriage proposal. Duff and McIntire find out their mines are worthless because Powers' father, Jackpot Wray (William Demarest), owns the mine containing the apex and thereby is entitled to all the gold that emanates from his mine. Needing money in a card game, Demarest sells the deed to his mine to Barker. Learning that both Duff and McIntire want to purchase the mine, Barker returns the deed to Demarest and convinces Demarest and Powers to dynamite their mine to see why it is now desirable. Barker discovers that Demarest owns the apex and goes to town to register the apex. McIntire sends Gordon and his men to stop Barker. When Gordon's efforts fail, McIntire starts to shoot Barker but instead is shot by Duff. Barker and Powers plan to marry and Demarest makes Barker a partner in the mine. Barker decides to share his interest with Duff.

NOTES AND COMMENTARY: Mala Powers, upon learning that most critics thought the film was only fair, stated, "I think that's a very just review. They came up with this idea of these two guys (Barker and Duff) that really loved each other but it never really paid off. It was never anything more than superficial. The whole thing was superficial. The character of the girl [Powers' role] was superficial. The relationship between the guys was superficial. I forgot it as soon as it was over. It was not a happy experience for me as an actress." Mala Powers and director Jesse Hibbs never saw the character of Nevada and her lines in the same perspective. Consequently, this was not a fun movie for Powers. Hibbs would tell Powers how he wanted a line delivered. Powers would then try pleasing Hibbs, but inwardly, Powers was fighting Hibbs' suggestion because she disagreed with him. Powers commented, "So it came out neither his way or my way but something amorphous in between. I wasn't pleased with my performance at all." After the film was completed, Powers went to her teacher, acting director Michael Checkov, and told him, "Please teach me how to take direction because I never want to go through this again." Checkov worked with Powers to teach her how to take "impossible directions." Checkov taught Powers to take an object, look at it, then move into the darkness and look at it again and told her, "Don't think about it, don't talk about it, just do it." Powers remembered, "And when I learned to do

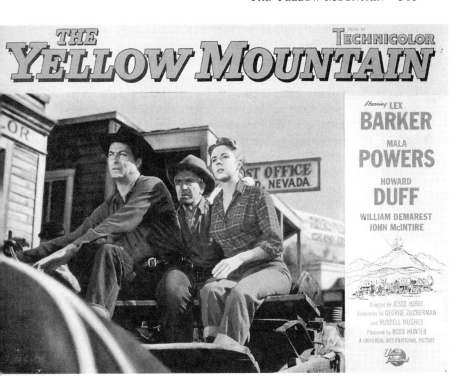

The Yellow Mountain (1954) scene card: Lex Barker, William Demarest, and Mala Powers arrive in town to register the mine's apex.

that, I found that everything is justifiable. You don't have to have all this motive, motive that makes sense. Motives do not have to make sense; you don't have to psychologically justify them. You don't have to think about it. You don't have to make a plot out of it. All you have to do is do it, and your own psychology will make it truthful if you're an actor. It was one of the best things that Jess Hibbs and I didn't see things to mean the same thing. I, then, had to go learn how to do that, to give the director anything he wanted whether I agreed or not. That's not to say I still wouldn't say, 'Oh, I see it this

way' and see if the director says, 'Oh, that's interesting, maybe we'll do it your way.' But if not, I know how to do it. It was a very great learning experience for me."

There was a scene near the beginning of the film in which Mala Powers had to slap Lex Barker across the face. From the camera angle that director Jesse Hibbs wanted, the blow could not be faked. To complicate matters, Powers and Barker were friends and she didn't want to hurt Barker or jeopardize their relationship. There were numerous retakes before the scene was completed. The first few takes were not acceptable because Powers softened the blow. Then, as Powers began to hit Barker harder, Barker first began to flinch and then to become angry. Powers said, "I could see the anger welling up in his eyes and there was nothing I knew how to do." Finally everything worked and the scene was completed.

Mala Powers did have fun the weekend she spent on location at Mojave. First, Howard Duff's wife, Ida Lupino, showed up and then Lex Barker's wife, Lana Turner, arrived. Lupino directed Powers in her first adult movie role in *Outrage* (RKO, 1950) and Powers was known as a Lupino discovery. Powers said the weekend was a lot of fun because of the wonderful sense of humor both Lupino and Turner possessed.

John McIntire impressed Mala Powers with his ability to raise one eyebrow independently of the other with great effect. Powers commented, "If you watched on the screen, a lot of fadeouts were always of McIntire raising this one eyebrow. I can't do it. He could get this one eyebrow to go straight up to the top of his head."

Reportedly Universal-International intended for *The Yellow Mountain* to play on double-feature bills in the larger markets and as a single feature only in the smaller markets. In the Norfolk, Virginia, area, the film played as an extra added attraction on a double-feature program only for a few days prior to the theater's big Christmas Day feature.

REVIEWS: "The outdoor market will probably put an okay stamp on *The Yellow Mountain.*" *Variety*, 11/24/54; "Fair Universal feature." *Western Movies*, Pitts.

SUMMATION: *The Yellow Mountain* is an okay western saga of gold mining in Nevada. Even with an engaging performance by Lex Barker as the hero and a fine chase on the desert flats, this picture doesn't have the necessary spark to elevate it to an above average status. Mala Powers, Howard Duff, William Demarest and John McIntire do what they can with a script and direction that can't make up its mind to play the story straight or tongue-in-cheek.

The Western Short Films of Universal-International

During the Universal-International years, 28 short films were released by the studio. Nineteen of these starred western music singer Tex Williams. Most of Williams' films were musical westerns featuring stock footage from the Universal "B" westerns that starred Bob Baker, Johnny Mack Brown and Rod Cameron. Eight of Williams' featurettes were paired to make four *Tales of the West* features for theatrical release.

(Author's note: The entries that follow are arranged chronologically. Most of the short films of Universal-International are not available for viewing. Therefore only a few entries will have full credits, synopsis, author's comments and other information.)

1. *Let's Sing a Western Song* (May 1947)

A *Sing and Be Happy* musical short

CREDITS: Director/Producer, **Harold James Moore**

2. *Tex Williams and His Western Caravan* (August 1947)

CAST: **Tex Williams and his Western Caravan** (Includes **Deuce Spriggins** and **Smokey Rogers**)

CREDITS: Director/Producer, **Will Cowan**

RUNNING TIME: 15 min.

3. *Hidden Valley Days* (February 1948)

CAST: **Red River Dave; Peggy Perron; Kenne Duncan; Curley Williams; The Texas Tophands**

CREDITS: Director/Producer, **William Forest Crouch**; Screenwriter, **Charles W. Curran**

RUNNING TIME: 27 min.

4. *Flight of the Wild Stallions* (February 1948)

CAST: Narrator, **Ben Grauer**

CREDITS: Producer, **Thomas Mead**

RUNNING TIME: 20 min.

NOTES AND COMMENTARY: *Flight of the Wild Stallions* was nominated for an Academy Award for Best Short Subject.

5. *Powder River Gunfire*
(February 1948)
CAST: **Kenne Duncan; Paula Raymond; Don Douglas; Dick Thomas; The Santa Fe Rangers**
CREDITS: Director, **Harold James Moore**; Screenwriter, **Irwin Winehouse**
LOCATION FILMING: Peekskill area, New York
RUNNING TIME: 24 min.

6. *Echo Ranch* (April 1948)
CAST: Red, **Red River Dave**; Curley, **Curley Williams**; Kurtz, **Kenne Duncan**; Peggy, **Diane Hart**; Father, **Ed Moran**; Kneehi, **Kneehi Holley**; Sheriff, **Jack Jackson**; **The Texas Tophands**
CREDITS: Director/Producer, **William Forest Crouch**; Screenwriter, **Charles W. Curran**; Editor, **Leonard Anderson**; Cinematographer, **Don Malkames**; Makeup, **J. Lynn Cook**; Sound, **Richard E. Byer**
SONGS: "Red River Valley" (Traditional)—sung by **Red River Dave**; "Echo Ranch"—sung by **Red River Dave**; "Cotton-Eyed Joe" (Wills and Duncan)—sung by **Curley Williams**; "I Can't Tell That Lie to My Heart"—sung by **Red River Dave**; and "I'm a Roving Cowboy"—sung by **Red River Dave**
RUNNING TIME: 25 min.
STORY: Rancher Ed Moran is robbed of money needed to pay the mortgage on his ranch. Red (Red River Dave) stages a rodeo and dance to raise money to help Moran. The robbers strike again and this time Dave brings the robbers to justice.

NOTES AND COMMENTARY: Red River Dave (McEnery) had an all too brief career in Hollywood. In addition to his work at Universal-International, Dave starred in *Swing in the Saddle* (Columbia, 1944), a short, *Pretty Women* (Sack, 1949), and 14 three-minute entries for Soundies Corporation of America between 1942 to 1946.

AUTHOR'S COMMENTS: *Echo Ranch* is a passable western featurette with one of the few screen appearances of Red River Dave. To the film's credit there is some good music by Dave and The Texas Tophands, some rodeo footage to add authenticity and a pretty good fistfight between Dave and Kenne Duncan. On the debit side is a slight story and some below par acting by most of the cast members.

7. *Western Whoopee* (June 1948)
CAST: **Tex Williams and His Orchestra; Patricia Alphin; Smokey Rogers; Judy Clark; Jimmie Dodd**
CREDITS: Director/Producer, **Will Cowan**
RUNNING TIME: 15 min.

8. *Six Gun Music* (January 1949)
CAST: Tex, **Tex Williams**; Judy Clark, **Lina Romay**; Smokey, **Smokey Rogers**; Kit Clark, **Patricia Alphin**; Deuce, **Deuce Spriggens**; Sheriff Harmon, **Hal Goodwin**; Mason, **Eddie Cobb**; **Tex Williams' Western Caravan**
CREDITS: Director, **Nate Watt**; Producer, **Will Cowan**; Story/Screenwriter, **Luci Ward**; Editor,

Frank Gross; Art Director, **Bernard Herzbrun**; Set Decorators, **Russell A. Gausman** and **Ruby R. Levitt**; Cinematographer, **Charles Van Enger**; Sound Directors, **Leslie I. Carey** and **Corson Jowett**; Music Arranger, **Milton Schwarzwald**

SONGS: "Go West" (Carling and Ohman)—sung by **Lina Romay**; "Big Hat Polka" (Williams)—sung by **Tex Williams** and **Lina Romay**; "You Got to Hand It to the West" (Carling)—sung by **Tex Williams**, **Smokey Rogers** and **Deuce Spriggens**

RUNNING TIME: 25 min.

STORY: Veterinarian Kit Clark (Patricia Alphin) and her sister, Judy (Lina Romay), take up residence on the wrong ranch by mistake. When the owners, Tex (Tex Williams), Smokey (Smokey Rogers) and Deuce (Deuce Spriggens), try to take possession, Alphin runs them off the ranch. Williams, Rogers and Spriggens fix up Alphin and Romay's ranch to allow Alphin to continue practicing her profession. Alphin still thinks she's on the right ranch until Sheriff Harmon (Hal Goodwin) delivers a tax bill, which Alphin is unable to pay. Not wanting to lose the talented veterinarian, the neighboring ranchers have taken up a collection to pay the back taxes.

NOTES AND COMMENTARY: Luci Ward's story of young ladies taking residence on the wrong ranch was used in both Gene Autry's *Springtime in the Rockies* (Republic, 1937) and Roy Rogers' *Utah* (Republic, 1945). Patricia Alphin was also billed as Audrey Young at Universal-International.

A publicity shot of Donna Martell and Tex Williams, who appeared in at least six featurettes together (courtesy of Donna Martell).

AUTHOR'S COMMENTS: *Six Gun Music* is a pleasant musical western with no action except Tex Williams chasing a runaway team of horses. The performances are adequate and the music is tuneful.

9. *Cheyenne Cowboy* (February 1949)

CAST: Cheyenne, **Tex Williams**; Kate Harmon, **Lina Romay**; Smokey, **Smokey Rogers**; Deuce, **Deuce Spriggens**; Mr. Harmon, **Stanley Andrews**; Jud Keller, **Riley Hill;** Cookie, **Helen Gibson**; Tex Williams' Western Caravan

CREDITS: Director, **Nate Watt**; Producer, **Will Cowan**; Story/Screenwriter, **Luci Ward**; Editor, **Frank**

Cheyenne Cowboy (1949) scene card: Riley Hill (*right*) holds Tex Williams at bay (*left*) after knocking Stanley Andrews to the ground, Lina Romay with him; right border—shows Romay and Williams.

Gross; Art Director, **Bernard Herzbrun**; Set Decorators, **Russell A. Gausman** and **Ruby R. Levitt**; Cinematographer, **Charles Van Enger**; Sound Directors, **Leslie I. Carey** and **Corson Jowett**; Music Arranger, **Milton Schwarzwald**

SONGS: "Sun in the Sky" (Carling)—sung by **Tex Williams**; "Man's Best Friend Is a Woman" (Carling)—sung by **Tex Williams, Deuce Spriggens, Smokey Rogers** and **Lina Romay**; "A Cowpoke Gits No Rest at All" (Carling)—sung by **Deuce Spriggens and Tex Williams' Western Caravan**; "That Good Old Western Music" (Washburne and Carling)—sung by **Tex Williams and Tex Williams' Western Caravan**

RUNNING TIME: 25 min.

STORY: Wandering cowboy Cheyenne (Tex Williams) gets a job on the Blue River Ranch, which is losing money. Actually Williams is the owner, having inherited the ranch from his father. After some cattle are sold, Williams gets an idea who is responsible for the loss. Top hand Jud Keller (Riley Hill) takes more cattle on a drive than has been contracted. Hill pockets the money for the extra cattle sold. When his scheme has been exposed, Hill tries to escape on horseback. Williams chases Hill down and brings him to justice.

NOTES AND COMMENTARY: Western great Buck Jones can be briefly seen in the trail-drive footage. The trail-drive footage was also used in Kirby Grant's *Trail to Vengeance* (Universal, 1945).

REVIEW: "Ace entertainment in condensed form" *Film Daily*, 6/6/49

AUTHOR'S COMMENTS: *Cheyenne Cowboy* is a good Tex Williams featurette. Some good music, especially "*Sun in the Sky*," and a swiftly moving narrative make this a most enjoyable tale.

10. West of Laramie
(March 1949)

CAST: **Tex Williams**; **Smokey Rogers**; **Deuce Spriggens**; **Patricia Hall**; **Patricia Alphin**; **Terry Frost**

CREDITS: Director, **Nate Watt**; Producer, **Will Cowan**; Story, **Bennett Cohn**; Screenwriter, **Luci Ward**; Music Arranger, **Milton Schwarzwald**

RUNNING TIME: 23 min.

11. Spade Cooley and His Orchestra (July 1949)

CAST: **Spade Cooley and His Western Caravan**; **Karel's Adagio Four**; **Les Anderson**; **The Pickard Family**; **Bill Roberts**

CREDITS: Director/Producer, **Will Cowan**

RUNNING TIME: 15 min.

12. Silver Butte (July 1949)

CAST: Tex, **Tex Williams**; Smokey, **Smokey Rogers**; Deuce,

Deuce Spriggens; Rita Landon, **Barbara Payton**; Don Hernandez, **Joe Grandy**; Del Randolph, **Lane Bradford**

CREDITS: Director/Producer, **Will Cowan**; Screenwriters, **Sherman Lowe** and **Victor McLeod**

SONGS: "In the Heart of the Cow Country" (Carling); That Fellow Manuelo" (Carling and March); "I Don't Like to Work" and "Fiesta" (Carling)

STORY: The Masked Bandit leads an outlaw gang plaguing Rita Landon (Barbara Payton) and Don Hernandez (Joe Grandy) by highjacking their silver bullion shipments. The Masked Bandit threatens to kill Payton if Grandy seeks help from the law. Foreman Del Randolph (Lane Bradford) decides not to ship more silver bullion, and the outlaws attack the mine. Tex (Williams) and his sidekick, Smokey (Rogers), see the robbery attempt and take a hand, forcing the bandits to retreat. Grandy hires Williams and Rogers. Williams plans to decoy the outlaws by appearing to ship the bullion by one route but actually sending the silver by another. The outlaws learn of the plan and steal the bullion and take Rogers and Grandy captive. Payton is able to lead Williams to the outlaw hideout. Williams and his men overpower the bandits and Williams bests the Masked Bandit in a tough fistfight. When the Masked Bandit is unmasked, Bradford turns out to be the leader of the bandit gang.

NOTES AND COMMENTARY: *Silver Butte* is a reworking of Johnny

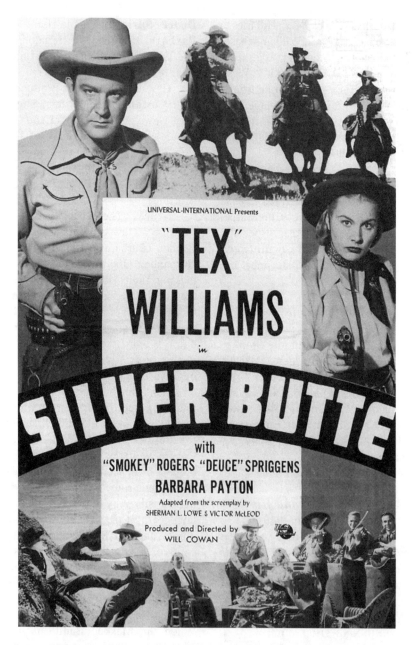

Silver Butte (1949) from pressbook: Tex Williams (*top left*); Lane Bradford (*masked*) and Williams in bottom left; Joe Grandy, Williams, Barbara Payton and unidentified actors (*bottom right*); Payton (*center right*); unidentified riders (*top right*).

Mack Brown's *The Masked Rider* (Universal, 1941).

Leading lady Barbara Payton made headlines in September 1951 when actors Tom Neal and Franchot Tone engaged in a fistfight over her. Initially, Payton was to marry Tone then changed her mind and was set to marry Neal. On the night prior to the Payton-Neal nuptials, Payton went out with Tone. Neal was waiting at Payton's home when the couple came home. Tone invited Neal to go out on the front lawn and initiated the fight. Neal quickly knocked Tone unconscious. A few weeks later, Payton wed Tone in a marriage that dissolved before the middle of 1952. Payton and Neal co-starred with Willard Parker in *The Great Jesse James Raid* (Lippert, 1953). According to the pressbook for *Silver Butte*, this Tex Williams featurette in 1949 was Barbara Payton's first screen appearance. James Cagney selected Payton to co-star with him in *Kiss Tomorrow Goodbye* (Warner Bros., 1950). By 1953, Payton was playing in low budget productions and, after her appearance in *Murder Is My Beat* (Allied Artists, 1955), her movie career had ended.

RUNNING TIME: 27 min.

13. *The Girl from Gunsight*
(September 1949)

CAST: **Tex Williams**; **Donna Martell**; **Smokey Rogers**; **Deuce Spriggens**; **Myron Healey**

CREDITS: Director/Producer, **Will Cowan**

RUNNING TIME: 24 min.

14. *Nevada Trail*
(September 1949)

CAST: Tex Williams, **Tex Williams**; Mayor Smokey Rogers, **Smokey Rogers**; Deuce Spriggens, **Deuce Spriggens**; Lucy Wollen, **Donna Martell**; Jack Wollen, **Norman Jolly**; Tom Benner, **Marshall Reed**; George Pierce, **Eddie Parker**; Miss Tucker, **Elizabeth Kerry**; Britt Macaulay, **George Slocum**

CREDITS: Director/Producer, **Will Cowan**; Adaptation from the Screenplay, **Ande Lamb**; Editor, **Russell Schoengarth**; Art Director, **John F. DeCuir**; Set Decorators, **Russell A. Gausman** and **Oliver Emert**; Cinematographer, **George Robinson**; Sound Director, **Leslie I. Carey**; Music, **Milton Schwarzwald**

SONGS: "The Big Bull Fiddle and the Old Banjo" (Carling)—sung by **Deuce Spriggens** and **Smokey Rogers**; "Ham and Eggs" (Carling and Washburne)—sung by **Tex Williams**, **Deuce Spriggens** and **Smokey Rogers**; "Happiness Corral" (Carter and Rosen)—sung by **Donna Martell**; "The Mayor, the Marshal and the Deputy Sheriff" (Carling and M. Cowan)—**Tex Williams**, **Smokey Rogers** and **Deuce Spriggens**

RUNNING TIME: 23 min.

STORY: New city marshal Tex Williams arrives in Dead River to find that Tom Benner (Marshall Reed) has control of the water rights in the area. Reed charges trail drivers to water their herds or he buys the herds at half the market price. Cattleman Jack Wollen (Norman Jolly) refuses to pay and tries to take water by force. Williams advises Jolly to use the water troughs in town since those are public property for use by anyone. Williams then discovers Reed altered the survey of his property to control the water rights. Meanwhile, Reed plans to stampede Jolly's cattle. Williams finds out Reed's plan and is able to stop Reed and bring him to justice.

NOTES AND COMMENTARY: Donna Martell's singing was dubbed. Martell has no idea who did her singing in any of the Tex Williams featurettes. Plot elements from James Stewart's *Destry Rides Again* (Universal, 1939) were used. Footage from *Frontier Badmen* (Universal, 1943) and *Riders of the Santa Fe* (Universal, 1945) can be seen.

SUMMATION: Nevada Trail is a fast-moving, exciting western featurette. This is one of the best Tex Williams productions. Enjoyable songs are intermixed with fast action, even though most of the action is stock footage.

15. The Pecos Pistol

(October 1949)

CAST: **Tex Williams**; **Smokey Rogers**; **Deuce Spriggens**; **Barbara Payton**; **William Cassidy**; **Forrest Taylor**; **George Lloyd**; **Monte Montague**; **Harry Calkin**; **Terry Frost**

CREDITS: Director/Producer, **Will Cowan**

RUNNING TIME: 26 min.

16. Coyote Canyon

(November 1949)

CAST: Tex, **Tex Williams**; Smokey, **Smokey Rogers**; Deuce, **Deuce Spriggens**; Jane Barlow,

Donna Martell; Marshal, **George Eldredge**; Steele, **Judd Holdren**; Barlow, **Leslie Kimmell**; Sheriff, **Jim Hayward**; Deputy, **Bob Wilke**; Guard, **Jess Fargo**

CREDITS: Director/Producer, **Will Cowan**; Story, **Norton S. Parker**; Screenwriter, **Joseph O'Donnell**; Editor, **Russell Schoengarth**; Art Director, **Richard Riedel**; Set Decorators, **Russell A. Gausman** and **Oliver Emert**; Cinematographer, **Charles Van Enger**; Sound Director, **Leslie I. Carey**; Music, **Joseph Gershenson**

SONGS: "High-Tailin' Along to Glory" (Carling)—sung by **Smokey Rogers, Deuce Spriggens, Tex Williams** and **Donna Martell**; "Waltz of the West" (Carling)—sung by **Tex Williams, Smokey Rogers, Deuce Spriggens** and **Donna Martell**; "Shoot Him" (Carling)—sung by **Deuce Spriggens and Chorus**; "High-Tailin' Along to Glory" (reprise) (Carling)—sung by **Tex Williams**

RUNNING TIME: 24 min.

STORY: Mistaken as desperate outlaws, Tex (Williams) and Smokey (Rogers) are arrested. Williams and Rogers are released on the condition they will bring in outlaw Steele (Judd Holdren). Deuce (Spriggens), a friend of Williams and Rogers, tips them to Holdren's hideout in Coyote Canyon. Wanted posters convince Holdren to allow Williams and Rogers to use his hideout. At the hideout, Williams and Rogers find when Holdren's next stage robbery will be. The marshal (George Eldredge) receives a copy of the

Tales of the West #1 (1950) scene card: This 55-minute featurette starred Tex Williams in *Cactus Caravan* and *South of Santa Fe.*

wanted poster and when Williams emerges from the outlaw stronghold, arrests him. Unable to convince Eldredge of his innocence, Spriggens frees Williams. Williams forces Eldredge to go with him to the holdup site. Holdren holds up the stagecoach. Spriggens brings a posse and, with Williams and Eldredge, swoops down on the bandits. In the ensuing gunfight, Williams shoots Holdren. Williams now finds time to romance the stage owner's daughter, Jane Barlow (Donna Martell).

NOTES AND COMMENTARY: Coyote Canyon is a remake of Bob

Baker's *Border Wolves* (Universal, 1938). Footage from *Border Wolves* with Bob Baker and his horse, Apache, can be seen in this western short subject.

Donna Martell's voice was dubbed. Martell remembered, "They asked me to sing. I could have. I don't know why I said no. But I said no. I had to mouth exactly how the words are and they would dub it in."

Coyote Canyon and *The Fargo Phantom* made up *Tales of the West #2* (Universal-International, 1950), a 50-minute feature presentation.

SUMMATION: *Coyote Canyon* is a pleasant undemanding western short. The musical efforts are the standout in this featurette. Tex Williams makes a good western hero, though.

17. South of Santa Fe

(November 1949)

CAST: **Tex Williams**; **Smokey Rogers**; **Deuce Spriggens**; **Donna Martell**; **William Tannen**; **Kenneth MacDonald**; **Ethan Laidlaw**; **Harry Calkin**

CREDITS: Director/Producer, **Will Cowan**; Story, **Norton S. Parker**; Screenwriter, **Joseph O'Donnell**; Music, **Joseph Gershenson**

RUNNING TIME: 25 min.

NOTES AND COMMENTARY: *South of Santa Fe* and *Cactus Caravan* made up *Tales of the West #1* (Universal-International, 1950), a 55-minute feature presentation.

18. The Fargo Phantom

(February 1950)

CAST: Tex, **Tex Williams**; Smokey, **Smokey Rogers**; Deuce, **Deuce Spriggens**; Pat Condon, **Shirlee Allard**; Hartley, **Forrest Taylor**; Shorty, **Stark Bishop**; Bill Watson, **Monte Montague**; Barnes, **Chuck Hayward**; Driver, **Ray Jones**; Agent, **Robert O'Neill**

CREDITS: Director/Producer. **Will Cowan**; Story, **Joseph West**; Screenwriter, **Joseph O'Donnell**; Editor, **Otto Ludwig**; Art Director, **Robert Clatworthy**; Set Decorators, **Russell A. Gausman** and **Roland A. Fields**; Cinematographer, **George Robinson**; Sound Director, **Leslie I. Carey**; Music, **Joseph Gershenson**

SONGS: "A Song in Your Heart" (Carling)—sung by **Tex Williams** and **Smokey Rogers**; "In Old Montana" (Carling)—sung **by Tex Williams** and **Smokey Rogers**; "Thar's Gold in Them Thar Hills" (Carling)—sung by **Tex Williams, Shirlee Allard, Smokey Rogers** and **Deuce Spriggens**

RUNNING TIME: 25 min.

STORY: Tex (Williams) and his sidekick, Smokey (Rogers), are on their way to Montana when they meet up with an old friend, Deuce Spriggens. Spriggens, working for stage-line owner Pat Condo (Shirlee Allard), is up against holdups where gold disappears mysteriously from strong boxes. Hartley (Forrest Taylor) is behind the stage robberies. Using specially built boxes, Taylor has one of his men, Shorty (Stark Bishop), hide in the box and sneak out of a side panel to steal the gold. Williams and Rogers stay to lend a hand. Finally, when Williams and Rogers are carrying a large gold shipment, the outlaws make their move. Distracted by other members of the gang, Bishop is able to steal the gold but the gold is too heavy and he has to jump from the stage. Williams and Rogers notice the box is much lighter than when it was placed on the stage. Williams finds the side panel and decides to hide in the box so he can be taken to the gang's headquarters. When Taylor picks up the box, he notices the weight and knows someone must be hiding inside. Williams arrives at Taylor's ranch, gets the drop on the gang but is rendered unconscious by a bullet. Then, Allard, Rogers and

Spriggens arrive to save Williams. Taylor is shot by Rogers and Spriggens, putting an end to his ingenious scheme.

NOTES AND COMMENTS: *The Fargo Phantom* is a remake of Bob Baker's final solo-starring western, *The Phantom Stage* (Universal, 1939).

The Fargo Phantom and *Coyote Canyon* made up *Tales of the West #2* (Universal-International, 1950), a 50-minute feature presentation.

SUMMATION: *The Fargo Phantom* is a neat Tex Williams featurette. This is a nice blend of music and action.

19. *Gold Strike* (March 1950)

CAST: Tex, **Tex Williams**; Smokey, **Smokey Rogers**; Deuce, **Deuce Spriggens**; Ruth Gorman, **Shirlee Allard**; Brady, **Jack Ingram**; Bart, **Bob Anderson**; Spike, **Fred Kohler, Jr.**; Marshall, **James Linn**

CREDITS: Director/Producer, **Will Cowan**; Story, **Joseph West**; Screenwriter, **Joseph O'Donnell**; Editor, **Otto Ludwig**; Art Director, **Robert Clatworthy**; Set Decorators, **Russell A. Gausman** and **A. Roland Fields**; Cinematographer, **George Robinson**; Sound Director, **Leslie I. Carey**; Music, **Joseph Gershenson**

SONGS: "Wide Open Spaces" (Carling)—sung by **Tex Williams** and **Deuce Spriggens**; "When You Dance the Old Year Out" (Carling)—sung by **Tex Williams**, **Shirlee Allard** and **Smokey Rogers**; "Chief Cook and Bottle Washer" (Rogers and Car-

ling)—sung by **Smokey Rogers**, **Deuce Spriggens** and **Shirley Allard**; "Wide Open Spaces" (reprise)—sung by **Tex Williams**

RUNNING TIME: 25 min.

STORY: Outlaws, operating from the ghost town of Stilwell, are robbing the stagecoach mail deliveries to prevent mail from falling into the hands of the town's owner. Gang leader Brady (Jack Ingram) plans to purchase the town for back taxes then advertise a false gold strike. Tex (Williams) and his partner, Deuce (Spriggens), trail-herding horses, arrive in town to rest for a few days. Ruth Gorman (Shirlee Allard), who has inherited the town from her father, comes to the town to look it over. Mayor Smokey (Rogers), who had been pretending to be a little touched in the head, tells Williams there is gold under the town and gives Williams enough gold dust to pay off Allard's back taxes. Ingram sends men to stop Williams, but Williams is able to get to the county seat and pay the amount owed. Williams then goes back to Stilwell and brings Ingram to justice. After delivering the horses, Williams plans to return to Stilwell to marry Allard.

NOTES AND COMMENTARY: *Gold Strike* is a remake of Bob Baker's *Ghost Town Riders* (Universal, 1938). Bob Baker and Apache can be seen racing across the plains in several scenes. *Gold Strike* and *Rustler's Ransom* made up the feature presentation *Tales of the West #3* (Universal-International, 1950).

SUMMATION: *Gold Strike* is a

SHOOTING COWBOY BRINGS LAW TO THE FRONTIER!

UNIVERSAL-INTERNATIONAL Presents

"TEX" WILLIAMS

IN

WESTERN COURAGE

with

"SMOKEY" ROGERS   "DEUCE" SPRIGGENS
DONNA MARTELL

Produced and Directed by
WILL COWAN

Western Courage (1950) title card: Tex Williams, Smokey Rogers and Donna Marshall.

slick, fast-moving entry in the Tex Williams series of featurettes. Some good songs and a nice performance by Smokey Rogers pretending to be a little "touched in the head" bolster this entertaining story.

20. *Rustler's Ransom*

(March 1950)

CAST: **Tex Williams; Deuce Spriggens; Smokey Rogers**

CREDITS: Director/Producer, **Will Cowan**

RUNNING TIME: 25 min.

NOTES AND COMMENTARY: *Rustler's Ransom* and *Gold Strike* made up the feature presentation *Tales of the West #3* (Universal-International, 1950).

21. *Prairie Pirates* (May 1950)

CAST: **Tex Williams; Smokey Rogers; Deuce Spriggens; Patricia Hall; William Haade: Lane Bradford**

CREDITS: Director/Producer, **Will Cowan**; Screenwriter, **Sherman Lowe**; Music Arranger, **Milton Schwarzwald**

RUNNING TIME: 23 min.

22. *Western Courage*

(June 1950)

CAST: Tex, **Tex Williams;**

Smokey, **Smokey Rogers**; Deuce, **Deuce Spriggens**; Ruth Eaton, **Donna Martell**; Frank Eaton, **Watson Downs**; Chuck Gorman, **Kenne Duncan**; Slim Farley, **Lane Bradford**; Dan Farley, **Judd Holdren**; Gunsmith, **Monte Montague**; Sheriff, **Bud Osborne**; Judge Meade, **Forbes Murray**; Rancher, **Ray Grimes**

CREDITS: Director/Producer, **Will Cowan**; Story, **Sherman Lowe** and **Victor McLeod**; Screenwriter, **Joseph O'Donnell**; Editor, **Ted J. Kent**; Art Director, **Alexander Golitzen**; Set Decorators, **Russell A. Gausman** and **Ruby R. Levitt**; Cinematographer, **Charles Van Enger**; Sound Director, **Leslie I. Carey**; Music, **Joseph Gershenson**

SONGS: "The Marshal (of Jackson Hole Wyoming)"—sung by **Smokey Rogers** and **Tex Williams**; "Western Courage"—sung by **Tex Williams, Donna Martell, Smokey Rogers** and **Deuce Spriggens**; and "The West Is Calling Me Home"—sung by **Tex Williams, Donna Martell, Deuce Spriggens** and **Smokey Rogers**

RUNNING TIME: 25 min.

STORY: Former marshal Tex (Williams) comes to Rawhide to settle down and raise cattle. Williams finds that brothers Dan (Judd Holdren) and Slim Farley (Lane Bradford) control the town. Williams turns down an offer to clean up the town. Rancher Frank Eaton (Watson Downs) spots rustlers taking his cattle. Riding to his ranch for help, Downs is shot by Bradford. Clues lead Williams to Bradford. Williams arrests Bradford and has him placed in jail. On the date of the trial, Holdren and his men lay siege to the jail in an effort to free Bradford. Downs' daughter, Ruth Eaton (Donna Martell), brings men to town to battle the outlaws. In the gunfight Holdren is killed and his men surrender. With peace now brought to the community, Williams has time to notice Martell.

NOTES AND COMMENTARY: Donna Martell's singing again is dubbed instead of using her own voice.

Footage from Johnny Mack Brown's *Law and Order* (Universal, 1940) and Franchot Tone's *Trail of the Vigilantes* (Universal, 1941) is utilized in this featurette. Kenne Duncan uses some familiar dialogue when he spots Tex Williams, "This town's not big enough for both of us." *Western Courage* and *Ready to Ride* made up *Tales of the West #4* (Universal-International, 1951), a 54-minute feature presentation.

SUMMATION: *Western Courage* is an above average, fast-moving western short with a good song, "The West Is Calling Me Home." Stock footage is nicely utilized to deliver action-packed entertainment.

23. *Thundering Rails*
(June 1950)

CAST: **Tex Williams**; **Deuce Spriggens**; **Smokey Rogers**

CREDITS: Director/Producer, **Will Cowan**

RUNNING TIME: 25 min.

24. *Cactus Caravan* (July 1950)

CAST: **Tex Williams**; **Smokey Rogers**; **Deuce Spriggens**; **Leslie Banning**; **Tris Coffin**; **Marshall Reed**; **Franklin Parker**; **Steve Clark**

CREDITS: Director/Producer, **Will Cowan**; Screenwriter, **Joseph O'Donnell**

RUNNING TIME: 26 min.

NOTES AND COMMENTARY: *Cactus Caravan* and *South of Santa Fe* made up *Tales of the West #1* (Universal-International, 1950), a 55-minute feature presentation.

25. *Ready to Ride* (October 1950)

CAST: **Tex Williams**; **Smokey Rogers**; **Deuce Spriggens**; **Donna Martell**; **Ann Pierce**; **Felipe Turich**; **Harry Lauter**; **Holly Bane**; **Edmund Cobb**; **Harry Vijar**

CREDITS: Director/Producer, **Will Cowan**; Screenwriter, **Joseph O'Donnell**

RUNNING TIME: 25 min.

NOTES AND COMMENTARY: *Ready to Ride* and *Western Courage* made up *Tales of the West #4* (Universal-International, 1951), a 54-minute feature presentation.

26. *Corral Cuties* (June 1954)

CAST: **Tennessee Ernie Ford**; Molly Bee

CREDITS: Director/Producer, **Will Cowan**

RUNNING TIME: 15 min.

Cactus Caravan (1950) title card: Tex Williams (*top left*); Tex Williams and Leslie Banning (*bottom left*); Marshall Reed and Tex Williams fight (*bottom right*); Smokey Rogers (*right*).

Ole Rex (1961) scene card: Bob Bray, owner of Rex, and Billy Hughes with Rex.

27. Webb Pierce and His Wanderin' Boys (June 1955)
CAST: **Webb Pierce** and His Band; **Hank Penny**; **Sue Thompson**; **Marion Colby**; **Red Sovine**
CREDITS: Director/Producer, **Will Cowan**
RUNNING TIME: 16 min.

28. Ole Rex (May 1961)
CAST: **Rex; Billy Hughes; William Foster; Robert Hinkle; Whitey Hughes; William Hughes; Richard McCarty; Bob Bray; Robert Marlow, Jr.; Dale Terry; Jim Cochran; Charles E. King**
CREDITS: Director/Screewriter, **Robert Hinkle**; Producers, **Robert Hinkle, Charles E. King**; Story, **Jack Specht**

LOCATION FILMING: Wichita Falls, Texas
EASTMAN COLOR by Pathé
RUNNING TIME: 40 min.
STORY: A young boy, Billy Hughes, and his dog, Rex, run away from home. In his journey, Hughes looses his footing and falls into a gully infested with rattlesnakes. Rex protects Hughes from the snakes. Hughes and Rex are reunited with his father, William Foster.

NOTES AND COMMENTARY: Bob Bray owned Rex. Robert Hinkle saw a story on Rex and the ferocity he displayed toward rattlesnakes. Originally intended to be a documentary on the dog, after the story was sold to Universal-International, the scope of the story was enlarged. One of the

local citizens supplied the rattlesnakes. Whitey Hughes remembered, "They had some vicious looking rattlesnakes there. This old boy
went out and gathered us up a whole
sack full of rattlesnakes. We had
then in cages all over the place."
Charles E. King of King Oil put up
the money so this featurette could be
made. King also had a small part in
Ole Rex. This Charles E. King is no
relation to the famous bad man of
countless "B" westerns.

REVIEW: "Fair featurette for the
family trade" Western Movies, Pitts

Alphabetical Listing of Universal-International Westerns

1. *All Mine to Give* with Glynis Johns, **January 1958**
2. *Apache Drums* with Stephen McNally, **June 1951**
3. *Back to God's Country* with Rock Hudson, **November 1953**
4. *Backlash* with Richard Widmark, **April 1956**
5. *The Battle at Apache Pass* with John Lund, **April 1952**
6. *Bend of the River* with James Stewart, **February 1952**
7. *Black Bart* with Yvonne De Carlo, **April 1948**
8. *Black Horse Canyon* with Joel McCrea, **June 1954**
9. *Border River* with Joel McCrea, **January 1954**
10. *Bronco Buster* with John Lund, **May 1952**
11. *Calamity Jane and Sam Bass* with Yvonne De Carlo, **July 1949**
12. *Cattle Drive* with Joel McCrea, **August 1951**
13. *Cave of Outlaws* with Macdonald Carey, **November 1951**
14. *Chief Crazy Horse* with Victor Mature, **April 1955**
15. *The Cimarron Kid* with Audie Murphy, **January 1952**
16. *Column South* with Audie Murphy, **June 1953**
17. *Comanche Territory* with Maureen O'Hara, **May 1950**
18. *Curse of the Undead* with Eric Fleming, **July 1959**
19. *Curtain Call at Cactus Creek* with Donald O'Connor, **June 1950**
20. *Dawn at Socorro* with Rory Calhoun, **September 1954**
21. *A Day of Fury* with Dale Robertson, **May 1956**
22. *Day of the Bad Man* with Fred MacMurray, **April 1958**
23. *Destry* with Audie Murphy, **January 1955**
24. *Drums Across the River* with Audie Murphy, **June 1954**
25. *The Duel at Silver Creek* with Audie Murphy, **August 1952**
26. *The Far Country* with James Stewart, **February 1955**
27. *Feudin', Fussin' and a-Fightin'* with Donald O'Connor, **July 1948**
28. *Four Fast Guns* with James Craig, **February 1960**

29. *Four Guns to the Border* with Rory Calhoun, **November 1954**
30. *Foxfire* with Jane Russell, **July 1955**
31. *Frenchie* with Joel McCrea, **February 1951**
32. *The Gal Who Took the West* with Yvonne De Carlo, **September 1949**
33. *The Great Sioux Uprising* with Jeff Chandler, **July 1953**
34. *The Groom Wore Spurs* with Ginger Rogers, March 1951
35. *Gun for a Coward* with Fred Mac-Murray, **March 1957**
36. *Gunsmoke* with Audie Murphy, **March 1953**
37. *Hell Bent for Leather* with Audie Murphy, **February 1960**
38. *Horizons West* with Robert Ryan, **October 1952**
39. *Joe Dakota* with Jock Mahoney, **September 1957**
40. *Kansas Raiders* with Audie Murphy, **November 1950**
41. *The Kid from Texas* with Audie Murphy, **March 1950**
42. *Kiss of Fire* with Jack Palance, **October 1955**
43. *The Lady from Texas* with Howard Duff, **October 1951**
44. *The Last of the Fast Guns* with Jock Mahoney, **July 1958**
45. *The Last Sunset* with Kirk Douglas, **July 1961**
46. *Law and Order* with Ronald Reagan, **May 1953**
47. *The Lawless Breed* with Rock Hudson, **January 1953**
48. *The Lone Hand* with Joel McCrea, **May 1953**
49. *Lonely Are the Brave* with Kirk Douglas, **June 1962**
50. *Lost in Alaska* with Abbott and Costello, **August 1952**
51. *The Man from Bitter Ridge* with Lex Barker, **June 1955**

52. *The Man from the Alamo* with Glenn Ford, **August 1953**
53. *Man in the Shadow* with Jeff Chandler, **January 1958**
54. *Man Without a Star* with Kirk Douglas, **April 1955**
55. *Mark of the Renegade* with Ricardo Montalban, **August 1951**
56. *Michigan Kid* with Jon Hall, **March 1947**
57. *The Mississippi Gambler* with Tyrone Power, **February 1953**
58. *Money, Women and Guns* with Jock Mahoney, **January 1959**
59. *The Naked Dawn* with Arthur Kennedy, **November 1955**
60. *Night Passage* with James Stewart, **August 1957**
61. *No Name on the Bullet* with Audie Murphy, **February 1959**
62. *Once Upon a Horse* with Rowan and Martin, **September 1958**
63. *One Desire* with Anne Baxter, **August 1955**
64. *Pillars of the Sky* with Jeff Chandler, **October 1956**
65. *Pirates of Monterey* with Maria Montez, **December 1947**
66. *Posse from Hell* with Audie Murphy, **May 1961**
67. *Quantez* with Fred MacMurray, **October 1957**
68. *The Raiders* with Richard Conte, **November 1952**
69. *Rails into Laramie* with John Payne, **April 1954**
70. *Raw Edge* with Rory Calhoun, **September 1956**
71. *The Rawhide Years* with Tony Curtis, **July 1956**
72. *Red Canyon* with Ann Blyth, **April 1949**
73. *Red Sundown* with Rory Calhoun, **March 1956**
74. *The Redhead from Wyoming* with Maureen O'Hara, **January 1953**

75. *Ricochet Romance* with Marjorie Main, **November 1954**
76. *Ride a Crooked Trail* with Audie Murphy, **September 1958**
77. *Ride Clear of Diablo* with Audie Murphy, **March 1954**
78. *River Lady* with Yvonne De Carlo, **June 1948**
79. *Run of the Arrow* with Rod Steiger, **September 1957**
80. *Saddle Tramp* with Joel McCrea, **September 1950**
81. *The Saga of Hemp Brown* with Rory Calhoun, **October 1958**
82. *Saskatchewan* with Alan Ladd, **March 1954**
83. *Scarlet Angel* with Yvonne De Carlo, **June 1952**
84. *The Second Greatest Sex* with Jeanne Crain, **December 1955**
85. *Seminole* with Rock Hudson, **March 1953**
86. *Seven Ways from Sundown* with Audie Murphy, **September 1960**
87. *Showdown* with Audie Murphy, **May 1963**
88. *Showdown at Abilene* with Jock Mahoney, **October 1956**
89. *Sierra* with Audie Murphy, **June 1950**
90. *6 Black Horses* with Audie Murphy, **June 1962**
91. *Slim Carter* with Jock Mahoney, **November 1957**
92. *Smoke Signal* with Dana Andrews, **March 1955**
93. *The Spoilers* with Anne Baxter, **January 1956**
94. *Stagecoach to Dancers' Rock* with Warren Stevens, **October 1962**
95. *The Stand at Apache River* with Stephen McNally, **September 1953**
96. *Star in the Dust* with John Agar, **June 1956**
97. *Take Me to Town* with Ann Sheridan, **June 1953**
98. *Tap Roots* with Van Heflin, **August 1948**
99. *Taza, Son of Cochise* with Rock Hudson, **February 1954**
100. *Tomahawk* with Van Heflin, **February 1951**
101. *Tomboy and the Champ* with Candy Moore, **April 1961**
102. *The Treasure of Lost Canyon* with William Powell, **March 1952**
103. *Tumbleweed* with Audie Murphy, **December 1953**
104. *Untamed Frontier* with Joseph Cotten, **September 1952**
105. *The Vigilantes Return* with Jon Hall, **July 1947**
106. *Walk the Proud Land* with Audie Murphy, **September 1956**
107. *War Arrow* with Jeff Chandler, **January 1954**
108. *The Wild and the Innocent* with Audie Murphy, **May 1959**
109. *Wild Heritage* with Will Rogers Jr., **August 1958**
110. *Winchester '73* with James Stewart, **July 1950**
111. *Wings of the Hawk* with Van Heflin, **September 1953**
112. *The Wistful Widow of Wagon Gap* with Abbott and Costello, **October 1947**
113. *Wyoming Mail* with Stephen McNally, **October 1950**
114. *The Yellow Mountain* with Lex Barker, **December 1954**

Chronological Listing of Universal-International Westerns

1. *Michigan Kid* with Jon Hall, **March 1947**
2. *The Vigilantes Return* with Jon Hall, **July 1947**
3. *The Wistful Widow of Wagon Gap* with Abbott and Costello, **October 1947**
4. *Pirates of Monterey* with Maria Montez, **December 1947**
5. *Black Bart* with Yvonne De Carlo, **April 1948**
6. *River Lady* with Yvonne De Carlo, **June 1948**
7. *Feudin', Fussin' and a-Fightin'* with Donald O'Connor, **July 1948**
8. *Tap Roots* with Van Heflin, **August 1948**
9. *Red Canyon* with Ann Blyth, **April 1949**
10. *Calamity Jane and Sam Bass* with Yvonne De Carlo, **July 1949**
11. *The Gal Who Took the West* with Yvonne De Carlo, **September 1949**
12. *The Kid from Texas* with Audie Murphy, **March 1950**
13. *Comanche Territory* with Maureen O'Hara, **May 1950**
14. *Curtain Call at Cactus Creek* with Donald O'Connor, **June 1950**
15. *Sierra* with Audie Murphy, **June 1950**
16. *Winchester '73* with James Stewart, **July 1950**
17. *Saddle Tramp* with Joel McCrea, **September 1950**
18. *Wyoming Mail* with Stephen McNally, **October 1950**
19. *Kansas Raiders* with Audie Murphy, **November 1950**
20. *Frenchie* with Joel McCrea, **January 1951**
21. *Tomahawk* with Van Heflin, **February 1951**
22. *The Groom Wore Spurs* with Ginger Rogers, **March 1951**
23. *Apache Drums* with Stephen McNally, **June 1951**
24. *Cattle Drive* with Joel McCrea, **August 1951**
25. *Mark of the Renegade* with Ricardo Montalban, **August 1951**
26. *The Lady from Texas* with Howard Duff, **October 1951**
27. *Cave of Outlaws* with Macdonald Carey, **November 1951**
28. *The Cimarron Kid* with Audie Murphy, **January 1952**

29. *Bend of the River* with James Stewart, **February 1952**

30. *The Treasure of Lost Canyon* with William Powell, **March 1952**

31. *The Battle at Apache Pass* with John Lund, **April 1952**

32. *Bronco Buster* with John Lund, **May 1952**

33. *Scarlet Angel* with Yvonne De Carlo, **June 1952**

34. *The Duel at Silver Creek* with Audie Murphy, **August 1952**

35. *Lost in Alaska* with Abbott and Costello, **August 1952**

36. *Untamed Frontier* with Joseph Cotten, **September 1952**

37. *Horizons West* with Robert Ryan, **October 1952**

38. *The Raiders* with Richard Conte, **November 1952**

39. *The Redhead from Wyoming* with Maureen O'Hara, **January 1953**

40. *The Lawless Breed* with Rock Hudson, **January 1953**

41. *The Mississippi Gambler* with Tyrone Power **February 1953**

42. *Gunsmoke* with Audie Murphy, **March 1953**

43. *Seminole* with Rock Hudson, **March 1953**

44. *Law and Order* with Ronald Reagan, **May 1953**

45. *The Lone Hand* with Joel McCrea, **May 1953**

46. *Column South* with Audie Murphy, **June 1953**

47. *Take Me to Town* with Ann Sheridan, **June 1953**

48. *The Great Sioux Uprising* with Jeff Chandler, **July 1953**

49. *The Man from the Alamo* with Glenn Ford, **August 1953**

50. *The Stand at Apache River* with Stephen McNally, **September 1953**

51. *Wings of the Hawk* with Van Heflin, **September 1953**

52. *Back to God's Country* with Rock Hudson, **November 1953**

53. *Tumbleweed* with Audie Murphy, **December 1953**

54. *Border River* with Joel McCrea, **January 1954**

55. *War Arrow* with Jeff Chandler, **January 1954**

56. *Taza, Son of Cochise* with Rock Hudson, **February 1954**

57. *Ride Clear of Diablo* with Audie Murphy, **March 1954**

58. *Saskatchewan* with Alan Ladd, **March 1954**

59. *Rails into Laramie* with John Payne, **April 1954**

60. *Black Horse Canyon* with Joel McCrea, **June 1954**

61. *Drums Across the River* with Audie Murphy, **June 1954**

62. *Dawn at Socorro* with Rory Calhoun, **September 1954**

63. *Four Guns to the Border* with Rory Calhoun, **November 1954**

64. *Ricochet Romance* with Marjorie Main, **November 1954**

65. *The Yellow Mountain* with Lex Barker, **December 1954**

66. *Destry* with Audie Murphy **January 1955**

67. *The Far Country* with James Stewart, **February 1955**

68. *Smoke Signal* with Dana Andrews, **March 1955**

69. *Chief Crazy Horse* with Victor Mature, **April 1955**

70. *Man Without a Star* with Kirk Douglas, **April 1955**

71. *The Man from Bitter Ridge* with Lex Barker, **June 1955**

72. *Foxfire* with Jane Russell, **July 1955**

73. *One Desire* with Anne Baxter, **August 1955**

74. *Kiss of Fire* with Jack Palance, **October 1955**

75. *The Naked Dawn* with Arthur Kennedy, **November 1955**

76. *The Second Greatest Sex* with Jeanne Crain, **December 1955**

77. *The Spoilers* with Anne Baxter, **January 1956**

78. *Red Sundown* with Rory Calhoun, **March 1956**

79. *Backlash* with Richard Widmark, **April 1956**

80. *A Day of Fury* with Dale Robertson, **May 1956**

81. *Star in the Dust* with John Agar, **June 1956**

82. *The Rawhide Years* with Tony Curtis **July 1956**

83. *Raw Edge* with Rory Calhoun, **September 1956**

84. *Walk the Proud Land* with Audie Murphy, **September 1956**

85. *Pillars of the Sky* with Jeff Chandler, **October 1956**

86. *Showdown at Abilene* with Jock Mahoney, **October 1956**

87. *Gun for a Coward* with Fred MacMurray, **March 1957**

88. *Night Passage* with James Stewart, **August 1957**

89. *Joe Dakota* with Jock Mahoney, **September 1957**

90. *Run of the Arrow* with Rod Steiger, **September 1957**

91. *Quantez* with Fred MacMurray, **October 1957**

92. *Slim Carter* with Jock Mahoney, **November 1957**

93. *All Mine to Give* with Glynis Johns, **January 1958**

94. *Man in the Shadow* with Jeff Chandler, **January 1958**

95. *Day of the Bad Man* with Fred MacMurray, **April 1958**

96. *The Last of the Fast Guns* with Jock Mahoney, **July 1958**

97. *Wild Heritage* with Will Rogers Jr., **August 1958**

98. *Once Upon a Horse* with Rowan and Martin, **September 1958**

99. *Ride a Crooked Trail* with Audie Murphy, **September 1958**

100. *The Saga of Hemp Brown* with Rory Calhoun, **October 1958**

101. *Money, Women and Guns* with Jock Mahoney, **January 1959**

102. *No Name on the Bullet* with Audie Murphy, **February 1959**

103. *The Wild and the Innocent* with Audie Murphy, **May 1959**

104. *Curse of the Undead* with Eric Fleming, **July 1959**

105. *Four Fast Guns* with James Craig, **February 1960**

106. *Hell Bent for Leather* with Audie Murphy, **February 1960**

107. *Seven Ways from Sundown* with Audie Murphy, **September 1960**

108. *Tomboy and the Champ* with Candy Moore, **April 1961**

109. *Posse from Hell* with Audie Murphy, **May 1961**

110. *The Last Sunset* with Kirk Douglas, **July 1961**

111. *Lonely Are the Brave* with Kirk Douglas, **June 1962**

112. *6 Black Horses* with Audie Murphy, **June 1962**

113. *Stagecoach to Dancers' Rock* with Warren Stevens, **October 1962**

114. *Showdown* with Audie Murphy, **May 1963**

Bibliography

Books

Aaronson, Charles S. *The International Motion Picture Almanac*. New York: Quigley Publications, 1965.

Adams, Les, and Buck Rainey. *The Shoot-'Em-Ups*. New Rochelle, N.Y.: Arlington House, 1978.

Alicoate, Jack. *Film Daily Yearbook of Motion Pictures 1948–1964*. New York: Ayer Company Publishers.

American Film Institute Catalog, Feature Films 1961–1970. New York and London: R.R. Bowker Company, 1976.

Bloom, Ken. *Hollywood Song the Complete Film and Musical Companion*. New York: Facts on File, Inc., 1995.

Blum, Daniel. *Screen World (1954)*. New York: Crown Publishers, 1955.

____. *Screen World (1956)*. New York: Crown Publishers, 1957.

De Carlo, Yvonne, with Doug Warren. *Yvonne: An Autobiography*. New York: St. Martin's Press, 1987.

Eames, John Douglas. *The Paramount Story*. New York: Crown Publishers, 1985.

Fetrow, Alan G. *Feature Films, 1940–1949*. Jefferson, N.C. and London: McFarland & Company, Inc., 1994.

Fitzgerald, Michael G. *Universal Pictures*. New Rochelle, N.Y.: Arlington House, 1977.

Fowler, Karin J. *Anne Baxter: A Bio-Bibliography*. Westport, Conn.: Greenwood Press, 1991.

Freese, Gene Scott. *Hollywood Stunt Performers*. Jefferson, N.C., and London: McFarland & Company, Inc., 1998.

Gaberscek, Carlo. *Sentieri del Western*. Germono, Italy: La Cineteca del Friuli, 1996.

Gossett, Sue. *The Films and Career of Audie Murphy*. Madison, N.C.: Empire Publishing, 1996.

Hardy, Phil. *The Western*. New York: William Morrow and Company, Inc., 1983.

Higham, Charles, and Joel Greenberg. *The Celluloid Muse, Hollywood Directors Speak*. New York: New American Library, 1972.

Hirschhorn, Clive. *The Universal Story*. New York: Crown Publishers, 1983.

Jackson, Ronald. *Classic TV Westerns*. New York: Citadel Press, 1994.

Jewell, Richard B., with Vernon Harbin. *The RKO Story*. New York: Arlington House, 1982.

Kaminsky, Stuart M. *Don Siegel: Director*. New York: Curtis, 1974.

Lentz, Harris M., III. *Western and Frontier Film and Television Credits: 1903–1995*. Jefferson, N.C., and London: McFarland & Company, Inc., 1996.

Mathis, Jack. *Republic Confidential Vol. 2: The Players.* Barrington, Ill.: Jack Mathis Advertising, 1992.

Michael, Paul. *American Movies Reference Book: The Sound Era.* Englewood Cliffs, N.J.: Prentice–Hall, 1969.

Miller, Don. *Hollywood Corral.* New York: Popular Library, 1976.

Mulholland, Jim. *The Abbott and Costello Book.* New York: Popular Library, 1975.

Munn, Michael. *Kirk Douglas.* New York: St. Martin's Press, 1985.

Nash, Jay Robert, and Stanley Ralph Ross. *The Motion Picture Guide.* Chicago: Cinebooks, Inc., 1985.

The New York Times Film Reviews, 1913–1968. New York: The New York Times and Arno Press, 1970.

Pitts, Michael R. *Western Movies.* Jefferson, N.C., and London: McFarland & Company, Inc., 1986.

Rainey, Buck. *The Shoot-'Em-Ups Ride Again.* Metuchen, N.J., and London: Scarecrow Press, 1990.

Rothel, David. *An Ambush of Ghosts.* Madison, N.C.: Empire Publishing, 1990.

Rutherford, John A., and Richard B. Smith, III. *More Cowboy Shooting Stars.* Madison, N.C.: Empire Publishing, 1992.

Server, Lee. *Sam Fuller: Film Is a Battleground.* Jefferson, N.C. and London: McFarland & Company, Inc., 1994.

Sherman, Robert G. *Quiet on the Set!* Chatsworth, Calif.: Sherway Publishing, 1984.

Siegel, Joel E. *Val Lewton: The Reality of Terror.* New York: The Viking Press, 1973.

Steinberg, Cobbett. *Film Facts.* New York: Facts on File, Inc., 1980.

Thomas, Tony. *The Best of Universal.* Vestal, N.Y.: Vestal Press, 1990 .

Tuska, Jon. *The Filming of the West.* Garden City, N.Y.: Doubleday & Company, Inc., 1976 .

Variety Reviews (3 volumes). New York and London: Garland Publishing, 1983.

Yarbrough, Tinsley. *Those Great B-Western Locations.* Albuquerque, N.Mex.: VideoWest, 1998.

Periodicals

Boxoffice (Kansas City, Missouri)
Boyd Magers' Western Clippings (Albuquerque, New Mexico)

Hollywood Reporter (Hollywood, California)
Screen Facts (Kew Gardens, New York)
The Westerner (Vienna, West Virginia)

Newspapers

The New York Times (New York, New York)
Richmond Times-Dispatch (Richmond, Virginia)

The Virginian-Pilot (Norfolk, Virginia)

Miscellaneous

The Universal Story (movie, Universal, 1995)

Songs of the Civil War (album liner notes—Columbia CK 48607)

Index